WOMEN *and* MEN *in* MINISTRY

WOMEN *and* MEN *in* MINISTRY

A COMPLEMENTARY PERSPECTIVE

ROBERT L. SAUCY
JUDITH K. TENELSHOF
General Editors

MOODY PRESS
CHICAGO

Library of Congress Cataloging-in-Publication Data

Woman and men in ministry : a complementary perspective / Robert Saucy and Judith TenElshof, editors.

p. cm.

Includes bibliographical references and index.

ISBN 0-8024-5291-4

1. Women clergy. 2. Women in church work. 3. Women in Christianity. 4. Women clergy--Biblical teaching. 5. Women in church work--Biblical teaching. 6. Women in the Bible. I. Saucy, Robert L. II. TenElshof, Judith.

BV676. W545 2001
262'.14'082--dc21

2001030223

1 3 5 7 9 10 8 6 4 2

Printed in the United States of America

To our beloved life complements:
Nancy Saucy and Gene TenElshof

CONTENTS

ABOUT THE CONTRIBUTORS

Clinton Arnold (Ph.D., University of Aberdeen) is Professor and Chairman of the Department of New Testament Language and Literature at Talbot School of Theology, Biola University. Published works include *Ephesians: Power and Magic, Power of Darkness: Principalities and Powers in Paul's Letters,* and articles in *Christianity Today, Journal of Psychology and Theology,* and *Journal for the Study of the New Testament*. Clint and his wife, Barbara, live in La Habra, California, and are the parents of three boys.

John Coe (M.A., Western Kentucky University; M.A., Talbot School of Theology; M.A., Ph.D., UC Irvine) is Associate Professor of Theology and Philosophy at Rosemead School of Psychology. He is also Director of The Institute for Spiritual Formation, Talbot School of Theology. John and his wife, Greta, are the parents of two daughters and live in La Mirada, California.

Thomas Finley (Ph.D., UCLA) is Professor of Old Testament and Semitics at Talbot School of Theology, Biola University. Published works include *Joel, Amos, Obadiah* in *Wycliffe Exegetical Commentary; Joel, Obadiah, Micah* in *Everyman's Bible Commentary;* and *A Bilingual Concordance to the Targum of the Prophets: Ezekiel* (3 vol.).

Sherwood Lingenfelter (Ph.D., University of Pittsburgh) is Dean of the School of World Mission, Fuller Theological Seminary. He formerly served as Professor of Intercultural Studies, Provost and Senior Vice President, Biola University. He is the author of *Ministering Cross-culturally: An Incarnational Model for Personal Relationship, Transforming Culture: A Challenge for Christian Mission,* and co-author or editor of six other works dealing with anthropology. Articles have appeared in *Current Anthropology, Journal of the Polynesian Society, Ethnology, Journal of Pacific History,* and others. Sherwood and Judy Lingenfelter live in Pasadena, California, and are the parents of a daughter and a son.

Robert Saucy (Th.D., Dallas Theological Seminary) is Distinguished Professor of Systematic Theology at Talbot School of Theology, Biola University. Published works include: *The Church in God's Program, The Case for Progressive Dispensationalism, Is the Bible Reliable?, The Common Made Holy* (co-author), *Are Miraculous Gifts for Today? Four Views* (co-author) and contributions to the *Expositor's Bible Commmentary, The Evangelical Dictionary of Theology,* and four other books, along with articles that have appeared in *Bibliotheca Sacra, Criswell Theological Journal, Journal of the Evangelical Theological Society,* and others. Robert and his wife, Nancy, live in Anaheim, California, and are the parents of a son and two daughters (one deceased).

Judith TenElshof (Ph.D., Fuller Theological Seminary) is Associate Professor of Christian Ministry and Leadership and Director of the Intentional Character Development at Talbot School of Theology, Biola University; Staff Therapist, Biola Counseling Center; and Founder of Hilltop Renewal Center for Christian Leaders. Published works include several journal articles and chapters in *Foundations of Ministry: An Introduction to Christian Education for a New Generation; The Short-Term Missions Boom: A Guide to International and Do-*

mestic Involvement; and *The Christian Education Dictionary*. Judy and her husband, Gene, live in LaPalma, California, where they raised their son and daughter.

Michael J. Wilkins (Ph.D., Fuller Theological Seminary) is Dean of the Faculty and Professor of New Testament Language and Literature at Talbot School of Theology, Biola University. Published works include *The Concept of Disciple in Matthew's Gospel, Following the Master: A Biblical Theology of Discipleship, In His Image: Reflecting Christ in Everyday Life, Matthew* in the *NIV Application Commentary,* and *Matthew* in the *Zondervan Illustration Bible Backgrounds Commentary.* He was the co-editor and contributor to *Worship, Theology, and Ministry in the Early Church* and *Jesus Under Fire: Modern Scholarship Reinvents the Historical Jesus.* His many articles have been published in venues as diverse as *Journal of Biblical Literature, Anchor Bible Dictionary, Dictionary of Jesus and the Gospels, Moody Monthly,* and *Discipleship Journal.* Michael and his wife, Lynne, live in San Clemente, California, where they raised their two daughters.

PREFACE

This book was born out of the questions of women seminary students: "What can women do in the church? We want to serve, but we don't want to disobey the Lord. What does the Bible teach concerning the role of women in church ministry?" Conveying these concerns to the dean resulted in the formation of a course at Talbot School of Theology to address this subject. At first two men taught it, I (Bob) and another of whom the same questions had been asked. But the complementary relationship of men and women that we found in the Scripture soon suggested a complementary teaching of the course. Thus the two editors of this work have taught the course together for several years, also using the expertise of the other contributors to this volume. As two individuals, we could never fully portray the characteristics of man and woman. Nevertheless, both men and women students often noted the masculine and feminine dimensions in the class with positive reaction, making their understanding of complementarity more comprehensive and holistic.

The confusion over this issue in the church today makes the questions of the women students completely understandable. On the one hand, some assert that there are no gender distinctions whatsoever in the roles of men and women in the church. Both can serve in the same functions and offices with no restrictions. On the other hand, we find churches where the ministry of women is stringently limited, particularly in the teaching and leadership roles. The focus is on those Scriptures that restrict them from certain functions. In many instances, women feel as if they have less voice in their church than in any other area of their lives, including their Christian families.

The thesis of this work is that neither of these positions adequately represents the complementary relationship of man and woman portrayed in Scripture. Created to complement each other, men and women are different, resulting in distinctions in life roles. The denial of these gender distinctions by much of our contemporary society has led to confusion among both genders as to who they are as man and woman.

But the created complementary nature of man and woman also leads to complementarity in all of life. Each needs the other to fulfill the human task to the glory of God. We see this most clearly in the family where husband and wife, working together, helping and teaching each other, contributing their strengths for the good of the other, serve and grow together. In Christ we, as man and woman, are being renewed to the true humanity for which we were created, a humanity of man and woman together in complementarity. The purpose of this work is to encourage the church toward a greater realization of this truth.

The collaborative effort involved in this work is evident by the many contributors. To them we express our thanks, not only for the written essays included, but for their willingness to present and refine their material in the crucible of class discussion. This work would also not be a reality without the support of the administration of Talbot Seminary, not only in the establishment of the class on this subject, but also by continual encouragement. The same goes for our faculty colleagues who regularly expressed the need of such a work in the present church situation. To all of them, we acknowledge our debt for their encouragement. Our thanks also go to the many students who patiently listened and interacted with the material, told their own experiences, and, through it all, helped to broaden and sharpen the thoughts presented in this work.

The people at Moody Press have also been a delight to work with from start to finish. Our thanks to James Bell Jr. and Dave DeWit for their help in bringing this project to reality. A special thanks to Cheryl Dunlop, who definitely made the end product better with her astute questions and detailed editing.

Finally, special thanks to our spouses, Nancy Saucy and Gene TenElshof, who, no doubt, heard about this book more than they ever desired. Without their support and great patience, this work would not exist.

It is our prayer that the Lord would use what in this work is in accord with His Word to guide His people into a fuller experience of His will for the relationship of men and women in the church and through the church to a culture burdened by gender confusion and its destructive consequences.

PART ONE

INTRODUCTION

CHAPTER ONE

A PROBLEM IN THE CHURCH

Robert Saucy and Judith TenElshof

Introduction

Some women (like me) who take the Scripture seriously and have great passion for theology and evangelism feel frustrated, not knowing whether we are to just "shut up and be passive wimps" being instructed by our husbands at home ("Yes, dear.") or can we use our minds and abilities to His glory? It seems there is very little "legal" ground for women. And yet wherever the church as a whole is enjoined to a task, we can reasonably assume women can take part, right? Evangelism—declaring the gospel—as well as apologetics—defending the faith from error/detractors—seems within the "legal" purview of women. . . . Excuse the ranting. . . . It's a difficult issue. Sometimes I'm so discouraged I want to leave the church—but where could I go? No. It's the best place to be, but frankly I don't feel I fit in—I don't like children's ministries (I know I'm weird, but some women actually don't like spending time with kids! I'm not good at it!) and in my church that's about all there is in terms of ministry opportunities. I love my pastor and am grateful for the strong male leadership. I don't know what the answer is. . . .

The note above from a personal friend represents the turmoil in the minds and hearts of many women and not a few men in the church today. The focus on the role and status of women in the culture at large, raised by the modern feminist movement, has evoked similar concerns in the church. The significance of the issue for the church is seen in the title of the cover story in *Time* magazine a few years back (November 23, 1992): "God and Women: A Second Reformation Sweeps Christianity." Although that article dealt more with the changes taking place in the more liberal mainstream churches, as the note above indicates, conservative Bible-believing churches are not immune from this troubling question. It may simmer below the surface in private hurt and anger or erupt in contentious conflict. But it is there.

The issue may be felt more personally by women; however, it cannot be dismissed or ignored by men. My own (Bob) pilgrimage in relation to this question perhaps reflects that of many men reared in the evangelical church. The role of women in church ministry was simply not a burning question until it asserted itself in recent decades in conjunction with the modern women's movement. The Bible taught man's headship and forbade women to teach men in the church. I cannot recall a great deal of teaching or controversy that delved into the real meaning and significance of these biblical statements. For the most part they were taught and practiced in a straightforward way that focused on obedient structure or form.

The eruption of the women's question into the limelight of our culture prodded me as a theology instructor who regularly taught the doctrine of the church to look more deeply into the scriptural teaching on the role of women in the church. What did these biblical passages dealing with women in the church really teach? What were the women who were asking hard questions really saying, and was there any biblical validity to the issues they raised? As noted in the preface, this probing was spurred on by women students who above all desired to obey God in their church ministry, but in the midst of confusing voices they were not sure what God's Word said on the subject.

My study led me to the realization that the injunctions concerning the ministry of women in the church were not instructions dealing with a specific somewhat isolated issue. The relationship of men and women, as one might suspect from its importance to human life, is a prominent theme of biblical instruction. For me, therefore, the answer to the question of their relationship in church ministry must be sought within an understanding of this entire teaching. In brief, along with affirming an order between man and woman in human community that recognized their created difference, I became more aware of the biblical teaching that they were created for a complementary relationship and more aware of what that really meant for their life and service together.

As a result, although I believe there is a rejection of biblical teaching on the part of many within the women's movement, I could not say that the biblical picture of God's design for the relationship of men and women was fully operative in most churches today. My participation in this work, therefore, represents part of my own process of hopefully coming not only to a fuller understanding of the biblical teaching, but also a greater enjoyment of God's plan for us as His people in this area of our life.

The significance of this issue makes it unlikely that it will go away. For the nature of man and woman and their relationship deals with the very essence of our humanity. Its scope touches every realm of thought concerned with human life, e.g., theology, philosophy, psychology, sociology. Most important, it is more than an academic debate over abstract truth. It inevitably and inescapably must be lived out in day-to-day relationships. The significance of this issue makes it difficult to avoid the conclusion of Piper and Grudem that "before the struggle ends, probably no Christian family and no evangelical church will remain untouched."[1]

The Source of Our Problem

The question of the role and status of women in society and the church is, of course, not a modern question. It is the most fundamental question of human society—the relationship of man and woman—which has existed from the beginning. As such, it is not simply the question of "a woman's place in the church," but involves the bigger question of the divine design of the relationship of man and woman in creation and redemption.

In creation God declared that it was not good for man to be alone, so He created woman as his complement. They were created for each other, to need each other, and thus together to be one. In the creation of *adam* (mankind) in God's image, Scripture tells us that "He created *him;* male and female He created *them*" (Gen. 1:27, italics added). Man and woman are different, "male and female," "them"; but they are also one, "him," i.e., one humanity, one *adam*.

The unity of man and woman according to the divine design is delightfully seen in the first recorded words of a human being in the Bible. At the sight of the woman whom God had made for him, the man cries out in rapturous exclamation, "This is now bone of my bones, and flesh of my flesh; she shall be called Woman, because she was taken out of Man" (Gen. 2:23).[2] Something of the excitement over the relationship is captured by Cassuto in his sense of the opening words: "This creature, this time [that is, at last], is in truth a helper corresponding to me! Thus the man exclaims in his enthusiasm and heart's joy."[3] "Bone of my bones, and flesh of my flesh" is more than the obvious physical relationship. It is the language of the relationship of mutual loyalty and responsibilities.[4] The man recognizes his unity with this new gift from God, giving her a name corresponding to his own: "She shall be called Woman, because she was taken out of Man." Created in the very image of a loving God, man and woman lived for each other, bound together in love.

But this loving relationship was soon broken by sin. Rather than gratefully accepting their relationship to their loving Creator, both man and woman succumbed to the tempter's lie that they could be like God themselves. Cut off from the only source of true love that gave them the ability to love each other with a self-giving love in likeness to God, they became hollowed, impoverished creatures. Instead of living out of the fullness of life with God's self-giving love that grows as it is given to the other, man and woman, alienated from God, now exerted their energies to protect their false, inadequate, god-playing self.

Pitiably they tried to hide from each other by hastily constructing makeshift clothing from fig trees. As God approached, they used the bountiful trees of the garden that He created for their delight and nourishment as shields to hide from Him. When finally confronted, they defended their threatened selves by laying the blame for their actions on another—the woman pointed to the Serpent, and the man charged the woman and God who gave her to him.

This early biblical picture of the created unity and alienating effect of sin captures all subsequent human relationships. Created in the image of the triune God and still bearing the remnant of that image, we yearn for relationship. We know in our heart the truth of the saying, "*Ein*

Mann ist kein Mann" ("One man is no man"). We are social beings created to live in the bond of love, mutually giving ourselves one to the other. But the nature of sin as the self-centered assertion of self destroys relationships through strife and jealousy as we seek to play God and get our own way.

If this situation is true of all human relationships as a result of sin, it is most true of man and woman in relationship to each other. Created as complementary partners in need of each other, the pull toward unity is greatest between them. But the closer the unity, the more sin's friction enters to bring tension and strife. Thus the saying of both men and women about the other sex, "You can't live with them and you can't live without them."

History continues to record this struggle, which will finally be overcome only when the presence of sin is banished from human relationships.

Focusing on the Issue

Posing the Right Question

In any problem, the way one poses the question is vital to arriving at the correct solution. Unfortunately, the question regarding women's ministry in the church has not always been framed in helpful ways. At times the issue has been confused by posing the question in such limited terms that it fails to get to the real underlying issue involved. In other instances it is stated in misleading global questions that purportedly solve the issue, but in reality beg the question by again not facing the central issue.

An example of the first type of question is to frame the issue as one of women's ordination. Should women be ordained? One's answer to this question depends on the meaning and application of ordination. Is it limited only to the highest office of the church, i.e., elders/bishops, or can others be ordained for specific service within the congregation as the seven men in Acts 6 were? One's answer to that question would surely affect one's answer to the question of whether a woman can be "ordained." Moreover, limiting the question to the issue of ordination does not address the more basic underlying question of the overall relationship of man and woman in the church.

More frequently, the topic of women's ministry is posed in broad questions that transcend the real issue and are therefore unhelpful and often misleading. Liefeld, for example, sees the entire issue revolving around the nature of Christian ministry. He writes,

> The conclusions we reach with regard to women and ministry are inevitably affected by the way the questions are posed. It could be said . . . that there is only one question: Should Christian ministry, which by all testimony of Scripture is *spiritual* in nature, be limited by the gender of the minister, which is by nature a *human* distinction? That is a basic and straightforward way of putting it. It cuts through to the heart of the issue and sets the agenda without ambiguity.[5]

In actuality this question presupposes a position that itself needs careful evaluation. Is it not possible that church ministry could be both "human" and "spiritual"? After all, is not "spiritual" ministry done by those who are "human"? Without a biblical answer to this prior question, any conclusion based on the proposed question is surely a case of question begging.

In a somewhat similar vein, the question is often said to be one of spiritual giftedness: Are the gifts gender-specific? Since Scripture does not explicitly assign spiritual gifts to specific genders, the conclusion is drawn that there can be no difference between men and women in ministry roles. Such a question again fails to encompass all of the data and allow for further questions, which must also be considered before one can arrive at a solution. For example, even though spiritual gifts are not gender-specific, does this preclude their functioning in certain relationships? The fact that both men and women are gifted in teaching surely does not preclude some distinctions in the practical use of these gifts.

Even more unhelpful ways of framing the problem involve global questions that attempt to determine the issue solely on such broad biblical doctrines as personhood and redemption. According to Patricia Gundry, "There is but one central and watershed question in this conflicted issue: Are women fully human? All other questions and issues are peripheral to this question."[6] Responding to Gundry's assertion, Gretchen Gaebelein Hull goes even further to ask: "Are Women fully redeemed?"[7]

To frame the questions in this fashion is, of course, to answer them. No one could possibly interpret Scripture as giving anything but a positive answer to both of these questions. Women in Christ are as fully human and as fully redeemed as men. But as significant as these questions may be to the issue, they overlook other biblical teaching related to the question at hand. The absence of distinctions at one level does not preclude their presence at another level. The fact that man and woman are fully human and redeemed manifestly does not remove all distinctions in life between men and women. If men and women are truly different and therefore complementary, to say that their differences cannot entail functional distinctions appears to assert more than can rightly be concluded from an equality of personhood and redemption.

This is not to deny the validity of the above questions. Specific questions such as the ordination of women are related to the issue of the role of women in church ministry. But their answers must be sought in further questions concerning underlying principles. Similarly, the issues of personhood and redemption have an important bearing on the entire question. All would agree that the controversy before the church involves those who are both persons and redeemed. But they are also men and women. So again, the question of the biblical teaching on men and women and their relationship must be addressed. If the Bible teaches that being human and redeemed eliminates all distinctions between men and women, then the matter of their roles in church ministry would appear to be solved, i.e., there can be no distinction of any kind. If, on the other hand, a distinction between the genders is still valid even among believers, then the categories of personhood and redemption do not close the issue. The basic issue in the question of women's ministry in the church is thus: Does God intend any role distinction between men and women in relation to ministry in the church?

Although this is the fundamental question in the present controversy, its answer and an understanding of the biblical picture of the role of women in church ministry must be sought in the context of other questions related to the total picture of New Testament church ministry. (1) What is the meaning and function of the biblical terms for church functionaries, e.g., elder, bishop, deacon, pastor, "minister," etc.? How did these people actually function as leaders in the church? (2) What is the "church" in relation to the question of ministry? Does it refer to all of our "church" functions (e.g., home gatherings, Sunday school, etc.)

or only "corporate" worship? What about so-called parachurch ministries —are they "church"? (3) What was the nature of the meeting of the New Testament church? Did it involve the participation of more people than our contemporary services? That is, did more people (men and women) have opportunity to exercise their spiritual gifts when the church met together than they do today? Have we structured our usual church service with certain functions (e.g., preaching) so dominant (and often restricted to men) that only a few individuals actually minister, thereby excluding the ministry of women (and most men)? The issue of the place of women in the ministry of the church today is more than the question of whether or not there is a gender distinction. Since according to Scripture the church grows through the ministry of every member (men and women), the question is finally an understanding of God's design for the complementary relationship of the ministry of man and woman in the church.

An Overview of the Positions

Although there is disagreement on some of the details of meaning and application, most interpreters agree on the central message of the primary passages dealing with the relationship of women and men both in the church and in the home. They are willing to acknowledge, for example, that there are several statements in the New Testament that instruct wives to be in submission to their husbands (e.g., Eph. 5:22; Col. 3:18; 1 Pet. 3:1). Similarly, Paul's prohibition against women teaching men, at least in some form, is also generally accepted (1 Tim. 2:12). The disagreement comes over whether these teachings are still normative for the church today.

The position that does not take the biblical teaching as normative for the church today is known as *egalitarianism*. Because it is generally included in the overall feminist stance, it is also described as the feminist position. According to this understanding, there are no distinctions between the roles of men and women in ministry; all functions and positions in church ministry are equally open to both genders. On the other side are those who see the biblical teaching of a distinction in roles between man and woman in the church (or in the home), who are commonly known as *complementarians*. This position has also been traditionally called *patriarchy* or *hierarchism,* although these latter terms are more limited in meaning, emphasizing only the headship of man rather than the complementary contribution of the distinct role of woman.

Egalitarianism

Egalitarians, those who see no distinction between women and men in church ministry, are broadly divided into two camps in their interpretation of the Scriptures that teach a distinction between men and women either in the home or in the church. One group, generally associated more with liberalism, understands all of the Scriptures that draw a distinction between men and women in the home or church as simply expressing the prevailing patriarchal opinion of the writers' day. It was not God's perspective, but the opinion of the fallible culture-bound writer.

Most evangelicals reject this understanding, affirming the biblical teaching as authoritative.[8] However, they restrict the apostles' teaching of distinct roles for women and men as applicable only to the particular historical situation addressed. For example, Paul's prohibition against women teaching or exercising authority over men in 1 Timothy 2:12 is related to a particular issue in the church of Ephesus at the time of its writing. Opinions vary as to the nature of the situation calling for this prohibition. Some see the apostle as teaching a temporary patriarchy as expedient for the sake of Christian testimony in the surrounding patriarchal culture. Others see specific issues such as the lack of women's education as the rationale for the prohibition.[9] Although the explanations for the apostles' teaching vary, there is agreement that this teaching is not normative for the church at all times.[10]

Complementarianism

Contrary to egalitarians, complementarians understand the biblical passages dealing with men and women as teaching a permanent normative order between man and woman in the home and in the church. With regard to the question of men and women in church ministry, the apostles are interpreted as teaching an order that entails the leadership of men in the church. There is, however, considerable variation among complementarians as to how this is to be worked out in the practical functioning of men and women in church life.[11]

At one end of the spectrum, some understand Scripture to teach that church leadership and the leadership of all public ministry is to be exercised by men. Women's participation in public worship is largely limited to group participation.[12] The prohibition of women ruling is interpreted as excluding women from such positions as choir director or Sunday school superintendent—in short, any church position that puts men under their authority.

A more common understanding of the meaning of the order between men and women in the church restricts women only from the office of pastor or elders, i.e., the teaching-ruling positions of the church. All other ministries and positions of authority are open to women.[13] Perhaps the least restrictive view held by advocates of a biblical gender order in the church is that women can do anything as long as it is under male leadership. It would be permissible, under this view, for a church to appoint a woman preacher as long as her ministry was under the authority of men.

Arriving at a Solution

For the believer in the authority of Scripture, the solution to the question of the relationship of women and men in church ministry must be sought in the considerable scriptural teaching on God's design for men and women and their relationship. This involves both that which is directly related to the ministry of women and the total biblical picture of the nature and relationships of men and women. In addition, although Scripture alone is canonical, the natural disciplines of psychology and anthropology are also useful in our understanding of the nature of man and woman and their life together.

The biblical teaching directly related to the ministry of women in the church and the role of women in the church is central to our question. This includes texts giving explicit instructions relative to the subject. In addition, the whole life and practice of the New Testament church plays a vital role in determining the biblical answer to the question of the place of women in church ministry. If we assume that the apostles and the churches under their authority sought to implement the apostolic directives, then these examples of actual ministry are valuable in showing what the apostolic teaching looked like in its practical outworking in the church.

Although the meaning of the explicit biblical texts dealing with the role of women in the church and the actual examples of women in ministry are central to the discussion of the role of women in the church, these can only be rightly understood in the context of the total picture of God's design for man and woman. The apostolic teachings and practices concerning the ministry of men and women in the church do not come as incidental or foreign elements thrust upon the new human community of the church. Nor is there any evidence that the apostles were bringing something radically different in God's design for the overall functional relationship of man and woman. The relationships of men and women in the church are clearly one with the general pattern of relationships discernible throughout Scripture.

Scripture, of course, contains many examples of sinful aberrations that must not be seen as part of God's pattern. There are also some changes that take place in the divine plan as a result of the progression of God's salvation history. The outpouring of the Spirit at Pentecost and the resultant universality of the priesthood of all believers bring about increased ministry for both men and women. Despite these changes, an underlying relationship pattern between man and woman is visible throughout biblical history. This total biblical picture of the nature of men and women and God's design for their life together as co-humanity is therefore essential as a background for the proper interpretation of the specific passages dealing with women's roles in the church.

An important element in this total biblical picture is an understanding of how men and women are designed by God to relate personally to each other. The issue of the role of women in the church is more than the questions of "what" with regard to the ministry of both men and women; it is also the question of "how." It is not enough to see the basic structure of relationships or a divine order between man and woman. An understanding of this order in terms of functioning relationships and attitudes must be fleshed out if men and women are to work together in harmony and fruitfulness in the church.

Foundational to this understanding is the biblical teaching of the complementary relationship of man and woman by creation. This complementarity means that two important realities are grounded in the very nature of all men and women: (1) They are different by nature, and (2) they require each other for fullness of their humanity. If such is the nature of man and woman by creation that they exist as co-humanity in a complementary relationship, this truth must find expression in all of life, including church ministry.

The truth of complementarity raises questions for both the new egalitarian interpretation of women's ministry and the traditional understanding. For the former we would ask, If men and women are different, what differences does it make in the actual life of the church? How does the full equality of men and women in the church harmonize with their created differences? Could it not be possible that one gender is more suited for a particular function by God's design than the other? It does not seem to be adequate to simply assert equality without also dealing with differences and how these play out in practical functioning together.

But advocates of a traditional viewpoint of the leadership of men in church ministry must also deal with the principle of complementarity. Does the interpretation of Scripture that often limits the role of women in church largely to social activities and ministry with children square with this principle of the need of men and women for each other? If men and women are basically complementary in life, including spiritual life, is a larger contribution of women somehow necessary in the whole of church life, as in the family, for all to mature into the fullness of the new humanity of Christlikeness?

The Approach of This Book

In our search for the biblical understanding of the role of women in church ministry and how both men and women can function in a complementary way for the good of the church, we will begin by laying the foundation of the overall picture of the relationship of men and women. Parts 2 and 3 will present the most significant biblical teaching concerning man and woman and their relationship. The biblical picture will include what can be gleaned from direct instructions as well as practice from the Old Testament, the teaching and example of Jesus, and the early church.

In an attempt to further understand God's design for the complementary functioning of man and woman, part 4 will attempt to gain an understanding of the meaning of femininity and masculinity. Both the light of the special revelation of Scripture and the insight given through natural revelation in the observations of human life and behavior by social scientists will be brought to bear on this subject. With the assumption that history gives support to the natural pattern for man and woman, part 5 surveys the relationship of man and woman within human societies throughout history.

This picture of the general pattern of the relationship of man and woman provides the background for the final major section, part 6, which focuses directly on the relationship and functioning of men and women together in the ministry of the church. The background of the total picture of the nature and relationship of men and women provides the picture of ministry together in a rich and necessary complementarity according to the divinely created order.

CHAPTER TWO

THE BACKGROUND OF THE CONTEMPORARY SITUATION

Robert Saucy and Judith TenElshof

The disintegrating effects of sin on the relationship of man and woman have continued from Eden down to the present. Within the diverse cultures of human history the gender struggle has manifest itself in many different forms. Without attempting to survey all of these, it will be helpful in our consideration of the contemporary situation to briefly consider the history of the relationship of men and women within the history that most directly influenced our Western culture.

An Ancient Problem

It goes without saying that men and women, being sinful, both contribute to the strife. But the general story of history is that man's leadership in all human communities has made it more possible for his self-centeredness to express itself in the domination of woman. At times this domination has expressed itself in raw physical abuse or through verbal and psychological humbling. More subtly, male domination takes the form of establishing community values according to which masculine characteristics and their corresponding achievements are awarded the greater value.

Cultures are formed by the shaping of children in their early years. That is, our societies are shaped to a great extent by those who nurture our children, and these are largely women, whose natural characteristics tend more toward nurturing and relational qualities than those of men. But it is not mothers and others who tend our young with these feminine qualities who are extolled in our popular culture. Rather, the movers and shakers of the political and economic and sports worlds, with the more masculine drives of initiation and competition, adorn our magazine covers and are deemed worthy of public recognition and adoration. Self-esteem is attached to job status and performance, a male tendency, rather than to relationships, the female strength. Throughout history, beginning with the Greek philosophers and especially since the Enlightenment of the seventeenth and eighteenth centuries, analytic reason, which is more associated with males, has reigned as the supreme human trait. Women, who were viewed as more emotional, were therefore seen as inferior. This, of course, is contrary to Scripture where the holistic "heart" including mind, emotion, and will is the most significant human dimension.

Classical Greece with its philosophies and sophistication in art and culture has strongly influenced Western societies, including their attitude toward women. According to Bullough,

> [T]he Greeks have the honor of demonstrating on a "scientific basis" that women were inferior, although there were conflicting beliefs and even considerable ambiguity. Greek philosophy and science are usually associated with the name of Plato and Aristotle . . . and it was their thinking about women which most often was reflected in later scientific and philosophic writings.[1]

Although Plato was somewhat ambiguous in his attitude toward women, he held that a woman's ability to learn was less than that of a man.[2] Woman needed man for her well-being, but man did not need woman.[3] The inferiority of woman was more consistent in Aristotle. It was part of Aristotle's "physiology and biology as well as his political, ethical, and aesthetic theories." The superiority of man was in the male principle in reproduction. According to Aristotle, the male semen provides the form (that which makes something what it is, e.g., a human being rather than an animal), while the female supplies the matter or material that is shaped by the form.[4] The female was not only meant to be passive, but inferior intellectually and morally.[5]

All of this had its practical effect on the relationship between man and woman. Because "the female character just had a sort of natural deficiency . . . it was only natural that women often loved and admired the male without receiving an equivalent love in return, since Aristotle held that love was proportionate to superiority and whoever was the superior must receive more affection that [sic] he gave."[6] Legally, women were almost entirely dependent upon their husbands, fathers, or male relatives. Although women were more emancipated in the Roman world, it was only relative, as Rome continued to be a man's world where the purpose of women was to serve men.[7]

Christianity tended to accept this supposed "scientific" portrayal of women as inferior to men. Clement of Alexandria, for example, recognized that women had the same human nature as men and were capable of the same degree of perfection, but nevertheless "taught that men were usually better at everything than women."[8] Typical feminine characteristics in the eyes of the Church Fathers included "fickleness and shallowness, as well as garrulousness and weakness, slowness of understanding, and instability of mind."[9]

Thomas Aquinas, later in the thirteenth century, expressed a similar natural superiority of man. Woman, he said, is naturally subject to man for the sake of good order in the human family "because in man the discretion of reason predominates." Following Augustine, Thomas understood woman as helper to man only in "the works of generation," but not "as a helpmate in other works, as some say, since man can be more efficiently helped by another man in other works."[10] Ignatius of Loyola, the founder of the Jesuits, also cast aspersions on the nature of woman, comparing Satan to women: "[T]he enemy conducts himself as a woman. He is a weakling before a show of strength, and a tyrant if he has his will."[11]

In addition to inheriting the attitude of a general inferiority of women from the Greek world in which the Christians existed, the asceticism that quickly developed in the post-apostolic church also contributed to misogynous attitudes. This asceticism was strongly associated with celibacy; since women reminded the men of sex, they were often viewed as temptresses and the source of evil, making it difficult for men to be holy. "Tertullian requested all women to remember that each one of them was an Eve, the devil's gateway, the unsealer of the forbidden tree, 'the first deserter of the divine law; you are she who persuaded him whom the devil was not valiant enough to attack. You destroyed so easily God's image, man. On account of your desert—that is, death—even the Son of God had to die.'"[12] Clearly for Tertullian, who was no doubt expressing the thought of many men of his time, man is the superior moral being, and woman is to blame for the Fall. This, of course, ignores the fact that Adam succumbed to the enticement of the "inferior" woman without even facing the direct attack of the devil.

The attitude toward women improved somewhat after the medieval period, with a greater recognition of their place as companions and helpers to men in all of life. Calvin provided one example of this in a note to a friend after the death of his wife, Idelette: "I have been bereaved of the best companion of my life, who, if our lot had been harsher, would have been not only the willing sharer of exile and poverty, but even of death. While she lived, she was the faithful helper of my ministry."[13] Such expressions of love and appreciation for women, however, should not be taken to mean that women generally were no longer viewed as inferior to men. The words of John Knox, the great Scottish Calvinist, writing in opposition to the possible rule of women in England and Scotland, reveal not only a belief that women should not rule, but also an underlying opinion of their lesser qualities.

> For who can denie but it is repugneth to nature, that the blind shall be appointed to leade and conduct such as do see? That the weake, the sicke, and impotent persons shall norishe and kepe the hole and strong? And finally, that the follishe, madde, and phrenetike shal governe the discrete, and give counsel to such as be sober of mind. And such be al women, compared unto man in bearing of authoritie. For their sight in civile regiment is but blindness; their strength, weaknes; their counsel, foolishnes; and judgment, phrensie, if it be rightlie considered.[14]

In early America, women were restricted in education and limited in what they might learn. This was not simply because of a belief in the subordination of women and their primary role as homemakers who did not require higher education, but also because of a prevailing opinion that their capacity to learn was limited. When women did go to school, "they often read special textbooks prepared for them in order to limit the strain on their faculties. Such titles as *Newton's Ladies Philosophy*, *The Lady's Geography, The Female Academy, The Ladies Complete Letter Writer,* and the *Female Miscellany* were often advertised."[15] "Even Thomas Jefferson held that girls were unfit in brains and character for serious study."[16]

This brief sketch of the history of men's attitude toward women is illustrative of what has been the general tenor in most societies throughout world history. A few voices, primarily in the last few centuries, spoke out for women's equality; but, for the most part, history records not only the subordination of women, but an attitude on the part of men that, to one degree or another, saw women's nature as inferior. No doubt this attitude contributed to many instances of physical and emotional abuse that man was able to inflict on woman due to his physical strength. But above and beyond this kind of abuse, the general effect was inequitable societal structures in many areas of life, from limitations on educational opportunities to the subordination of women's legal rights to men. At times they were considered legally incompetent and not fit to give testimony in court. In the medieval period, even church canon law allowed the husband to beat his wife as long as he did not mutilate or kill her. He was in control of his wife's actions, except that he could not ask her to do something contrary to the Christian religion.[17] All of this is not to excuse woman's contribution to the friction in the relationship of the genders, but simply to demonstrate that man's strength has often enabled him to express his sinfulness in a self-exalting domination of society and its structures, often justified by an alleged superiority of nature over woman.

Tragically for the life and witness of the Christian community, this attitude was not absent among God's people. It not only limited women from participating in church ministries in ways that seem contrary to the biblical picture of men and women ministering in the family of God as complementary equals, but brought a hurtful devaluation of women in the church. The feeling of Teresa of Avila in the sixteenth century has, no doubt, been felt by many thoughtful women in the church.

> When thou wert in the world, Lord, Thou didst not despise women, but didst always help them and show them great compassion. Thou didst find more faith and no less love in them than in men. . . . We can do nothing in public that is of any use to thee, nor dare we speak of some of the truths

> over which we weep in secret, lest thou shouldst not hear this, our just petition. Yet, Lord, I cannot believe this of thy goodness and righteousness, for thou art a righteous Judge, not like judges in the world, who, being after all, men and sons of Adam, refuse to consider any women's virtue as above suspicion. Yes, my King, but the day will come when all will be known. I am not speaking on my account, for the whole world is already aware of my wickedness, and I am glad that it should become known; but, when I see what the times are like, I feel it is not right to repel spirits which are virtuous and brave, even though they be the spirits of women.[18]

Woman's Response

Although there would be conflict between man and woman as part of the strife between all people due to sin's self-centeredness, it cannot be denied that the present gender struggle owes much to the history noted above in which women were seldom acknowledged as fully equal, complementary partners in the human endeavor. A brief look at the response of women to the inequalities of male-dominated societies will help us understand the present situation.

The Feminist Movement

For the most part, women throughout history submitted to the domination of men. A few gained considerable power in the church, such as abbesses during the Middle Ages, some of whom even had jurisdiction over parishes, and a few were prominent in the secular world.[19] But most women simply accepted their situation, although some like Teresa questioned and chafed under their lot as women.

It was only in the latter 1700s that a more general response began to take place in what could be termed the first "women's movement." Led by such influential feminists as Elizabeth Cady Stanton, Susan B. Anthony, and John Stuart Mill, this early push dealt basically with inequalities in the legal and political realms, the workplace, and educational opportunities. They also fought the double standards of morality that condemned women and exonerated men for the same sexual misconduct. By 1930, with the achievement of many of its goals, this initial women's movement began to lose its impetus.

The cause of women that has come to be known as feminism

emerged again as part of the social upheaval of the early 1960s. The political climate of the period was one of rebellion against traditional structures that were seen as causes of the domination of one group over another. Civil rights, student rights, and the peace movement were linked together by the assertion of individual and class rights in the pursuit of freedom from domination. The feminist participation in this call for social change was initiated largely through the writing of journalist Betty Friedan. It was her book *The Feminine Mystique* (1963), along with an earlier work by the French philosopher Simone de Beauvoir, *The Second Sex* (1953, Eng. ed.), that became the basis for the new feminist stirring.

In an excellent discussion of the modern feminist movement, especially in relation to the church, Mary Kassian traces the movement through three stages.[20] The first phase during the 1960s focused on the cause of women's oppression and found it to be rooted in woman's biological differences, primarily related to the reproductive function, which were deemed to be weaknesses. To overcome this disadvantage, social and political changes were sought that would minimize these biological differences and overcome the traditional roles of women. Legalized abortion, day care for children, and greater equity in the workplace, including affirmative action programs, were all seen as beneficial in overcoming the traditional role of women as childbearers and nurturers, which was viewed as the source of oppression.

During the 1970s, the second phase of the feminist movement arrived. Instead of the woman's differences being viewed as weaknesses, they were now seen as superior to those of the male and became a source of pride and confidence. On the basis of their presumed superiority, the feminists began to reinterpret all of the world about them through the "superior" perspective of women's characteristics and experience. The traditional viewpoints and values that had shaped society were said to have been structured by men and therefore were to be rejected. These male-inspired traditions were not only not normative; they were inferior. The world would be better off under the leadership of women. On the basis of woman's "instinct . . . to tend, to nurture, to encourage healthy growth, and to preserve ecological balance," one feminist explained, "[s]he is the natural leader of society and of civilization, and the usurpation of her primeval authority by man has resulted in the uncoordinated chaos that is leading the human race inexorably back to barbarism. . . . Today . . . it is to the women that we look for salvation."[21]

The third phase of the modern feminist movement, beginning in the late 1970s and early 1980s, joined feminism with spirituality. The redefining of reality by the feminists now led to the redefining of God. The external "male god," as the Judeo-Christian God was termed, was replaced by the goddess, which was essentially a symbol of the divine in all things. Thus feminists' spirituality was substantially a feminized version of the New Age beliefs that were emerging about the same time.

A primary theme of feminist philosophy is the elimination of all traditional distinctions, such as class, race, sex, etc. The purpose of such distinctions, it is argued, is solely so that one group can oppress another. The primary distinction responsible for all racial and class oppression, according to feminists, is patriarchy. Thus their central drive is to eliminate distinctions between the sexes. For many feminist leaders this extends to the acceptance of homosexuality as equal with heterosexuality. The success of the feminist movement in affecting the culture and political mainstream of our society with their agenda is readily apparent.

Feminism in the Church

The feminist movement emerged in the church about the same time as its secular counterpart, spawned largely by the same issues.[22] As William Douglas noted in 1961, "[T]he major impetus for reexamining the relationship of men and women in the churches has come from a changing society."[23] Feminists pointed to a second-class status for women in the church that in some ways was worse than that in society around them. They sought to change a situation that Douglas characterized as one in which "women do most of the work, while men exercise most of the authority."[24] Based on their demonstrated abilities in earlier activities, including women's suffrage and the Women's Christian Temperance Union and active participation in educational and social services, especially world missions, women sought greater participation in the leadership of the church itself.

Like the secular feminists, the first Christian feminists argued for the essential similarity between men and women except for the biological differences. Alleged emotional or intellectual differences were said to be only culturally conditioned.[25] There was no reason therefore to exclude women from any ministry of the church. Women were equipped with the same spiritual giftedness and the same personal capabilities as men. Since the epitome of church ministry was viewed as the ordained pastorate, the initial push of Christian feminism was for the ordination of women based upon their equality with men.

But like their secular counterparts, they also began to look at patriarchy as the underlying problem and to seek ways to overcome it. Mary Daly, in her influential work *The Church and the Second Sex* (1968) and her later work *Beyond God the Father* (1973), identified the source of women's oppression as theological error. The picture of God as "male" along with His character as "an all-powerful, all-just God who evidently willed or at least permitted oppressive conditions to exist" was to be rejected, according to Daly.[26] The belief in the Bible as a changeless revelation also needed revision in favor of a dynamic model that gave "women in the Church . . . as much right to direct current theology as the Apostle Paul did in his day."[27]

The theological changes proposed by Daly led to the full-blown feminist theology of the second phase of church feminism throughout the 1970s. In their theology the feminists adopted the principle of biblical interpretation that had been established in liberation theology, namely, the use of experience, especially the experience of the oppressed peoples, as the norm for finding the meaning of the Bible. According to feminist theologian Letty Russell, the feminist theory of interpretation begins by "asking what is 'appropriate in light of personally and politically reflected experience of oppression and liberation.'"[28] In Kassian's words, these church feminists "judged the truth of the Bible by their experience. If a doctrine or text did not agree with women's experience of oppression and quest for liberation, then it was freely revised in order to make it agree."[29] In their attempt to reinterpret Scripture according to their experience, the church feminists, like those in the outside world, were no longer seeking to deny their differences from men. Women's characteristics were now a source of pride and confidence.

The theological trends developed in feminist theology continued to develop in the most recent stage of feminist theology from the early 1980s until the present. The rejection of any patriarchal or hierarchical dimensions in Scripture led to the changing of biblical descriptions of God. God was to be known as She/He, and any descriptions of God such as Father, Judge, and King were to be changed so as to neutralize their masculine overtones. God was to be described equally as feminine and masculine or as androgynous.[30]

In the interpretation of Scripture, women's experience became increasingly the norm of authority. Since they believed that Scripture and its historic interpretation was simply theology from the male's perspective, they had every right to do theology from their own perspective. Women were now "to *believe in their own equivalent personhood as the normative starting point of theology* more than they can believe in any past accumulation of tradition which has been carried on without and against women's participation."[31] Feminist Letty Russell argues that "the text only has authority as I agree with it and interpret it to my experience." Any passage with which she did not consent was not authoritative.[32] Feminist theologians also felt free to look to material outside of Scripture as authoritative sources for theology.[33]

Theologically, the contemporary church feminist movement is edging ever closer to the spirituality that has developed within secular feminism. The freedom to change the biblical descriptions of God into terminology more suitable to feminism has led all the way to acceptance of goddess worship in some circles.[34]

Evangelical or Biblical Feminism

Evangelicals had been in the forefront of much of the movement for women's rights and involvement in society in the nineteenth century. Women ministers were common in many Holiness and Pentecostal churches, with some also among Methodist, Presbyterian, and other Protestant groups.[35] It is important to note that the usual rationale for the ministry of these early women preachers was quite different from that of modern feminism. As Chaves explains, "Before the Civil War, proponents of female preaching almost always based their arguments more on the extraordinary abilities of the few women who wanted to preach or on the special religious sensibilities of women or on the practical need for effective workers for Christ than on the principle of gender equality."[36] Commenting specifically on women preachers of this era within Methodism, Catherine Brekus notes that few of them were involved with the women's rights movement. "Instead of demanding political or legal equality to men, [female preachers] continued to laud the virtues of female subordination."[37]

Evangelical involvement in the modern feminist movement did not take place until the mid-1970s, after the modern feminist movement had been spreading for some time within the general culture and the more liberal churches. Some of the early works that introduced feminism into evangelical circles were *Women, Men and the Bible* (1977) by Virginia Ramey Mollenkott; *All We're Meant to Be* (1974) by Letha Scanzoni and Nancy Hardesty; and *Man as Male and Female* (1975) by Paul K. Jewett. The influence of the cultural feminism of the time on its introduction into the evangelical church is evident in the following letter written by one of the early evangelical feminist leaders to *His* magazine in 1973.

> At the historical moment when secular society is just beginning to wake up concerning centuries of injustice to women, it is unwise and unjust for evangelical publications to stress biblical passages concerning ancient inequalities between the sexes. By continuing on such a course, evangelicals will only add fuel to the widespread secular concept that the Christian church is an outmoded institution dedicated to the maintenance of the status quo no matter how unjust and inhuman.[38]

In order to promote feminism within the church, a number of evangelical feminists founded the Evangelical Women's Caucus International in 1974. Because of later affirmation of gay and lesbian rights by the EWCI, a number of evangelicals withdrew in 1987 to form another feminist group, Christians for Biblical Equality.

Evangelical feminists claim a strong allegiance to the historic doctrines of the evangelical faith, including the full authority of Scripture. Their writings, which have continued unabated since the mid 1970s, have, in general, focused on the relationship of men and women without following the theological developments of liberal feminist theology noted above.[39] Evangelical feminists, however, share the same starting point of many of the earlier church feminists, namely, that the texts traditionally understood as teaching an order between man and women are to be reinterpreted or otherwise made to harmonize with equalitarianism.[40] A few who began as evangelicals, and in some cases still claim that description, have moved increasingly in the direction of some of the more liberal positions of mainstream feminist theology.[41]

Scanzoni and Hardesty, for example, in the latest edition of their work, *All We're Meant to Be* (1992) see feminism touching "upon every aspect of the church's life" including "theological concepts." They go on to cite approvingly other feminist theologians who speak of "revisioning Christian categories" and provision of a "new apprehension of God and of Christ."[42]

This is not to say that all evangelical or biblical feminists will follow this same path. It is only to note that the journey away from a more conservative beginning taken by many within feminist theology in general has also been followed by some evangelical feminists.[43] No doubt many biblical feminists will remain solidly within evangelical orthodoxy and not let their interpretation of Scripture with regard to the relationship of men and women affect the other areas of their faith. Whether the feminist interpretation can be so isolated logically, however, may not be so evident.

This problem may be illustrated in the biblical language used of God. Although God is neither male nor female, He is portrayed predominantly in masculine terms in Scripture, including pronouns and masculine descriptions such as King, Shepherd, and Judge. He is especially seen as Father, both in relation to His people and perhaps even more basically in terms of the Trinity, which Scripture terms Father, Son, and Holy Spirit.

On occasion, feminine imagery is also used to describe God, so that in a very real sense his Fatherhood includes motherly traits. But contrary to the Canaanite religions where God was depicted as mother, the God of the Bible is nowhere addressed as Mother. He always chooses to relate to people in the form of the masculine.

Now the question comes as to what this imagery means to us. Clearly, both the masculine and feminine imagery related to God convey certain concepts that in biblical times were associated with men and women. For example, the feminine imagery is used to convey something of the nature of God's faithful loving care for His people. Similarly, the masculine imagery often conveys His power and leadership.

If feminism is correct, however, and these characteristics do not truly belong to masculinity and femininity, but rather were erroneous traits applied to men and women within a sinful patriarchal society, then how should the believer deal with this scriptural portrayal of God? The traditional evangelical interpretation that accepts the masculine language as validly portraying masculine characteristics uses these characteristics in relation to God as instructive and corrective for human relations. Instead of a sinful domineering patriarchy, the masculine image must be formed after the loving servant, Father-Husband picture of God.

Biblical feminists, on the other hand, seemingly must take one of the following two tacks in relation to the Bible's masculine God language. Either this masculine language conveys genuine masculine traits and is therefore applicable to humans as well (e.g., loving provision, protection, leadership, etc.), or it was applied to God as an adaptation to the sinful patriarchy of the culture into which the divine revelation came. The latter option would mean that this language has no relationship to the characteristics of human fathers and husbands; nor, for that matter, does the feminine language related to God have any relationship to women. It would seem very difficult to continue to refer to God with the biblical language while believing that it was only a cultural adaptation. As many feminists have asserted, to continue to use the patriarchal biblical language reinforces a patriarchal dimension within human relationships. Thus there seems to be an impetus of logic for egalitarians, whether liberal or evangelical, to move toward inclusive language for God. And with the move toward inclusive language has come a modification of the very nature of God. Feminist theology clearly demonstrates the validity of Bloesch's contention that "when we change the language about God we are basically moving into another religion. To re-symbolize is to redeify."[44]

Thus far, the writings of evangelical feminists do not say much about the issue of God language. How this question will be dealt with, as well as other questions related to the possible effects of the general feminist hermeneutic that allows the reinterpretation of certain texts as limited to certain cultural situations, will no doubt become clearer as feminism continues to influence the evangelical church through various means.[45]

In response to this feminist challenge within evangelicalism, advocates of the traditional viewpoint of a divine order between man and woman have also produced significant works seeking to blunt the inroads of feminism within the evangelical church. Their concern was not simply to counter the feminist arguments but also to elaborate the traditional understanding with more sensitivity to the contemporary concerns for equality of personhood.[46] The Council on Biblical Manhood and Womanhood was formed in 1987. Composed of evangelical pastors, academicians, and laypeople, the declared purpose of the CBMW is the promotion of what it calls the "Biblical vision of sexual complementarity," which includes distinctive roles for men and women in the church and in the home.[47]

Conclusion

History demonstrates that along with enjoying a measure of the love for each other according to the design of their Creator, man and woman throughout history have also known continual conflict in every realm of life. Sadly, this includes the evangelical church. The significance of this problem among evangelicals is evident in the expenditure of time and energy along with financial resources on both sides of the issue. Most recognize that the question of the role of women in the church cannot be isolated from the similar question of the relationship of men and women in the home. The issue of the role of women in the church therefore extends beyond what some might view as the limited arena of church life. It is finally a question that touches the very fabric of culture and society.

PART TWO

WOMAN AND MAN IN THE OLD TESTAMENT

CHAPTER THREE

THE RELATIONSHIP OF WOMAN AND MAN IN THE OLD TESTAMENT

Thomas Finley

Introduction

The Old Testament has a great deal to say about the relationship of women and men, and it is hardly possible to exhaust its wisdom on the subject in a brief chapter. In this chapter, I will look first for key issues about the relationship between man and woman within creation in Genesis 1–3 and what those relationships might reveal about order.

Does the Old Testament teach that a man is worth more than a woman? Some passages in the Mosaic Law have been taken that way, and I will consider some of these controversial verses in light of their cultural background and the basic theological principles established from Genesis 1–3.[1]

Foundational Matters (Genesis 1–3)

The first three chapters of Genesis are crucial for understanding what the Bible teaches about how men and women relate together. The creation account of Genesis provides the foundational understanding for the relation of man and woman. When Jesus dealt with the issue of divorce, He grounded His discussion in Genesis 1:27 and 2:24. Even what Moses taught must be understood in light of the way things were in the beginning (Matt. 19:3–9). Other New Testament teaching on the relation of man and woman also expressly looks back to the creation account (see 1 Cor. 11:2–16; 1 Tim. 2:11–15).

The first chapter of Genesis teaches the relationship of mankind as a whole, both male and female, to the rest of creation and to the Creator Himself. Chapter 2 of Genesis (v. 4ff.) shifts the focus from man in relation to the whole creation to the interrelationships between the first man and the first woman. Then chapter 3 describes how the man and the woman were alienated from each other, from God, and even from the rest of creation.

Man and Woman in the Image of God (Genesis 1:1–2:3)

Mankind (in Hebrew the same term is also used for "the man" or Adam) is clearly the climax of the entire creation laid out in Genesis 1, and God makes them rulers over all life. In addition, mankind stands in special relationship to God, in that God created them in His own image and likeness. In the words of Genesis 1:27–28:

> So God created man in his own image, in the image of God he created him; male and female he created them. God blessed them and said to them, "Be fruitful and increase in number; fill the earth and subdue it. Rule over the fish of the sea and the birds of the air and over every living creature that moves on the ground." (NIV)

Why does this passage give the sequence man—him—male and female—them? From the standpoint of the structure of the text, the reference to "male and female" prepares the way for the divine blessing: "Be fruitful and increase in number." It is verse 26 that first mentions God's desire for mankind to rule over the earth, and that appears to be the primary reason for the stress on the image of God. However, two things stand out about the creation of man. First, God uniquely used the plural to refer to Himself: "Let us make man in our image, in our likeness" (1:26 NIV). Second, it is only for mankind that the passage mentions the two categories of male and female. Such categories could be assumed to apply to the animals as well. Indeed, the Hebrew terms are frequently used of animals (cf. Gen. 6:19; 7:3, 9, 16; Lev. 3:1, 6), but not so in Genesis 1. With the statement about the image so closely juxtaposed to "male and female," the thought may be that "the divine plurality expressed in v. 26 is seen as an anticipation of the human plurality of the man and woman, thus casting the human relationship between man and woman in the role of reflecting God's own personal relationship with himself."[2] Caution must be exercised here, though, not to assume that there are sexual distinctions within the Godhead. Susan Foh notes that the reference to sexual differentiation explains what is meant by "man," not the "image of God": "God created Man the species on the sixth day, but more specifically he created a man and a woman, the two basic types of Man."[3] People must be "male and female" because God gives them the task to "fill the earth."

The idea of the social relationship between man and woman does reflect the relationship between the persons in the Godhead (Father, Son, and Holy Spirit), but the ordering of the text helps us to understand that the reflection is not through sexuality per se but through intimacy. Sexuality defines us in relation to the rest of creation, not in relation to God: "There is neither . . . male nor female . . . in Christ Jesus" (Gal. 3:28). Genesis 1, which talks in terms of "male and female," flows into chapter 2, which moves to "man and woman" and the way they connect with each other. There is something deeper in the difference between a man and a woman than merely the reproductive functions. The gender aspects of their relationship will become more explicit through the unfolding of the dynamics between "the man" and the "helper" specially created for him that he will name "Woman." Those dynamics in turn are reflective of the triune God, three distinct persons, each of whom "is dependent on the other for his own identity."[4]

Several important issues derive from the way that Genesis 1:27 is stated. First, God is responsible for the different sexes. The division of the human race into "male" and "female" is part of God's plan for His creation, and He calls "all" that He made "very good" (1:31). There is nothing bad or evil about the fact that human beings exist as both "male and female." In fact, it is *good* that they are divided into those categories. There is no indication in Scripture of the first person as an androgynous being, as some have taught.[5] Scripture teaches simply that God created mankind "male and female."

Second, there is an essential unity between the two sexes; they together comprise two parts of "man" or "mankind." The Hebrew term *adam* is normally a collective noun. That is, it groups all people together under the same general term.[6] The word has no plural form, and sometimes a singular pronoun can refer to it, as here in 1:27, "He created *him*" (italics added). Once the plurality of "male and female" is made explicit, then the narrator refers to "them." The same Hebrew word has a different sense in Genesis 2:7, where it refers to the first man, Adam ("the man" NIV).

Third, it is clear that creation in God's image applies to both male and female. Commentators cannot agree on exactly what the "image" of God is, but they do concur that the most significant implication of that image in people is brought out by the text itself. They are given the responsibility to "rule over" and "subdue" the rest of creation. Unlike English, the command form of the verb in Hebrew distinguishes between singular and plural, and all of the commands in 1:28 use the plural. There is no change in the persons referred to by "them": "Male and female He created *them*. God blessed *them;* and God said to *them* . . ." (italics added). Another way to state this implication is that man and woman are equal as persons in their standing before God, a fact that the apostle Paul underlines for believers in Christ: "There is neither Jew nor Greek, there is neither slave nor free man, there is neither male nor female; for you are all one in Christ Jesus" (Gal. 3:28).[7]

Paul's teaching in 1 Corinthians 11:7 (that man is the image and glory of God, and woman is the glory of man) does not deny this truth (cf. Col. 3:10–11 where he asserts that all believers are being renewed according to God's image). In 1 Corinthians 11 he is not referring to image of God as that which is common to all humanity, as in Genesis 1. His concern is much more limited, focusing on "headship." In his headship man images God in a way that woman does not. Woman is the "glory" of man in responding to his headship even as man is the "glory" of God in responding to His headship (cf. Prov. 12:4).

Since both man and woman are created in God's image, it is also true that they both share in the task of subduing the rest of creation. They will need each other just as much for this task as for multiplying and filling the earth. The latter task they share with the animals; only the task of subduing brings out the implication of their creation in the divine image.

Man and Woman in Relationship to Each Other (Genesis 2:4–25)

Whereas Genesis 1 used the terms "male and female," thus referring primarily to sexuality within the human species, Genesis 2 uses first "the man" *(adam)* and then "a helper suitable for him," whom "the man" *(adam)* names "woman" *(ishshah)* because she was taken from "man" *(ish)*. The terms used, then, have various implications for how the man and the woman relate to each other, and that is the primary point of the chapter.

In Genesis 1 the creation of mankind climaxes God's work and shows how He appointed people to rule over the rest of creation. In Genesis 2 the woman appears at the climax of the chapter, with God creating "the man" *(adam)* first. The apostle Paul argues in two places that the woman/wife in some sense needs to recognize the authority of the man/husband because of the order of creation: the man first and then the woman (1 Cor. 11:8–9; 1 Tim. 2:12–13). The source for Paul's argument must be Genesis 2. Some have argued, though, that Paul doesn't have a logical argument, because on the analogy of chapter 1 the woman should be the ruler of all creation. "It cannot be maintained that woman was inferior to man even if, as asserted in chapter ii, she was created after him without at once admitting that man is inferior to the creeping things, because he was created after them."[8] This argument, besides assuming falsely that a subordinate relationship has to mean inferiority, fails to take into account the different structures of the two chapters. In chapter 1 heaven and earth are the realm where mankind rules, and therefore it is created before the man is placed there. Chapter 2 focuses instead on the relationship between the man and the woman, the two divisions of mankind. That is, while man is the climax of the sequence of creation in Genesis 1, in Genesis 2 woman is the climax of the search for a helper. She was the only one who was the "helper corresponding to" Adam. By creating man first and then the woman from the man, God determines an order that is not seen for any other creature.

Even more to the point, God gave the man his responsibility before He created the woman. First God places the man in the garden "to cultivate it and keep it" (2:15), and then He gives him the prohibition about "the tree of the knowledge of good and evil" (2:16–17). All this is prior to any discussion at all of the woman. The reader's attention first turns to her when God says in the very next verse (2:18), "It is not good for the man to be alone; I will make him a helper suitable for him." What is it here that is "not good"? Partly it would seem to be lack of companionship, but a key issue from the immediate context is that he needs someone to help him carry out his responsibilities; he cannot accomplish them by himself.

What are those responsibilities? Chapter 1 spoke of filling the earth and subduing it, of having dominion over it as a representative of God. The major work of chapter 2 appears to be gardening (2:15). Later in the chapter the statement is made that the man and his wife "shall become one flesh." By inference, one of the purposes for the woman is that she will help the man in the process of reproduction, something that obviously cannot happen without her. But is there more to her help than that? Is her sole purpose only the means to bearing and nurturing children? (That is not to say that such a purpose is not a noble one!)

Many have answered the question in the affirmative. Both Augustine and Aquinas believed that for any other type of work, another man would have made a better helper.[9] More recently, David Clines argued that God was not thinking of Adam's good in creating the woman but rather "of himself and of his designs for the human race." He also pointed out that the punishment on the woman in chapter 3 concerns making difficult "the one thing she has been created to do."[10]

The context of Genesis 1–3 will not allow such a simple answer. First of all, as was pointed out above, the sexual distinctions that God created were good. Reproduction did not have to be through sexual differentiation; there are other ways it could have been accomplished. Yet God chose to have most of creation participate in a reproductive process that would involve both a male and a female, and the fact was singled out especially for mankind. If Aquinas's negative view of women were accepted, one would wonder why God didn't create some other way for reproduction to take place.

Second, there is no reason to think that women are excluded from the dominion over all creation that was given to mankind. Women are not excluded from the image of God, and that entails that God's plan for them is to be part of ruling the rest of creation. The same thing is true of 2:18. God makes no comment at that point about how the one who is "suitable for" ("corresponds to") the man is to help. The Hebrew here is literally "like opposite him." According to Gordon Wenham, "It seems to express the notion of complementarity rather than identity." Wenham's translation is "a helper matching him."[11] By default, it would seem that the Lord at least has in mind that the woman would help her husband care for the garden.

God spoke of the need for a helper for the man, but then He immediately turned to the animals. Why did God have the man name the animals first before He created the woman? It seems that the man must learn some lesson about his need for her, and therefore Clines cannot be right that God is thinking only of His own plan and not of the man. God could have simply brought the woman to the man and told him her function. Instead He forces the man to discover his need so that he will recognize the suitable helper when she arrives. This is a key point. It is not good for men to function alone; they have to recognize that they need women in order to carry out their task of ruling and subduing properly. Women were designed to help men, and it is to the detriment of both women and men when their help is rejected or not sought.

By giving each animal a name, Adam saw into its essential nature and also exercised his authority over it. In Genesis 1, God did all of the naming; now the man who bears God's image assigns the names. After God made the woman and brought her to Adam, he immediately recognized her as the suitable helper, as the person who was in essential oneness with him. By giving her a name, he also exercised his authoritative headship in the relationship. As Raymond Ortlund Jr. put it, "God did not explain to the woman who she was in relation to the man, although He could have done so. He allowed Adam to define the woman, in keeping with Adam's headship."[12]

There are some differences between how Adam named the woman and how he named the animals. The narrator points out that for the animals, "Whatever the man called a living creature, that was its name" (2:19). The man's statement with regard to the woman is pointedly indirect and could be paraphrased: "People will call her 'woman,' for she was taken from 'man.'" In giving her a name, he also gives himself a new name. "Adam" is a general term meaning man and applies to both of them (cf. 5:2, "and [God] named them Man") with Adam himself functioning as the representative head. He continued to bear that name the rest of his life. Her name, "woman" *(ishshah)*, relates to his new name, "man" *(ish)*. Adam recognized a new relationship and saw himself in a new light: the one from whom "woman" was "taken."

God also often changed the name of a person when the person's relationship to Him changed. Some examples are Abram/Abraham (Gen.

17:5), Sarai/Sarah (Gen. 17:15), and Jacob/Israel (Gen. 32:28). In similar fashion, the man gave his wife the new name "Eve" after some essential changes in their relationship with each other and with God (Gen. 3:20).

Looking further at the man's reaction to the woman (2:23), he is impressed by the fact that she is of the same substance as he is, "bone of my bones, and flesh of my flesh." The identical sequence, bone and flesh, is used elsewhere of kinship relations (Gen. 29:14; Judg. 9:2; 2 Sam. 5:1; 19:13; 1 Chron. 11:1). What the man failed to find in any animal he found in the woman: someone who could be in relationship with him. That relationship implies a sense of connectedness and mutual feelings. It is a family relationship. The narrator expressed it best: "For this reason a man will leave his father and mother and be united to his wife, and they will become one flesh" (Gen. 2:24 NIV).

This last passage raises a new question: What is meant by "they will become one flesh"? In one sense, it refers to the physical union of a man and his wife, a union that founds a new relationship that is different from that between a man and his parents. In another sense, the passionate tenor of the naming statement and its climactic position in the chapter help the reader to infer that there will be a partnership here that goes beyond merely reproducing their own kind. For the first pair, the relationship between them resulted from the fact that the woman had been taken from her husband's side. For all subsequent marriages, it will be established when the man leaves one relationship with his parents and enters a new one with his wife.[13]

To return to the original question: How will the woman help the man? Except for the issue of bearing children, this is not a question that can be answered with a straightforward, "She will do such-and-such." The answer is that she will help him through her relationship with him. As the head, he will guide them in focusing on the task, and she will partner with him to accomplish it.

The term "helper" carries no idea of personal inferiority or weakness; it is frequently used in the Old Testament of God helping His people (e.g., Gen. 49:25; Exod. 18:4; Deut. 33:7; 1 Sam. 7:12). Neither does the word "imply that the helper is stronger than the helped; simply that the latter's strength is inadequate by itself (e.g. Joshua 1:14; 10:4, 6; 1 Chron. 12:17, 19, 21, 22)."[14] Still, the fact that the woman was created to help the man and not the other way around gives the man a certain centrality (cf. 1 Cor. 11:8–10). He is created first, provided with a garden and an occupation. Now God, like a father, provides the man with a wife to help in order that together they might fulfill their purpose as mankind. Her role is not leadership over the man or somehow to be in competition with him, but she will work alongside him in a relationship of support and help.

To some, this may appear to assign the woman to an inferior role, but one must remember that this is the Garden of Eden, the ideal Paradise that God created for the first couple. There was no sense of competition or of worthlessness or of superiority. The negative effects would come later when the man and his wife disobeyed their Creator. As Susan Foh put it so aptly:

> God's assignment of functions may sound like job discrimination to us. Men get to be bosses, and women have to be secretaries. We feel a twinge (or maybe a pang) of resentment because we do not know what a sin-free hierarchical arrangement can be like. We know only the arbitrariness, the dominance, the arrogance that even the best boss/underling relationship has. But in Eden it was different. It really was. The man and the woman knew each other as equals, both in the image of God, and thus each with a personal relationship to God. Neither doubted the worth of the other nor of him/herself. Each was to perform his/her task in a different way, the man as the head and the woman as his helper. They operated as truly one flesh, one person. In one body does the rib rebel against or envy the head?[15]

God gave the first man, then, a leadership role, and He created the first woman as a partner who was of the same substance as the man. She "corresponded" to him in a complementary way, unlike the animals who could help him, but not as an equal partner. The man exercised his leadership by assigning the woman a name that showed her essential oneness with him. God's plan was for the two of them to work hand in hand in tending the garden and in filling and subduing the world. There was no intent on God's part or the man's part to place the woman into an inferior position. She, like the man, is made in the image of God. She, along with the man, is called to tend the garden, to reign over the animal kingdom, and to populate the earth. Together they stand before each other, naked but not ashamed (Gen. 2:25).

The relationship of man and woman in the creation account involved an equality and complementary order that resulted in oneness. Stephen Clark expressed this succinctly:

> There is subordination in Genesis 2, but it is a very specific kind of subordination—the kind that makes one person out of two. According to Genesis 2, woman was created to be a help to man, not to be a servant or a slave. She was created to be a complement to him, making a household and children possible. He in turn protected her, provided for her, and considered her part of himself, a partner in life. He was the head of the relationship, head of a relationship that was "one flesh."[16]

Although Genesis 2 deals primarily with man and woman in the marriage relationship, it also provides something of the foundational model for the broader relationship between man and woman. Adam and Eve represent man and woman as well as husband and wife.

Man and Woman Fall into Sin (Genesis 3)

When the text said in chapter 2 that the two were naked but unashamed as they stood before each other, it set up a contrast that occurs in chapter 3. After they ate the forbidden fruit, "the eyes of both of them were opened, and they knew that they were naked; and they sewed fig leaves together and made themselves loin coverings" (Gen. 3:7). The immediate result of their sin was a rupture in their relationship with each other. They now experienced something new: shame because they were naked.

Many dynamics about the story of the temptation and its consequences relate directly to the issue of man/woman relationships. One of the first questions that arises is why the serpent chose to deceive the woman rather than the man. It is important to remember that the text does not actually say why the woman was singled out this way. Based on the overall context, one could say that the serpent chose the woman because she was not the one with the lead role. Since she was supposed to be the man's helper, what better way to persuade the couple to turn against God than to undermine her desire to cooperate with the conditions that God had laid out? Possibly she had received those conditions secondhand from her husband, but the text is silent about how she came to know about them.

One issue that needs special clarification concerns the interpretation of 3:6, "She gave also to her husband with her, and he ate." Was her husband "with her" during the entire time of the temptation? Some have suggested this with the implication that he watched the entire process but refused to step in and stop it.[17] This is unsatisfying in terms of the account itself, because the text focuses only on the intimate conversation between the serpent and the woman. It is at the point that she "gave also to her husband" that the text says, "with her." The Hebrew indicates no more than that he was with her when she gave him the fruit. The comment seems incidental to the narrative rather than defining for his guilt. This would also agree with the reason God gave for His pronouncement against the man: "Because you have listened to the voice of your wife, and have eaten from the tree about which I commanded you, saying, 'You shall not eat from it'" (3:17). He is guilty because he chose to follow what his wife said instead of what God had commanded. Had he been present during the temptation, his responsibility would have been to step in and expose the serpent as a liar. Also, when Adam passed the blame for their sin to his wife, she could have responded that her husband had been there through the whole time of temptation and yet had remained silent. She would have had every right to blame him first and the serpent second.

After the couple ate the fruit, God came into the garden and called for the man. Even though the woman had succumbed to the deceit and persuaded her husband to join her in rebellion against God, God held the man primarily responsible for what had happened. This is clear first from God's summons to Adam, "Where are you?" In the Hebrew, the word "you" has a form that is appropriate for addressing one individual who is also a male. It is also brought out through the fact that God issues an indictment only for the man, not for the woman: "Because you have listened to the voice of your wife, and have eaten from the tree about which I commanded you, saying, 'You shall not eat from it'" (Gen. 3:17). Paul also recognized this when he singled out Adam as the one man through whom "sin entered the world" (Rom. 5:12 NIV).

Even though Adam was the head of the relationship, he tried immediately to deny his responsibility: "The woman whom You gave to be with me, she gave me from the tree, and I ate" (3:12). God gave the woman to him as companion, and now he blames her for what happened. Ultimately, he blames God for giving her to him in the first place. Adam's attempt to shift the blame here was devastating for the relationship. Now rather than two functioning as one, there are two at cross-purposes. The leader tries to disassociate himself from his helper. He says, in effect, "She acted on her own initiative; I'm not involved."

When God turns to the woman, she points to the serpent: "The serpent deceived me, and I ate." Consequently, God makes a pronouncement against the serpent first. The judgment refers in the first line to the offspring of the woman as her descendants, but the second line with the singular pronoun "he" and the direct reference to the serpent himself ("you") justifies viewing the passage as the *protevangelium,* the first hint in the Scriptures of the coming Messiah and of God's plan to gain victory over evil in the world.[18] Many have stressed how Eve was the one deceived, but God points out in His curse on the serpent that it is through the children whom Eve will bear that eventually a son will be born who will gain the ultimate victory over the serpent. So through this statement God elevates the role of the woman in His plan for winning back the world to Himself.

God next turns His attention from the serpent to the punishment for the woman (3:16). Because she failed to tend to her relationship by consulting with her husband and allowed herself to be deceived by the serpent, she would experience great difficulties in the related areas of bearing children and partnering with her husband. There are two major interpretations of Genesis 3:16. Susan Foh thinks that the verse refers to "the beginning of the battle of the sexes," and this view has become widely popular: "The woman's desire is to control her husband (to usurp his divinely appointed headship), and he must master her, if he can."[19] Claus Westermann takes a more traditional view: "[J]ust where the woman finds her fulfillment in life, her honor and her joy, namely in her relationship to her husband and as mother of her children, there too she finds that it is not pure bliss, but pain, burden, humiliation and subordination."[20] Even though Foh views the meaning of the woman's "desire" differently, she arrives at a similar conclusion: "And so, the rule of love founded in paradise is replaced by struggle, tyranny, domination, and manipulation."[21] This state of affairs is what it is like after the man and his wife disobeyed God, and much of the "pain, burden, humiliation and subordination" can be struggled against through obedience to Christ.

In like manner, the man, who listened to his wife rather than to God, also finds the very ground from which he was taken cursed. His initial occupation of caring for a fruitful garden will be turned into the hard labor of struggling against a ground that will yield its fruit only with great difficulty. Ultimately, he will return to that very ground.

While the focal point of the punishments moves from serpent to woman to man, it is also true that both the man and his wife share together, though to different degrees, in each of the pronouncements. Blessing will come to both when "the seed of the woman" ultimately triumphs over the serpent; both will face together the difficulties associated with her pregnancy and labor in childbirth; both will struggle with getting bread from the ground; and, finally, both will return to the ground in death. Yet one should also note the formal indictment that introduces the punishment for Adam: "Because you have listened to the voice of your wife, and have eaten from the tree about which I commanded you, saying, 'You shall not eat from it' . . ." (3:17). This indictment against Adam has no counterpart in the judgment concerning the woman, and this also shows that Adam bore the primary responsibility for the sin as the head or representative of mankind.

What was the effect of the Fall in Genesis 3 on the relationship of man and woman? First, it is clear that the man had the primary responsibility before God as the head of the relationship. Second, God's ideal intention for the man and his wife has been grossly distorted through disobedience. Instead of leading in the context of a mutual relationship, the man will dominate his wife. Where they should work together for a common God-given goal, the couple will find themselves, instead, competing against each other. This sense of competition is implied by the contrast: "Your desire will be for your husband, [but] he will rule over you" (v. 16 NIV). Third, the nature of the punishments helps to uncover the roles that were already there from creation. "The woman's punishment struck at the deepest root of her being as wife and mother, the man's strikes at the innermost nerve of his life: his work, his activity, and provision for sustenance."[22] Finally, the only hope for redemption from this bondage is to trust in the Lord's plans for the ultimate defeat of the serpent.

The Worth of a Woman

A commonly heard complaint is that the Old Testament, or at least parts of it, devalues the worth of women by validating a patriarchal society. The general principles established from the early chapters of Genesis, though, help us to understand that women are not considered of any less value than men in God's eyes. Women are created in God's image equally with men. Therefore, we should expect the rest of Scripture to teach things that are in harmony with what is taught in the early chapters of Genesis. Jesus Christ Himself upheld the authority of the Old Testament in what it teaches (Matt. 5:17–19). Because of Genesis 1:26–28 the issue is settled: Any woman can cling to the truth that as a human being she is just as valuable in God's sight as any other human being. Paul reaffirms the same truth in the New Testament: "There is neither . . . male nor female . . . in Christ Jesus" (Gal. 3:28). Further, Genesis 2:23 affirms her kinship relationship with man. She is not his slave but of his same substance.

I suspect that a large part of the issue that some have with the position of women in the patriarchal society seen in the Old Testament stems from not considering the immense cultural difference between ancient Israel and modern life. Moderns are almost obsessed with issues of individual rights, and families come in all sizes and shapes, including the single-parent family. In biblical times, there was more a sense of community, and families would normally be extended, sometimes with numerous related people living together in the same dwelling. The families of Abraham (Gen. 24:67) and Jacob (Gen. 37:2–4) illustrate the practice of extended families living in at least close proximity. Even if each couple within a broader family had separate houses (Job 1:4, 13), there was still a strong sense of family solidarity that would operate to make sure that anyone in the family was provided for (cf. the book of Ruth). This great cultural distance must be kept in mind when considering the "rights" of women in Old Testament times. If we had a chance to interview Sarah or Ruth or Hannah, would they even be able to understand what we meant by questions of individual rights?

The Patriarchal Focus of Genesis

Clearly the book of Genesis focuses on men. The genealogies, even though they sometimes mention "daughters" as a general category, trace lineage through the sons.[23] God establishes His covenant with men, and it is the men Abraham, Isaac, and Jacob who carry forward the promise. The wives of the patriarchs are not completely absent from the narrative, of course, but they appear mainly in the background as those who stand behind their husbands.

Does this mean that God devalues the position of women in terms of His plan of salvation for the human race? That hardly can be the case considering that God made His first promise of salvation to Eve (see Gen. 3:15). Once again we are faced with the issue of role. As people, we tend to think that the actors in the play are more important than those who work "behind the scenes" to make the play possible, but is that really true? The actors will receive more exposure and outward honor than the set designers, but both are equally necessary to the play. In the same way, the men at center stage of the book of Genesis do not render the women of less value or importance to God's plan of redemption.

Actually, God worked through the men as representatives of the people. Abraham was chosen by God to represent all people of faith (Rom. 4:16), and what God did through Jacob represented the Lord's intentions for the entire nation of Israel. Jacob was also given the name of "Israel," the name in turn given to the whole nation (Gen. 32:27–28). When God chose a man, He also chose a people that included both men and women.

It is also true that there are moments when a woman takes center stage in the narratives of Genesis. For example, even though Cain and Abel stand out as the major figures of chapter 4, the passage is framed by two occasions when Eve named her sons. Of Cain she said, "I have gotten a manchild with the help of the Lord" (v. 1), and of Seth, "God has appointed me another offspring in place of Abel, for Cain killed him" (v. 25). From 5:3 it would appear that Adam rather than Eve named Seth. Apparently Adam concurred with his wife's choice of name, and 5:3 stresses Adam's role as the leader of the couple. Some other examples of a woman as the center of attention in Genesis include the narrative of Hagar's flight from Sarah (Gen. 21:17–21) and the story of Tamar's method of ensuring she would have a son to carry on the line of her deceased husband (Genesis 38).

When Eve named Cain, she used the term "man" uniquely of a baby (hence "manchild" in the NASB). It is the same word used in Genesis 2:23 when Adam named Eve, "She shall be called Woman, because she was taken out of Man." Probably readers are supposed to notice the connection between the two incidents of naming.[24] When God created Eve, He separated her from the man, but Eve herself from now on would bear offspring, some of whom would be men. The second name that Adam gave her, "Eve," reflects this reality, for she became "the mother of all living."[25] Either parent can name a child, and there are other cases in Genesis where the mother names her son (29:32–35; 30:6–24; 35:18; 38:4–5). It is interesting that in the parent-child relationship, either parent could exercise the authority indicated by giving a name to the child.

At the risk of stating the obvious, regardless of how prominent the men are in the book of Genesis, it was impossible for any of them to even exist apart from the women. Without a mother there can be no birth, and the patriarchal narratives in Genesis do not suppress that fact.

Indeed, the identity of the mother of one of the patriarchs was crucial; it was important that she be within the chosen circle. This is most evident in the case of Sarah, Abraham's wife. For many years she was barren (Gen. 11:30), so Abraham at first thought that his servant Eliezer might be the one chosen by God to inherit the promise (Gen. 15:2–3). However, God made it clear that the heir would come from Abraham's own body (15:4). When Sarah continued in her barrenness, she suggested that her husband have a child by her Egyptian handmaiden, Hagar (16:1–2). Even though Hagar proceeded to bear Ishmael for Abraham, God told Abraham that Sarah herself would have a son, despite her advanced age (18:9–11). Later, God confirmed that Isaac, the son of both Abraham and Sarah, was the son of promise (21:12). Some other incidents that point to the importance of the right mother for the son who is to inherit the promise of God include the times when the mother's purity was endangered by the possibility of adultery (Gen. 12:10–20; 20; 26:6–11), the search for a bride for Isaac (Genesis 24), and Tamar's efforts to bear an heir for Judah (Genesis 38). Genesis stresses that the ancestry of the mother was just as important as that of the father (see also Gen. 26:34–35; 27:46; 28:1–2).

Even though Hagar was not the chosen mother for the promised seed, the Lord still appeared to her and gave her a promise: "I will greatly multiply your descendants so that they shall be too many to count" (16:10). The words God used remind us of His promise to Abraham (15:5; 22:17). Also, just as Abraham and other patriarchs often named a place after some encounter they had with the Lord (Gen. 22:14; 26:20–22, 33; 28:17–19; 32:30), so Hagar gave a name to the Lord in honor of her experience: "You are El-roi" ("the God who sees") (see 16:13).

In sum, the women are generally less prominent in Genesis than the men, but God does not view them as any less important. The patriarchs were representative figures, even as Adam represented the entire human race. In certain instances, the women figure more prominently in the narrative, especially in situations related to family issues.

Leviticus and the Evaluation of Women

Certain passages in Leviticus require special study because it is easy to misinterpret them as lessening the value of women. As with any biblical text, it is necessary to study what the text meant in its original context before making applications to what it means now. Even many commentators who should know better are guilty of jumping too quickly from the ancient context and culture to modern issues.

Purification After Childbirth (Leviticus 12)

A case in point is Leviticus 12, which deals with the purification of a woman after she gives birth. If an Israelite woman gave birth to a boy, she was to be ceremonially unclean for seven days until her son was circumcised (12:2–3), after which time she would have thirty-three days "to be purified from her bleeding" (12:4 NIV). However, if her baby was a female, her initial period of uncleanness was for two weeks, "as in her menstruation" (12:5), and her time of purification from her blood was sixty-six days. In other words, she would need to avoid touching sacred things or entering the sanctuary twice as long after having a girl as for a boy.

One commentator says, "The cultic inferiority of the female sex is expressed in giving the female birth a double 'uncleanness' effect, shown also in the double period required in this case before the mother is once more clean."[26] The text does not directly state why there is a longer period of uncleanness when a female child is born, so it is only an assumption to say that it teaches the inferiority of females. Other explanations have been given. Further, the mother had to bring the same sacrifice for her purification whether her child was a son or a daughter (12:6), so it cannot be that the birth of a girl led to a higher state of sinfulness. Perhaps the Law was merely attempting to differentiate men and women without meaning to indicate difference in value.[27]

Without a direct statement in the text about the reason for the different lengths of unclean or impure status for the mother, it is impossible to settle the issue, but some important features of the context give some help. The time during which the mother remains in a state of uncleanness has two parts. The first part corresponds to "the days of her menstruation" (vv. 2, 5), while the second part includes "to be purified from her bleeding" (vv. 4–5 NIV). The circumcision of the boy on the eighth day brings the first part to a conclusion (v. 3), while for the daughter it continues for a second week (v. 5). In similar fashion, the time of purification for the mother of a girl lasts twice as long as that for the mother of a son. Thus it appears that the child has an influence on the mother's status. Why should this be so?

With regard to the worship of the Lord, men served as priests and men received circumcision, the mark of the covenant. They did this in a representative manner, standing for the nation as a whole. In a similar way, boy babies may have resulted in a briefer period of uncleanness for the mother simply to indicate the role the boy would someday assume as head over his future family. A daughter, on the other hand, would be destined to be under the protection or authority of first her father and then her husband. Both a son and a daughter would also be under the authority of their mother, of course, but the status of the mother during the time of uncleanness and purification could be a reminder of the representative role that sons have. With respect to the daughter herself, as a woman she would in general be subject to more seasons of uncleanness and purification throughout her life because of events such as menstruation and childbirth.[28]

Ultimately, we do not know why the regulation prescribed a longer period of ceremonial isolation for the birth of a daughter than of a son. In any case, it is not reasonable to charge the Levitical law with saying that women are less valuable than men.

The Value of a Woman for a Vow (Leviticus 27:2–8)

According to Leviticus 27:2–8 (NIV), "If anyone makes a special vow to dedicate persons to the LORD by giving equivalent values," the value is to be fifty shekels for a male between the ages of twenty and sixty but only thirty shekels for a female within the same age range. Likewise, "If it is a person between the ages of five and twenty, set the value of a male at twenty shekels and of a female at ten shekels." Finally, if the person is over sixty, the value is fifteen shekels for a male but ten shekels for a female. This is another passage that some have thought teaches that women were not valued as much as men. According to one author, "Females are thus worth between 50% and 66% what males are worth. Women, in other words, are not worthless or negligible, but they are not equal to men."[29] This *assumes* that the figures of Leviticus are given to indicate absolute worth of a man and a woman in relation to each other. There are reasons for rejecting this assumption, though.

First, the passage also makes distinctions based on age. Does this mean that the law valued the young more than the elderly, and children the least of all? That hardly seems likely in light of the great value that the Old Testament assigns to advanced age and the teaching that children are a blessing from the Lord.[30]

Second, the passage is not about absolute value in any and every situation but about value in a particular setting. That setting is work or service in the sanctuary. That is, an Israelite might promise the Lord to spend his or her life in the sanctuary doing various kinds of service. Or he or she might dedicate a child to such service, even as Hannah who dedicated her son in advance of his birth (1 Sam. 1:28; 2:18).[31] Since Levites normally served in the sanctuary, however, it was possible for someone to substitute a monetary value instead. Because of the type of work involved, the young and strong male would be more valuable than a child (whose future is unknown), an old person, or a female of comparable age. As John Hartley puts it, "In this law the price was set on the basis of a person's strength, not on the basis of a person's intrinsic value as a human being."[32]

Women and the Taking of Vows

If a minor daughter made a vow or an oath to the Lord and her father heard it, he had the power to either approve it through silence or to forbid it (Num. 30:3–5). If she didn't carry out the vow because of her father's wishes, then "the Lord will forgive her because her father had forbidden her." For an adult woman, the same passage in Numbers deals with three situations. First, if she had made a vow while in her father's house but then got married, her husband can either remain silent and approve it or speak up and annul it (vv. 6–8). Second, a widow or a divorced woman who makes any vow is obligated to fulfill it (v. 9). Third, a husband has the opportunity to annul his wife's vow as soon as he hears of it. If he remains silent, it must stand, even if he should disapprove of it at a later time (vv. 10–15), though the guilt for not carrying it out would rest on his shoulders rather than on the woman's.

The text is silent about the situation of a son living at home who might take a vow. Some have assumed this meant that a vow for any male was always binding, but it is better to conclude that the discussion was not intended to cover every possible situation.[33] Perhaps the situation of the need for a wife's vow to be validated by her husband led most naturally to the discussion of the daughter. It might be assumed that a similar circumstance would hold for the unmarried son living at home. Later Jewish tradition interpreted the passage to mean that a man was obligated to his vows after he was thirteen and that the situation described for a daughter not yet betrothed pertained only if she was under twelve.[34]

Clearly, the father/husband had authority that extended over the desire of a girl or woman to carry out a religious act. The vow would typically involve the offering of a sacrifice (Lev. 22:21, 23; Num. 6:13–21; 15:2–12; Deut. 12:11; Isa. 19:21) and so could have an economic impact on the household. With the man having the primary responsibility for deriving a living for the family (Gen. 3:17–19), the man would have a say in what might have an effect on the economy of his family.[35] A woman could also take a Nazirite vow (Num. 6:2), and that might have implications for the diet of the rest of the family if a daughter living at home or a married woman took the vow. The purpose of the law was not just to give men authority over women but also to allow the husband/father in a family unit to have veto power over an action that might affect the household. It also served to protect the woman, who might make a vow under the emotion of the moment without fully considering all of its consequences for the family. Naturally, the man might also make a rash vow, as in the case of Jephthah (Judg. 11:30–40), but as the head of the family unit he bore full responsibility for whatever he vowed.

It also needs to be noted that women could participate in vows to the Lord, and widows and divorcées could do so without any input from a man. In fact, a husband or father could annul a vow only upon first hearing of it. This probably meant that only vows that were obviously extravagant or "rash" (Numb. 30:6) were likely to be annulled. The man could of course abuse his privilege by making a general practice of forbidding any vows.

Was Marriage Unfair to the Woman?

Apparently, the Old Testament permitted a man to have more than one wife but absolutely prohibited a woman from having more than one husband. That is, her marital status automatically made liaison with any man, married or not, adultery; but a man could only commit adultery by joining up with a woman who was already married. Does this mean the Old Testament was unfair, after all, in how it treated men and women?

God did not prohibit polygamy (or, more accurately, polygyny) directly in the Law of Moses, but He regulated it. Various incestuous relationships were prohibited (Leviticus 18). A man was not permitted to marry two sisters (Lev. 18:18). If a man acquired a woman sold into slavery for his wife and then married a second wife, he was not allowed to reduce the food and clothing allowance of the first wife or to deprive her of conjugal rights (Exod. 21:8–10). If a man's oldest son was born to a wife who became disfavored, he was not permitted to deny the rights of the firstborn in deference to the son of a more favored wife (Deut. 21:15–17). By doing so, the Law of Moses chose to focus on the evil consequences of polygamy rather than to abolish the practice. This divine viewpoint toward polygamy is analogous to how God dealt with divorce and slavery. They were permitted for "the hardness of men's hearts," but certain passages in both Testaments underscore God's ultimate desire for marriage to be permanent and for people to be free.

When the Lord Jesus was questioned about divorce, He rightly referred to Genesis 2:24, a pronouncement that stands outside the Mosaic Law and that encapsulates a universal principle: "For this reason a man shall leave his father and mother and be joined to his wife, and the two shall become one flesh." This verse clearly envisions marriage as between one man and one woman, and as our Lord concluded, it was to be permanent: "What therefore God has joined together, let no man separate" (Matt. 19:5–6). Also, the principle that the husband is the head of the marriage relationship underlies all the regulations of the Old Testament. This was not to put the woman in her place, but to make for a smooth running of the family unit and to protect and provide for women in the society. Additionally, many regulations of marriage in the Old Testament were, as the Lord Jesus stressed, necessary because of the "hardness" of people's hearts (Matt. 19:8; Deut. 24:1–2).

What about the prohibition of adultery in the Ten Commandments

(Exod. 20:14; Deut. 5:18)? Did that commandment in effect prohibit more than one wife? The wording of the adultery commandment was given in such a way that it addressed the man as the head of the relationship. It was his responsibility to turn away from a relationship with another man's wife. Behind the negative wording of the command, though, stands also a more positive emphasis.

The commandments are divided into two parts, responsibilities toward God and responsibilities toward one's neighbor. Surely, the responsibilities toward God included the positive attitude expressed in Deuteronomy 6:5 that one should "love the Lord your God with all your heart and with all your soul and with all your might." One's duty to God included more than merely avoiding idolatry, refusing to take the Lord's name in vain, and observing the Sabbath. Those were mere outward signs of the inner attitude of total devotion. So it was with the commandments about a neighbor. They were aimed not merely at an absence of conflict but at a true harmony in human relations: "Love your neighbor as yourself" (Lev. 19:18). The commandment about adultery was aimed, then, at a harmonious relationship between the husband and wife, and that harmony would ideally include exclusivity as part of it. That certain deviations from it were regulated in the Mosaic Law was due to hardness of heart.[36]

Concluding Issues: Equal Before God but Different from a Man

Women and men are both in the image of God and therefore stand equal before God. That is the point of Galatians 3:28, which states that in Christ "there is neither male nor female." This fundamental equality means that it is wrong to treat a woman as though she is less valuable as a person. When the Old Testament is approached with the bias that it teaches that women are not as valuable as men, something is wrong with the methodology. The main problem may be that those who use such a method are equating value with function.

It is biologically impossible for a man to take on the function of being a mother. Perhaps some men might make better mothers than some women. They might take better care of themselves during the pregnancy, and they might work harder at bonding with the baby when it is born. No matter—they don't meet the one essential qualification. Only women need apply! Does that mean a man is of less value than a woman, who can be a mother? Neither is it really possible for a woman to be a father. She can try to do all the things that fathers do, but she will never really be quite the same as a man in that role.

The Old Testament teaches that from the beginning of creation there has been male and female, man and woman, husband and wife. They are different in their essential roles of head and helper, and those differences are expressed throughout the structure of human society.

God's perfect will was not for men to oppress women through patriarchal structures. He does not support abuse or injustice or belittlement; those evils are a result of sin. When the first couple was disobedient, a corruption of everything that is good entered the world. Headship degenerated to domination, and helping deteriorated to competition.

God does desire for men and women to face together the task of filling and subduing the world. Mothers and fathers are desperately needed; godly husbands and wives are in constant demand; and men and women whose interaction with each other is grounded in their relationship with the Lord are essential.

CHAPTER FOUR

THE MINISTRY OF WOMEN IN THE OLD TESTAMENT

Thomas Finley

Introduction

In this chapter I will examine how Old Testament women participated in worship and in the life of the community. From this examination, a general picture should emerge of the relationship of women and men as far as leadership in the community is concerned. The reader should keep in mind that the culture of the people in the Old Testament is not the same as modern culture. Hence one needs to be careful about assuming that the way something was done in the Old Testament should be normative for today. Rather it is important to look for general principles that are universally valid and preferably specifically taught as doctrine in the Bible.

Women and Leadership in Ancient Israel

The two basic institutions of leadership in ancient Israel were the priesthood and the monarchy. Prophets also stepped in to bring a word from the Lord to His people, but the phenomenon of prophecy was more situational than constant in nature. That is, although prophecy occurred throughout the history of Israel, individual prophets arose only at specific times and under special circumstances. Some prophets spent virtually their entire adult lives in ministry, but it was also possible for a prophet to receive a call at a particular point in life with a commission to deliver a message, after which time the prophet no longer functioned in that capacity. That seems to be the force of Amos's words to Amaziah: "I am not a prophet, nor am I the son of a prophet; for I am a herdsman and a grower of sycamore figs" (Amos 7:14). Kings and priests, by contrast, were perpetuated through hereditary succession and served for life.

The fact that kings and priests constituted official institutions of the state meant that they also had the power to enforce their decisions on the people. The king had control of the army, and the priests controlled access to God through the sacrificial system. God revealed His will and gave direction to His people through the prophets. They could function as a check on the monarchy and the priesthood, in that God often sent a prophet when the king or priests became corrupt.[1] Of course it would be up to the king or priest to recognize the divine authority of the prophet or to reject him or her. Israel had false prophets as well as true prophets of the Lord. Sometimes a prophet or a group of prophets would have fairly constant access to the king, who might even have certain prophets that he would call on regularly when he needed guidance from the Lord (see 1 Kings 22:1–14).

It is a well-known fact that women were excluded from the priesthood in Israel. This probably reflects the creation order that was revealed in Genesis 1–2. The priests represented the people before God, and the man as the head of the relationship between man and woman also represents humanity before God. Another reason for limiting the priesthood to men may have been because of the direct authority of the priest over the system of worship. A third reason might be suggested: Hereditary succession typically occurred from father to son, even as property was passed on to the sons.

Even though she could not serve as a priest, it was possible for a woman to serve in a special capacity at the tabernacle in the wilderness. When Bezalel constructed the tabernacle, he made the bronze basin and its stand "from the mirrors of the serving women who served at the doorway of the tent of meeting" (Exod. 38:8). What were these "women who served" doing? The Hebrew word that describes this activity is not the normal term for "serving," but a special word that is otherwise used only of the service of Levites in "the work of the tent of meeting" (Num. 4:23; 8:24), of some women "who served at the doorway of the tent of meeting" when it was at Shiloh (1 Sam. 2:22), and of military service (Num. 31:7; Isa. 29:7–8; 31:4; Zech. 14:12). The ancient interpreters thought the women were either praying (Syriac and Targums) or fasting (Greek Septuagint). Jerome, who translated the Latin Vulgate, said they were "guarding" the entrance to the tabernacle. Since the word for their service is the same as that used for the service of the Levites, they probably had a parallel type of work, possibly taking care of the entryway.

Whether these women did religious service or physical work, they had a function that was complementary to the Levites, who worked inside the wilderness tabernacle. The women helped the men to keep the sanctuary in order, and their service for the Lord calls to mind the New Testament women who served in the church (Rom. 16:1; 1 Tim. 3:11; 5:9–10).[2] Solomon's temple does not seem to have included these women servants, possibly in order to avoid the kind of scandalous activity that took place in the days of Eli (1 Sam. 2:22). Luke in the New Testament mentions the prophetess Anna who "never left the temple" after her husband died, "serving night and day with fastings and prayers" (Luke 2:37). It is tempting to see a continuation or renewal of an old tradition, but it is not certain that Luke means she actually lived in the temple. She may have spent long hours there but actually slept in her own home. The evidence is too weak to posit that she was part of a "special order of widows with religious duties at the temple."[3]

Women also participated in all the essential elements of worship besides the priestly functions. To quote Susan Foh:

> Women are not men, and God requires different things from men and women in some areas. On the other hand, the woman stands in the same relation to God as the man. When a man or woman sins, the guilt is the same (Num. 5:6). She is responsible for her own obedience; she is to know and obey God's law. She prays to God without mediation of husband or priest (Gen. 16:7–13; 1 Sam. 2:1ff.). God spoke to women directly (Gen. 25:22–23; Judg. 13:3–5). She offers her own sacrifices. The woman is a full-fledged member of the covenant community.[4]

Women were also able to participate in the three annual feasts at Jerusalem: Unleavened Bread (Passover), Weeks (Pentecost), and Tabernacles. In fact, the Lord encouraged them to participate: "You and your son and your daughter and your male and female servants . . . the orphan and the widow who are in your midst" (Deut. 16:11, 14). The men, on the other hand, were required to appear at these three festivals (Deut. 16:16). Apparently, the women were exempt from the requirement because of family responsibilities or because of possible ritual uncleanness through childbirth or menstruation.

Looking at the monarchical government of Israel, a woman also did not become the supreme ruler of the country except in extraordinary circumstances (2 Kings 11:1–3). The reason for having a king as the supreme ruler rather than a queen is probably also related to the creation order and to the Davidic king as a type of Christ (see especially 2 Sam. 7:12–16). However, the position of the queen mother seems to have been especially important and influential. She could have some say in the naming of her son as successor to the king (1 Kings 1:11–31). She could also have a strong spiritual influence on her son that would have an effect on the quality of his reign (1 Kings 15:13; 22:52), and Scripture often preserved her name along with that of her son (1 Kings 11:26; 14:21; 15:2, 10; 22:42; 2 Kings 12:1; 14:2; 15:2, 33; 18:2; 21:1, 19; 22:1; 23:31, 36; 24:8, 18). When Nebuchadnezzar of Babylon deported the nobility from Judah, the queen mother was included among the exiles (2 Kings 24:12, 15). Other influential women in Israelite civil service include David's wife Abigail (1 Sam. 25:3–42), a wise woman from Tekoa (2 Sam. 14:2–23), and a wise woman from Abel Beth-maacah (2 Sam. 20:15–22). In foreign courts, the Bible singles out for special mention Queen Esther and the unnamed mother of Belshazzar (Dan. 5:10–12).[5] Esther's story is noteworthy as showing that God could elevate a woman into a position of great influence even as he elevated Joseph to such a position.

Although the offices of priest and king were not open to a woman in the Old Testament, the function and office of a prophet was. When two men were filled with the Spirit of God and began to prophesy among the Israelites while they were encamped in the wilderness, Joshua wanted to restrain them. Moses, though, replied, "Are you jealous for my sake? Would that all the Lord's people were prophets, that the Lord would put His Spirit upon them!" (Num. 11:26–29). God's Spirit could come upon any of His people to inspire them to prophesy, whether man or woman. Deborah and Huldah are two outstanding examples of women who discharged the prophetic function. Miriam, sister to Aaron and Moses, was also called a prophetess (Exod. 15:20), and at least one woman was a false prophetess (Neh. 6:14). The "prophetess" of Isaiah 8:3 appears to be the wife of Isaiah. Perhaps she was given the title because her children had prophetic significance. Finally, Joel 2:28–29 tells of a time when the Lord will "pour out" His Spirit upon both men and women: "And your sons and daughters will prophesy, your old men will dream dreams, your young men will see visions. Even on the male and female servants I will pour out My Spirit in those days."

Why should it be that a woman could not serve as priest or king but she could prophesy? The prophet's message had authority to the extent that he or she spoke for the Lord, but prophets did not have personal authority to make things happen in the same way as the king or a priest. Naturally, when the people chose to ignore a true prophet, they placed themselves in danger of the judgment of God. Still, they could so choose, whereas the king's word had to be obeyed. Also, while the king and the priest in some way represented the people before God, the Lord could speak to anyone in the community through the prophet. This served as a check against authority wielded in the wrong way by the crown or by the priesthood. These two institutions had males who stood at their head and represented all the people. The prophet often had the task of praying for the people (see Gen. 20:7; 1 Sam. 12:19–23; Jer. 7:16), but he or she stood outside the more fixed institutions of Israel and brought God's message directly to bear on whatever was lacking in them. This noninstitutionalized and nonhereditary nature of prophecy made it possible for anyone to take it up, man or woman. Of course, many did take it up who were not qualified, because the Lord had not called them to it. Only prophets sent by the Lord had a legitimate authority.

Part of the prophetic role included recording Scripture; the Holy Spirit moved upon the prophets either to utter God's message, which would eventually be written down, or to write it down themselves. Women also participated in this process for the Old Testament. Deborah and Barak sang a song together, but Deborah's name is listed first, and Deborah refers to herself in parts of the song (Judg. 5:7, 12). The words have rightly been called the "song of Deborah." Huldah starts her prophecy with "thus says the Lord," just like the classical writing prophets, and she predicted judgment on the kingdom of Judah (2 Kings 22:16). Other important excerpts of Scripture given through a woman include Hannah's hymn of praise (1 Sam. 2:1–10) and the words that King Lemuel's mother taught him (Prov. 31:1–9 and possibly also verses 10–31).

Some think that Miriam's song (Exod. 15:20ff.) should also be included here, but there are indications that the song was really composed by Moses. The first reference to the opening words in Exodus 15:1 states that "Moses and the sons of Israel sang this song to the Lord." Moreover, Revelation 15:3–4 contains language that echoes Exodus 15 and labels it "the song of Moses, the bond-servant of God, and the song of the Lamb." Strong arguments can be given that Moses was viewed as the composer of the song.[6] Robert Hubbard speculated that the writer of the book of Ruth may have been a woman, reflecting a "female perspective" and a "female assertiveness which drives the story's action."[7] A Jewish tradition names Samuel as the author, but the book is really anonymous. Nothing seems inherently improbable about Hubbard's conjecture. The tradition of a woman uttering an inspired hymn of praise continued into the New Testament with Mary's Magnificat (Luke 1:46–55).

Four Prominent Women of the Old Testament

In the remainder of the chapter, I will discuss particular women of the Old Testament who had a highly significant role in the history of the nation, keeping in mind the general principles established in the previous chapter. First, I will highlight three prophetesses: Deborah, Miriam, and Huldah. Then I will examine the ideal wife of Proverbs 31.

Deborah

Deborah has to be one of the most colorful characters in the entire Bible. Certainly the song that she wrote and sang (Judges 5) is among the most stirring poems in Scripture. The images of pounding hooves and of stars fighting from heaven draw our minds into the great battle with Sisera, and the high drama of Jael's murder of Sisera both attracts and repels in its vividness. Even though Barak sang the song of victory with her (v. 1), Deborah's role as author of the poem cannot be missed: "Village life in Israel ceased, ceased until I, Deborah, arose, arose a mother in Israel" (v. 7 NIV). Judges 4 gives a prose account of Deborah's career. Scripture nowhere else mentions her name, though Psalm 83:9 does refer to the great conflict in which she participated.

Here is how Judges 4:4 first describes Deborah: "Now Deborah, a woman, a prophetess, the wife of Lappidoth—she was judging Israel at that time."[8] Deborah, who played this significant role in Israel's history, was a woman. Furthermore, she was married to Lappidoth, but he did nothing memorable; nowhere else does his name occur in Scripture.[9]

Judges 4 and 5 as a whole emphasize the role of the two women in the account, Deborah and Jael, as ultimately more honorable than that of the men. Because Barak refused to act immediately upon what the Lord told him through Deborah, she prophesied that the honor of the victory would not fall to him but to a woman (4:8–9). Jael, the wife of Heber the Kenite, fulfilled that prophecy when she struck down Sisera while he slept in her tent (4:17–22; 5:24–27). Warfare was normally a man's domain; the emphasis on the role of women in this account stresses as well that the battle was really fought by the Lord. Deborah's song plays out the theme of the role of women in the victory even further when she speaks so powerfully of Sisera's mother waiting in vain for the return of his chariot (5:28–30). She expected that he would be dividing the spoil as a victorious conqueror; instead, he lay dead at the feet of the woman in whose tent he had sought refuge.

Deborah had three basic roles. First, she was a prophetess. She delivered the word of the Lord to Barak (Judges 4:6), predicted the role of a woman in the victory over Sisera (v. 9), and composed the victory song that eventually became a part of the inspired book of Judges. Second, she "was judging Israel at that time" (v. 4). That is, at the time when Israel cried out to the Lord about Sisera's oppression, the Israelites were coming "to her for judgment" as she sat under the "palm tree of Deborah" in the hill country of Ephraim (v. 5). As the NIV puts it, "the Israelites came to her to have their disputes decided." She would make decisions in various legal disputes or act as an arbitrator. In addition, she also acted like one of the charismatic leaders who delivered the people from their Canaanite oppressors when she accompanied Barak into the battle (v. 9). Third, Deborah was a wife and perhaps a mother (4:4; 5:7). According to her own song, she was "a mother in Israel" (5:7). The context implies that she was like a mother to her oppressed people. She presumably brought the characteristics of a mother to her other roles of prophetess and judge as well.

What are we to make of this rather remarkable woman? Does her assumption of the roles of a prophet and of a judge prove that the Bible does not really teach any distinctions in the roles of men and women? Does the fact that she was functioning in a time when "every man did that which was right in his own eyes" (Judg. 17:6 KJV) show that she was wrongly usurping a man's role? Or is there some other way to account for her actions?

First, the expression "every man did that which was right in his own eyes" occurs only twice in the book of Judges (17:6; 21:25) and refers in each case explicitly to some gross action of Israel that was plainly wrong. The author of Judges also referred to the lack of a king in Israel in conjunction with this expression (see also 18:1; 19:1), so he evidently meant a situation that could be remedied by a king who would unite the tribes and enforce the rule of law in a way that the charismatic judges couldn't. Although the various judges had character flaws, they still were raised up by the Lord to deliver the people (Judg. 2:16). The fact that the writer of Judges applied the term "prophetess" to Deborah indicates he had a positive view of her. This term would imply, when used of a prophet of the Lord, that the individual was specially called of God and served as His mouthpiece. There is no evidence from the text that the author viewed her as incorrectly assuming her role of leadership.

In fact, Deborah did not attempt to usurp the role of a man. She told Barak that the Lord had chosen him to lead the people in the battle (Judges 4:6). When Barak refused to go if Deborah didn't go with him, she then delivered her prophecy that the glory for the victory would go to a woman. Even so, Deborah accompanied Barak as he led the way.

Even though Deborah assumed leadership functions, she nevertheless brought to her work the unique perspective of a woman. She sat under a palm tree while people came to her with their disputes,[10] giving her opportunity to become acquainted with the many ways in which the people were suffering. She highlighted this in her song when she called herself "a mother in Israel" (5:7). It is unclear from the text whether she solved the people's disputes by prophetic revelation or simply by her great wisdom. In either case, the positive attitude of the author toward her implies that she was at least guided by God in her decisions. Even though she appears somewhat charismatic, she was content to let Barak lead the people. He still conducted the battle, albeit a woman dispatched

Sisera. The "hall of faith" in Hebrews 11, emphasizing the military leaders in Judges, includes Barak but not Deborah. In the ancient Near Eastern culture it was a normal function for women to compose and sing victory anthems. Deborah showed unusual skill in the composing of her victory song, demonstrating her prophetic insight. In sum, Deborah was willing to submit to the military leadership of a man, while at the same time she assumed leadership functions that were sanctioned by God for a woman in her social situation. The text doesn't dwell on it, but surely she could have been described as a "woman of God," even as a prophet like Elijah was called "a man of God" (1 Kings 17:24).

Miriam

Miriam held a position of honor, along with her brothers, Moses and Aaron, as one of those responsible for leading the Israelites out of their slavery in Egypt and guiding them through their wanderings in the wilderness. The Lord would later speak through the prophet Micah concerning these three leaders: "Indeed, I brought you up from the land of Egypt and ransomed you from the house of slavery, and I sent before you Moses, Aaron and Miriam" (Mic. 6:4). This suggests an even larger role for Miriam than is apparent from the account of the Exodus from Egypt and the wilderness wanderings.

Miriam first appears in the Bible as the sister of baby Moses who watched over him for her mother (Exod. 2:4–8). She is not mentioned again until just after the Israelites passed through the Red Sea on dry ground. At that time she led a group of women in singing and dancing to celebrate the great deliverance (Exod. 15:20), a traditional function of women (Judg. 5; 11:34; 1 Sam. 18:6–7; Ps. 68:11). Prophets sometimes used music and poetry to enhance the effect of their message (1 Sam. 10:5; 2 Sam. 23:1; 2 Chron. 29:30; 35:15), which may be why Exodus 15:20 stresses that Miriam was a "prophetess." Miriam led the Israelites in singing the song (15:21), and Moses was also a prophet, and he composed it.

On a later occasion, Miriam and Aaron challenged the authority of their brother, Moses (Num. 12:1–15). Miriam took the lead in this incident; her name is mentioned first,[11] and the Lord struck her but not Aaron with leprosy (Num. 12:10; Deut. 24:9). Since the dispute concerned Moses' marriage to a Cushite woman, it may be that there was some bad feeling between the two women. Even though Aaron apparently was not punished, he was still guilty of sin for siding with Miriam and using the occasion to question the authority of Moses. Moses interceded for his sister, yet the Lord decreed that she must bear her punishment for seven days (Num. 12:13–15). The final glimpse of Miriam comes with the notice of her death at Kadesh (Num. 20:1).

Miriam and Aaron challenged the authority of Moses when they said, "Has the Lord indeed spoken only through Moses? Has He not spoken through us as well?" (Num. 12:2). The pretext for this complaint was Moses' Cushite wife. This became an occasion to place the prophetic gift within its proper limits. Moses, according to the Lord's answer (vv. 6–8), stood in a unique position in relation to prophets: "He is faithful in all My house." This was reiterated in Deuteronomy 34:10: "Since then no prophet has risen in Israel like Moses, whom the Lord knew face to face." Aaron and Miriam exercised leadership alongside Moses, and their individual prophetic gifts were useful to the Lord. Yet, as E. J. Young notes, "Important as was the revelation granted to Miriam and Aaron, they were in a subordinate position. They were under Moses, and for them to seek to compare the revelation granted to themselves with that given to Moses was sinful indeed."[12]

A broader lesson emerges from this incident. Prophets, be they men or women, have to be subject to the Lord; they cannot act on their own initiative or question God's program. The priests instructed the king in the Law of Moses (Deut. 17:18–19), and no prophet could be accepted who taught anything contrary to what the Law had said or who predicted anything that didn't come true (Deut. 13:1–5). The Lord gave Miriam a position of high responsibility, but she took a wrong path when she questioned why she was not given as much honor as Moses. Aaron participated in the same sin and was also rebuked by the Lord. The Lord valued servant leadership from His Old Testament saints just as much as He still values it among church leaders. A proud spirit is always incompatible with servant leadership.

Miriam was able to have a key role in the life of Moses and to help him and Aaron lead the Israelites from Egypt to Canaan. We might speculate that she had some special responsibility to work with the women in the camp. As a woman, she devoted her talent to the Lord as a prophetess. On at least one occasion, she sought to usurp the authority of Moses. Still, she acted in concert with Aaron, who was likewise guilty. Her sin was not that she was a woman filling an improper role, but that she failed to exercise her role in proper submission to the Lord.

Huldah

Huldah was God's woman at a critical point in the history of Judah. The only thing the Bible records about her is that she delivered an important message from the Lord to Josiah, the king of Judah. King Josiah began to reign when he was only eight years old, about 640 B.C. After he had reigned for eight years, "he began to seek the God of his father David" (2 Chron. 34:3). When he had reigned for eighteen years, he decided to repair the temple in Jerusalem as part of a general religious reformation. At that time Hilkiah, the high priest, gave Josiah the "book of the law" that he had found in the temple. When the scribe read from the book to Josiah, the king said: "Great is the wrath of the Lord which is poured out on us because our fathers have not observed the word of the Lord, to do according to all that is written in this book" (2 Chron. 34:21; cf. 2 Kings 22:13).

At this point, Josiah sent Hilkiah along with some others to speak "to Huldah the prophetess, the wife of Shallum the son of Tikvah, the son of Harhas, keeper of the wardrobe (now she lived in Jerusalem in the Second Quarter)" (2 Kings 22:14). The fate of the nation hung on the word that Huldah would give from the Lord.

When Huldah responded to the king's request, she prefaced her remarks with a phrase that established the authority of her message: "Thus says the Lord God of Israel" (2 Kings 22:15). In effect, she let the king and his delegation, which included Hilkiah the high priest, know that what she was about to say did not come from her but from God. There was no higher authority for the words she would utter. She even repeated the phrase for emphasis: "Thus says the Lord" (v. 16).

Huldah spoke in the first person, as though she were directly quoting God: "I bring evil on this place and on its inhabitants, even all the words of the book which the king of Judah has read" (2 Kings 22:16). Like her prophetic predecessors (Micah, Isaiah, and Zephaniah) and her successors (Habakkuk and Jeremiah), she foretold the destruction of the nation and of the temple because of disobedience to the Lord. Unlike the prophets who left behind entire books, though, this single prophecy is all that remains of her words. It seems obvious that her ministry must have included many occasions when she gave a word for the Lord, because the text implies that the delegation sought her out immediately. She must have had a reputation as a true prophetess of the Lord.

Why would Josiah receive a word from the Lord via a prophetess when other prophets might have been available? Convenience could have been a factor; Huldah resided right in Jerusalem, whereas Jeremiah was from Anathoth, a few miles to the north. Habakkuk may have begun his ministry later than Josiah's eighteenth year, and his hometown is not known.

One might also ask: Why not seek a woman for a word from the Lord? The Historical Books (Joshua to Esther) have numerous references to occasions when the Lord used a woman to bring a message to His people. Hannah, Samuel's mother, prayed a prayer that was really a psalm that exalted the Lord's power to intervene on behalf of His oppressed people (1 Sam. 2:1–10). Centuries later, Mary drew on Hannah's powerful words for inspiration in composing the Magnificat (Luke 1:46–55). Later Abigail spoke in a near prophetic manner concerning David, who recognized that God "sent you this day to meet me" (1 Sam. 25:32). When Saul became afraid on the eve of his battle with the Philistines, he consulted the woman who was a medium when he could not get any word from the Lord[13] (1 Sam. 28:6–19). The Lord used her, even though she was practicing forbidden things, to convey the message of disaster to Saul. When Sheba the Benjamite rebelled against David following the defeat of Absalom, David's captain, Joab, pursued Sheba to Abel Beth-maacah. Joab was about to conquer the town to get at his prey when a "wise woman" intervened and saved her city from destruction (2 Sam. 20:14–22). The Scripture gives no indication that anyone thought it strange that Josiah would seek a woman in order to hear from the Lord. Presumably, the people didn't think of it as unusual, even though references to prophetesses in the Old Testament are rare.

The Ideal Wife (Proverbs 31:10–31)

An alphabetic acrostic poem at the end of the book of Proverbs extols the virtues of the "wife of noble character" (NIV). Possibly it was part of the teachings of King Lemuel's mother (Prov. 31:1), although many commentators prefer to think of it as anonymous.[14] It summarizes many of the themes of the book of Proverbs, focusing various virtues of godliness on this one woman. She is an ideal woman who cannot be located in history, but she still reflects the Israelite society in which the author places her. She is not merely "a demonstration of what the life of Wisdom herself would look like, were she to manage the home,"[15] but the "excellent wife" who is "the crown of her husband" (Prov. 12:4). The same Hebrew phrase translated "excellent wife" in the NASB of Proverbs 12:4 is the "wife of noble character" in 31:10 (NIV). As a model woman who comes to us through the inspiration of God, she has much to teach about what it means to be a godly woman. This teaching comes from general principles that the woman illustrates, not from the details of what she does.

One of the most striking characteristics of this woman is her extremely high value. Each one of the twenty-two verses of the poem stresses in some fresh way her worth to her husband, her children, herself, and God. From the outset we hear that she is "worth far more than rubies" (Prov. 31:10 NIV). The full impact of that comparison becomes more acute within the context of the book of Proverbs, where wisdom and knowledge are said to be more valuable than rubies (3:15; 8:11; 20:15; cf. Job 28:18 NIV).[16] Moreover, her value stems from the fact that she is a *woman* of noble character. Even though her virtues—industry, attention to home, care for the poor, fear of God—would also be valuable for a man, the point of the poem is how she demonstrates her value to her husband and family by expressing these virtues as a woman.

Perhaps the Proverbs 31 woman could be placed alongside Eve in the garden, filling out some of the details about a woman that were not mentioned for Eve. The Proverbs 31 woman clearly reflects the image of God as much as her husband. She participates not merely in procreation but in the broader task of subduing the earth. She makes things of wool and flax (v. 13); she brings "food from afar" and provides for everyone in the household, including some servant girls or "maidens" (vv. 14–15); "she considers a field and buys it; from her earnings she plants a vineyard" (v. 16). She acts on her own initiative and goes about her work energetically, but her labors are not for her own benefit but for the household. She is really an entrepreneur and a manager of her household.[17] "She looks well to the ways of her household" (v. 27): "The implication of this picturesque language is not only the overseeing of household chores, but also of the behavior and relationships among household members."[18]

The relationship with her husband also reflects in certain ways that between Adam and Eve. Adam expressed his delight in his wife by recognizing that she was at last the helper who corresponded to him; she was flesh of his flesh and bone of his bones. The husband of the Proverbs 31 woman trusts her implicitly (v. 11) and affirms her value with words of praise: "Many daughters have done nobly, but you excel them all" (v. 29). They are not competing with each other. By her contribution to the household, he is able to rise to a position of leadership in the community, possibly even in the nation. According to verse 23, he "is respected at the city gate" and "takes his seat among the elders of the land" (NIV). The major business and judicial affairs of the city took place near the gates. The statement could be paraphrased, "He is respected at city hall." He is also among the "elders of the land," which possibly means the leaders of the country,[19] something like the Congress or Parliament. William McKane gives a nice summary of this point:

> Such a woman makes a notable contribution to her husband's success in public life, for he has no domestic worries and can build his reputation on the basis of an honourable and prosperous household. By virtue of her character and genius for sound management he is well set to exert himself as a counselor and man of weight.[20]

The wife of noble character is "a woman who fears the Lord" (v. 30), reflecting by her life the image of God that she bears. The evidence for that evaluation comes from how she exemplifies values that have been developed throughout the book of Proverbs. Like the "wise woman [who] builds her house" (14:1), she focuses her efforts on her own family (cf. 24:3). With her diligent hands, she brings wealth to her household (10:4). When she "extends her hand to the poor and . . . stretches out her hands to the needy" (31:20), she receives a blessing from the Lord (19:17; 28:27). She also "opens her mouth in wisdom" and teaches with "kindness" (31:26). Wisdom and instruction are highly valued throughout Proverbs (cf. 1:2, 7–8; 4:13; 10:13, 17, 31; 13:14; 18:4). Formal instruction that she does is probably in a family setting (cf. 6:20), but her wise speech is valuable for any who happen to encounter her.

Does the Proverbs 31 woman feel insignificant or oppressed because her husband gets to sit with the elders while she runs the household? No, she "works with her hands in delight" (v. 13) and "senses that her gain is good" (v. 18). The poet concludes the work by saying, "Let her works praise her in the gates" (v. 31). Thus are both she and her husband respected in the community; they form a team with complementary roles.

Conclusion

The Old Testament provides examples of women who served the Lord in significant ways. Often a woman brought something to her role that a man could not, and there were certain areas where she was not to intrude on a function that would be reserved for a man.

Deborah and Miriam both sang songs of victory. This was a function typically reserved for a woman, though it appears to be cultural rather than normative. It was complementary, however, to the role of the men as warriors. The men fought the battles, and the women supported them and encouraged them by commemorating their accomplishments for future generations. Barak by his own admission was not ready to go into battle unless Deborah agreed to go along, even after she proclaimed God's word to him that he was to go. So she went along and helped to rally the tribes of Israel to come together for the fight (see Judg. 5:9, 12). Afterward, she celebrated the victory by singing the song she crafted. Moses led the people through the Red Sea when God parted the water, after which the water returned to its place and drowned the Egyptians (Exod. 14). Miriam at that point led the women in singing the victory hymn that Moses composed to celebrate the victory.

Huldah acted more like one of the classical prophets than either Deborah or Miriam, in that she proclaimed the Lord's judgment to the people for their lack of obedience. Deborah had something like a pastoral role with the people when she settled their disputes, but she did not seek to gain dominance over men. Miriam and Deborah stand at the beginning of a long tradition of women celebrating the victories of the Lord on behalf of His people. This tradition includes Hannah's song in 1 Samuel 2 and extends all the way to Mary's song of praise when she met with her cousin Elizabeth (Luke 1:46–55). The ideal wife of Proverbs 31 is characterized above all by her fear of the Lord. From that wellspring of her life, she was able to devote her life to helping her family and the poor, finding fulfillment in the process.

One final thing can be noted about these women. It was legitimate for each of them to work together with a man and to accomplish ministry together. In fact, they illustrate something of the ideal synergism between men and women working together that ought to be present in the church. Each one of these women in leadership fulfilled the purpose for which she was created by helping carry out the task given by God, without seeking to control or manipulate the situation for her own ends.

Deborah helped Barak, agreeing to go with him and helping him to face the battle. Miriam, despite the one incident Scripture records of her rebellion in cooperation with Aaron, worked alongside Moses and Aaron. Huldah became God's mouthpiece to deliver a message of vital importance to King Josiah.

Finally, the whole family unit of the Proverbs 31 woman was energized by her faith and diligence. Both she and her husband were honored in the community, and her children and husband benefited from her wisdom and gentle instruction.

PART THREE

WOMAN AND MAN IN THE NEW TESTAMENT

CHAPTER FIVE

WOMEN IN THE TEACHING AND EXAMPLE OF JESUS

Michael Wilkins

Introduction

Jesus' teaching about, and ministry to, women is both radical and conservative. It is radical because He challenged and changed some of the prevailing attitudes about women that were found within Judaism in the first century. He offered spiritual life and opened doors of ministry opportunity that many in Israel would have denied women. But Jesus was conservative as well, because He was carrying forward God's will for women that had been revealed in the Old Testament. Jesus' earthly ministry was intended to fulfill the Law and the Prophets (Matt. 5:17), which meant to bring to completion what God had intended from the very beginning. Where the people of His day had deviated from God's will for women, Jesus will stand out as a radical revolutionary who challenged the status quo of the religious elite as He asserts His authoritative statement about women and their roles. Where the people of His day had correctly sustained God's will for women, Jesus will appear to be a firm conservative who reasserts attitudes and roles for women already extant within Israel.

Ultimately, Jesus will bring a dignity, value, and worth to women and their roles that God had intended from the very beginning, when humans were created male and female and given the mandate of being complementarian co-laborers in ruling God's world for Him (Gen. 1:26–28). Where this had been lost to women because of misinterpretation of the Old Testament, or because of cultural bias, Jesus will bring restoration. Where the people of Israel had been correct in their interpretation, Jesus will bring affirmation. Therefore, we will find in the first place that Jesus restores and reaffirms to women their dignity and worth as persons who are fully equal to men as humans created in the image of God. In the second place, Jesus preserves the male-female distinction of humans, so that they are restored and affirmed in the different roles that God had intended from the beginning. And in the third place, He restores and affirms to women the status of co-laborers with men in God's plan for the outworking of His will on this earth.

Women in First-Century Judaism

"Judaisms" and Women in the First Century

Jesus came into a mixed social, cultural, and religious milieu within Judaism of the first century. Indeed, it has become quite commonplace to hear Jewish and Christian scholars refer to the "Judaisms" of the first century.[1] Various subgroups within Israel had distinctive worldviews and ways of life that expressed themselves differently in their social world. Each thought that theirs was the "right" way to think and express oneself in their everyday world.

Such is the case in the way that various groups within Judaism understood the status and roles of women in the first century. All took the same Old Testament Scriptures seriously, but each group tended to focus on particular teachings as representative of the status of women and the roles women should play within their subgroup.[2] A further complication is that we sometimes find in the Old Testament depersonalized attitudes and treatment of women that were recorded, but that were not intended as God's endorsement of such attitudes or behavior. For example, women were sometimes treated almost as property in polygamous marriages in the Old Testament, but simply because those actions are recorded does not imply that God condoned either the depersonalization of women or polygamy.[3] But some groups took those *descriptions* and turned them into *prescriptions* intended as being from God to validate their improper treatment of women (similar to the Mormons today). So we must try to be as balanced as possible if we want to gain a clear understanding of the status and roles for women in the first century.

Within Judaism at the time of Jesus, we find contrasting attitudes about women and contrasting expectations about the roles that women could play. Although the rabbinic material from Mishnah and Talmud was not recorded until much later, and may reflect only later attitudes, they do help give an indication of rabbinic attitudes that may in part go back to Jesus' time. In addition, we can look to the Dead Sea Scrolls, the writings of Josephus and Philo, and various legal documents from the time that give us an indication of the status and roles of women within Judaism of the first century.

A Somber Picture of Women in Judaism

We do find a fairly strong strain of passages within Jewish literature that paint a rather somber picture of the status and role of women. Josephus states, "The woman, says the Law, is in all things inferior to the man" (Josephus, *Against Apion* 2:201), apparently interpreting Genesis 3:16 to indicate that women are not only under the authority of men, but also have a lower personal status. Women are categorized in the repeated rabbinic formula, "women, slaves and minors" (*m. Berakoth* 3.3; *m. Sukkah* 2:8), demonstrating that a woman, like a Gentile slave and a minor child, was under the authority of a man and had limited participation in religious activity. One of the most widely cited rabbinic sayings from the early Mishnaic period that reflects an inferior position of women was included in a threefold daily prayer: "Praised be God that he has not created me a gentile! Praised be God that he has not created me a woman! Praised be God that he has not created me an ignoramus!" (*Tosephta Berakoth* 7:18). This prayer is still included today in some of the more conservative Jewish prayer books, a fact that modern Jewish scholar C. G. Montefiore laments was a rabbinic attitude toward women that was "very different from our own."[4] One passage in the Mishnah discourages too much conversation between men and women, even with one's own wife, because it distracts the rabbinic disciple from studying Torah: "He that talks much with womankind brings evil upon himself and neglects the study of the Law and at the last will inherit Gehenna" (*m. Aboth* 1:5).

The later rabbis overall regarded the woman's primary sphere of influence to be in the home. Some considered a woman to be the equivalent of the property of her father, or, when married, her husband. In the same context of discussing how slaves, cattle, and property are acquired, one passage from the Mishnah gives the means by which a woman is acquired as a wife: money, contract, or arrangement (*m. Kiddushin* 1:1–5).

An Encouraging Picture of Women in Judaism

Honor to Women

On the other hand, the rabbinic literature in various places reiterates the Old Testament directive that honor is to be given equally to the father and mother. One passage indicates that since the father is listed first in Exodus 20:12 and the mother is listed first in Leviticus 19:3, Scripture teaches that "both are equal" (*m. Kerithoth* 6:9; cf. *m. Nedarim* 9:1). One saying attributed to a third century A.D. rabbinic authority indicates his attitude toward the spiritual status of his mother. When Rav Yosef (Rabbi Joseph) would hear the footsteps of his mother approaching, he would say, "Let me arise before the approach of the Shekinah [Divine presence]" (*b. Kiddushin* 31b). Honoring wife and mother was considered to be of enormous spiritual value. Although most rabbinic sayings confine the influence of women to the home, there is evidence of wider impact.[5]

The Influence of Women

Evidence of wider influence for women surfaces in the Old Testament and Second Temple Jewish literature, and that influence carries over into the first century A.D. First, in the Old Testament we find evidence of women who were actively involved alongside men in public life. As discussed in the previous chapter, Deborah was a prophetess who was also a good judge over Israel (Judg. 4:4), and she joined Barak to defeat Sisera (Judges 4–5). Athaliah had national influence in Israel when she ruled (2 Kings 11:1–20), although it was a negative influence, because she was a wicked queen who usurped the rightful reign of Joash. One of the most remarkable pictures of a woman's role and influence in daily Jewish life is found in Proverbs, especially in the acclaim given the virtuous woman. She not only cared for the daily needs of home and family, but she was also involved in public life as she purchased and worked the fields and engaged in selling supplies to tradesmen (Prov. 31:10–31).

Second, Jewish literature tells us that in the decades prior to the birth of Jesus, a woman—Queen Salome Alexandra—ruled Israel during the Hasmonean dynasty. She had an exceptionally prosperous reign, and her nine-year rule from 78–69 B.C. is looked upon as a miniature golden age in Jewish history.[6]

Third, we find in archaeological discoveries from caves in the Judean wilderness the archives of two Jewish women, Babatha and Salome Komaise. Their legal papers and other artifacts date from around A.D. 130. These personal archives indicate that, away from some of the more restrictive rabbis, women enjoyed a great deal more freedom than we otherwise might expect if we only had the writings of the rabbis. The rabbinic literature speaks for those who were under the influence of the early rabbis of the Pharasaic strain, but many if not most people were influenced more by a variety of local practices, customs, and laws. As one scholar states, "Clearly, Babatha and her friends were not influenced by the early rabbis, who promoted an all-encompassing halakhic system."[7] These women carried documents to prove their relationship to their husbands,[8] indicating a subservient role, but their documents also indicate that these women were actively engaged in fairly widespread public business, legal, and political activities with other Jews and also with Gentile Romans, Greeks, and Nabateans.[9]

It is quite likely that women experienced a more elevated status and more personal freedom than the somber picture painted in much of the rabbinic literature. The gospel record of Jesus and His relationship with women seems to confirm a more balanced attitude toward women.[10] That is where we now turn.

Jesus Restored and Affirmed the Worth and Dignity of Women

Jesus inaugurated His earthly ministry with a dramatic message: "The time is fulfilled, and the kingdom of God is at hand; repent and believe in the gospel" (Mark 1:15). This was the beginning of the restoration of humanity that had been anticipated ever since the entrance of sin into the world had distorted God's intended purposes for His creation. Jesus told the religious leader Nicodemus that one could gain access to God's kingdom only by being born again by the Spirit (John 3:1–8).

Jesus did not make a distinction between women and men in this ministry of restoration. Women are addressed equally with the invitation to experience Jesus' offer of eternal salvation through their inclusion as full members in His band of disciples. In this inclusion, He realigns some of the prevailing attitudes found in the religious and social culture of first-century Judaism, restoring to women their full worth and dignity as humans created in the image of God.

Women Were Equally Worth Jesus' Saving Activity

Both in His teaching and in His activities, Jesus reached out to women as persons who were equally worthy as men of His saving activity. A classic passage in this regard is Jesus' interaction with the Samaritan woman. This is a remarkable exchange, since Jesus was not only interacting with a Samaritan, a member of a race that was despised by Jews, but also a woman. Women were not encouraged to have interaction with male strangers. But Jesus went beyond the cultural ethnic and gender barriers and treated her as a person who was worth His offer of the living water of eternal life (John 4:10, 14). He establishes the principle that whoever accepts His offer of living water, that person will receive it (vv. 13–15). The woman saw the barrier as ethnic (v. 9), whereas the disciples returned and made an issue of gender (v. 27). But for Jesus, gender and ethnicity are irrelevant in His offer of salvation. Jesus treated her as a *person* needing salvation. The Samaritan woman was alert enough to the spiritual realities of Jesus' messianic identity and ministry that she was then able to lead the men of the city to Jesus (vv. 28–30), and they believed on Jesus as the "Savior of the world" (vv. 39–42).

When Jesus went about His public ministry, we see Him giving open invitations to the crowds that followed Him. Men may have had more opportunity to free themselves of daily responsibilities to hear Him, but women were regularly a part of the crowds who were healed and who heard Him teach and proclaim the gospel (e.g., Matt. 14:15–21, esp. v. 21; 15:29–39, esp. v. 38). When Jesus healed the poverty-stricken hemorrhaging woman (Mark 5:25–34) and the demon-possessed daughter of the Gentile Canaanite mother (Matt. 15:21–28), He saw in both of these women the kind of faith that was an example even to the Twelve. He felt compassion for those who were at the mercy of the tragedies of life, especially for those who would be at a disadvantage because of the social restrictions women often experienced, such as the bereaved widow whose son had died (Luke 7:11–17). On the Sabbath when He healed the demon-caused, eighteen-year illness of the woman, He declared to the indignant, hypocritical synagogue leaders that the woman was a daughter of Abraham, and so deserved to be healed on the Sabbath (Luke 13:10–17). As a "daughter of Abraham," this woman is paralleled to Zacchaeus, who later will be called a "son of Abraham" (Luke 19:9). Both are God's chosen people and heirs of the promises to Abraham, so both equally deserve the spiritual status and salvation guaranteed Abraham's descendants.[11] These examples are simply representative of the fact that Jesus' ministry to women transcended gender, purity, legal, social, economic, and ethnic barriers. As Jesus offered salvation and healing to the people, women were equally worthy of His full-orbed ministry.

Women Were Called to Be Jesus' Disciples

Discipleship in the ancient world was a diverse phenomenon.[12] Within the Greco-Roman world, a disciple could be an apprentice of a craftsman, a pupil of a teacher, an adherent of a particular culture or lifestyle, or a committed follower of a philosopher or religious figure. Within Judaism we find a similar diversity, so that followers of religious figures as different as John the Baptist and the Pharisees are called "disciples" (Mark 2:18).[13] Especially among the rabbis, a man chose a master teacher under whom he would study, with the intention of becoming a rabbi himself at the end of the prescribed period of preparation.

But Jesus' saving activity initiates a unique form of discipleship. Jesus' disciples are all those who have responded to His call to salvation. The crowd of people, including both men and women, are those to whom Jesus extends an invitation to salvation. As a person in the crowd responds positively and accepts Jesus as the Messianic Savior, he or she comes out of the crowd to become a disciple of Jesus. On one occasion, Jesus was requested by His mother and brothers to come outside the house where He was speaking to the crowds, but He retorted, "'Who is My mother and who are My brothers?' And stretching out His hand toward His disciples, He said, 'Behold My mother and My brothers! For whoever does the will of My Father who is in heaven, he is My brother and sister and mother'" (Matt. 12:48–50). The implication is that when Jesus points to His disciples, He intentionally broadens the gender references to include women by stating "sisters and mother."[14] Obedience to the will of the Father was the hallmark of Jesus' disciples, whatever the gender.

This was a unique form of discipleship, which Jesus carefully defined and articulated, so that in His final Great Commission the central imperative is "make disciples of all the nations" (Matt. 28:19). Any person—woman or man, young or old, Gentile or Jew—who believes on Jesus for eternal life is His disciple. The book of Acts confirms that identification, where Luke clearly uses the word *disciple* to refer both to men and women (Acts 6:1–7; 9:10, 36; 16:1), a term synonymous to *believers,* which is also used of both men and women (Acts 5:14). Together they comprise the "church" (Acts 8:3).[15] Luke even uses the rare feminine form of the word "disciple" *(mathētria)* to refer specifically to Tabitha/Dorcas in Acts 9:36.

Because other forms of discipleship within Judaism were especially oriented toward acquiring particular secular or religious skills in the public arena, discipleship was primarily restricted to men. But Jesus' form of discipleship is instead oriented toward transformation of the person's life to be like Him. One of the remarkable, revolutionary truths about Jesus' call of women and men to be His disciples is that they can be like Jesus in a way that no other disciples can be like their masters. In fact, becoming like Jesus is the overarching goal of the entire Christian life, laying the foundation for later New Testament teaching on sanctification. The apostle Paul declares, "And we, who with unveiled faces all reflect the Lord's glory, are being transformed into his likeness with ever-increasing glory" (2 Cor. 3:18 NIV). This transformation is a process throughout our earthly life that is concluded in eternal life. Paul elsewhere confirmed that the ultimate goal for those God called from eternity was to be "conformed to the image of His Son" (Rom. 8:29). From a different perspective, Paul proclaims that the goal of spiritual formation and discipleship is that "Christ is formed in you" (Gal. 4:19).

Within the disciples, we can see concentric circles around Jesus. In the outer circle are the large number of disciples who believed in Jesus and became His followers. Within that larger circle, we find seventy (-two) who were appointed and sent out on a preaching tour (Luke 10:1–17).

Then we find a group of women (not included in the Seventy) who traveled with Jesus and the Twelve to support Jesus' missionary tour (Luke 8:1–3), some of whom also followed and ministered to Jesus all the way to the cross and the tomb (Matthew 27:55–56 and parallels). Forming a smaller circle are the Twelve who were called to be trained as apostles (Luke 6:13). And then within the Twelve was the inner circle, composed of Peter, James, John, and sometimes Andrew (e.g., Mark 13:3). These concentric circles did not indicate levels of spirituality or personal worth. These circles were not related to personal standing with Jesus, but were circumscribed according to function.[16] All disciples were equal as believers, but some had specialized ministries that brought them into closer proximity to Jesus. For our purposes, we will look most closely at the Twelve and the women who followed Jesus and served Him.

As disciples of Jesus, women have restored to them the full dignity that was theirs in the creation, when men and women were both created in the image of God. Jesus affirmed the Genesis intention when He declared, "Have you not read that He who created them from the beginning made them male and female" (Matt. 19:4; cf. Gen. 1:26–27). Men and women, originally created as equal partners in the mandate to rule God's creation for Him, are equal followers of Jesus as His disciples.

Women Received Instruction and Nurture as Jesus' Disciples

Education was valued highly in ancient Israel. The data are debated, but there is evidence that all children, girls and boys, were given the rudiments of education, including reading and writing. Most of this took place in the home, with the father taking the primary lead in teaching the children. Education was notably directed to learning the Old Testament Scriptures, especially so that boys and girls would know how to pray and worship properly.[17] Some rabbis assumed that both sons and daughters would receive instruction in Scripture,[18] whereas others denied daughters even the basics of Torah instruction.[19] This difference of opinion reflects the overall conflicting attitudes toward women found in the rabbinic literature, even in the same context.[20] What seems to be consistent, however, is that girls were excluded from admission to formal rabbinic schools. Although the schools of Shammai and Hillel held opposite views about candidates for admission, with the former opting for higher social class students and the latter preferring a more democratic clientele, neither opened their doors to female students.[21]

Jesus did not open a formal school, but He was known as a profound Teacher whose authoritative instruction far surpassed the scribes and the Pharisees (Matt. 7:28–29). However, as profound as it was, His teaching was not limited to only a few privileged students. Jesus' instruction was directed to the curious crowds of men and women (cf. Matt. 14:21; 15:38), giving an open invitation to come and learn from Him (Matt. 11:28–29). But the focus of His teaching, especially as He neared the end of His earthly ministry, was directed to His disciples, which included women.

One particularly poignant example is in the well-known story of the two sisters, Mary and Martha (Luke 10:38–42). Jesus and the Twelve were traveling about and were invited by Martha into her home. While Martha was "distracted" with the preparations for the guests, Mary was "seated at the Lord's feet, listening to His word" (v. 39). The position Mary assumed is the traditional position of a disciple. When the apostle Paul described his education under the great rabbi Gamaliel, he used the stereotypical expression "at the feet of Gamaliel" (Acts 22:3 KJV). Jesus not only allowed Mary to be taught, but He chided her sister Martha for not having chosen this good part of learning from Him (Luke 10:42). In this intriguing scene, Jesus makes clear that women are included among disciples, whose responsibility it is to sit at Jesus' feet and be taught by Him.[22]

This episode prepares us for a central element of the Great Commission. Once a person, male or female, is converted from among the nations to be a disciple of Jesus, he or she is to be baptized and to be engaged in the lifelong process of "teaching them to observe all that I commanded you" (Matt. 28:20). This restores equal opportunity for women to learn God's will as He has revealed it in the Scriptures. Women and men are equal disciples of Jesus, and their development depends upon being taught how to obey all that Jesus had originally given His disciples during His first-century ministry and how that was developed throughout the New Testament Scriptures.

Jesus Restored and Affirmed Women to His Ministry Team

Out of the mixed social and religious setting of first-century Judaism, Jesus drew a team of co-laborers who would join Him in ministering to the people of Israel. The very first statements in the Bible about men and women indicate that they were to be co-laborers created in the image of God to rule God's creation (Gen. 1:26–28). In Jesus' ministry, women are being restored to their role of co-laborers with men in proclaiming the gospel of the kingdom.

The incident of His interaction with the Samaritan woman is a beginning glimpse of the way that Jesus would enlist women to join Him in ministering to His people. Once the woman accepted Jesus' messianic identity and ministry, she was sent back by Jesus to tell the rest of her village, and she then led the men to Jesus (John 4:28–30, 39–42). At the very end of His earthly ministry, the women who were the first witnesses of the empty tomb were privileged to carry the message of the risen Christ back to the apostles.

A prominent place is given in the Gospels and Acts to women who were disciples of Jesus and who were called into ministry with and to Him. These women were included in Jesus' ministry in a unique manner. They were a part of the band of disciples in a way not common in many circles of Judaism. Some later rabbinic writings indicate that it would have been considered scandalous for women to follow a rabbi/teacher around. However, Jesus' form of discipleship and ministry included women (e.g., Luke 8:1–3; Matt. 27:55–56, 61).

The Twelve

The four Gospels witness unanimously to a core of twelve disciples who were called by Jesus into a special relationship with Him. Luke tells us that on one occasion, after Jesus spent the night in prayer, "He called His disciples to Him and chose twelve of them, whom He also named as apostles" (Luke 6:13). The term *disciples* points to their identity as those who have believed on Jesus, whereas the title *apostles* points to the function of the Twelve as those whom Jesus will now train to be the leadership of the church. The distinction is made even clearer as Luke continues with the narrative. After listing the names of the twelve apostles, Luke says that Jesus descended with the Twelve "and stood on a level place; and there was a large crowd of His disciples, and a great throng of people from all Judea and Jerusalem and the coastal region of Tyre and Sidon" (v. 17). Three groups are listed here: the twelve apostles, the great multitude of disciples, and the large throng of people from all over. The apostles are those selected from among the other disciples to play a leadership role, the great multitude of disciples are those who believe in Jesus, and the great throng of people are those who are interested, but who have not made a decision for or against Jesus.

The Women on a Mission Trip (Luke 8:1–3)

Luke also tells of another group that had joined Jesus to participate in a particular preaching tour.

> Soon afterwards, He began going around from one city and village to another, proclaiming and preaching the kingdom of God. The twelve were with Him, and also some women who had been healed of evil spirits and sicknesses: Mary who was called Magdalene, from whom seven demons had gone out, and Joanna the wife of Chuza, Herod's steward, and Susanna, and many others who were contributing to their support out of their private means. (Luke 8:1–3)

Only one woman was mentioned in Luke's narrative to this point as having been cured (Luke 4:38–39), but the reader is assumed to know of Jesus' ministry to women and that they were included in the summaries of Luke 4:40–41 and 6:17–19.[23] Now a group of women are mentioned as having received healing, and they joined Jesus and the Twelve on a preaching tour through Galilee. This passage reveals several important points about Jesus' ministry to, and with, women.

The Women and the Twelve Were "with Jesus" as His Disciples

In the first place, the women mentioned here are parallel with the Twelve in the grammatical structure. The Twelve are "with Jesus," as are also the women. The phrase "with Him" *(sun autō)* is a technical expression in Luke's gospel (cf. Luke 8:38; 9:18; 22:56), indicating much more than mere immediate presence; it indicates the discipleship of both the Twelve and the women.[24] This is parallel to Jesus' challenge that one is either with Him or against Him (Luke 11:23). The scene is consistent with Jesus' overall inclusion of women in His saving ministry of extending a call to all who heard to join Him as His disciples. One of the qualifications for becoming one of the Twelve, replacing Judas, would later be that the individual had first been "with"[25] the Twelve and Jesus as His disciple. The wording in the Luke 8:1–3 passage indicates that these women were themselves disciples of Jesus who joined Jesus and the Twelve on a mission. Some of this same group of women "followed Jesus" up to Jerusalem, where they were in attendance for the Crucifixion and were the first ones to the empty tomb after the Resurrection (Luke 23:49, 55; 24:9).

The Women and the Twelve Were Jesus' Supporting Team

In the second place, the women are parallel with the Twelve as Jesus' supporting team. Jesus alone is the One who is "proclaiming and preaching the kingdom of God" (Luke 8:1–3). Although we know that the Twelve and the Seventy(-two) themselves went out on preaching missions at other times during Jesus' earthly ministry (e.g., Luke 9:1–6; 10:1–12, 17–20), on this occasion neither the Twelve nor the women are said to be preaching.[26] Both groups on this mission tour had supporting roles in what we might call Jesus' ministry team. Women disciples of a great master were an unusual occurrence in Palestine of the first century, as even the reaction to Jesus' interaction with the Samaritan woman by His early disciples reveals (John 4:27). Although Jewish parallels can be found for women supporting rabbis and their disciples out of their own money, property, or foodstuffs, they were not considered disciples of the rabbis, and there is no evidence of them traveling around with a rabbi and his disciples. However, the women in Luke 8:1–3 certainly exhibited the twin characteristics of Jesus' disciples—cost and commitment—and they are explicitly described as traveling around with Jesus and the Twelve. Although the women were not considered members of the circle of the Twelve *apostles,* they were within the wider circle of Jesus' *disciples,* and here they are included in a missionary outreach in Galilee. They had a significant part in His earthly ministry.

There Was No Hint of Scandal or Criticism

Third, we may be surprised to realize that there is no hint of scandal or criticism of these women traveling with Jesus and the Twelve. This may be an indication that there was more freedom within Judaism at that time for women to move about and even join with men in religious activity than we may be led to think. It may be that some of the rabbinic comments about the lowly status of women were either from a later date and/or from only one spectrum of Jewish leaders, because we demonstrated above that we also find in later rabbinic literature a high regard for women. It is possible that women had more freedom than some rabbis indicated, or that the level of their acceptance varied. Otherwise, we would have expected to hear criticism of Jesus and His relations with women thrown at Him by His enemies.

We noted above that, although the home was the typical sphere within which women operated, away from the cities and the restrictiveness of Pharisaic rabbis, women had more freedom of movement and interaction with men. Without mention of any criticism directed at Jesus or the women, traveling on this preaching mission appears to have been an acceptable activity. Although this is an argument from silence, it seems appropriate to argue this way in this instance. The Gospels quite often note criticism of Jesus by religious leaders, and even laypeople, when He went contrary to social custom or religious tradition. This would have been a prime opportunity for Jesus' critics to try to accuse Him of serious moral charges, or at least serious social charges of disrupting appropriate gender roles and relationships. We find Jesus freely and frequently interacting with women, yet there was virtually no condemnation of His attitudes or actions. The Pharisees condemned Jesus and His disciples for many things, but nothing significant is stated as a direct criticism about His relationships with and treatment of women. Rather, the criticism He received was when He treated women as *sinners* worthy of His saving attention, not the fact that they were women (e.g., Luke 7:39; John 8:4). There seems to be some amazement from His own disciples when He was discovered talking with a woman (John 4:27), but this apparently reflected simple social customs of women and men not having casual contact, or the fact that He was talking to a *Samaritan woman*. With no hint of that criticism during His ministry in Galilee, we are led to believe that Jesus included women on His ministry team in a way that was appropriate. Jesus provides a precedent for women to join with men in a ministry team.

Jesus Broke Down Barriers by Including Women

Fourth, we can see in this passage that Jesus broke down a number of barriers—gender, social, sectarian, spiritual, economic—by the inclusion of these women. The occurrence of this group of women traveling with Jesus and the Twelve is a remarkable phenomenon. Within rabbinic circles in Judaism, it would have been inappropriate to include women as disciples, but Jesus breaks through that barrier. Mary Magdalene would have been considered a social misfit prior to her exorcism, but being listed first probably displays a position of prominence she showed among these women. Joanna was a woman from the higher echelons of Jewish social/political life, since her husband was a steward in the household of Herod Antipas. Nothing is revealed to us about Susanna's background, and we are told that there were "many other" women along. "Here Luke gives evidence of how the Gospel breaks down class and economic divisions, as well as social barriers, and reconciles men and women from all walks of life into one community."[27] The doors that may have been locked to women in various avenues of life in the past are now opened to the one community that is gathered equally around Jesus.

Jesus Selected Only Men from Among the Disciples to Be Apostles

Fifth, although the women are included equally as Jesus' disciples and are included in the ministry team, Jesus selected only men from among the disciples to be apostles (cf. Luke 6:12–16). Out of the qualifications later stipulated in the early church for replacing Judas Iscariot in the twelve apostles (Acts 1:21–22), the women in the ministry team qualified on at least one count, having been "with" Jesus and the Twelve. Some of them even witnessed the Resurrection, thereby having what may be the most prominent qualification. Mary Magdalene especially would have seemed to be a likely candidate, because she met several of the qualifications. She is quite prominent in the gospel records, obviously more so than either of the two men put forward, including Matthias who was ultimately chosen, because neither man is mentioned in the Gospels. But the wording in the qualifications stresses that the person chosen was to be a "man," using the term for the male gender *(anēr)*, not the more generic term *(anthrōpos)*.

Selection of only men does not appear to be simply accommodation to a patriarchal culture, because Jesus broke religious, cultural, and social customs when He saw it to be necessary to establish the kingdom and the church in distinction from prevailing practices. For example, against religious custom, Jesus criticized the scribes and Pharisees publicly (Matt. 23:13–36), and He cleansed the temple (Matt. 21:12–13). Against cultural and social custom, Jesus spoke to the Samaritan woman (John 4:7–9), He ate with tax collectors and sinners (Matt. 9:11; Mark 2:15), He did not require His disciples to fast when even the disciples of John and the Pharisees were fasting (Matt. 9:14–15; Mark 2:18–20), and He did not require His disciples to perform ritual purification, allowing them to eat with unwashed hands (Mark 7:1–23). On several occasions, Jesus found Himself at odds with the religious establishment of Israel, whose "traditions of the elders" regarding Sabbath observance and ritual washings were far stricter than what the Law originally intended, and Jesus did not back down from conflict with them when the principle was at stake (cf. Matthew 12:1–14; 15:1–20).

Jesus did not bend easily to cultural pressure. He could have included women as apostles if He was correcting inappropriate religious or cultural custom. If Jesus had wanted to go contrary to social custom by including women as apostles, He surely would not have hesitated, especially when we recognize that some of the ways in which He offended the religious leaders got Him crucified. There must be another reason for not including women as apostles, yet indeed including them as disciples who were part of His ministry team. We can see clearly that women and men are treated as equal persons who are called to equal status as Jesus' disciples. But we can also see that when Jesus did not call women to apostleship, this is an indication that there are different roles for women and men that will maximize their creation in the image of God as male and female. Jesus retains the distinctiveness of men and women, which includes roles appropriate for the way He created them to operate in this world. The hint here is that there are certain positions of leadership that are appointed for men, but that in no way minimizes the status of women as persons or hinders them from participating as equal members of Jesus' ministry team. It will remain for the rest of the New Testament to clarify those purposes.

The Role of the Women in the Ministry Team

Finally, what exactly was the role of the women in the ministry team while on the preaching tour?[28] Luke states that they "were contributing to their support out of their private means" (Luke 8:3). At the very least, these women were called to a ministry to provide material support for the group.[29] Similarly, we find a number of women who functioned as patronesses in the wider Greco-Roman world and as benefactors of Jewish religious and synagogue life (e.g., Josephus, *Antiquities* 17.2.4 §§41–44),[30] but there is no firm evidence that they traveled with or joined in the work of their beneficiaries. The women disciples of Jesus could have given financial support to Jesus and the Twelve without leaving their homes, and apparently, in the case of Joanna, leaving her husband, so more than just financial support seems to be implied.

Some suggest that since they were considered disciples, they were also involved in proclamation along with Jesus and the Twelve.[31] This stretches the context further than is appropriate by making an unwarranted connection between public proclamation and discipleship. Although the women joined Jesus so that they could support the proclamation ministry, it is problematic whether they were themselves involved in public proclamation. In fact, neither the Twelve nor the women are said to be preaching on this occasion.[32] Jesus Himself is the One who is preaching and teaching. The Twelve and the women both had supporting roles on Jesus' ministry team as He proclaimed the gospel.

Although they were not involved in actual proclamation, it is unwarranted to imply that the term *serve (diakoneō)* indicates that these women accompanied Jesus and the Twelve simply to cook and clean for them.[33] The expression "serve" comes to have much more significant connotations in Jesus' ministry than simply "waiting on tables." "To serve" encapsulates Jesus' entire redemptive purpose for coming to earth (Matt. 20:28; Mark 10:45), and it will characterize both the mission of the apostles (1 Cor. 4:1) and the calling of the disciples in the early church (cf. Luke 22:24–27; Gal. 5:13). It also indicates here that instead of simply providing for the economic well-being of Jesus' mission, "these women are far more intimately caught up in the enterprise in which Jesus is engaged."[34]

Perhaps we can say that, besides providing financial support for the missionary outreach, the women joined the Twelve as Jesus' companions and as witnesses of His ministry.[35] This diverse collection of women had received healing themselves, and so they were powerful witnesses to the reality of Jesus' ministry. Perhaps in that cultural setting it may have been easier for these women to speak personally with the large throngs of women who also were in attendance at many of the public appearances of Jesus (cf. Matt. 14:21; 15:38). Both the women and the Twelve played essential roles as those who would later testify to the reality of Jesus' ministry, death, and resurrection (cf. Luke 23:49; 24:1–10; Acts 1:21–22).

But further, it appears as well that both the women and the Twelve provided companionship for Jesus during His earthly ministry. It is well known that Jesus often took the inner circle of three or four of the Twelve with Him on special occasions,[36] such as at the Transfiguration (Matt. 17:1–3) and for His time of prayer in the Garden of Gethsemane (Matt. 26:38). In the latter case, Jesus had brought the inner group to share with Him this difficult time as He faced the cross. He wanted their fellowship, support, and encouragement as they watched with Him. Unfortunately, they failed Him at His moment of personal need by falling asleep, but New Testament scholar Leon Morris states, "There is a sense in which [Jesus] had to be alone in prayer, for only he could pray the prayer he prayed. But there is also a sense in which he could have been encouraged by the support of his closest followers nearby."[37]

It may be difficult to grasp that the Son of God had such needs, but to understand this gives us a more adequate understanding of His incarnation. The relationship between Jesus and the sisters Mary and Martha and their brother, Lazarus, demonstrates the depth of loving companionship that women and men provided Jesus. Jesus loved Mary, Martha, and Lazarus (John 11:3, 5), which made the death of Lazarus all the more difficult as He shared their grief. It was at their home that Jesus probably stayed while in Bethany for the Passion Week, and it was Mary who performed the beautiful deed of anointing Jesus (cf. John 12:1–8). Although Jesus must endure the cross Himself, He needed the support and fellowship of His closest companions, women and men. His loving friendship with His disciples will provide a pattern for the love that disciples are to have for one another (John 15:12–17). The group of women who traveled with Jesus and the Twelve on the mission trip in Galilee had received the touch of Jesus' messianic ministry, and they displayed the essence of discipleship as they traveled with and served Him.

The ministry team of the Twelve and the women foreshadows the community of faith that would comprise the church, where women and men join together as witnesses to the reality of the Christian life and as brothers and sisters in Christ who share equally in the life of the Spirit. Jesus broke down barriers—economic, racial, religious, gender—by calling people into a spiritual family based on equality of discipleship. There are different ministry roles within the family, but each person has equal value as a family member. The spiritual family of disciples today is called the church. We are the family of God because we are His children by faith (cf. John 1:12–13). We are brothers and sisters in Christ; we need each other as a spiritual community of faith (see Hebrews 10:24–25).[38]

The Women at the Cross and the Empty Tomb

All of the evangelists mention a group of women who followed and served Jesus in the Galilee region, who also "followed" Jesus to Jerusalem, witnessing the events of the final week, including the Crucifixion[39] and the Resurrection.[40] Some of these women were among those who had been included with the Twelve on Jesus' missionary ministry team, including Mary Magdalene and Joanna (Luke 8:1–3; 24:10).[41] Others included Mary, the mother of Jesus; Mary, the mother of James and Joseph (if not the same); the mother of the sons of Zebedee; and many other women who followed Jesus from Galilee, ministering to Him (Matt. 27:55). They did not desert Him at the cross, but witnessed the Crucifixion from a distance (vv. 55–56). Mary Magdalene and the other Mary even maintained a vigil after Jesus was placed in the tomb (v. 61).

Exemplary Disciples of Jesus

The expressions used to describe these women concur with the evidence elsewhere that they were Jesus' disciples.[42] They had "followed" (*akoloutheō*) Jesus from Galilee,[43] which can be used in simply a spatial sense, as, for example, people "followed" Jesus from one point to another (Luke 22:54), or even as Jesus "followed" the ruler to his house so that He could heal his daughter (Matt. 9:19). But here the context indicates the metaphorical sense of the word—accompanying Jesus as His disciple. The disciple is the one who has counted the cost, has made a commitment of faith, and has then "followed" Jesus.[44] As the women "followed Jesus" they "ministered" to Him (Matt. 27:55; Mark 15:41), called Him "Lord" (John 20:2, 13, 18), and "worshiped" Him after the Resurrection (Matt. 28:17). These descriptions not only designate the women to be disciples, but also describe them as *exemplary* disciples of

Jesus. They were displaying a commitment to Jesus that the Twelve themselves should have displayed.

Witnesses to Jesus

One of the most important perspectives on the women here is that God used them as witnesses not only to the central redemptive act of history, Jesus' death on the cross, but also to the attestation of that act in His resurrection from the dead. Since the women were present for Jesus' death on the cross and His burial by Joseph of Arimathea (cf. Matt. 27:55–56, 61), they could verify that He was truly dead, not just unconscious. Several of the women witnessed the sealing of the tomb (cf. Matt. 27:60–61; Mark 15:46–47; Luke 23:55) and then were among the first witnesses of the empty tomb and the resurrected Jesus (Matt. 28:1–6; Mark 16:1–6; Luke 24:1–8; John 20:1–16). And then the women were designated by both the angel and Jesus to be the ones who would carry their witness to the other disciples as the first to testify of the reality of the Resurrection (Matt. 28:10; Mark 16:7; John 20:17).

Many scholars consider God's choice of women as the first witnesses to be one of the bedrock truths of the Resurrection narratives and of the historicity of the Resurrection itself.[45] It is unlikely, for a variety of reasons, that any Jew would have created such a story as fiction.

In the first place, because of the debated status of women in Judaism at the time, there was disagreement among some of the rabbis as to the acceptability of a woman giving testimony in a court of law. Josephus recorded a traditional ruling that stated, "From women let no evidence be accepted, because of the levity and temerity of their sex."[46] Nevertheless, a number of others did allow women to give testimony.[47] Because of the varied opinions over their acceptability as witnesses, however, the testimony of the women to Jesus' resurrection could either be rejected out of hand or at least considered shaky. This would make it much less likely that a Jew would fictionalize a woman's testimony in the case of Jesus' resurrection. In the second place, the cowardly picture painted of the men hiding away in Jerusalem while the women boldly carried out their responsibilities to prepare Jesus' body for burial would certainly offend the sensibilities of Jewish readers, and doubtless would not have been recorded unless it were true. Third, the listing of the names of the women weighs against being fiction, because these women were known in early Christian fellowship and would not easily have been associated with a false account. Fourth, Jesus' appearances to these women with debated status lend credibility to the account, because again, they would be unlikely selections for a fictionalized account trying to be understood as believable. For these reasons and more, the selection of women as the first witnesses yields high credibility to the Resurrection narratives, and to the Resurrection itself.[48]

The Crucifixion and Resurrection accounts tell us a decisive number of things about God's purposes for women in the life and ministry of Jesus. First, God was bestowing a special honor on these women. They are exemplary of true discipleship to Jesus, and because of their faithfulness and courage, they were given the special honor of first witnesses to the empty tomb and the post-resurrection appearances of Jesus. Second, contrary to the way that some cultural groups of His day lowered the status of women, Jesus restored women within His community of faith to their original status as equal with men. Men and women were both created in the image of God and were to receive that equal status among believers. Third, women are validated as worthy of the most privileged service in the community of faith, bearing witness to the reality of the risen Lord Jesus. This is an indication that within the community of faith they are to be restored to be co-laborers with men in the community of faith, a role they had been assigned from the beginning of creation (Gen. 1:26–28).

These women are exemplary of what it means to be faithful disciples of Jesus Christ who battle through the fears and the uncertainties to be obedient to God's will for their lives. As such, they are held up, along with the Twelve and other very human disciples like Joseph of Arimathea and Nicodemus, and Mary and Martha and Lazarus, as examples of what is to be accomplished in Jesus' final commission, to "make disciples of all the nations."

Conclusion

Jesus is both radical and traditional in His treatment of women and in His inclusion of them in His ministry team. He is radical because He goes contrary to some of the prevailing negative attitudes and treatment of women in first-century Judaism. However, He is traditional in that He is not establishing a new order. He came to fulfill the Old Testament's prescription for God's will for women and men. His call to men and women did not create a kind of genderless Christian species of disciples. Rather, in coming to Jesus to be His disciple, a person has begun to have restored and affirmed to him or her God's intention for humans from the creation: They are male and female, created in the image of God to serve Him as complementarian co-rulers of God's creation.

Male and female, every race, every person in every culture on the face of the earth is made in the image of God. This is what makes for true equality of persons and helps us to understand that all humans have an inherent value to God. All human life is sacred. Jesus restores and reaffirms to women their dignity and worth as persons who are fully equal to men as humans created in the image of God. He also preserves the male-female distinction of humans, so that they are restored and affirmed in the different roles that God had intended from the beginning. Distinctions among Jesus' followers relate to function, not spiritual standing or commitment or essential personal worth. And Jesus restores and affirms to women the status of co-laborers with men in God's plan for the outworking of His will on this earth. Unless men and women work together as a complementary team, neither can fulfill God's purposes apart as well as they can together. The fulfillment of that goal has begun in the ministry of Jesus.[49]

CHAPTER SIX

WOMAN AND MAN IN APOSTOLIC TEACHING

Robert Saucy and Clinton Arnold

Introduction

The Old Testament and the Gospel accounts of the life and ministry of Jesus show that women played an important part in human society. They participated in the work and worship of God along with men in the fulfillment of their common goal as humans on earth. Living together in a complementary relationship, the ultimate responsibility for community leadership rested with men. The record of God's people reveals that the experience of this leadership was marred by sin. But whether practiced in the loving relationship intended by God from creation or in sinful selfishness, the leadership of men was the normal experience of the people of God. Grounded in the creation account of Genesis as we saw in chapter 2, this pattern was clearly expressed in some of God's instructions relative to religious leadership, e.g., the priesthood.

For the most part, the relationship of men and women in the Old Testament and the ministry of Jesus is presented simply in the description of their lives together with little explicit teaching. For example, we have no direct teaching on the topic by Jesus. It is only with the instruction of the apostles to the New Testament church that we come to the Bible's most direct teaching on our subject.

In this chapter, we will examine this apostolic teaching around these questions: (1) Does the Bible teach a specific relationship between man and woman that is permanent? In other words, do the apostles teach a normative order between men and women that is in harmony with the descriptions of the relationship seen in the Old Testament and the ministry of Jesus? (2) What does the apostle Paul mean when he calls man the "head" of woman? We will reserve for the next chapter the related teaching that "in Christ" there is neither "male nor female" (Gal. 3:28) and what it has to contribute to our understanding of the relationship of men and women.

Our primary concern in this chapter is thus the apostolic teaching on the structure of the relationship of man and woman and not on the dynamics of its actual practice. Although something of the attitudes and actions of the relational partners will be included in the later sections of this chapter, the primary discussion of the manner of relating will be reserved for the final chapter. However, as we approach the question of order in this chapter, we will do well to keep in mind that its actual practice involves imperatives for both relational partners. The apostles do not instruct woman in her responsibility toward man without at the same time exhorting man in his obligations toward woman. In almost every passage dealing with the relationship between man and woman, God has something to say to both partners, calling each to an obedience in attitude and action that is necessary for the relationship to be what He intended for fullness of life together.

The "Ordered" Relationship of Man and Woman

The Apostolic Concern for Order

In their concern for the new human community founded on the work of Christ and empowered by the Spirit, the apostles gave a wide variety of instructions. Many of these concerned the day-to-day life of believers as they related to one another in the home and the church. As members of the new "alien" community, their lives were to be lived differently than previously in the old sinful communities of the world.

The manner in which believers related to one another, including men with women, was also important for the sake of the testimony of the gospel to the world around them.

The Teaching of an Order

In their instructions concerning men and women, the apostles covered a variety of subjects ranging all the way from their responsibilities to each other and the manner of their relationships to dress codes. A prominent theme in their teaching is the maintenance of the proper order between men and women. Specific instructions are given for the purpose of promoting and maintaining this fundamental relationship. We may find some of the specifics related to this teaching, such as the "head covering" in 1 Corinthians 11, to be difficult to relate to our present culture. But in the particular cultures addressed by the apostles, these practices were somehow expressive of this basic relationship between man and woman.

This underlying concern for the order between men and women is evident first in the use of a particular Greek term found in several passages dealing with instructions concerning men and women. The verb form of the word is *hypotasso,* which has the basic meaning "to order or arrange under" or "to subordinate." In his instructions concerning women's silence in the church, the apostle Paul wrote, "The women are to keep silent in the churches; for they are not permitted to speak, but are to subject themselves, just as the Law also says. If they desire to learn anything, let them ask their own husbands at home; for it is improper for a woman to speak in church" (1 Cor. 14:34–35). The words "let them subject themselves" translate a form of this Greek word.

Exactly what the apostle means by keeping "silent" in this text is not clear. We will see in our discussion of this text in chapter 12 that it cannot refer to the absolute silence of women in the church. But what is important to note at this point is that whatever this prohibition of speaking in church meant in terms of actual practice, it was given to uphold a basic order between men and women in the Corinthian church. Women were to "subject themselves" or "order themselves under" men in the church. The speaking that the apostle prohibits, whatever its nature, would somehow indicate a disregard for this order. The apostolic instruction was thus for the sake of maintaining the proper order between men and women.

The noun form of the same Greek word translated "submissiveness" is found in the key passage dealing with women's teaching in the church. Writing to Timothy, Paul said, "A woman must quietly receive instruction with entire submissiveness. But I do not allow a woman to teach or exercise authority over a man, but to remain quiet" (1 Tim. 2:11–12). Without getting into the specific meaning of the prohibitions at this point, it is important to see that they are again related to the apostle's concern for the underlying relationship between men and women in the church. A woman was to receive instruction with "entire" (NASB) or "full" (NIV) "submissiveness" or "subordination." She was to be "ordered under" the leadership of men in the church. In other words, the manner of her learning or receiving instruction was not to violate this relationship. Like the instruction to silence mentioned above, the specific instructions concerning teaching and exercising authority over men are given to maintain the proper relationship between men and women in the Christian community. For women to practice what is prohibited would be to overturn this order.[1]

In addition to these two passages dealing with men and women in the church, the apostle Paul used the same Greek term four times to express the relation of men and women in marriage. Wives are to "be subject to [ordered under]" their husbands (Col. 3:18; cf. Eph. 5:22, 24; Tit. 2:5). Peter also used the same word twice in his instructions to husbands and wives in 1 Peter 3:1, 5.

The same concept of an ordered relationship between man and woman is expressed in other terminology. Wives are exhorted to "fear" or "respect" their husbands (Eph. 5:33; cf. also 1 Pet. 3:2). Sarah, who "obeyed" her husband Abraham, calling him "lord," is portrayed as an example for godly women to emulate (1 Pet. 3:6). This terminology must not be pressed so as to confuse the wife's relationship to Christ as Lord with that of her husband. But it does express the apostle's concern that the wife show deference and respect to her husband.[2]

The prominent use of the Greek term denoting an "order," along with the other terminology expressing the same concept, makes it clear that the apostles believed and taught that men and women in the home and in the church were to live together according to a certain order. Their activities and responsibilities toward each other were to be undergirded and lived out in accord with this order. Because terms like "submissiveness" and "subordination" carry such a negative connotation in our contemporary culture, it is vital that we understand their biblical meaning when used in the relationship of women and men.

It is important to note that the biblical teaching concerning an ordered relationship of man and woman in the home and the church is not talking about the relationship of every man to every woman in these human communities. The reference is rather to an order between man and woman with reference to the family and church as human communities. For example, should there be grown brothers and sisters living in a family household, there is no instruction indicating that the sisters should be "subordinate" to their brothers. Similarly, the order related to the church does not mean that every woman is subordinate to every man in the church. In both instances, the order applies to the leadership of the community (i.e., family or church) and not every member. In the home, the reference is thus between husband and wife, while in the church it refers to the leadership of the church and all others. As will be seen especially in chapters 9 and 10, we exist in our gender as men and women in all of life. Our very natures therefore cannot help but impact all of our relationships in every situation. The specific scriptural teaching concerning an order between man and woman, however, focuses on the human communities of the family and the church.

The Meaning of "Subordination"

As noted above, the primary biblical word used to express the relationship of the woman to the man *(hypotasso)* has the basic meaning of "subordination." It is the compound of the preposition *hypo,* "under," and the verb *tasso,* "to arrange, order, or appoint." In this case, both elements continue to carry their separate meaning when joined in the compound. *Hypotasso* thus expresses the idea of "ordering or arranging under." That which is "ordered under" is therefore in a "subordinate" position. Although obedience is often the sign of subordination, it is important to note that the term "subordinate" does not itself mean "to obey." Its central meaning has reference to a position or order.[3]

More insight into the meaning of this term can be gained by seeing how it is used throughout the New Testament.[4] First, we are all told to be in subjection to God (Heb. 12:9; James 4:7), and since Christ represents the authority of God, "all things" are said to have been put in subjection under Him (1 Cor. 15:27–28; Eph. 1:22; Phil. 3:21). Specific mention is made of angels, including evil angels, and the church being subject to Christ (1 Pet. 3:22; Eph. 5:24). The evil powers are also subject to His disciples (Luke 10:17, 20). In the end, Christ Himself is going to be "subjected" to the Father (1 Cor. 15:28).

In the realm of human relationships, we are to be in "submission" to human governmental authorities (Rom. 13:1, 5; Titus 3:1), and, in fact, to "every human institution" (1 Pet. 2:13). In addition to the order between women and men mentioned in the previous section, God instructs slaves to be subject to their masters (Tit. 2:9; 1 Pet. 2:18; cf. Eph. 6:5–7; Col. 3:22–23) and children to their parents (Luke 2:51; 1 Tim. 3:4). Finally, believers are exhorted to "submit" to their church leaders (1 Cor. 16:16 NIV; cf. also 1 Pet. 5:5), and all are to be in mutual submission to one another (Eph. 5:21).[5]

This brief overview of the uses of subordination helps us to put this concept in its proper biblical perspective. It is important to note that the idea of a negative servility is not inherent in the biblical concept of the subjection of one person to another. This is apparent both in Christ's subordination to the Father and in the divinely ordained orders within human society. Apart from the forced servitude of those who oppose the authority of God or Christ, the other orders in which some are subordinate to others do not necessarily contain any idea of a cringing thralldom. Rather they are given for the sake of a properly ordered society that works for the good of all.

We may not be happy with the governmental leaders under whom we are ordered and to whom we are therefore in subjection. But no one would argue that society would be better off without any order of leaders and those subject to them. The same is true of the orders that subject children to their parents and believers in the church to their leaders. Even the order between slaves and their masters, which in the ancient world undoubtedly involved forced servitude in many instances, has its contemporary application in the ordered employee-employer relationship that most would agree is preferable for all concerned than no order at all.

When we look more closely at the order between men and women, we will see that there are important differences in the dynamics of the different orders. Nevertheless, they all share the same basic relationship in which some are ordered under others. Far from being negative, God in His wisdom has ordained these orders within human relationships during this present age for the good of human society. People are ordered under other people, not that some may enjoy advantage and others suffer in subjection, but for the mutual benefit of all.

The Orders and "Mutual Submission"

To say that an arrangement where one is subordinated to another is good for both seems difficult for us to understand. Too often, we see people who are over others obviously enjoying many advantages and perks over their subordinates. God's plan can only be worked to the benefit of both the superior and the subordinate in the context of obedience to the overriding principle that is to be operative among all believers, namely "mutual subordination." As the apostle explains, one of the results of being filled by the Spirit will be that believers live "subject to one another in the fear of Christ" (Eph. 5:21).[6]

God's plan for order thus includes the subjection of some under others, and yet at the same time the subjection of all to each other.[7] To some these seem like contradictory teachings. How can some be ordered under others when all are to be ordered under each other? For many egalitarians the exhortation to mutual submission takes precedence over other teachings about women being subordinate to men. According to them, these latter thoughts are given only for certain historical situations, whereas the command for mutual submission is normative for all time.

But the egalitarian explanation is impossible when we recognize that the apostle's teaching of mutual subjection is directly related to his teaching of the other specific societal orders for believers. While grammatically related to the prior command to be filled with the Spirit, the statement about mutual subjection also leads into and "forms an essential element of the section . . . which follows."[8] In this following section, the apostle gives specific instructions concerning the relationships between husbands and wives, children and parents, and slaves and masters. Wives are specifically exhorted to be in subjection to their husbands in this teaching (Eph. 5:24; cf. also vv. 22, 33). Although the explicit terminology for subordination is not used in connection with the other groups in the passage, the idea of order and subordination is clearly present. Thus we find that the apostle's teaching of mutual subordination is "indissolubly tied" to his teaching of the "specific subordination of one group to another."[9] After noting that "justice has to be done *both* to the force of v. 21 [mutual submission] *and* to the force of the specific types of submission" in what follows, Lincoln rightly says, "Modern interpreters might perceive the first admonition as undermining or deconstructing the others, but clearly the original writer did not find them incompatible."[10]

The error of the egalitarians' insistence that the exhortation to mutual subjection negates the order between man and woman is also apparent when we realize that this command also covers the other groups in the context—parents and children and masters and slaves. No one would argue that because of this overriding principle, there are not specific orders remaining in these relationships.

Instead of negating the various societal orders that God has ordained for this age, the teaching of mutual subjection provides the attitude and motivation by which believers are to live out their roles in the orders in which they find themselves. It teaches us "about the specific respect [believers] . . . owe because of Christ to those with whom they live together either by choice, or by birth, or by historical circumstances."[11] This respect is expressed by the same Greek word meaning "to order under" or "to subordinate."

That people who live in a relationship in which one is subordinate to the other but at the same time both are subordinate to each other may at first sight appear to be an impossible paradox. But it becomes clear when we consider Paul's exhortation to the Philippian believers: "Do nothing from selfishness or empty conceit, but with humility of mind regard one another as more important than yourselves; do not merely look out for your own personal interests, but also for the interests of others" (Phil. 2:3–4). The "humility of mind" that is enjoined on all believers signifies an "unselfish" manner of life that places the interests of others ahead of their own. It is nothing other than mutual submission, "the resolution to subject oneself to others and to be more concerned about their welfare than one's own."[12]

The example of Christ's self-emptying that follows this exhortation in Philippians 2 demonstrates that this attitude of humility of mind or subjection to another has nothing to do with one's position in an ordered relationship (cf. Phil. 2:5ff.). The One who existed in the form of God came to earth and took on the form of a servant. He humbled Himself to the point of death in His service for those over whom He was Lord. As He taught His disciples, not only is it possible for a leader in an ordered relationship to place himself under those whom he leads in service to their needs, but such "subjection" is inherent in God's pattern of leadership.

Another example of the attitude of "humility of mind" and the "mutual subjection" operating within a functional order is evident in the life of Paul himself. It is his heart's desire, he says to the Philippians, "to depart and be with Christ." That is, if he were to live for himself and place his desires first, this would be his goal. But because he was convinced that it was "more necessary" for their sake to stay on in ministry, his desire to remain and serve them took precedence over his desires for himself (Phil. 1:23–24). In doing so, he "subjected himself" to those believers who were themselves "subject" or "ordered under" him as an apostle of Christ.

The understanding of "mutual subjection" as seen in other Scriptures and the examples of this practice in the lives of Christ and the apostle thus make it clear that the apostle's exhortation to the mutuality of subjection in Ephesians 5:21 cannot be set in opposition to his other teaching of societal orders, including man and woman. Not only are these principles not contradictory, but it becomes apparent that the various orders ordained by God for human life in society can only function according to His plan for the good of all concerned when they are done so within the context of true "mutual subjection."

The Basis of the Order Between Man and Woman

Most biblical interpreters acknowledge that the Bible does in fact teach a variety of ordered relationships, including that between man and woman. The real dispute with regard to the latter order is whether the biblical teaching is still pertinent today or whether its application was intentionally limited by certain historical or cultural factors that may or may not be present in modern times. The answer to this question must be sought in an apostle's own rationale for his teaching.

For the most part, the apostles gave their teaching concerning the proper deportment of men and women in the home and church without supporting arguments or evidence. The same is true with regard to the injunctions concerning other orders, e.g., the responsibilities of parents and children. Often they simply teach what should be done, with comments that this behavior is "right" or "fitting in the Lord" (cf. Eph. 6:1; Col. 3:18). On occasion a concern for living rightly so that no reproach will come to the gospel is given as a reason. After instructions to both older and younger women that includes "being subject" to their husbands, Paul adds, "that the word of God will not be dishonored" (Titus 2:5; cf. also 1 Tim. 5:14, although this passage contains no reference to the man-woman order).

These last explanations for the apostle's exhortation concerning the relationship between men and women are frequently cited as evidence that his teaching of the subordination of women was only for the sake of testimony within a patriarchal culture.[13] To defy the cultural norm would hinder the progress of the gospel. According to this view, egalitarianism, and not a specific order, was God's real design for the man-woman relationship and should be the norm when Christian testimony is no longer at stake. The apostolic teaching concerning the subordination of women is therefore not permanently applicable.

To do something for the sake of testimony in a certain culture may indicate that that practice is only related to that particular culture and is not God's permanent will. But this in no way is a necessary conclusion. Frequently the apostles challenged believers to live in a way that would have an impact upon the world around them. These challenges included general exhortations to a behavior of good works and integrity, which no one would say are only related to certain cultural contexts. The apostles obviously believed that even unbelievers in the world respected certain behaviors that were good and right, even though they did not always practice them (e.g., 2 Cor. 8:20–21; Titus 2:8; 1 Pet. 2:11–12, 15; 3:16). For the apostles to teach a certain action because of the outside world, therefore, does not by itself determine whether that action is a temporary accommodation to a particular culture or a permanent norm of what is good and right. Which one of these alternatives is valid can only be determined in each instance by other data.

We have seen in earlier chapters that the Old Testament and the example of Jesus give no support for the claim that God's ideal is an egalitarian relationship between man and woman. Although they clearly teach the full equality of men and women as human persons, a complete similarity as far as societal roles is never found.[14] As we will see in this chapter, the teaching of the apostles yields a similar picture. An alleged biblical teaching of egalitarianism, therefore, cannot be used to demonstrate that the apostle's teaching of an order between men and women is limited to a particular cultural context.

The real data for the proper interpretation of the apostolic teaching of a man-woman order are supplied by the apostles themselves. The divine order is not only useful as a testimony to those outside; it is grounded in the creation of man and woman. After asserting that women are to "receive instruction with entire submissiveness" and not to "teach or exercise authority over a man," Paul adds, "for it was Adam who was first created, and then Eve" (1 Tim. 2:11–13). The particular word *(plasso)* translated "created" (NASB) or "formed" (NIV) is a direct link to the creation account in Genesis 2 where the man was created before the woman. (See Gen. 2:7–8, 15 in the Greek translation of the Hebrew Scripture.)[15]

The statement concerning the creation is introduced by the Greek term *gar* ("for"), which is normally used as a conjunction introducing the cause or reason for the preceding statement.[16] Thus, according to the apostle, his instructions concerning women, including their ordering under men, are based on the truth of the creation of man and woman and not on some particular local problem facing the church of that time.

Some have attempted to get around this conclusion by arguing that instead of supplying the reason for Paul's instructions, the references to creation and Eve's deception in 1 Timothy 2:13–14 are only given for the purpose of illustration. Payne says that "the example of Eve's deception leading to the fall of mankind is a powerful illustration of how serious the consequences can be when a woman deceived by false teaching conveys it to others."[17] The order of creation is said to indicate that Eve was less educated than Adam in spiritual things, perhaps not being taught directly by God concerning the trees in the garden. It was this uneducated state that resulted in her deception and caused her leadership to fail.

According to this understanding, therefore, Paul is simply teaching that women who at this time were less educated than men should not be teaching in their uneducated state. But since verse 11 indicates that they were to learn, there would come a time when they would be educated in spiritual things. At that time, the restriction would no longer apply, and they would then be qualified to teach along with the men teachers.

This interpretation fails on several counts. First, as noted above, the most prominent use of the Greek term *gar* ("for") at the beginning of verse 13 is to introduce the cause or reason for the previous statement rather than simply giving an explanatory illustration. In fact, its use to introduce an explanation is relatively rare.[18] The causal use is especially common in Paul's writings when, as in this passage, a command is followed by a statement beginning with *gar:* "I do not allow . . . for [*gar*] it was . . ." (vv. 12–13). With regard to twenty-one instances in the Pastorals alone where this same sequence is found, Moo states that "in each case the causal idea appears to be required."[19] The use of *gar* ("for") at the beginning of the statement concerning the creation of Adam before Eve (v. 13), therefore, *does not introduce an example* related to the teaching of the subordination of women. Rather *it gives the reason or basis* for the previous command concerning the ordered relationship between man and woman.

A second evidence against the illustration interpretation is that the content of verses 13–14 simply does not provide good illustrations of what Paul is said to be commanding in verse 12. His command, according to this view, concerns women who lack the educational background to teach. But the statements relative to the order of creation and Eve's deception say absolutely nothing about woman's lack of education. This is especially true concerning the sequence of creation. To make the fact that Adam was created prior to Eve say something about their relative spiritual knowledge is obviously to read something into the text that is patently not there. Even the statement about Eve's deception says nothing about its being caused by a lack of knowledge.

Finally, the view that the temporary lack of the woman's education is the background of Paul's teaching in this passage fails in relation to the specific commands of the apostle. If the lack of education were the problem, there is no reason that the prohibition against teaching and exercising authority should not include untaught men as well. In this connection, it is often noted that the background of this teaching concerning women was a false teaching going on in Ephesus that particularly enticed women (cf. 1 Tim. 4:7; and esp. 2 Tim. 3:6–7). Although this may well have been true, it should be noted that there is no indication that the teachers of these deceptive doctrines were women. Rather, it was men who were leading women astray (cf. 2 Tim. 3:6–9). If his prohibition of teaching in this passage was concerned only with the teaching of false doctrine, one would have expected him to include men as well as women in his instruction.

The application of the restriction to all women on the ground that they are untaught also seems particularly out of place in an epistle destined for Timothy at Ephesus which was the home of Priscilla at that time (cf. 2 Tim. 4:19). She, along with her husband, Aquila, obviously had considerable theological knowledge as they were able to instruct Apollos "more accurately" in theological matters (cf. Acts 18:24–26). Surely she along with others like her would have been excluded if Paul's concern was to prohibit from teaching only those women who lacked education in spiritual truth. The fact that the apostle's words in this passage address women in general is evidence that the idea of their lack of education is not involved in this instruction.

The causal use of *gar* ("for") to introduce 1 Timothy 2:13–14, as well as the content of these verses, therefore indicates that the apostle is not using Adam and Eve as an illustration of the negative effects of teaching by an untaught woman. He is basing his teaching of the order between man and woman on the fact that Adam was created first. No explanation is given as to how the order of creation leads to an order of relationship. It may be related to the familiar pattern of the primacy of the firstborn son.[20] But no matter what the explanation, the understanding that the apostle was basing his teaching of an order between man and woman on the prior creation of man has been the generally recognized interpretation throughout church history and remains so today, even among most feminist scholars. The latter simply don't agree with the apostle's teaching. The attempt by evangelical egalitarians to harmonize this passage with an alleged overall biblical egalitarianism and thus avoid rejecting the apostle's words has led to improbable and, for the most part, unconvincing reinterpretation of the passage.

That this passage in 1 Timothy 2 teaches an order between man and woman based on the creation account is supported by the use of the same argument in 1 Corinthians 11. In support of the headship of the man, which he has taught in verse 3 ("the man is the head of a woman"), the apostle wrote, "For man does not originate from woman, but woman from man; for indeed man was not created for woman's sake, but woman for the man's sake" (vv. 8–9). This statement clearly teaches the temporal priority of Adam, but then goes on to add a further dimension, namely, that he was the source of the woman, that Eve was taken out of Adam. There was a causal as well as a temporal priority involved in the headship of man in relation to the woman. And this causal priority, as well as the temporal one, carries the idea of authority in social relationships.[21]

This understanding of verses 8 and 9 has often been challenged on the basis of the apostle's teaching of the mutual dependence of man and woman on each other in verses 11–12: "However, in the Lord, neither is woman independent of man, nor is man independent of woman. For as the woman originates *from* the man, so also the man has his birth *through* the woman; and all things originate from God" (italics added). These verses that are interpreted as teaching egalitarianism are said to demonstrate that verses 8–9, which teach that woman was created out of man and for his sake, are not meant to support the subordination of woman,[22] or, conversely, that the order that is taught in verses 8–9 is now invalid "in the Lord," i.e., in the church.[23]

In response to the last alternative, the idea that the apostle would teach something (i.e., the subordination of woman, vv. 8–9) and even draw out from it an inference for the functioning of women in the church (cf. v. 10), and then immediately negate (vv. 11–12) what he had just taught, seems impossible. As for the first alternative, the question might be asked as to why the apostle felt it necessary to add this supposed egalitarian teaching in verses 11–12 in order to "qualify" the previous verses (i.e., vv. 8–10) if these prior verses have nothing to do with an order between man and woman. More important, in regard to both attempts to deny the teaching of an ordered relationship between man and woman in this passage, Paul's teaching about the relationship of man and woman "in the Lord" (vv. 11–12) does not necessarily support functional egalitarianism. It simply affirms the equality of nature and the complementary mutual need of each other that is inherent in the original creation account.

The Corinthian passage adds one further point from the creation account in support of the ordering of man and woman. Not only is there a priority of man both temporally and causally, but woman was created "for the man's sake" and not "man . . . for the woman's sake" (1 Cor. 11:9; cf. Gen. 2:18–23). According to the Genesis record, woman was made to be "a helper suitable for him" (Gen. 2:18). Now as we have seen earlier in the chapter on man and woman in the Old Testament, nothing in this description of the creation of woman suggests that she is in any way personally inferior to the man. Nevertheless, the apostle sees in the fact that man was created first and then woman expressly as his complementary helper the establishment of a certain functional order between them.

The Nature of Woman's Subordination

If we would understand the biblical teaching concerning the relationship between man and woman, we cannot be satisfied with simply affirming the fact of a divine order. Equally important is the nature of that order. The teaching of the traditional order between man and woman has suffered much from the failure to understand and, even more, to practice that order in conformity with its true design.

Subordination Within Equality

It must be asserted at the outset that the ordering between man and woman in no way affects their more fundamental equality as human persons. According to the creation account of Genesis, man and woman stand in a perfectly equal position under God and above the rest of creation. Both are created in God's image, and both are appointed rulers of the rest of creation (Gen. 1:27–28). This absolute equality of personhood, which is affirmed throughout Scripture, especially in the ministry of Jesus, is also plainly taught by the apostle Paul. His statement that in Christ, "there is neither male nor female" (Gal. 3:28) asserts without equivocation the absolute equality of man and woman in God's sight. Similarly, Peter calls the women that he has just encouraged to be submissive to their husbands, "fellow heir[s] of the grace of life" with their husbands (1 Pet. 3:7). They are equal before God and equally share in the inheritance of eternal life.

This equality of man and woman as human persons found in the original creation and again in the new creation of the church provides the fundamental framework in which any order between man and woman is to be understood and practiced. Any thought or practice of the "subordination" of women that conveys to the man that he is somehow superior as a human being or to the woman that she is in any sense less of a human person than the man fails to understand the true nature of the biblical order. Any distinctions between men and women are not distinctions in the value of personhood. It is totally contrary to God's design to rank some human characteristics above others in a way that elevates the gender in which these traits are predominant to a superior position as human beings. Examples of this error may be seen in the masculine exaltation of reason over emotion that was part of the fruit of the Enlightenment and in some feminists' claim today for the superiority of women's traits, e.g., caring and concern for relationships. The God-given distinctions of woman and man are all essential for full human life and must not be allowed to convey a different value of personhood between the genders. Although woman is ordered under man in the functional arrangements of the home and the church, she is fully his equal as a human being.

Subordination Within Mutuality

As we have already seen, the creation of woman as the "helper" of man suggests the essential mutuality of their existence together. As Franz Delitzsch says, "Human beings cannot fulfill their destiny in any other way than in mutual assistance."[24] The thought of mutuality is strengthened with the further description of the "helper" as one "suitable for him" (Gen. 2:18). The Hebrew term for the latter expression literally means "that which is over against, counterpart." Woman is the one who "corresponds" to the man.[25] What is expressed is "the mutual understanding in word and answer as well as in silence which constitutes life in common." These two concepts of mutual help and mutual correspondence "describe in an extraordinary way what human community is; it has to do primarily with man and woman, and determines human existence for all times."[26]

The creation account thus teaches forcefully that man and woman are designed to live together in a relationship of total mutuality. It is God's purpose that human existence be "the personal community of man and woman in the broadest sense—bodily and spiritual community, mutual help and understanding, joy and contentment in each other."[27]

The same mutuality between man and woman is taught by the apostles. After asserting the headship of man in 1 Corinthians 11, Paul desires to make it clear that he is neither teaching an arrogant independence of self-sufficient males nor encouraging a disposition of reticence on the part of women. Men and women are interdependent "in the Lord, neither is woman independent of [lit. without] man, nor is man independent of woman. For as the woman originates from [lit. out of] the man, so also the man has his birth through the woman" (vv. 11–12). As the woman's existence was originally out of the man in creation, so in the process of procreation, man comes into being through woman. Thus, as Barrett says, "each owes his existence to, and cannot continue without, the other."[28]

The fundamental mutuality between man and woman, which determines all life and therefore underlies all functional order, is powerfully underlined by Barth:

> All other conditions of masculine and feminine being may be disputable, but it is inviolable, and can be turned at once into an imperative and taken with the utmost seriousness, that man is directed to woman and woman to man, each being for the other a horizon and focus, and that man proceeds from woman and woman from man, each being for the other a centre and course. This mutual orientation constitutes the being of each. It is always in relation to their opposite that man and woman are what they are in themselves.[29]

This teaching of the mutuality of man and woman in all human life must be brought alongside the equally biblical teaching of functional orders in the home and church. God's design for the relationship of man and woman is that both of these truths be lived out together. It is especially important, in seeking to uphold the biblical teaching of order with regard to the place of women in the ministry of the church, that the place of woman as the mutual partner of man not be overlooked.

A Subordination in Love

Finally, and most important, the order of subordination of woman to man both in the home and in the church is one of voluntary love. Although the same terminology meaning "ordered under" is used for all of the divine orders, all of the relationships are not the same.[30]

The active sense of the verb "to subordinate" is used only in relation to God's subjection of creation to "futility" (Rom. 8:20) and the subjection of all things to Christ (1 Cor. 15:25–28; Eph. 1:22; Phil. 3:21; Heb. 2:8).[31] The thrust of this active use is on the forcible involuntary nature of the subjection, that is, subjugation. The apostle says that it was "not of its own will" that the creation was subjected, nor did the "principalities and powers" willingly submit to the power of Christ. In this active use of "to subordinate," "the weaker is put 'in its place'; he has to obey and serve; law and order are thus established."[32]

The thought is quite different when the teaching deals with the subordination of believers. This is true of all of the orders in which believers find themselves, whether the relationship is with another believer or an unbeliever, for example, an unbelieving spouse or master. In all instances involving believers, the biblical writers use a form of the verb that views the person in the subordinate position as willingly assuming that position rather than being forced into it. In the words of Markus Barth, this use of the verb "describes a voluntary attitude of giving in, cooperating, assuming responsibility, and carrying a burden."[33]

Only believers in Christ, who Himself willingly submitted to His Father, are expected to practice this form of subordination. As with Christ, this subordination does not connote the status of miserable servitude. Rather it is the action of "the free children of God, or persons in high standing, even of princes." It is a "subordination as it were *inter pares* ('among equals')," and does not affect the essential equality or intrinsic worth of the individuals within the orders.[34]

The absence of certain terminology that is present in connection with other ordered relationships further reveals the distinct character of the order between man and woman. With only two exceptions, those who have authority in the divinely ordained orders are given power *(exousia)* or rule (dominion or force, *arche*) with which to function.[35] Christ has been granted *exousia* by which He subjects to Himself all the principalities and powers who oppose Him (Matt. 28:18).

Within the orders of human society, the master has *exousia* over his servants (Luke 19:17). The same *exousia* belongs to the government of the state (Rom. 13:1; Titus 3:1). Government officials are called "authorities" (*exousiai*, Rom. 13:1; Titus 3:1) and "rulers" (*archai*, Titus 3:1). In all of these instances, power or authority is granted to some within the ordered arrangement to be used in relation to those who are subordinate to them.

The two exceptions mentioned above where these terms of power or rule are not present are the orders relating to parents and children and men and women.[36] Instead of the term *exousia,* "authority" or "power," Scripture employs the term "head" *(kephalē)* when speaking of the man's relation to the woman (1 Cor. 11:3) or that of husband to wife (Eph. 5:23). The nonuse of *exousia* in the man-woman relationship may be due to the legal authoritarian connotations found in many uses of this term. In the words of Foerster, *exousia* describes "power which decides." It is active in "a legally ordered whole, especially in the state and in all the authoritarian relationships supported by it." These relationships involving *exousia* thus reflect God's lordship and authority in "a fallen world."[37]

Both the rather impersonal sense of the "authority" and especially the nature and structures of the power exercised in a "fallen world" are contrary to the original divine intent for the relation of man and woman. As a matter of fact, Scripture gives no evidence of any divinely intended orders among mankind before the entrance of sin except that of man and woman (Genesis 2). No doubt there was also to be some order between parents and children. But human governmental orders clearly entered and became useful only with the entrance of sin (cf. Gen. 9:6 and Rom. 13:1ff.). The concept of people subordinate to others in the present orders of master-slave or employer-employee are probably also present only under fallen conditions. The absence of the authority terminology, thus, signifies that leadership of man in relationship to woman is of a radically different nature than that exercised by other authorities in God's ordained orders.

This distinction in authority is seen further in the fact that nowhere in Scripture are women commanded to obey men. This is all the more significant in light of the centrality of obedience as the expression of the Christian faith. Believers are to obey Christ (Heb. 5:9) and the Word (2 Thess. 1:8; 3:14). Obedience is also commanded as an expression of subordination in the other orders of the people-government authorities, servant-master, and child-parent.

The absence of the command to obedience does not mean that it is totally absent from the concept of woman's subordination. Sarah, an example of the "holy women," obeyed her husband, Abraham (1 Pet. 3:6). But the lack of commanded obedience points to the nature of the subordination: It is done voluntarily out of love. This unique nature of the man-woman order is noted by Zerbst.

> The woman is merely told that she has been subordinated to man, that man is her "head," and that she should willingly accept this divine arrangement.

> In these contexts the New Testament always addresses the woman. It never tells man to subject woman unto himself. It never speaks of the "power" of man. It never draws the deduction from woman's subjection that she should obey her husband in the manner in which children and servants are to obey their parents and masters, or in which soldiers are to obey their commanders, and citizens their government. All this accentuates that distinctive nature of woman's subjection and indicates that the divine institutions of the state, of the social structure of the family, and of marriage must not be regarded as being on the same plane. The man-woman relationship is distinctive in nature.[38]

Consideration of the above biblical teaching leads to the conclusion that, in a special sense, the order between man and woman is uniquely grounded in love. It is not structured in power and dominion. The leadership of man and the subordination of woman are to be willingly and sacrificially motivated by a love that respects, honors, and seeks the highest good of the other and the entire family or church, as the case may be. Although the record of the first man and woman speaks of the concept of marriage in becoming "one flesh," it is also possible to see in this first relationship of man and woman something fundamental to human society as a whole. The most basic relationship of human society in which the complementary needs of every individual are evident is in the relationship of man and woman. In addition to everything else that may be said about the dynamics of that complementariness, its most fundamental basis and outworking is the sphere of love, the same love that characterizes the relations between the Father and the Son. As in this love, it does not negate the possibility of an order involving subordination in the outworking of God's will. Rather, it demonstrates that such an order does not involve a selfish demonstration of power and authority on the one hand or a chafing submission on the other. Both sides of the order are finally really one in the fulfillment of the divine will and purpose.

The "Headship" Relationship

The order between man and woman, as we have already noted, is portrayed as the "headship" of the man. The meaning of this concept is vital to the proper understanding and practice of God's design for the relationship between man and woman. Concerning the relationship of men and women in the church, Paul tells the Corinthians, "The man is the *head [kephalē]* of a woman" (1 Cor. 11:3, italics added). In Ephesians, he uses the same concept to clarify the nature of the relationship between a husband and a wife when he says, "The husband is the *head* of the wife, as Christ also is the head of the church" (Eph. 5:23, italics added). Both of these passages have traditionally been understood to mean that the man has been designated by God as the one to exercise leadership and authority both in the home and in the church.

This view, however, has been challenged in recent years by a few Bible scholars who have attempted to set forth a new view that interprets the metaphor as "source" (in the sense of origin).[39] They contend that the figure does not at all convey a sense of authority or role distinction. Thus, in 1 Corinthians 11:3, the man is the source of the woman in the sense that Paul speaks about a few verses later in 11:8: "For man does not originate from woman, but woman from man" (see also v. 12).[40] Similarly, Ephesians 5:23 is understood as teaching that the husband is the *source* of his wife in a temporal and creational sense, but does not signify a hierarchical role distinction. By reinterpreting the metaphor of headship as source and by stressing Paul's injunction to mutual submission (Eph. 5:21), these interpreters lay a foundation for an egalitarian family structure. In this view, leadership in the home and the church is not determined by gender but by giftedness and mutual consent.

Dr. Wayne Grudem, a theology professor at Trinity Evangelical Divinity School, has provided the most detailed and thorough response to this new view. After analyzing numerous occurrences of the term *head* throughout Greek literature, Grudem reached the conclusion that there is not one clear instance of the term *head* used in the sense of "source." He also concluded that the meaning "authority over" is a well-established meaning when the term is used in a metaphorical sense. Consequently he argued that "authority over" is the meaning that best suits the interpretation of "head" in 1 Corinthians 11:3 and Ephesians 5:23.[41] At the same time, and working independently from Grudem on this issue, the eminent Roman Catholic scholar Joseph Fitzmyer of the Catholic University of America reached the identical conclusion that *kephalē* was typically used in the sense of "authority over" in the Greek Old Testament and in Jewish writings of the time. He also concluded that this is the best sense in which to take 1 Corinthians 11:3.[42]

In a more recent development, P. G. W. Glare, the current editor of the standard lexicon for Greek literature (the Liddell, Scott, Jones *Greek-English Lexicon* [Oxford]), has stated that the supposed sense of "source" for the Greek word *kephalē* "does not even exist," and that a future edition of the Oxford lexicon would not list "source" as a possible meaning for *kephalē*.[43] This would be consistent with the standard lexicon for New Testament Greek, Bauer's *Greek-English Lexicon of the New Testament and Other Early Christian Literature* (Univ. of Chicago, 1979), which never mentions "source" as a possible meaning. It is also true of the latest German edition of Bauer's lexicon (1988).[44]

The case made by Grudem and Fitzmyer—supporting the traditional interpretation of the passages—is compelling at numerous points. At the minimum, they clearly demonstrate that the metaphorical use of "head" to signify leadership and authority was the common usage and was widespread in Jewish and Hellenistic traditions. One of the strongest pieces of evidence for this view comes from the Old Testament. The Hebrew word for "head" *(rōsh)* was used in a figurative sense for "leader" or "chief." When these figurative uses were translated into Greek, the translators used an array of Greek words for "leader"; included among these terms was the Greek term "head" *(kephalē)* (see, for example, Judg. 11:11: "Then Jephthah went with the elders of Gilead, and the people made him *head* and chief over them" (italics added); see also Judg. 10:18; 11:8–9; 2 Sam. 22:44).

When Paul asserted that "the man is the head of [the] woman" in 1 Corinthians 11:3, the overall context has to do with the role relationships of men and women in the church. He hereby indicated that males have been given the role of leadership. In laying down this principle, however, Paul made two other important statements regarding the relationship of Christ to men and to God. He remarked, "Christ is the head of every man," and "God is the head of Christ." Both of these are theological statements that have meaning that transcends the specific local situation at Corinth. The first clearly affirms that Christ wields authority over men and functions as their leader. The second conveys significant insight for us into the nature of the relationship of the persons of the Trinity; namely, there is a distinction of roles, and Christ fulfills a role of responding to the leadership and authority of the Father. Of course, this does not create a rupture in their relationship because the Father is all-loving and all-wise and the Son is well-pleased to carry out the will of the Father. Neither does this relationship imply an inequality between the Father and the Son; their equality is based on their equality of being or essence, not in fulfilling the same roles. As Paul then declared that "the man is the head of [the] woman," he was affirming what appears to be a creational principle—that males should assume the role of leadership—which is not contingent upon any historically limited situation in the church of that time. As noted previously, he went on in the passage to ground this principle in the truths of the creation of man and woman (cf. 1 Cor. 11:8–9).

The meaning of headship is more fully elaborated in the apostle's extended application of the metaphor to the relationship of husband and wife in Ephesians. Although the husband-wife relationship involves an intimacy beyond that of simply man and woman in the church, the use of the same imagery of "headship" suggests that similar principles are being taught in both relationships—man-woman and husband-wife. Both are also grounded in the creation account of Genesis 2 where Adam and Eve represent both man-woman and husband-wife.[45]

In the husband-wife application in Ephesians, the term *head* is part of a larger metaphor in which the head is discussed in terms of its relationship to a body. Paul elaborated on this metaphor in Ephesians 4:15–16 where he applied the imagery to Christ and the church: "We are to grow up in all aspects into Him who is the head, even Christ, from whom the whole body, being fitted and held together by what every joint supplies, according to the proper working of each individual part, causes the growth of the body for the building up of itself in love." In this passage, the head not only serves a leadership function, but also functions as the ultimate source of supply for all of the body's needs. The head, therefore, performs the dual function of *leadership* and *source of provision*.

An extensive study of the use of head/body imagery in the world of the New Testament demonstrates that this interpretation of the dual function of the head in relationship to the body was the common use of the metaphor.[46] One passage out of the writings of Philo, a first-century Jewish writer who lived in Alexandria, Egypt, serves to illustrate this usage.

> The soul innervates and strengthens sense perception by directing its energies to what is suitable for it, with the participation of the parts of the body. And the center, in one meaning, is the chief and head, as is the leader of a chorus. (Philo, *Questions and Answers on Genesis,* 1.10)

In this passage, both the leadership of the head and its ability to provide for the body by directing the energies to the various members are stressed.

We find Paul again using this imagery to convey the nature of the relationship of Christ to His church in the letter to the Colossians. In that context, he was warning the church against a dangerous and threatening teaching that some were advocating who were really not in touch with "the Head": "He has lost connection with the Head, from whom the whole body, supported and held together by its ligaments and sinews, grows as God causes it to grow" (Col. 2:19 NIV). By speaking of Christ as the "head" of the church, Paul was insisting that Christ alone is *the leader* of the congregation. He alone possesses authority over His people—not the ringleaders of this deviant teaching who were judging and condemning the Colossian Christians. Paul was also affirming that Christ is the *source of provision* for the church. It is from Him that the entire church draws its nourishment for growth. The church can only mature as it submits to Christ's leadership and receives His nourishing strength and support.

Paul now applied this imagery to clarify the role relationships between husbands and wives in marriage: "For the husband is the head of the wife, as Christ also is the head of the church . . . the body" (Eph. 5:23). It is important to recognize, however, that Paul did not use the imagery absolutely (i.e., "the husband is the head of his wife"), but he qualified it based on the analogy of Christ's relationship to the church (i.e., "the husband is the head of the wife, as Christ also is the head of the church"). This established the vital significance of gaining a proper understanding of how Christ functions in relationship to His church as "head."

As we have already established based upon Ephesians 4:15–16 and Colossians 2:19, in headship there is a dual function: leadership and source of provision. The notion of leadership is implied in the fact that the church subjects itself to Christ (Eph. 5:24). This, in turn, serves as an example of how the wife should respond to her husband. The nature of Christ's leadership is governed by selfless love (Eph. 5:2, 25) with the welfare of the church always in view. In the same way, the husband should exercise his leadership out of a selflessness that puts the welfare and growth of his wife chiefly in view. The Gospels clearly distinguish Christ's form of leadership from the concept of leadership known in the world. Jesus modeled a servant pattern of leadership. He told His disciples, "For even the Son of Man did not come to be served, but to serve, and to give His life a ransom for many" (Mark 10:45).

Christ is also presented in this passage fulfilling His role as "head" by providing for the church. The husband is called to nourish and to cherish his wife because this is what Christ does for the church (Eph. 5:29–30). Providing for the wife's physical needs is an essential part of the husband's responsibility. It goes beyond this, though. The husband has a duty to be concerned about his wife's emotional needs. "Cherishing" implies that the husband needs to communicate in a variety of ways the high degree of value he places on his wife and the depths of his love for her. She needs to know that she is like a precious jewel in his eyes.

The headship of the husband in marriage thus involves the exercising of leadership, but it is a special kind of leadership. The husband will "lead" his family rather than boss his partner; the husband will be in tune with his wife's needs and strive to meet them; the husband will value what his wife can give him that he needs and does not have without her; the husband will recognize his wife's giftedness and seek to support her and give her opportunity to express her gifts; the husband will cast a vision and direction for the family oriented around God's kingdom purposes—in other words, he will have a strategic plan for how his household will serve the Lord in the church and community.

Our discussion of these important texts dealing with "headship" thus leads us to a number of instructive implications for the role relationship of men and women in the church, in which the ultimate official leadership is the responsibility of certain men:

- The kind of leadership that these men give to the church should not be an overbearing and harsh use of authority. It is not "bossing" or "lording it over" (inappropriate leadership models that Jesus roundly condemns; Mark 10:42).
- Leaders in the church will provide whatever is essential for the health and well-being of the church in terms of time, energy, resources, and care.
- Leaders in the church will help women to identify their giftedness, facilitate the development of these gifts, and provide opportunities for them to serve.

- Leaders in the church are called to serve in a selfless way, leading the congregation as virtuous examples.
- Leaders in the church will cherish the congregation with a deep and sincere love.
- Leaders will recognize their needs for women and value what the church receives from them.

Women (along with all members of the church) are accordingly called to respect the leaders of the church and to "order themselves" under their leadership. If this were to happen in the way God has designed it, women would not be denied the right or opportunity to serve in a variety of ways in the church. The leaders would affirm the women in their giftedness and free them to serve accordingly, including functions of leading under the ultimate leadership of the church. They would also recognize the critically important contribution of women—they have a complementary and necessary contribution to make precisely because they are women. They are equal partners with men in the work and service of the church.

Conclusion

Our examination of the extensive apostolic teaching on the relationship of man and woman demonstrates a complete harmony with what we have seen earlier in the teaching and examples of the Old Testament and Jesus in the Gospels. Man and woman are designed by their Creator to live in an ordered relationship of complementarity in which there is an absolute equality of value and personhood and yet divinely ordained functional distinctions. There is a security in identity because there is an essential equality and fitting together of the two. There is a relationship of warmth, because it is rooted in authentic love—a self-sacrificial love modeled by Christ. There is a sense of purpose because both sexes have equally important roles to fulfill in the service of Christ and His overall kingdom program.

CHAPTER SEVEN

THE "ORDER" AND "EQUALITY" OF GALATIANS 3:28

Robert Saucy

Introduction

"There is neither Jew nor Greek, there is neither slave nor free man, *there is neither male nor female*; for you are all one in Christ Jesus" (Gal. 3:28, italics added). This statement by the apostle Paul declaring that there is neither male nor female "in Christ," although not directly addressing women's activity in the church, has important bearing on the issue. Located within a discussion of the changes brought about by the coming of Christ and the end of life under the old Mosaic Law for the believer in Christ, it signals a newness of relationships. The question of the nature of this change is therefore a central issue in the discussion of women's place in ministry.[1]

Some interpreters see the fact that "there is neither male nor female . . . in Christ" as pointing to the end of all distinctions between men and women in the realm of social functions. For some, such as F. F. Bruce, this applies only in the church. Distinctions between man and woman in the family are valid and useful.[2] Most who understand this text in this way, however, apply it to all man-woman relationships.[3] This latter position seems the most consistent as people "in Christ" are not only so in their church roles, but in all of life. For those who understand Galatians 3:28 in this way, it is the key text in relation to the subject of the relationship between man and woman today—"the locus classicus,"[4] "The Magna Carta of Humanity."[5]

This text, with its denial of distinctions between man and woman, thus takes precedence over the teaching that we have seen in the previous chapter that woman is to be "ordered under" the headship of man. The texts that teach an order between man and woman must be interpreted in light of this overarching egalitarian understanding of their relationship taught in Galatians 3:28. Some do this by saying that Paul simply failed to carry out the implication of his theological "breakthrough" in Galatians into all of the realms of man-woman relationships. That is, in the passages in which he teaches an ordered relationship of man and woman he was still under the influence of his traditional patriarchal background.[6] Others, including most evangelical egalitarians, harmonize these different teachings by seeing the apostle's instructions concerning an order between man and woman as limited to particular historical situations and thus not intended by the apostle as normative for all time. The egalitarian teaching of Galatians 3:28 is what the apostle intended to be the normative universal teaching for the relationship of men and women.

For most interpreters throughout the history of the church, the apostle's teaching concerning male and female in Christ in Galatians 3:28 is not contrary to his other teaching concerning their ordered relationships in society and the church. Rather, the two teachings are complementary —there is an order and yet a profound equality. That is, the statement that "there is neither male nor female . . . in Christ," when interpreted in its context, does not contradict an ordered relationship. But it does have much to say about the nature and conduct of that relationship. Man and woman "in Christ" are returned to their original created relationship of loving complementarian unity.

The Meaning of Galatians 3:28

The Theological Emphasis of the Context of Galatians 3:28

In distinction from Paul's other letters, the book of Galatians focuses on the single issue of the threat of the heresy of "a different gospel"

(1:6–7). In the words of Lightfoot, "The Galatian apostasy in its double aspect, as a denial of his [Paul's] own authority and a repudiation of the doctrine of grace, is never lost sight of from beginning to end."[7] The broad context of the entire book in which our statement concerning man-woman distinctions is found is thus a discussion of the doctrine of salvation, including how a person becomes rightly related to God (i.e., justification) and how that justified person lives his or her life (i.e., sanctification). Unlike the apostle's other writings, Galatians does not address a variety of issues related to the practical life of the Christian in the different spheres in which he or she lives, e.g., the church, home, work, or the world. The so-called "house tables" of ethical instructions for the various stations of life (including that between husband and wife) that are found in other epistles (cf. Eph. 5–6; Col. 3–4) are not included in Galatians. Doctrine, of course, is always vitally related to practical life. But the fact that the apostle was dealing directly with doctrine and not matters of practical social functioning in Galatians must be kept in mind when interpreting the various texts of this book, including 3:28.

Turning from the broad context of the book to the more immediate context, we find that the teaching of the equality of male and female in Christ is found in the center of the passage (3:19–4:7) in which New Testament scholar Richard Longenecker says the apostle "comes to the heart of his differences with the Judaizers."[8] The theological nature of this discussion is further seen in Longenecker's descriptive title of this section: "The Believer's Life not 'Under Law' but 'in Christ': Against Nomism [living under Law]."[9] The discussion concerns changes that have taken place now that Christ has come and the believer in Him no longer lives "under the Law." The verses surrounding 3:28 (vv. 26–29) contain numerous statements asserting the truth that now that Christ has come all believers have come to a unity "in Christ" through faith in Him. Their equal sharing of the position "in Christ" gives them equal status as God's "sons" (v. 26) and equal participation in the promised inheritance (v. 29). The thrust of the passage thus deals with the "'objective' state of salvation" common to all believers.[10] The emphasis is on the unity of believers in Christ and their equal participation in all that belongs to those in Him without distinction.

The equality of believers in Christ, however, does not negate all distinctions in role and responsibility among the believers. Differences in gifts and roles of responsibility still remain. This harmony of diversity and equality in Christ is seen in the apostle's teaching on spiritual gifts and the body of Christ. In language similar to Galatians 3:28, Paul writes to the Corinthians, "We were all baptized into one body, whether Jews or Greeks, whether slaves or free," but we all have different functions in the church according to the diversity of God's gifts (1 Cor. 12:13–18).

The apostle's teaching to the Colossians also shows that an equality "in Christ" does not negate the distinctive roles of man and woman. All believers joined to Christ, he says, are involved in "a renewal in which there is no distinction between Greek and Jew, circumcised and uncircumcised, barbarian, Scythian, slave and freeman, but Christ is all, and in all" (Col. 3:10–11). The male and female distinction is not mentioned, but it is generally agreed that this passage expresses the same truth as that found in Galatians 3:28—there is an equality of *all* believers "in Christ."[11] Yet only seven verses after this teaching of the equality of all in Christ, the apostle gives the instruction, "Wives, be subject to your husbands, as is fitting in the Lord" (Col. 3:18). Apparently, the apostle does not intend his teaching on the equality of all believers in Christ (v. 11) to deny the functional distinctions between man and woman in the home (v. 18).[12] This is further seen in the motivation that is given for the wife's action. She is to be in this relationship with her husband "as is fitting in the Lord," which as Bruce explains means fitting "within the new fellowship of those who own Christ as Lord."[13] Thus being "in Christ" with its equal participation in all of the blessings of salvation in Him does not abolish divinely ordained functional distinctions.

The Religious and Personal Distinctions of Galatians 3:28

The theological emphasis of Galatians 3:28 that we have seen in the broad context is also evident when we consider the nature of the distinctions transcended "in Christ"—Jew/Greek, slave/free, male/female. Just prior to verse 28, the apostle explained that with the coming of Christ, the believer's relationship with God is no longer related to living under the Law: "Therefore the Law has become our tutor to lead us to Christ, so that we may be justified by faith. But now that faith has come, we are no longer under a tutor. For you are all sons of God through faith in Christ Jesus" (vv. 24–26). The distinctions of verse 28, therefore, are now abolished because they all belonged to the Law and the contemporary Jewish application of it.

It is possible that when Paul wrote these distinctions he had in mind a Jewish morning prayer that goes back to the first century. In this prayer the Jewish man expressed gratitude to God for not making him a Gentile, a slave, or a woman. The rationale of this prayer, as Bruce notes, was "not any positive disparagement of Gentiles, slaves or women as persons but the fact that they were disqualified from several religious privileges which were open to free Jewish males."[14] This is seen in the comments on the prayer from Rabbi Jehuda: "Blessed be God that he had not made me a Gentile: 'because all Gentiles are nothing before him' [Isa. 40:17]. Blessed be God that he has not made me a woman: because woman is not obligated to fulfill the commandments. Blessed be God that he has not made me a boor: because a boor is not ashamed to sin [he does not follow the Rabbinic or Pharisaic rules]."[15]

The issue of all three categories of distinction was thus a question of religious status according to the Law at that time. As Strack and Billerbeck explain, "This thought (Gal. 3:28) simply could not be realized in the synagogue, because it was precisely those natural differences which significantly determined the relationship of the individual to the law: the born Jew had a different relationship to the law than the proselyte, the man a different relationship than the woman, the free man a different relationship than the slave."[16]

The Jew-Greek (or Gentile) distinction under the Law is well-known. Gentiles were outside the provisions of the Law. They were limited to the temple's outer court of the Gentiles, separating them from the inner court of women (Jewish) and the still more inner courts of the Israelites and of the priests. Paul's message to the Galatians was that in Christ this distinction was gone. All are equally sons of God through faith in Christ apart from the Law. The distinction abolished was a religious distinction that pertained first to their relationship with God, but also to their relationship with each other—they were now one.

As the Jewish prayer indicated, there was also a religious distinction between men and women under the Law.[17] In the first instance, circumcision, which was the sign of the covenant relationship under the Law, was limited to men. Women participated in the covenant through men. But now they come into the new covenant through their own faith and baptism even as men (Gal. 3:26–27). Women also were not obligated to keep all of the commandments of the Law that had to do with public religious observance.[18] Not being priests, they were unable to perform priestly or Levitical functions and were therefore excluded from the holiest parts of the temple. In the temple they were excluded from the court of the priest and even from the court of the Israelites, being permitted entrance only as far as the court of women. Again, as with the distinctions between Gentiles and Jews, these religious distinctions between men and women that had to do with the external and ritual of the Law were no longer present in Christ.

Finally, the Law made similar distinctions between slave and free men. Perhaps because of the requirements of the work, slaves were not obligated to observe all of the provisions of the Law. According to Rengstorf, their religious obligation was limited, like that of a wife.[19]

The abrogation of distinctions in Galatians 3:28 thus relates directly to the historical transition in God's plan of salvation. These various distinctions were part of the external rites and ordinances of Old Covenant Law, which was operative for the people of God before Christ. But with the coming of Christ and His fulfillment of the Law, this old economy with its distinctions no longer has any religious significance. Salvation is found in union with Christ and His work through faith alone. The apostle's words near the close of Galatians related the status of circumcision, the most prominent marker of separation between Jew and Gentile, to all of the old distinctions within all three pairs in 3:28: "For neither is circumcision anything, nor uncircumcision, but a new creation" (Gal. 6:15). The first and primary meaning of Galatians 3:28 thus has to do with the new and direct relationship to God now available to *all* people through Christ without any of the distinctions contained in the prior Old Testament Law.

However, these distinctions, which were introduced as part of God's wise plan to bring salvation to all peoples, had also become occasions for sin to turn them into sources of personal and social antagonism. Paul spoke of the removal of "the Law of commandments" as "abolishing . . . *the enmity*" between Jew and Gentile (Eph. 2:14–15, italics added). There is no doubt that the prayer of the Jewish man who was thankful he was not a woman, a Gentile, or a slave became for many a source of pride and an attitude of superiority over those distinct from him. A prayer very similar in content was also known among the Greeks in which the man gave thanks "that I was born a human being and not an animal, that I was born a man and not a woman, and that I was born a Greek and not a barbarian."[20]

In both Jewish and Greek cultures, then, these distinctions carried with them not only differences in religious obligations between the categories, but evaluations of personal superiority and inferiority. Concerning women, Jeremias notes that some Jewish statements praised the virtuous and righteous woman. But the total evidence points to the conclusion that women were considered religiously and personally inferior to men at the time of the New Testament.

> We have therefore the impression that Judaism in Jesus' time also had a very low view of women, which is usual in the Orient where she is chiefly valued for her fecundity, kept as far as possible shut away from the outer world, submissive to the power of her father or her husband, and where she is inferior to men from a religious point of view.[21]

Although women enjoyed greater freedom the further west one went toward Greece and Rome, they were still considered less than men even in these cultures.[22] Slaves were likewise considered on a lower level of humanity in Judaism as well as in the Greek world.[23]

The prayers of the Jewish and Greek man therefore provide a poignant picture of the divided world of humanity toward which the apostle directed his teaching. It is these distinctions in religion, especially those related to the Mosaic Law, and the sinful devaluing of certain human persons that accompanied them, that the apostle taught as abolished by seeing all equally sharing in Christ and therefore one—not all distinctions in the practical functional relationships.

The Apostle's Reference to Genesis 1 and Not Genesis 2

The fact that the apostle uses the specific language of "male" and "female" in Galatians 3:28 rather than "man" and "woman" also points to the equality of all people as human persons and not to an equality that negates all orders between human beings in their societal relationships. When discussing the *functional order* between man and woman or husband and wife, the apostles always use the Greek terms *anēr* (translated "man" or "husband" depending on the context) and *gune* ("woman" or "wife") (cf. 1 Cor. 11:3ff.; 1 Tim. 2:11–15; Eph. 5:22, 25, 28; Col. 3:18–19; Titus 2:5; 1 Pet. 3:1–7). These same words are used for "man" and "woman" in the Greek translation of the creation account of Genesis 2, which details the creation of woman in relation to man.

In Galatians 3:28, however, Paul does not say "man" and "woman," but "male" *(arsen)* and "female" *(thelus)*, terminology which he uses in only one other place (Rom. 1:27). Significantly, this is the same terminology that is used in the Greek version for "male and female" in the creation record of Genesis 1. Like the Greek words, the Hebrew terms for "male" and "female" in Genesis 1 are also distinct from those used for "man" and "woman" in Genesis 2.

The apostle's choice of the words "male" and "female" in Galatians 3:28, therefore, shows clearly that he is thinking of the creation story of Genesis 1, where the equality of both sexes is emphasized.[24] In this account, everything that is said about the "male" is also said about the "female." Both are created in the image of God and both are appointed rulers over creation. The thrust of Genesis 1 is to establish the place of humanity in the creation, i.e., under God and over all other creatures. Genesis 1 thus teaches the equality of "male and female" as human persons in relation to God and the rest of creation.[25] As we have seen, it is this equality of personhood that was denied in the cultural and religious distinctions that provided the background for the apostle's teaching in Galatians.

The apostle's use of the male-female language of Genesis 1 in Galatians 3 thus makes it clear that he is concerned in this passage with the equality of human persons taught in the first creation account. He is not overturning the functional ordered relationship between man and woman that in other passages he derives from the Genesis 2 record of creation, in which man is created first and woman is created as his "helper" and "complementary counterpart," and the language is "man and woman," not "male and female."

The particular meaning of "male and female" in distinction to "man and woman" also lends support for the view that the apostle is not concerned in Galatians 3:28 with the functional relationships between man and woman. The pair of words, "man-woman," refers to man and woman in their relationship. On the other hand, "male-female," which are used for animals species as well as mankind, are the primary terms for expressing sexual differentiation.[26] This distinction is noted by Bratsiotis in his comment on the fact that in Genesis 2 the man named the woman with the feminine of his own name (Heb. *'ish*, "man," *'ishshah*, "woman"). In so doing, the man

> recognizes their mutual relationship (*'ishshah me'ish*, "woman from man"), as well as the position of both in creation. Therefore, it is worthy of note

> that *zakhar,* "male," and *neqebhah,* "female," which serve only to denote a person's sex, are not used here, as they are in 1:27, but rather *'ish* [man] and *'ishshah* [woman]. While these words also mean "husband" and "wife" respectively, they also indicate their position in creation as well as their relationship to and with each other.[27]

The terms "man-woman," and not "male-female," are also used when speaking of the dominant characteristics of each. The distinct meaning of the Hebrew and Greek terms for "man" and "woman" therefore make these words the ones that are used in all discussions concerning the social relationships of life between man and woman. The fact that Paul does not use "man" and "woman" in Galatians 3 indicates that he is not directly concerned with the matter of the functional social relationships of man and woman. Rather, he is asserting their equal position and equal worth as human beings, truths which sin had perverted in the case of women, Gentiles, and slaves in that culture.

The Similarity Among the Groups in Galatians 3:28 Is Not Total

Although many evangelical feminists agree that the real point of the apostle in Galatians 3:28 is the abolition of distinctions in personal equality, they argue that this logically leads to equality in all areas of life. They point out that the change of relationship between Jew and Gentile in Christ led to a change in their relationship in the practical functioning of the church. Prior to the coming of Christ, the Jew held a privileged position in relation to God. But now Jews and Gentiles were perfectly equal as far as church ministry was concerned. Similarly, although slavery was not immediately abolished by the truth of the gospel, it was the outworking of the teaching of the biblical equality of all human persons that led to the emancipation of the slaves in Western cultures. Paul already suggested this conclusion in his treatment of the former slave Onesimus (Philem. 15–16). The cases of the Gentiles and slaves therefore show, according to the egalitarian argument, that the new position of a personal equality "in Christ" led to a practical functional equality.

The issue of slavery in particular is often cited by biblical egalitarians as a parallel to that of women. Since slavery was contrary to the real meaning of the gospel, it is argued that the apostles did not intend their exhortations for slaves to obey their masters as normative for all time. Rather, these instructions were only given for that particular time when to be a rebellious slave as a Christian would hinder the testimony of Christ. In a culture where slavery did not exist, they would therefore no longer apply. The exhortations for women to be ordered under men, they argue, were given for exactly the same reason, to avoid offense in the patriarchal culture of the New Testament era. When the full meaning of the equality of men and women in Christ became the norm of society, these instructions concerning women's subordination, like those related to slavery, would no longer apply.[28]

This argument breaks down, however, when we realize that the various distinctions or orders between groups in Galatians 3:28 are not totally analogous. The distinction between Jews and Gentiles came into being in the Old Testament when God called Israel as a special nation for the service of His salvation for all peoples. This gave the Jews a relationship to God that was not shared by the Gentiles (cf. Eph. 2:11–12). But with the coming of Christ, the "dividing wall" that kept these two groups distinct was broken down (Eph. 2:14). The distinction between Jews and Gentiles in relation to God was, therefore, not intended to be permanent. It was part of God's historical plan of salvation enacted as a result of sin, and not part of the original good creation.[29] The same is true with the religious distinctions between men and women that were related to the Mosaic Law and were abolished with its end.

The institution of slavery was also not part of God's original creation. All biblical instructions toward both slaves and their masters are God's instructions to control a practice that came into human life as a result of sin. As we noted earlier in the case of the slave Onesimus, the apostle himself expressed a negative attitude toward slavery. Even more significantly, he encouraged slaves who could gain their freedom to do so: "Were you a slave when you were called? Don't let it trouble you—although if you can gain your freedom, do so" (1 Cor. 7:21 NIV).

Unlike the Jew-Gentile, master-slave, and male-female distinctions that were related to religious distinctions in the Law and sinful devaluations of persons, the distinction of the complementarian man-woman relationship is grounded in the creation order. It was God's design for the relationship of man and woman from the very beginning of human life and, most importantly, before the entrance of sin.

Scripture makes it abundantly clear with vast teaching that the Law with its distinctions has come to an end. This is especially true concerning the new relationship of Jew and Gentile. In contrast, there is no *clear* teaching of the abolishment of the order between man and woman established at creation. If being in Christ did radically alter the relationship between man and woman that, as we have seen in previous chapters, is present throughout all of biblical history, including apostolic teaching, one would expect far more explanation of it than one text.

Finally, the express teaching for slaves to use their freedom, if it can be gained, clearly demonstrates that the issue of slavery cannot be used as a direct analogy for the man-woman relationship. Nowhere in all of biblical teaching is there a similar teaching directed toward women. Nowhere are women told that they should live under the headship of their husbands or the male leadership of the church so that they will not upset the cultural norm, but, if the opportunity presents itself to live in an egalitarian relationship, they should rather choose this. Since according to biblical egalitarians, Jesus displayed an egalitarianism in His practice, and even the apostles did at times, the absence of any scriptural encouragement toward this practice in real life is impossible to explain. To affirm that Galatians 3:28 provides the *theological* basis for a new egalitarian relationship for believers and then find no teaching of an encouragement toward this in the *actual life* of marriage or church relationship suggests that the egalitarian understanding of Galatians 3:28 is in error.

It is also important to note that the abolishment of distinctions between slaves and masters does not eliminate all of the functional order that these represented in biblical times. Although the institution of forced servitude is contrary to the gospel and its teaching concerning the equality of human personhood, the principles of functional distinctions and ordered relationships in the workplace are not. Most interpreters readily apply the many biblical exhortations to slaves and masters to the present societal functional relationships of employee and employer. In other words, the removal of all distinctions between slaves and masters in Christ does not remove all functional distinctions between Christians in the practical area of working life. In a very real sense, it is not the "order" involved in slavery that believing abolitionists saw as contrary to Scripture, but rather the characteristics of that order, namely, the forced servitude and inhuman treatment of a person as property.

Contrary to the egalitarian view, then, Galatians 3:28 is far from a clear statement of the abolishment of all social and functional distinctions between man and woman. This conclusion is strengthened when we consider that the many other passages where such functional distinctions are taught give no indication that they were only temporary or less than harmonious with the new gospel of Christ.

The theological issue of the context, along with the religious nature of the distinctions related to the Law said to be abolished "in Christ" and the specific language of "male and female," show that this Galatian text is dealing with spiritual and personal equality brought about by a new relationship with God through faith in Christ. The apostle was not addressing the issue of the functional orders in human society and was therefore not negating his teaching of an order between man and woman. Personal equality and social order are not incompatible for him. Madeleine Boucher, an evangelical feminist, acknowledges that "the ideas of equality before God and inferiority in the social order are in harmony in the NT. To be precise, the tension did not exist in first-century thought, and it is not present in the texts themselves. The tension arises from *modern man's* inability to hold these two ideas together."[30] Klyne Snodgrass, an egalitarian, apparently agrees when he says, "Paul obviously did not give up on the idea of hierarchy, and I would argue that equality and hierarchy are not necessarily antithetical ideas."[31]

For centuries, the church agreed that Galatians 3:28, the numerous passages by the same author, and others that teach an order between man and woman do not have contradictory messages. The fact that for many modern interpreters such a harmony is untenable raises the question of whether this more recent interpretation stems more from our modern outlook than from understanding this text correctly for the first time. For example, F. F. Bruce, the highly respected evangelical New Testament scholar, states the following principle in support of his egalitarian interpretation: "Whatever in Paul's teaching promotes true freedom is of universal and permanent validity; whatever seems to impose restrictions on true freedom has regard to local and temporary conditions."[32] The question is whether Scripture or our modern culture provides the definition of "true freedom" in Bruce's statement. Does the apostle really teach a "true freedom" in some passages that he denies in his many passages affirming an order between man and woman? In our opinion, there is no evidence that Paul or any other writer of Scripture felt any tension between his teaching of a complementarian order between man and woman and the true freedom of the believer in Christ.

Having said this, however, does not mean that a text like Galatians 3:28 has nothing to say with regard to functional human relationships, including that of man and woman. Differences in religious status and personal worth did have social consequences. The theological teaching of equality in relationship to God and personal worth was intended to transform practical relationships. For example, the physical ancestry that was so important to Jews is now submerged into the more important familial ties of the family of God, in which the bond is a spiritual relationship, not a racial one. The relationship of slave and master is similarly transformed. Paul encouraged Philemon to receive back his runaway slave, Onesimus, who was now a believer, "no longer as a slave, but more than a slave, a beloved brother . . . in the Lord" (Philem. 16). Whether Onesimus continued to be externally the slave of Philemon or was given his freedom is not the point. A new relationship was established between them that took precedence over the master-slave relationship. Philemon and Onesimus were through Christ brothers in the family of God, and their relationship should be characterized by Christian brotherly love.[33]

The practical effect of the new spiritual equality of all believers in Christ that is taught in Galatians 3:28 is seen in the other two passages where similar language is used. In connection with his discussion of spiritual gifts, Paul wrote to the Corinthians, "For even as the body is one and yet has many members, and all the members of the body, though they are many, are one body, so also is Christ. For by one Spirit we were all baptized into one body, whether Jews or Greeks, whether slaves or free" (1 Cor. 12:12–13). Diversity is not abolished; different individuals have different gifts and functions. But the apostle went on to show that their equal participation in Christ and in the Spirit must show itself in practical life together. Thus all are to be treated as necessary for the functioning of the body, and all are to be honored (cf. vv. 21–26).

The parallel teaching in Colossians 3 provides even more insight into the impact that equality in Christ should have in practical relationships. In the midst of an exhortation for believers to put on the qualities and characteristics of the "new man" (v. 10 KJV), the apostle declared that in this new man "there is no distinction between Greek and Jew, circumcised and uncircumcised, barbarian, Scythian, slave and freeman, but Christ is all, and in all" (v. 11). Two things in this discussion are particularly significant for our purposes. First, the characteristics and qualities of the "new man" that the believer is to put on are all attitudes and actions that have to do with personal relationships—"a heart of compassion, kindness, humility, gentleness and patience" (3:12, see also v. 13). The same is true of those belonging to the "old man" that believer is to discard—"anger, wrath, malice, slander, and abusive speech . . ." (v. 8). The mention of the abolition of these social distinctions, as Moule says, "throws light on the kind of friction which Christianity had to overcome."[34] The abolishing of these distinctions in the "new man," therefore, called for a radical change in attitudes and actions toward those who were different. Although the "male and female" distinction in Galatians 3:28 is not mentioned in this Colossian passage, the effect of the removal of distinctions here would surely be applicable to that distinction as well. The theological truth of equality of spiritual status and privilege and equal worth as persons in Christ must be lived out in relationships. Our common participation in God's gracious love along with our common possession of human nature must lead to a fellowship in which distinctions of this world have no bearing and all persons in Christ, brothers and sisters, are equally loved and valued. Eadie captured something of this truth when he said, "The slave does not obtrude though he mingle his voice in the same song of spiritual freedom with his master, and drink out of the same sacramental cup."[35]

The second truth in this Colossian parallel to Galatians 3:28 is the apostle's explanation that this "new man" into which we have come through faith in Christ and into which we ourselves as believers are being transformed is in reality a renewal "according to the image of the One who created him" (Col. 3:10). The removal of distinctions involved in this renewal thus means a return to the relationship with God and with one another that was present when God originally created mankind in His own image. If we see this same thought as encompassing the significance of the abolishing of the distinction between "male and female" in Galatians 3:28, it suggests that men and women are restored to their original situation as created in the image of God. In Christ we are called to recognize one another, women and men, as equally of human value and dignity, because we equally are created in the image of God. Moreover, we were created to be united in love in a relationship of complementarity in which both need the other and therefore love the other as themselves.

The Question of "Order" and "Equality"

Although some egalitarians like Snodgrass admit that a functional order *and* equality of personhood in relation to man and woman is possible, many argue that such a distinction based on gender is absolutely illogical and unjustified. Without attempting to be exhaustive, it will be helpful to consider some of the reasoning behind this conclusion set forth in a recent egalitarian work.[36]

It is acknowledged by egalitarians that difference in *function* or *role* and equality in *being* is valid under certain circumstances. Legitimate distinctions that do not affect equality of person may be based on individual abilities as, for example, leaders and followers, pupils and teachers. But they must be limited both in *scope* (i.e., for the accomplishment of a certain task) and in *time* (i.e., they are not permanent). The permanent order between man and woman in this life, egalitarians argue, does not meet these criteria and is therefore "unjustifiable."[37]

It is difficult to understand how a distinction in role or rank based on "individual abilities" can allow for equality of personhood for a limited time, but not for all of life. If being subordinate to another individual does not mean you are unequal as persons for a temporary period, then it would appear that subordination on the basis of different abilities does not *in principle* deny equality of person. It is unclear how more or less time changes that principle.

It may also be asked whether there are not some distinctions based on individual abilities that are rather permanent. For example, one of the qualifications for the position of elder in the church is the ability to teach. Assuming that this ability is related somehow to one's natural ability and especially to the gifting of the Spirit, which is diverse, not every person would meet this qualification. It is possible therefore that some individuals could be ordered under the elders of their church throughout their entire Christian life.

The real issue in rejecting functional distinction and personal equality in relation to women and men is therefore not that distinctions in role or rank make the subordinate person less important, or even that such subordination is temporally limited or unlimited. Rather, it is simply that whatever the distinctions between man and woman, they are not sufficient to justify distinction in role. This becomes clear when Groothuis says, "The sexually based difference in abilities that do exist between men and women . . . do not justify the subordination of one gender to the other."[38] The egalitarian argument thus appears to be that subordination does not entail less personhood if it is explainable on the basis of ability. But if it is not explainable on this basis, then it renders the subordinate person inferior as a person.

The question in all of this, of course, is who determines that the distinctions between men and women are or are not sufficient to account for different roles? Just exactly what qualities and what quantities of these are required to justify some legitimate distinction in roles? If psychiatrist Scott Peck is correct in concluding after twenty years of practicing psychotherapy that there is a "profound difference between the *spirit of maleness* and the *spirit of femaleness*,"[39] then what qualities are involved in this difference of "spirit"? Groothuis's suggestion that the "function of government of one's own life and the lives of others" involves wisdom, maturity, responsibility, and rationality that are not gender different may be valid.[40] But could it be that the difference in "spirit," seen by Peck, not only impacts these qualities, making them somewhat different, but also adds additional qualities that might relate to the role of leadership beyond the four listed?

All of this leads to the question noted above: Who determines whether the differences between men and women are sufficient to justify some role distinction? Do we as humans—particularly, fallen humans—understand the nature of our "maleness" or our "femaleness" sufficiently to declare that the differences are not sufficient to justify distinctions in role? Or do the numerous passages in Scripture that teach an ordered relationship of complementarity between man and woman in the home and church indicate that from God's perspective our differences do justify these distinctions?

A second element in the egalitarian reasoning against distinct roles but equality of persons should be cause for concern to all Christians, complementarians as well as egalitarians. Groothuis writes,

> It won't do simply to assert that we must value women equally because they are equal in God's eyes. We must be more specific: Given that women and men stand on equal ground before God, is it biblically warranted for men

> to claim exclusive access to higher-status positions solely on the basis of their gender. . . . In reserving leadership positions for men, traditionalists deny women the opportunity to demonstrate their equality of ability and maturity, and thereby to earn equality of status and social value.[41]

Does Scripture teach, as this statement suggests, that differences of positions, e.g., elder, teacher, helper, etc., mean higher and lower "status and social value"? Must a believer have the "opportunity to demonstrate . . . equality of ability and maturity" in order to "earn equality of status and social value"?

Aside from the fact that God's giftedness does not provide for all (men as well as women) to have "equality of ability" in relation to giftedness, this way of looking at things, although common in the world, seems foreign to Scripture. Using the metaphor of the members of the body for the diversity of spiritual gifts in the church, Paul says, "The parts that we think are less honorable we treat with special honor. . . . God has combined the members of the body and has given greater honor to the parts that lacked it, so that there should be no division in the body, but that its parts should have equal concern for each other" (1 Cor. 12:23–25 NIV). Commenting on the "greater honor" given to the parts that lack it, Fee says, "Most likely he means that the parts that appear to be weak and less worthy are in fact accorded the greater honor of having important functions or receiving special attention."[42]

The issues of higher and lower status and social value somehow seem out of place in this picture of the diversity of ministries in the church. This is not to deny that they are often reality in our churches. Special honor and value along with perks are frequently bestowed on those in certain positions or who exercise certain gifts while others are ignored and thereby silently devalued. Seldom is much thought (and even less action) given to the exhortation to "treat with special honor those that we think are less honorable," i.e., those who are hidden and whose ministry is not as widely visible as others, but equally necessary and valuable. Our response to failures in this area, of course, should be obedience to the biblical pattern. The world's pattern of a hierarchy of status and value must not be allowed to condition church ministries, either men's or women's.

Finally, egalitarian thought (some, at least) rejects the most fundamental principle in the complementarian understanding of the relationship of man and woman, namely, that any distinctions of roles is not for personal privilege, but for the good of the other person and the whole community. Again, to cite Groothuis as an example:

> Traditional male privilege and authority will be spoken of as a man's "responsibility" to "serve" his wife and his church, and to "provide" spiritual leadership and instruction. John Piper and Wayne Grudem illustrate this euphemistic tendency when they say that men "bear the responsibility for the overall pattern of life." This makes it sound as though men are saddled with an onerous obligation, of which women are fortunately free. What is meant, however, is that men and not women have the exclusive right to decide and determine the direction of things in both the home and the church. . . .
>
> [T]he central question concerns who has the ultimate "right to direct the actions of others." . . .
>
> When authority of this nature is reserved for men and denied to women, it is meaningless and misleading to talk of it as not being a privilege but a responsibility, and not a position of superiority but of servanthood.[43]

The idea of a loving leader whose concern is the welfare of the other person is clearly rejected. Leadership is simply having "the exclusive right to decide and determine the direction of things" or "the 'right to direct the actions of others.'"

This, of course, is not the full picture of man's leadership in Scripture, which is commanded to be motivated and exercised in a love that puts others ahead of self. Moreover, man's leadership is always subordinate to God's direction. Woman is directed to be "ordered under," but that is "in the Lord." She is not to follow man against the clear teaching of God.

Aside from this biblical instruction as to the nature of man's leadership, one wonders how the examples of God-given leadership in Scripture relate to this egalitarian understanding of leadership as essentially privilege to control and direct things. Is that the best way to describe the leadership of Moses and the apostles? Was their responsibility simply the "exclusive right to decide" for those under their leadership? What about Christ's leadership, which at least in some way is a model for the husband in relation to his wife (Eph. 5:23ff.)? Although it may be correct to consider that any God-given task is a privilege to carry out, the examples of these biblical leaders reveals that leadership was far more than the right to direct others. With Moses, and no doubt others, the costly and sacrificial demands of leadership were enough to make him prefer not to be in that position. And I would suspect that there were many others at the time who were perfectly satisfied not to be in the shoes of Moses.

Again, as with the hierarchy of status and social value, the concept of leadership simply as a privileged position of control over other people's lives is foreign to the picture of leadership commanded in Scripture and portrayed by our Lord and the apostles in the church. True leadership among believers is the privilege to be a servant, even a slave, of others (Mark 10:43–44). As with spiritual gifts in the church, leadership, whether in the home or in the church, is an activity that does not end on the person doing it, but rather is "for the common good" (1 Cor. 12:7).

To be sure, the remaining presence of the sinful tendency to self-centeredness in all believers has caused church leaders and Christian husbands, including complementarians, to frequently fail in living out this biblical model of leadership. But it is this kind of leadership that is inherent in the biblical teaching of the relationship of man and woman. Rather than devaluing the subordinate person, it is only seeing the other person as having genuine value that will motivate such an unselfish leadership that seeks the good of the one led.

That leadership with consequent subordination does not necessarily mean inequality of persons is in a way tacitly acknowledged by Groothuis. Without affirming the eternal subordination of the Son to the Father, she nevertheless grants that possibility. In doing so, she is seemingly acknowledging that distinction of position does not necessarily deny equality of persons. She goes on, however, to deny that this relationship of Father and Son in the Godhead is analogous to any such relationship between man and woman, asserting that the "voluntary submission (as in Christ's submission to the Father) is not of the same order as the necessary and unilateral submission that the traditionalist agenda required of women to men."[44]

This statement again reveals something of a misunderstanding of the biblical teaching. Woman's submission to man, as we saw in the previous chapter, is, in fact, like Christ's, "voluntary." It is a slave who has no control over what he does and is forced to do what another person wills. But Scripture never portrays the relationship of woman to man with such a picture. The biblical commands for her to be subject to man come to her from God, who asks her to willingly and lovingly exercise her own will to live according to the ordered relationship of the commands because they are good. The man has no command from God to force her submission. Even as the commands of God associated with the proclamation of the gospel, such as "repent" and "believe," are voluntarily obeyed, so the responsibilities of woman are to be voluntarily obeyed. No human power has been given authority to force the husband to obey God's command to "love" his wife. So also, no human has the authority to force the wife to obey her God-given commands. But as the church proclaims the commands of the gospel and seeks to structure its life by their meaning (e.g., not welcoming to the Lord's Table those who have not "believed"), so the complementarian seeks to proclaim the command of God and live accordingly in the belief that such is good for both men and women in their life together.

All of this is to say that it is vitally important in thinking about the legitimacy of distinct roles and yet personal equality that we think according to God's perspective and not that of the world around us. Hierarchies of status and social values have no place in God's evaluation of our distinct ministries. Biblical leadership's first concern is not directing or controlling someone else's life. And, finally, the woman's subordination is not like some other human orders in which the subordinate one is forced into subjection. Analogous to the relation of the Son to the Father at this point, it is an ordered relationship of love for the sake of unity and wholeness. When humans live out their created diversity under the control of true love, such diversity, including that of gender, cannot lead to devaluation of any person.

All of this is to say that great care must be taken by both egalitarians and complementarians that we look at all of the issues related to the relationship of persons and gender from God's perspective. The biblical teaching must be our canon, and not either the thought patterns that shape the world about us or the practice of these same patterns, which sadly all too often are present in our churches.

Conclusion

The apostle's teaching that there is "neither male nor female; for you are all one in Christ" is a profound statement about the relationship of men and women "in Christ." There is absolutely no distinction in their relationship to Christ. They equally participate in all that Christ has done for His people and all that He is to them today and forever. They are "one" in Him. However, as we have seen, this teaching of an equality in Christ is not contrary to all functional distinctions between God's people. The biblical teachers give no evidence that a spiritual equality in relation to Christ and His salvation was somehow contrary to the broad teaching and examples found in both the Old and New Testaments of a divinely ordered relationship of complementarity between man and woman established in their creation.

The teaching of an equality and oneness in Christ in Galatians and other passages should, however, have a profound effect on that relationship. It calls for a perspective and practice that transcends much of the actual practice of men and women throughout history, including that of God's own people. Equality of persons in Christ means the rejection of placing more value on one person than another, whether based on social status, particular ministry, or position in social orders. Galatians 3:28 points both men and women back to God's original design. Although created with differences and a distinct relationship and responsibility to each other, man and woman were equal and therefore equally valued in every respect as human beings in the image of God. The outworking of this equality has always been marred by sin, but it must be the goal of all believers. We will fulfill God's desire in relationships only if we fulfill this teaching on the equal value of persons, only if we truly love the other, both men and women, as ourselves.

CHAPTER EIGHT

THE MINISTRY OF WOMEN IN THE EARLY CHURCH

Robert Saucy

Introduction

The biblical record reveals that women played a significant role in the ministry of the early church. As in the Old Testament and the ministry of Jesus, men still had the responsibility of ultimate leadership of the community of believers. But there was a new emphasis of spiritual equality of those "in Christ" regardless of who they were or their rank in the social structure of the day. Symbolic of this new equality, the new initiatory rite symbolizing membership in the new Christian community was baptism for both men and women, as opposed to circumcision in the Old Testament community that applied only to males.

The new covenant salvation brought about by the finished work of Christ also brought a new democratizing of ministry. Previously only men served as priests. Now all believers belonged to the "priesthood" (cf. 1 Pet. 2:5). All are "ministers" in the church. The Spirit, rather than coming only on certain individuals to minister in the community as in the Old Testament economy, now comes on all believers, equipping every one to serve in the "ministry" of the church (cf. Eph. 4:7–16). Different functions remain as depicted in the apostle Paul's favorite church metaphor, the body. But every member is necessary for the proper functioning of the church and the fulfillment of its mission. All are equally related to Christ the Head and equipped with the Spirit.

The new elements related to ministry brought about by the new spiritual realities should caution us about indiscriminately applying Old Testament ministry patterns to ministry in the church. Frequently in the post–New Testament church we find the argument for restricting certain ministries to men because they serve as "priests" in church, and in the Old Testament all priests were men. The new universalizing of the priesthood clearly negates such reasoning. Christ's work brought about a newness that affected ministry as well as spiritual life. Something of the universalization sought in the desire of Moses that "all the Lord's people were prophets, that the Lord would put His Spirit upon them" (Num. 11:29) has been inaugurated in the church. The need for structure and order is not abolished, but there is a newness of unity and equality of all who are in Christ. Beyond the necessary order of organizational leadership within the community is the overarching truth that we are all "brothers and sisters," "brethren of Christ," in the family of God.[1] This newness of ministry is apparent in the pattern of women's ministry alongside men in the early church of the New Testament.

The Prominence of Women in the Early Church

The leading figures in the early church were men. But the biblical record also clearly reveals that women played prominent roles in the New Testament church. In the book of Acts alone, there are thirty-three references to women. At the very beginning they are mentioned along with the apostles and other men as praying together and seeking the Lord's will for the replacement of Judas's apostleship (1:14), and they apparently spoke with tongues along with men on the Day of Pentecost (2:1–4, 16–18). Women are mentioned along with men as responding to the gospel message and becoming full members of the church. "Multitudes of men and women were constantly added to their number" (5:14). In response to Philip's preaching in Samaria, "men and women alike" believed and "were being baptized" (8:12; cf. 17:4, 12, 34; 21:5). In one instance, Luke even mentioned women before the men: "Many of them believed, along with a number of prominent Greek women and men" (17:12). Paul's first convert in Europe was a woman, Lydia (16:14), and probably the second also; that is, the demonized slave girl (cf. vv. 16–19). Women provided houses for church meetings. In fact, we are more often given the names of women in whose homes churches met than we are of men (cf. Acts 12:12; 16:40; Rom. 16:3–5 [cf. 1 Cor. 16:19]; Col. 4:15).

As we will see later, women served alongside men in the propagation of the gospel in obedience to the Lord's command to be witnesses. Their equality in witness brought an equality of suffering. Acts records that they were bound and dragged off to prison for the sake of the gospel along with men (8:3; 9:2; 22:4). This continued in the post-apostolic period when women were martyred along with men and respected as spiritual equals by the Christian community.[2] They were also equally responsible with men morally. Sapphira died along with Ananias for lying to the Holy Spirit (Acts 5:1–11). As Keener notes, the early church rejected the male condescension toward woman's moral weakness that was typical of that day.[3]

The apostle Paul's greetings to certain people in the church at Rome also provides insight into the prominence of women (Romans 16:3–15). Of the twenty-six people greeted, nine are women if the Greek name often translated "Junias" (masc. v. 7) is rather "Junia" (fem.).[4] Eleven out of the twenty-six are given a specific description rather than simply being greeted or called "beloved," and of these five are definitely women (six, if Junia is included) and five men. Mary and Persis are described as having "worked hard" (vv. 6, 12), Tryphaena and Tryphosa as "workers in the Lord" (v. 12), and Priscilla as one of "my fellow workers in Christ Jesus" (v. 3). The latter is mentioned six times in the New Testament and always with her husband, Aquila. In four of the instances, she is mentioned first, perhaps because she was the more prominent and influential in the church (cf. Acts 18:2–3, 18, 26; Rom. 16:3; 1 Cor. 16:19; 2 Tim. 4:19). One wonders whether the same prominence of women's names would appear in a letter written to the average conservative evangelical church today.

The General Ministry of Women

Leaving aside for the moment the question of whether women held any official ministries or "offices" in the early church, they clearly served the church in varied and significant roles.

In the important ministry of evangelism and church planting, women are seen alongside men. The wives of apostles accompanied their husbands in their evangelistic ministries (1 Cor. 9:5). Although this text gives us no insight as to what they actually did, Clement of Alexandria expressed an early tradition that the wives accompanied their husbands as "fellow ministers" that the gospel might penetrate "the women's quarters without any scandal being aroused." In other words, they were co-laborers with their husbands, ministering to women.[5]

Beyond this hint in connection with the wives of the apostles, the participation of women in church-planting endeavors is forcefully evident in Paul's naming of women as his "co-workers." Although the apostle applied this term to all believers (e.g., 2 Cor. 1:24), he usually reserved it for certain individuals who participated with him in the ministry of the gospel. Fourteen men were specifically called "co-workers," among them such well-known associates as Timothy (Rom. 16:21), Titus (2 Cor. 8:23), Luke (Philem. 24), Epaphroditus (Phil. 2:25), and Apollos (1 Cor. 3:9).[6] In addition, three women are described by the same term: Priscilla (Rom. 16:3) and Euodia and Syntyche (Phil. 4:2–3). The application of the same terminology to the "household of Stephanas" and other unnamed individuals (1 Cor. 16:15–16; cf. also 1 Cor. 3:9) may add additional women as well as men.

If we add to the list of "co-workers" those who are said to have "toiled" or "labored hard" in ministry, a description that is used with the "co-workers" (cf. 1 Cor. 16:16) and frequently used to describe the ministry of the apostle himself as well as other significant servants of the church (e.g., 1 Cor. 15:10; Col. 1:29; 1 Thess. 5:12), we find four more women specifically noted for their ministry in the church, i.e., Mary (Rom. 16:6), Persis (v. 12), and Tryphaena and Tryphosa (v. 12). Finally, the term "servant" or "minister" (Gk. διάκονος) is also frequently used as a virtually equivalent term for a certain group of people who had significant roles in the church.[7] Paul and Apollos are not only "co-workers" with God, but "servants" (1 Cor. 3:5, 9; cf. also Timothy in 1 Thess. 3:2 and Rom. 16:21). Thus calling Phoebe "a servant of the church which is at Cenchrea" (Rom. 16:1) indicates that she had a significant ministry among the believers there.

Care must be taken, however, in assigning specific roles to the individuals who are described by these different terms. On occasion, all of the terms are ascribed to all believers in the church. All are involved in serving or ministering. For example, all of the saints serve or minister in the church (Eph. 4:12; 1 Pet. 4:10), all are "co-workers" (see 2 Cor. 1:24), all "labor hard" (1 Thess. 1:3). The terms, therefore, provide no ground for suggesting, as some do, that these co-laborers of the apostle are his equals in authority.[8] Nevertheless, their bestowal on certain individuals was more than the apostle's way of showing them honor; it marked them out as having a particularly significant ministry.

After studying the references to "co-worker," Ollrog defined such a person as "one who labors together with Paul as commissioned by God at the shared 'work' of mission preaching."[9] The two women in the Philippian church, Euodia and Syntyche, illustrate something of this definition. The apostle said that they "have shared my struggle in the cause of the gospel" (Phil. 4:2–3); that is, in the proclamation of the gospel,[10] probably especially reaching women. Their participation with Paul in the spread of the gospel exposed them to the same opposition and suffering that the apostle endured. They were truly Paul's "highly valued coworkers who had energetically participated in the apostolic mission, perhaps even when the congregation at Philippi was founded."[11] Their reconciliation, which Paul sought, was therefore because of their importance in the church. "They were surely mainstays of the believing Philippian community" or as the fourth-century church father Chrysostom put it, "These women seem to me to be the chief of the Church which was there."[12] No doubt Priscilla and Aquila were also "co-workers" in a similar participation with the apostle in the proclamation of the gospel, possibly through social contacts in relation to their business (Rom. 16:3).

The apostolic application of terminology that signified significant ministry to women as well as men does not of itself indicate that women held all of the same positions of leadership in the church identically with men. But it does give evidence that women were important co-workers in the ministry of the New Testament church. Whatever its particular nature, which is not always described, it was seen as an equally valuable complementarian ministry to that of men in the proclamation of the gospel and building up of the churches.

Some women's ministries are included in the New Testament record of general ministries of women in the church. One of these was prophecy, which they shared along with men. This, of course, had been true already in the Old Testament. But the coming of the Spirit at Pentecost in fulfillment of the eschatological promise resulted in the prophetic gift being bestowed more widely on both "your sons and your daughters" (Acts 2:17). Luke named the four daughters of Philip the evangelist as "prophetesses" in the record of Acts (21:9). And apparently the prophetic ministry of women was common, as the apostle Paul gave instructions with regard to head coverings for women "praying or prophesying" in the church assembly (1 Cor. 11:5). On the basis of the apostle's later call for women to be "silent in the churches" (1 Cor. 14:34), some have argued that chapter 11 refers to private worship in the home and not public meetings. However, although praying can be done in private, prophecy, according to the apostle's later description, was directed toward the community of believers for their instruction and encouragement (cf. 1 Cor. 14:1–5).[13] Others have suggested that the apostle's instruction concerning head coverings was a concession to what was going on in the Corinthian church. He would prefer women not to speak at all in the church gathering, but if they were going to do it, at least they should do it with the correct decorum with their heads covered.[14] However, all of the apostle's writings, and especially the epistle of First Corinthians in which this instruction is found, demonstrate that the apostle had no problem confronting things that he believed to be contrary to God's will. It is best therefore to see this exhortation dealing with women praying and prophesying as similar to the following discussion of the Lord's Supper. The apostle pointed out improper attitudes and actions connected with their practice of this ordinance, but not with the practice itself. So here, the restriction relates to the manner of the public praying and prophesying and not with the practice itself.

If, with most interpreters, we take 1 Corinthians 11:5 to refer to women prophesying in church gatherings, then we are no doubt to understand that women participated in the meetings of the first-century church at Corinth described in 14:26. "When you assemble, each one has a psalm, has a teaching, has a revelation, has a tongue, has an interpretation" (1 Cor. 14:26). Although prophecy is not mentioned here, the use of "revelation" in connection with prophecy (v. 30) probably indicates that we are to include prophecy and perhaps other inspired speaking gifts in the "revelation" that took place in the meeting. The fact that women participated in the prophetic ministry probably indicates that they also exercised the other ministries mentioned, as no gender restriction is noted. As we will see in chapter 13, the call for their "silence" in the church (v. 34) cannot indicate a complete exclusion from exercising speaking gifts in the congregational meetings.

The linking of prophecy with prayer suggests that prophecy was an ordinary and significant ministry in the church of the New Testament. Prophets ranked right after apostles in the importance of the role they played in the church (1 Cor. 12:28; cf. also Eph. 2:20; 3:5). The ministry of prophecy was to be sought above all others, and Paul even expressed the wish that all "would prophesy" because of the value of this gift in edifying the church (1 Cor. 14:1–5). Women who prophesied, therefore, participated along with men in a very significant church ministry.

This fact is often seen as evidence for women's equal authority and leadership in the church. However, as we saw in the previous chapter, the same apostle who gave instruction concerning women prophesying also taught an order between men and women that places the ultimate responsibility of leadership in the hands of certain men. The ministry of prophet was to declare the word of God that was given to him or her through direct revelation from God. Being the revealed word of God, prophecy by its very nature carried God's authority. However, this must be distinguished from the authority of the prophet. The question is: Who has the practical authority to authoritatively interpret the prophecy and, most significantly, authority to apply its revealed truth to the community of God's people? The Old Testament prophets similarly spoke the revealed Word of God, but the authority to implement it did not belong to them. That was the king's God-given responsibility.

Thus while the personality of the prophet or prophetess was involved in the expression of that communication, as Scripture clearly demonstrates, the personal authority of the prophet was not involved in what was said. The prophet or prophetess was simply the channel of God's revelation that carried His authority. Anyone could be used of God to bring His word to the church (1 Cor. 14:31). The spiritual gift of prophecy is therefore not equated with gifts of leadership or teaching or authoritative church "offices" in Scripture.

Women were also involved in teaching in the church of the New Testament.[15] The older women are expressly charged with "teaching what is good" to younger women (Titus 2:3). The "enrolled" (RSV) widows of the church ("on the list," NASB, 1 Tim. 5:3–16) no doubt also participated in this ministry.[16] In light of the prohibition against women teaching men (1 Tim. 2:12), many commentators view this teaching as taking place privately and primarily by example of life.[17] Scripture, indeed, does place great instructional value on the example of a godly life. But nothing in the New Testament precludes purposeful classes among women for this teaching as well. Nor is it clear exactly what private versus public teaching means given the early church meetings in homes. There is no reason that the apostle's instruction for the older women to teach the younger ones could not take place within the variety of teaching venues available in most contemporary churches, that is, Sunday school, home studies, seminars, etc.

In their teaching and counseling ministry, older women and widows performed an important service not only to younger women but to the community at large. Their significance to the church is illustrated in a story told by E. F. Brown who was a missionary in India when that country was still under the rule of Great Britain. A friend of his who was on furlough in England was once asked, "What is it you most want in India?" His reply: "Grandmothers." Because those who were engaged in governmental administration in India in those days often retired from their service and returned to England at a fairly young age, there were few older women in that society. Their absence left a serious lack. Brown went on to say, "Old women play a very important part in society—how large a part one does not realize, till one witnesses a social life from which they are almost absent. Kindly grandmothers and sweet charitable old maids are the natural advisers of the young of both sexes."[18]

In addition to the older women teaching the younger ones, women in general participated in the teaching ministry of the church in a variety of ways. This will simply be noted here, as it will be discussed more fully in chapters 13 and 14 in relation to women teaching men. Although not in the gathered church assembly, Priscilla provided a notable example of a woman involved in Christian doctrinal teaching. Listing her name before that of her husband, Aquila, indicated to many early interpreters, including Chrysostom, that she was the more prominent of the two. She, along with her husband, explained "the way of God more accurately" to the eloquent evangelist and church planter Apollos (Acts 18:24–26). Although this is the only recorded instance of such teaching, Scripture gives no indication that this was an exception, and we may assume that it occurred on other occasions.

More generally, Scripture makes reference to a general teaching ministry that took place in the church in which all members could participate. Along with the gift of prophecy and other manifestations of spiritual giftedness in the church meeting, the apostle says, "Each one . . . has a teaching" (1 Cor. 14:26). We do not know the nature of all of this teaching nor how it took place, but there does not appear to be any gender restriction implied. If the call for women's "silence" a few verses later (vv. 34–35) allowed women to prophesy, as we have argued earlier, then it would not seem to preclude them from this ministry as well.[19] The possibility for all to teach in some way is also suggested in the chiding remark of the writer to the Hebrews. Addressed to the church at large, he says, "By this time you ought to be teachers" (Heb. 5:12), suggesting that all who were mature were able to teach the less mature.[20]

Finally, if we follow the translation of the NIV and most modern versions, Paul's instructions to the Colossian believers suggest a general teaching in which all, including women, should be involved. "Let the word of Christ dwell in you richly as you teach and admonish one another with all wisdom, and as you sing psalms, hymns and spiritual songs with gratitude in your hearts to God" (Col. 3:16). According to this interpretation, the medium of teaching is the spoken word. Others favor connecting the teaching with singing as in the NASB, "with all wisdom teaching and admonishing one another with psalms and hymns and spiritual songs, singing with thankfulness . . ."[21] Although one hears little of song as a medium of teaching in today's church, the early church following the practice of Judaism held singing in high regard as a vehicle of instruction. Recent studies of New Testament hymnody show that early Christian hymns featured "both didactic and hortatory elements," that is, instruction and exhortatation.[22] The Psalms of the Old Testament, sung in the church, provide rich examples of such elements. The church also composed new songs declaring the new work of God in Christ. Many scholars identify the Christological teaching of Philippians 2:6–11 as an early Christian hymn (cf. Rev. 5:9–10; possibly Eph. 5:14; Col. 1:15–20; 1 Tim. 3:16). We are not told who composed these hymns, but Mary's song known as the Magnificat (Luke 1:46–55) suggests that women participated in the composition of these early Christian hymns as well as in their singing, which constituted a "mode of the Word in which Christ makes Himself heard" in the community of believers.[23]

Women's forms of ministry of the Word of God other than those described as "teaching" or "instruction" will be discussed in chapter

13. But the evidence above indicates that even though the final responsibility for this ministry in the church rested with the official leaders of the church, who were men, the women actively participated in the teaching ministry of the church in manners and venues that complemented those of men.

Continuing in the tradition of those who ministered to the daily needs of Jesus and His disciples, women in the early church also helped to build up the church by their practical "good works." If, as historian Chadwick says, the "most potent single cause of Christian success" in the early church was "the practical application of charity," then women contributed their share to that success.[24] They not only provided their homes for church meetings, with all of the arrangements that would entail, but they labored to help meet the various practical needs of the members. Tabitha, described as a woman who "was abounding with deeds of kindness and charity which she continually did" (Acts 9:36), no doubt models the actions of many women in the New Testament church.

The "enrolled" widows of the church discussed in 1 Timothy 5:3–16 also served the church in a number of significant ministries. Paul's primary concern for those who were "widows indeed" was that they be "honored."[25] As used with elders (v. 17) this term indicated that these widows were to be respected and provided with material provisions by the church.

But there is also an indication that they served the church. The qualifications for one to be enrolled as a church widow required that her life had been devoted to the ministry of helping others. She was to be one who has "shown hospitality to strangers" and has "washed the saints' feet," two services probably performed for traveling believers, including itinerant evangelists and teachers. She was also one who "has assisted those in distress, and . . . devoted herself to every good work" (v. 10). Although the text indicates that these tasks are ones that she has already done that qualify her for church care, most interpreters see them also as tasks that she would be asked to continue doing in the church as the need arose. In addition to doing "good works," like Tabitha, widows, no doubt, served with other older women in the counseling and teaching of younger women. Above all, like Anna in the Gospels, they ministered in the most important task that they could perform for the community: faithful prayer (v. 5; cf. Luke 2:36–37).[26] The records of the early post-apostolic church shows widows (sometimes difficult to distinguish from deaconesses) performing all of these services. They are especially seen as appointed to prayer. But they also visited and cared for the sick, in some instances accompanying deacons in this task; they visited prisoners and were responsible for hospitality for traveling preachers. In some instances in the Eastern churches, widows even seemed to attain a semiclerical status. This order of widows that existed in the New Testament and early church died out later, probably due to the rise of nunneries and the ministry of nuns.[27]

Phoebe illustrates another ministry of some significance in the early church provided by certain women. In Paul's commendation of her to the church at Rome, he described her as "a helper of many, and of myself as well" (Rom. 16:2). Because the verbal forms of the word for "helper" (*prostatis*, προστάτις) are most often used in the New Testament in the sense of "leadership" (cf. 1 Tim. 5:17, the "rule" of the elders; 1 Thess. 5:12, "those who . . . have charge"), some see Paul's description of Phoebe as a *prostatis* to mean that she held an office of authoritative leadership in the church.[28] This is unlikely, however, since it is improbable, if not impossible, to understand how she could have been a leader of Paul himself, which is what he would have been saying if that's what the word meant. Moreover, she is not called "a *prostatis* of the church," as in verse 1 where she is called "a servant of the church," which is probably a reference to something like an official deaconess in the church.

The verb also carries a strong sense of caring for or helping others and sometimes simply has this meaning.[29] Such an instance is seen in Paul's discussion of various ministry gifts in Romans 12:8 where the verb form is translated in the RSV "he who gives aid" (cf. also Titus 3:8, 14).[30] This is no doubt something of the meaning intended by Paul in using this term for Phoebe. But more than simply "helper," the term in secular Greek often denoted a "patron" or "benefactor," described by Moo as "one who came to the aid of others, especially foreigners, by providing housing and financial aid and by representing their interests before local authorities." It is probable that we are to understand Phoebe in the port city of Cenchrea ministering in this way as a patroness, "a woman of high social standing and some wealth, who put her status, resources, and time at the services of traveling Christians, like Paul, who needed help and support."[31]

Official Ministries of Women

There is no doubt that women played a significant role in the life and expansion of the New Testament church. Their ministry involved not only the general type of a wide variety of "good works," but also some roles in which they would have been viewed as "leaders" along with men. Phoebe and Priscilla, along with those who served with Paul as his "co-workers," would surely have been looked up to by the average members of the church as functional leaders in church ministry. But what is the nature of women's leadership? In reality, the exercise of a spiritual gift by any member is an exercise of leadership in the church. For the ministry of a spiritual gift is in truth the manifestation of the Spirit of God to which all must submit.

But for the sake of order, there were also certain ministries in the church that might be termed "offices" in that they were recognized functions of leadership. One, usually called "elder" or "overseer" (traditionally, "bishop"),[32] dealt with the general oversight of the church. The second provided leadership in the realm of "organized service." It was appropriately termed "deacon" or "deaconess," the transliteration of the Greek word for "servant" (*diakonos*, διάκονος) and related to the terms for "service" (*diakonia*, διάκονία). Did the leadership of women also involve being appointed to these official ministries?

Aside from apostles, whom most interpreters view as belonging to the foundational period of the church (cf. Eph. 2:20) and therefore not a permanent office, the elder or overseer represented the highest authority in the church. It might be noted that the elder's authority was related only to the local church, as there is no higher organizational structure seen in the New Testament. Authority in the church was radically different from that exercised among unbelievers and the religious authorities of Jesus' day (cf. Matt. 20:25–28; 23:1–12). It rested on the effectual ministry of the person and not simply the position or office. Nevertheless, the oversight responsibility of the elders in the churches included governing authority. They are "leaders" to whom the believers are to submit (Heb. 13:17); they "rule" in the church (1 Tim. 5:17) and "have charge over" others (1 Thess. 5:12; cf. also Acts 20:28; 1 Tim. 3:5; 1 Pet. 5:2–3).

There is no evidence in the New Testament that women served in this position of elder/overseer. Certain stipulations in the qualifications for this office make it evident that they apply only to men. The overseer is to be "the husband of one wife" (1 Tim. 3:2; Titus 1:6). That a similar qualification could have been given for women if they were considered for this office is seen in the later instruction that an enrolled widow was to be "the wife of one man" (1 Tim. 5:9). But nothing of this is mentioned in either passage on the qualifications for elder/overseer. In view of what the apostle teaches elsewhere about the relation of husband and wife, the requirement that the overseer manage his own household surely pertains to men and not women (1 Tim. 3:4–5). Also, the requirement for the elder to be able to teach (1 Tim. 3:2) so that he may "exhort in sound doctrine" and silence the false teachers who are "upsetting whole families" in the church (Titus 1:9–11) clearly fits with the apostle's emphasis in these same Pastoral Epistles on men having the leadership in authoritative teaching (cf. 1 Tim. 2:11–12).

Finally, the fact that the apostle states qualifications for "women" when he is writing about deacons, as we will see, most likely refers to deaconesses (1 Tim. 3:11). But the fact that he does not mention any qualifications for women in relation to elders indicates that women were not considered for the office of elder. This is further supported when we consider that women are frequently mentioned along with men in other instructions in these epistles (cf. 1 Tim. 2:8–9; 5:1–2; Titus 2:2–3).

Some see the "older women" in Titus 2:3 as "female elders."[33] But such an identification has little basis. If women elders were meant, the apostle could have used the feminine form of the normal word for elders, *presbytera*. Instead he used a word that simply means an older woman *(presbytis)*. The choice of words used for the "older men," *presbytes*, in the immediately preceding verse rather than the term for official elders, *prebyteros*, further supports the fact that "older women" are in view in this text.[34] In addition to "older men" and "older women," the apostle goes on to discuss "young women" (v. 4) and "young men" (v. 6), making it clear that he is giving instructions concerning various age groups in the church, not three age groups and one office.

Although women did not serve the church in the office of elder in the New Testament church, there is good evidence that they were appointed to serve as deaconesses. Some difficulty in the matter lies in the fact that the Greek term for "deaconess" or "deacon" is simply the word for "servant" *(diakonos)* which, with its related noun and verb forms, are widely used in the New Testament with a variety of applications. Christ is the "servant" supreme (e.g., Matt. 20:28; Rom. 15:8). Church leaders including the apostle Paul are "servants" (sometimes translated "ministers") (1 Cor. 3:5; 2 Cor. 3:6; Col. 1:25; 1 Thess. 3:2). Every believer ministering a spiritual gift is likewise a servant who is serving the Lord and His people (1 Cor. 12:5; Eph. 4:12; 1 Pet. 4:10). Even human governors are God's servants (Rom. 13:4).

But "servant" is also used for individuals who exercised a special function in the church. Paul addressed one of his letters to "all the saints . . . in Philippi, including the overseers and deacons" (Phil. 1:1). The addition "overseers and deacons" may be understood in a functional sense as simply describing the activity of some church workers. But most find it more likely that the reference is to certain individuals who were specifically appointed to leadership responsibility in these functions and were known in the church by these titles; otherwise, these two additions would seem to be pointless.[35] Sure evidence for an office of deacon is provided by the apostle when he stipulates requirements for "deacons" along with the requirements for the "overseer" (1 Tim. 3:8–13).

The question of whether the New Testament shows women serving as official deacons is debated. Although the word *diakonos* used in Paul's description of Phoebe as a "servant *[diakonos]* of the church which is at Cenchrea" (Rom. 16:1) may be taken to indicate that Phoebe had simply served the church in a variety of ways, it may also point to her as belonging to an official group of women servants; i.e., deaconesses (cf. NRSV, JB). The fact that she is specifically stated to be a "servant of" a particular church rather simply "serving" (cf. 15:25) or devoting herself to service or ministry (cf. 1 Cor. 16:15) suggests that the reference is to a definite recognized ministry. Furthermore, the nature of her service as "helper" or "patroness" providing material assistance to the needy in the church as well as hospitality for visitors and strangers, and other services to the church at large, fits well with what is known of the ministry of deacons.[36] With most interpreters, therefore, we are probably to understand Phoebe as an illustration of an early deaconess ministry in the New Testament church.[37]

This understanding of Phoebe as a "deaconess" is further supported by Paul's mention of the qualifications for "women" in the midst of his setting forth of the requirements for deacons (1 Tim. 3:8–13, cf. v. 11). The fact that this reference to "women" is simply found in the middle of a discussion of deacons, in addition to some other reasons, leads some interpreters, with the Authorized Version, to see these women as the wives of deacons (the Greek term can be translated "women" or "wives" depending on the context).[38] However, there are good reasons for seeing these women as deaconesses.[39]

1. If "wives" had been meant, we would have expected either a possessive pronoun, i.e., "their wives," or the Greek article that can be used in a possessive sense. But "women" are introduced without any grammatical indication of a relation to the deacons.

2. It would seem strange to state qualifications for the deacons' wives when no such qualifications are given for the wives of elders, although the latter have the more important role in the church. If, on the other hand, the reference is to women who served as deacons, then the absence of any mention of women in connection with elders is because there were no women elders.

3. The word "likewise" or "similarly" (*hosautos*) used to introduce the statement concerning women appears to be used as a transition to introduce a different group. "An overseer . . . must be above reproach. . . . Deacons *likewise* must be men of dignity. . . . Women must *likewise* be dignified" (vv. 2, 8, 11; cf. Titus 2:3, 6, italics added). Although a different group, the women are inserted in the discussion of deacons because they belong to this category. Because the New Testament does not know of a feminine form for deacon (Phoebe is called a *diakonos* [masc. form] in Rom. 16:1), the apostle had no way to introduce the women as "deaconesses." They are simply women deacons.

4. Finally, the clear evidence of the office of deaconess in the later church suggests that it developed from a biblical foundation, including this text along with the example of Phoebe. Early evidence is provided by the Letter of Pliny written to Emperor Trajan in A.D 112. In his investigation of Christians, he indicates that he tortured two Christian women who were called *"ministrae"* (deaconesses in Latin). References to "women deacons" are later found in the writings of the early church including Clement and Origen; Alexandrian fathers of the third century; the *Didascalia Apostolorum,* a book of church order from the same period; and the *Apostolic Constitutions* and Chrysostom, along with others in the fourth century.

The task of distinguishing the ministry of widows and deaconesses in these church writings is not always easy. But it appears that a ministry of deaconess is found immediately following the New Testament era with such an order taking clear shape in the third century. It might be noted in passing that this was primarily in the Eastern church as "an independent order of deaconesses never developed in the Roman Church." It later died out in the East in the early Middle Ages.[40]

The ministry of the deaconess, like that of the male deacon, was important in the early church. What little evidence we have from the New Testament indicates that their ministry was concerned primarily with the physical and material needs of people both in and outside of the church.[41] But their ministry probably also involved a wide variety of services in support of the overall leadership of the elders, as is seen in the explicit descriptions of their service in the postapostolic church.[42] The *Apostolorum* calls for the bishop to appoint "workers of righteousness . . . deacons . . . a man for the performance of most things that are required, but a woman for the ministry of women." The document goes on to explain the "many . . . matters" for which "the office of a woman deacon is required." These include (1) to assist at the baptism of women, especially in their anointing; (2) to "teach and instruct . . . [the baptized women] how the seal of baptism ought to be (kept) unbroken in purity and holiness"; (3) "to go into the house of the heathen where there are believing women, and to visit those who are sick, and to minister to them in that of which they have need, and to bathe those who have begun to recover from sickness." Both men and women deacons were to be diligent in the ministry, "even laboring more than" the bishop. They were to know the people of the congregation so that "for every one they may provide the ministry which is proper for him."[43]

In sum, the New Testament provides no evidence that women served in the office of elder/bishop providing overall authoritative leadership of the community of believers. They were, however, appointed along with men to the recognized function of deacon, giving leadership to the church's ministry of mercy, and probably also a wide variety of other tasks complementing and supporting the ministry of the elders.

The Question of Women Apostles

The most significant ministry during the New Testament foundational period of the church was that of apostle. The apostle Paul's description of Andronicus and Junias as "outstanding among the apostles" in his greetings to individuals at Rome (Rom. 16:7) raises the question as to whether women were part of this ministry. The Greek form, *Iounian*, translated in many versions "Junias" (masculine, RSV, NIV, NASB, NEB; cf. also BAGD[44]) could also be translated "Junia" (feminine). The man's name Junias is not found elsewhere and must be understood as a shortened form of the common name Junianus. On the other hand, the name Junia was a well-known woman's name in the ancient Roman world, leading most contemporary commentators to conclude that Paul is referring to a woman. The Fathers of the church even up to the Middle Ages predominantly support this understanding.[45] For example, in the fourth century, Chrysostom, who was no egalitarian, exclaims, "And indeed to be apostles at all is a great thing. But to be even amongst these of note, just consider what a great encomium this is! But they were of note owing to their works, to their achievement. Oh! how great is the devotion of this woman, that she should be even counted worthy of the appellation of apostle!"[46]

Assuming that Junia was a woman and that along with Andronicus she was outstanding as an apostle rather than "outstanding in the eyes of the apostles," which is grammatically possible but much less likely,[47] how are we to understand her ministry? The term apostle is actually used four ways in the New Testament.[48] (1) It could refer to the original twelve apostles, but this required that the qualifier "twelve" be added (cf. Matt. 10:2). (2) It could refer to those who had seen the risen Lord and had been commissioned by Him for ministry (cf. 1 Cor. 9:1). This category probably included the Twelve, Paul himself, plus some others (cf. 1 Cor. 9:1; 15:5–8). It appears that Paul identifies apostles of this kind as "apostle[s] of Jesus Christ" (1 Cor. 1:1; 2 Cor. 1:1; Col. 1:1). (3) It could refer to one sent out by a particular church to perform a certain task, i.e., "apostles of the churches" ("messengers," NASB, 2 Cor. 8:23; cf. Phil. 2:25). (4) Finally, "apostle" could have the meaning of missionary, such as Barnabas (Acts 14:4, 14).

Whether one agrees with this particular categorization, it is clear that the concept of an "apostle" had a range of meanings with differing status and function. Although the language makes it possible that Andronicus and Junia were among those directly commissioned by Christ, the fact that they are said to be "outstanding" makes this highly doubtful. As Stott cogently argues, "[I]t is impossible to suppose that an otherwise unknown couple have taken their place alongside the apostles Peter, Paul, John and James." Andronicus and Junia are most probably to be understood as a husband-and-wife team who were noted for their outstanding ministry among a group of missionaries that participated along with the apostles of Christ in spreading the gospel.[49] To say the least, it is clearly impossible from this single reference to one woman as an "apostle" to assert with certainty that women shared with men in the foundational ministry of the "apostles of Jesus Christ."

Conclusion

Our survey demonstrates that women were prominently engaged in ministry in the churches of the New Testament era. They served both in the practical ministry of meeting the physical and material needs of people, a vital ministry of the church of that time, and in the ministry of the Word. Along with apostles and evangelists, they were engaged in evangelistic church planting. They hosted churches in their homes and in some instances provided significant support as patronesses. They ministered the Word in prophecy and teaching. The latter was probably especially with women, although the example of Priscilla teaching Apollos and the general teaching of one another among the members at large suggests that women's teaching was not rigidly restricted to their own gender.

This picture of the prominence of women in ministry and especially their involvement in significant roles where they would undoubtedly be viewed as leaders have led many to understand that there was no longer any distinction between men and women in church ministry roles. Women are seen as serving in the same positions as men. Their leadership roles have equal authority with those of men. For example, Grenz says, "Although the New Testament probably does not directly designate a specific woman as an elder or bishop, we do find women acting in the kind of leadership functions normally associated with this office."[50] This reasoning leads easily to such questionable conclusions as that the "description of Phoebe *implies* that she was a 'ruling elder' as well as a deacon"[51] (italics added).

As acknowledged by Grenz, however, such *implied* conclusions go beyond any explicit examples of women in the New Testament. Women certainly held positions of leadership, but leadership has various applications and cannot be indiscriminately equated without further evidence. The apostle Paul's "co-workers" no doubt were all viewed as leaders. But their similar description surely does not imply that they were his equals, or for that matter, that all the "co-workers" functioned over the similar spheres with exactly the same authority. There are simply no clear New Testament examples of women ministering in the church that contradict the biblical teaching of an order between man and woman in the church as well as in the home.

Although egalitarianism presses the picture of women's ministry in the New Testament too far, there is also the danger of not recognizing the full extent of their ministry. The evidence suggests that they served in a wide range of ministries, using gifts and strengths as women to complement the ministry of men and thus provide a holistic ministry to the church. The gospel of Christ, along with the record of Christ's relationship with women and the picture of women in the early church, reveals a new status and opportunity for service for women over the Jewish or Greco-Roman cultural norms of the day.

It is beyond our purpose to trace the course of women's ministry in the centuries immediately following the apostolic period, except to note that for a variety of reasons there was a growing restriction on the roles of women. For example, deaconesses were specifically an ordained ministry in the post-apostolic period as witnessed by the ordination ceremony contained in the fourth-century document on church order, *Apostolic Constitution*. However, in the fifth and sixth centuries, at least three church councils mandated that the ordination of deaconesses be stopped.[52] Oepke concisely sums up this decline of women's role in the churches: "In both East and West the decisions against women exercising priestly functions became increasingly stricter. The history of the ministry of women finally ended for the time being in the convent."[53]

It is helpful to briefly note some of the reasons for this decline and ask whether some may still be influencing the role of women in the present church.[54]

1. *An unbiblical asceticism that included a deficient view of human sexuality.* A negative view of human sexuality accompanied the ascetic tendencies that gained ground in the churches of the Ante-Nicene period (prior to A.D. 325). Along with the exaltation of celibacy, singleness, and even continence in marriage, sexuality itself came to be viewed as impure. Women, who were viewed primarily in relation to their sexuality, came to be viewed negatively as temptresses or sources of sin and thus as inferior to men. The tendency to identify them with their sexuality

also identified them exclusively with certain related roles—wife, mother, homemaker—which minimized their roles in the church. As a result, some gifted women retreated to the convents of the monastic movement, which in its beginnings was motivated somewhat by this prevalent view of sexuality with its celibacy. Here, outside of the regular church, women could exercise their gifts freely among women.

2. *Increasing institutionalism and its likeness to the Old Testament practices.* A significant factor in the decline of women's roles in the early church, noted by Witherington, was "the hermeneutical move in which OT institutions and ideas are used to describe, reorient, or even replace NT teachings and practices." As a result of this development, "as the Church became increasingly viewed as a 'temple,' and ministers became increasingly viewed as 'priests,' and the Lord's Supper became increasingly viewed as a 'sacrifice,' Christian worship and ministry reverted to the OT order of things in which males assumed all the priestly functions."[55] This understanding is clearly seen in the reasoning of the author of the *Apostolic Constitutions,* where women are prohibited from baptizing because it is a priestly act on the same level as offering the sacrifice of the Eucharist, ordination, and the benediction. Moreover, underlying the rejection of women from the priesthood is the belief in natural inferiority of women, noted previously. Since the priesthood was a "ministry of salvation," in the opinion of the early church writers, it "implied mental superiority in the one exercising the ministry over those for whom it is exercised, they felt it right . . . that 'the weak should be saved by the strong' i.e., woman by man, and not the reverse."[56]

Along with the reversion to the Old Testament ministry of the priesthood and, no doubt, closely related to it, the church became increasingly institutionalized. Church ministry became more closely related to the official leaders with less and less recognition of the spiritually gifted ministry of all believers. This development had particular effect on the roles of women as seen in Burtchaell's comment that "in its earliest generations women were prominent; when the salient leadership passed over into the hands of the officers, those avenues of prominence were no longer so open."[57]

Other consequences on the role of women in the church also ensued with this reversion back to Old Testament institutions. Equating the Table of the Lord with the Holy of Holies and following the Old Testament regulations on the clean and unclean, Dionysius, the second-century bishop of Alexandria, gave instructions that women in their menstrual period should be prohibited from approaching the Table of the Lord and partaking of the sacrament when they are not "perfectly pure both in soul and body."[58] It is not difficult to imagine that such regulations had a negative effect on women's place in the church.

3. *The significance of women prophetesses in apocryphal writings and marginal movements.* The apocryphal writings of the late second and early third centuries, such as the *Acts of Paul and Thecla,* the *Acts of John, Peter, Andrew,* and *Thomas* all portrayed women in prominent church roles, including that of prophetess. In line with their ascetical tendencies, including the exaltation of celibacy and virginity, this ministry of women was at the expense of their traditional roles in the family. Although the assumption of leadership positions by women portrayed in these writings and their adherents bothered the early church leaders, it was the prominence of prophetesses in the Montanist movement of the late second century that evoked the strongest response. In their rejection of this movement with its emphasis on new revelations by the Spirit, the orthodox church sought not only to curtail excessive prophecy, which they more and more associated with a church official, but also to deny women the prominent roles that they had played in the leadership of this deviant movement. In general, the prominence of women among heretical or marginal sects discouraged the church from appointing women to similar functions and "contributed to a certain distrust of women."[59]

4. *Gnosticism.* The Gnostic teaching that salvation involved the transcending of the material, including sexuality, led to the conclusion that sexuality no longer made any difference. This tended to create an egalitarianism in church ministry in some circles. How much Gnosticism's increased sexual freedom and some new roles for women in their communities influenced a reaction toward restricting women's role in the orthodox church is unclear. Witherington is probably correct when he concludes that "it is quite believable that it was *an* important factor that could have nudged the Church in that direction especially when some Gnostic communities claimed to base their theology on the traditions passed on by Christian women of the apostolic age."[60]

These reasons suggest that the restriction of women's roles came primarily from (1) a failure in biblical theology, especially the understanding of the newness of ministry in the church that resulted from the forward movement of God's salvation program in Christ, and the equality of man and woman by creation, and (2) overreaction to the perceived assumption by women of biblically unwarranted roles. As understandable as these reasons might be in light of sinful human nature, one is still left with the question of the underlying forces that led to them, especially in view of the fact that they represent a deterioration from the new position of respect and status gained in the time of Jesus and the New Testament.

No doubt part of the explanation is that the church "began to reflect the more conservative values of the majority culture"[61] as the patriarchy of the day was not without some elements reflecting a lesser view of women. But accommodation to the culture cannot be the sole rationale for the church's action. Many of the functions of leadership denied to women by the church were open to women in the Greco-Roman world around them. Clearly, another factor was an excessive reaction against what was perceived as unbiblical activities by women in some Christian communities as well as in the surrounding culture. The reaction was ostensibly supported primarily by arguments from theology, some of which were clearly erroneous.

Although different outwardly, succumbing to the temptations of accommodation and overreaction reveal a similar source, namely, the propensity to live according to our human sinful nature rather than according to the values and power of the new creation in Christ. Interestingly, the same change that took place in the post–New Testament church occurred within Judaism following the Old Testament. According to Evans, from what we know of first-century Judaism, "it is possible to see a dramatic decline in the position and status of women in every sphere as compared to the situation described in the Old Testament."[62] The early deviation from God's Word by His people of both Testaments should alert us to carefully examine not only God's Word, but also our deep heart motives as we search for His will in the matter of the ministry of women along with men in the church today.

PART FOUR

FEMININITY AND MASCULINITY

CHAPTER NINE

BEING FAITHFUL TO CHRIST IN ONE'S GENDER: THEOLOGICAL REFLECTIONS ON MASCULINITY AND FEMININITY

John Coe

Introduction: A Confession

"Man never exists as such, but always as the human male or the human female" (Karl Barth, *Church Dogmatics*).

Who am *I?* Am I a man—a person? Who is she, whom I need and am so mystified over? Who is it that cries out from the deep, "Deliver me, have mercy on me, O Lord"? Is it not me, John, the man; is it not she, the woman? But how can I be a man when I fail at this so utterly? *Who,* then, is the failure? Who else but me, the one reflecting upon the truth that I am a male. I open my heart to You, and *in* the truth, am opened to what is infinitely more than male or female—a sinner, now clothed in Christ *alone*. Are You not my new Self, O Christ in me? Are you not the same new Self as that of my sister who cries to you? But who is it that cries within herself or myself but Your Spirit, the Spirit of Christ? This *I and she* now joined by, with and in You and Your body must be the most universal and true person. Here, at the core of human identity, all is mystery, all is openness. So, who am *I?* I and my sister with and in all our gender, in the presence of our brethren, cry to You as *more than* male or female: *We* need You, *we* wait for You, *we* love You.

Most everything I have of value to say is contained in my confession. The language of prayer best guards me from the conceit of knowledge, self-assertion, and egoism, though even this heavenly language should not be beyond suspicion in a sinner. To understand and, especially, be faithful to one's gender is a difficult task after the Fall, and all the more when the body of Christ is in so much turmoil over this issue.

Biblical Principles Related to Gender

The Bible asserts that it is something to be male or female that is not reduced merely to biological differences, socialization, or personal choice. Rather, God calls us to be *faithful* to our gender by journeying together as man and woman in full unity of personhood in the church. Moreover, this gender relational journey is thoroughly conditioned by the fact that gender finds its ultimate meaning and fulfillment in mystical union one to another in Christ and His church. That is, gender is not an end in itself or merely a servant to the family but serves the love of God and neighbor in complementary fashion as men and women are faithful to their genders. Each brings something unique to the life of self-giving love. In that case, what I have to say is not aimed only for the married but for man and woman in general. As I will argue, even the traits and virtues related to man and woman in marriage reflect a deeper ontology of what it is to be male and female as lived out for the good of mankind, whether one is married or single. I will develop these ideas in terms of (a) the Covenantal-Relational Nature of Gender, which reflects the gender-shared dimension of personhood, and (b) the Covenantal Typology of Gender, which reflects the gender-specific dimension of personhood, each of which radically conditions the other. The chapter then looks at a biblical typology of male and female. My ultimate goal is to provide a view of male and female that does justice to the Scriptures and human experience in such a complementary way that it lessens unnecessary alienation in the body of Christ.

The Covenantal-Relational Nature of Gender

The covenantal view of human gender focuses upon the radically relational nature of personhood and human identity. Gender finds its true ontology in being a finite reflection or analogy of the relationality of God as He chose to create this into finite human forms. As Kirschbaum stated, following Barth,

> Thus, God created not a solitary human being but human beings in relationship, that is, in a manner corresponding to his own non-solitariness. He placed human beings in a mode of existence similar to his own. Existing then as male and female together, human beings are made in the image of God.[1]

Gender was to reflect God's relationality and ultimately the human need for completeness, relationship, and union with God and one another. Human gender informs us that we are fully persons only with the other. A number of issues flow from this.

First, gender is not understood most fundamentally as isolated sets of male and female traits and capacities, but as openness to relationship, being an analogous expression of the triune God. By definition, God as an infinite Being has no gender; He is neither male nor female.[2] This must inform our view of personhood at the very core.[3] As an analogy of God, gender is a quality of created finitude, particularly human image bearers, which in some way reflects the fact that personhood in its very essence, both in the essence of God and in its reflection in gender, is relational. From this theocentric viewpoint, then, gender is not most fundamentally about peculiar male or female traits and capacities. Rather, it is about a deep relationality at the core of personhood that is clearly reflected in the gendered pair of man and woman who need and call to each other, and ultimately to God, for intimacy and union. It is important to note that this relational call is not limited to marriage, but rather is universalized to man and woman in general (single and married) in the church. Marriage, in fact, is merely a taste of what we all hunger for, which can be satisfied alone in God. In that sense, human gender points to the deep truth that the self is not an end in itself, but transcends itself in being for the other. Thus, human gender portrays the self not as an enclosed entity striving for self-fulfillment but as an opened horizon in search for and with the other.

Both Old and New Testaments reflect this thoroughly exocentric or relational nature of gender and personhood. This is expressed, particularly, with respect to the image of God in the human couple, their spousal union and relationally paired ruling (Gen. 1:26; 2:24). God did not try to express His relational nature in a single, isolated individual but in a gendered pair of male and female. The creation of this original gendered pair has not only to do with marriage but points to a deeper relational ontology between persons in general, of which marriage is merely the relational model. That is, the metaphor of "marital union" expressed in this first couple goes beyond the concrete marriage to reflect the possibility of human relationality in general, of man to woman, man to man, and woman to woman in general in Christ and in the church. The New Testament clearly supports this view that gender does not find its full meaning and fulfillment in marriage but in the eschatological relationship of all men and women in the mystical body of Christ (Eph. 5:32).[4] Marriage itself is portrayed in a transitional state from individual male-female pairings in this life to a universal church of (humanly unmarried) males and females as the bride wed to Christ, joined to God and one another by the Spirit in the eschatological kingdom.[5] Thus, male and female (married and single) find their true selves in union with Christ and one another in the church by the Spirit. Though human marriage is abolished in the kingdom, this is not true of all the virtues related to marriage and the family. Rather, these virtues point to a deep set of traits of the masculine and feminine soul that are expressed in more universal and profound ways in Christ and the church, as man and woman are faithful to their gender for the common good in complementary fashion. Thus, the beautiful metaphors of "marriage" and "family" find their full expression in the complementary relatedness of man and woman in the kingdom, which, in part, has begun in the church. This truth has particular relevance to those single persons who willingly make "themselves eunuchs for the sake of the kingdom of heaven" (Matt. 19:12) and, thus, eschatologically foreshadow a life that will be true of all of us. This will be discussed more concretely under the biblical typology of man and woman.

Consequently, the covenantal view points to gender's own transcendental nature in its capacity to receive not only the other but God Himself into the very dynamics, capacities, and powers of the human heart, to become "partakers of the divine nature" (2 Pet. 1:4). This new covenant union is a relationship beyond whatever could be realized by man and woman alone, for God is capable of literally inhabiting them in their psychological structures at the place of their agency and core identity, binding them in union with Himself and one another in the church. Thus, gender (and marriage itself) points to a new horizon of relationality. The new covenant does not abolish gender in human nature, functioning, or role distinctions. Rather, the Spirit glorifies gender (and marriage) in Christ by bringing it to its full relational telos in the church. In this sense, men and women are *more than* their genders, this "more" referring to their capacity to receive a new identity in Christ and the Spirit, to unite with another Person in their persons.

To say that gender is inessential to the human being is to deny and confuse the self, to split off self from self, to live a lie. However, to identify oneself most essentially with one's gender functioning within the finite horizon of experience alone is to misidentify oneself. Gender functioning in Christ opens to new horizons of relating to one another in God. Here in the depths of union we discover the very mystery and radical relationality of personhood that thoroughly conditions all of our gender-specific functioning. This conditions all else that can be said about being man and woman and is the only safeguard against trying to live out our gender in the flesh.

The Covenantal Typology of Gender

The Bible and human observation reveal not only a gender-common but also a gender-specific dimension of personhood that is grounded in covenant with God. By creation and covenant, it is something to be male or female, and failure to understand and consent to one's gender (masculine and feminine possibilities and intensities) results in distortion and often havoc in the home, church, society, and personal experience. In this sense, Barth is correct: I am not a person; I have never met a person. Human finitude only comes packaged as male and female. Kirschbaum, who worked intimately with Barth on his *Church Dogmatics,* comments on this very point.

> Humankind exists as male and female and only in the unity of this twofold nature. A human being taken on its own in isolation is not a real human being, but an abstraction in human thought. The real human being exists as a man alongside a woman, a woman alongside a man. There is no such thing as a woman existing in isolation any more than there is a such a thing as a man existing in isolation.[6]

Both the Bible and reality teach that gender is a necessary or essential element of our personhood, identity, and ontology and, thus, an element that impinges upon the manner in which we live out our new identity in Christ. The contemporary tendency to divorce gender from sexuality and reduce gender to unconscious socialization, autonomous choice, prejudice, or bigotry has resulted in a deep confusion intellectually and existentially regarding our human nature, function, and purpose. Although it is a kind of idolatry to find one's identity solely in finite, isolated gender functioning, it is perhaps a more unnatural misidentification to deny one's gender altogether or to insist that there is no natural or ontological relationship between gender and sexuality. A covenantal gender typology reflects a whole range of gender-specific functioning that, in turn, reflects the very relationships and dynamics between God the Father, God the Son, and God the Spirit. They are not identical persons, but have their own uniqueness and relational distinctives one to the other, within the same nature. This takes us into the very heart of the mystery of personhood, of which male and female are merely a finite glimmer. To fail to properly express to the earth God's image in human gender is to distort the analogous, relationally dynamic presence of God in persons.

Consequently, it turns out that within human ontology there are overlapping, gender-shared and gender-specific levels of essential human capacities and corresponding virtues, some of which are more central than others in explicating, defining, and aiding one in experiencing and understanding one's nature and personal identity. Whether there is one common, shared human nature or unique, individuated male and female natures is difficult to determine from the Bible. Because there is so much continuity shared between genders, there must be in some sense a gender-shared dimension to human nature. However, because there is, according to the Bible and observation, a gender typology with clear gender distinctions, there must be some gender-specific dimension to human nature and identity that individuates male and female in some sense. Thus, we can say that either there is one human nature with overlapping, unique gender-individuated possibilities and dimensions or there are two specific natures of the genus, human nature, which have overlapping gender-shared and gender-specific possibilities, manners, and intensities. In either case, these levels of gender-shared and gender-specific functioning experience dynamic interplay that accounts for

(1) gender distinctions within (2) shared humanness and (3) particularized uniqueness. They each condition the other, though ultimately they all serve identity and functioning in Christ. This corresponds to the shared Christian virtues and fruit of the Spirit, which are recommended to all believers, both male and female. Clearly, the New Testament is not centrally a manual on gender growth, but on the process and virtues of being a disciple of and formed into the image of Jesus (Eph. 4:24; Col. 3:10). As we will see, however, there are gender-specific implications to Christlike living that condition humanness at every level.

Clearly, then, gender is not done away with, but both is a means to growth in Christ and is glorified by Christ. Moreover, cooperation with one's gender serves as a catalyst in the growth of the other gender. Man and woman are not meant to grow in isolation, even in their gender. As we shall discuss, gender interaction and interdependence is necessary for healthy gender growth and ultimate growth in union with God and one another. In Pauline terms, woman was made *for* man, and man was made to be *with* woman *for* Christ to the end that they both, in this mutual interdependence, be made fully into the image of Christ by union with the Spirit in the church. This is not fulfilled ultimately, i.e., eschatologically in marriage but in reference to man and woman in general in the church, whether married or single. This is to be contrasted with any attempt to live out one's gender in a way that obscures or underemphasizes the *relational interdependence* necessary to fathom and actualize man and woman. Man and woman are ultimately made for and become full persons in union with one another by the Spirit. This is meaningful complementarity. Thus, one is called by God to be faithful and consent to one's gender, the nature of which the Scriptures in part explicate.

Gender Typology Overview

Before going into the details of a list of particular gender-specific traits, it will be helpful to understand them in the context of an overarching gender characteristic or capacity unique to man and woman. In general, man's capacity for "with-ness" and woman's capacity of "forness" seem to capture, more than other gender-specific traits, what is central to their distinct gender. Moreover, these meta-capacities to some degree condition all of their distinct gender traits and provide some conceptual linkage between the traits. Before introducing these gender meta-capacities and specific traits, let me make a few introductory remarks relevant to developing and thinking about a gender typology in general.

First, though there is a biblical typology of gender traits, nevertheless, we must safeguard against gender idolatry by bearing in mind that only in Christ and in the relational context of male and female in His body by the Spirit can we avoid strained and unnatural ways of living out our gender. Barth is entirely correct in his profound observation that we cannot truly be faithful to our gender in isolation.

Second, as stated earlier, the gender-specific traits or virtues we are about to discuss, while often reflected in marriage for this life, most profoundly reflect deeper dimensions of the male and female soul. Thus, both single and married participate in them, though with a distinct application to one partner for those who choose marriage in this life.

On the practical side, embracing one's gender was meant to work best in the context of both men and women mutually submitting to one another and to what their gender calls them to do in Christ for the other. However, there is always the risk in living out one's gender that the other gender will not respond: The man may be relationally open to woman, who refuses to help him; the woman may help man, who is not open to her as a person. Grounding their identity and relatedness in Christ will aid man and woman in having the courage to risk being faithful to their genders. Only His love is utterly constant.

Finally, a few important hermeneutic issues arise in any attempt to develop a biblical typology of gender. Apart from a number of explicit gender-related texts, in general one must look more subtly into the penumbra of the text, much like the systematic theologian who appropriately employs the text to answer specific questions, which perhaps the biblical author was not directly asking or answering, and do this without wrenching or reading into a text. Thus, my attempt to discover morsels of gender theology are based upon the following principle. I will assume that any command or description in the Bible that (a) appears to be gender-specific (e.g., Prov. 31; Gen. 3, etc.) and (b) does not appear to be merely descriptive of existing cultural viewpoints implies the existence of a corresponding gendered function or intensity element in the nature of male or female.[7] In those cases in which there is no contextual indicator to think the command or description regarding gender is merely culture bound or idiosyncratic, but is for general human-gender flourishing, the act of compliance corresponds to some virtue that in turn corresponds to some gender capacity or function in human nature that allows for the particular gender to function and flourish. That is, there is a corresponding gender psychology or nature and character possibilities that makes sense of God's prescribing such actions or describing such traits.

Male Typology Overview: Man as "With-ness"

Perhaps more than any other metaphor ascribable to the male in his gendered role is his relational capacity for "with-ness." Apart from ruling and subduing the garden, the primary task God gives to Adam is to embrace or be with the woman (Gen. 2:24). Adam is created "alone," incomplete, and, thus, in need of the other gender (2:18). The command to embrace the woman implies that man was not merely to rule nature, but to do it in relational connectedness with the woman. That is, man was to rule *in love*. By creation, man has a capacity to rule *with* her, to be *with* her, to let the embrace of her be part of his life and not merely to go after his own pursuits in ruling as an individual. In short, he would be completed by her as the result of his drawing her to himself. This relational openness to woman is at the heart of the complementary position, in which man in general is to affirm and relate to woman as a person, as a fellow heir, and as one having great significance in her identity, in her work, and in how man, society, and the church need what she has to contribute.

Man's compliance with this "with-ness" dimension of his nature, by being open to and properly relating to woman, would help realize the relational nature of humanity expressed in male and female. God created them male and female and "named them Man," or humanity (lit. "Adam" Gen. 5:2). Neither gender was complete in itself, but each served for the making of a whole "Adam." Man's "embrace" or relational openness to woman would ensure this. With respect to marriage, the Old Testament Wisdom Literature highlights the point that the wise life involves man rejoicing in his wife and being satisfied in her whole person.[8] It was a man's virtue to desire his wife, to know her intimately, and to crave her. Both polygamy and adultery are perversions of this order of relationality, the latter particularly condemned by the Lord as a treacherous way of dealing with one who "is your companion and wife by covenant" (Mal.

2:14). The New Testament strengthens this idea that the man is to nourish and care for his wife as he does his own body (cf. Eph. 5:28–29). Man was to be with woman in marriage, bringing her alongside him for the sake of the relationship and ruling relationally.

Importantly, this concept of man's "with-ness" in the Genesis account not only applies to marriage but points to a deeper ontological relationship between man and woman in general, that man is to psychologically embrace or be relationally open to woman while woman is to give of herself for man and mankind in general. In 1 Corinthians 11, Paul universalizes the creation account of gender in order to understand new covenant male-female relations in the church. After employing the creation account to affirm distinctions in gender roles and hierarchy in 1 Corinthians 11, Paul asserts that these creation realities do not alter the fact that man and woman are interdependent in general. As he states, "However, *in the Lord,* neither is woman independent [χωρις, lit., "separate from, apart from, or without"] of man, nor is man independent [χωρις] of woman" (1 Cor. 11:11, italics added).

Paul's use of creation-nature metaphors to establish his point of mutual dependence, viz., of woman owing her existence to man by creation and man to woman by birth (v. 12), is not merely to establish their natural dependence. Rather, these are employed to illustrate his point that in the Lord, that is, now in Christ and in the church, man and woman are interdependent and need each other to fulfill Christ's purposes in the church.

Thus, the new covenant reveals the true and full universal implications of man's "with-ness" dimension to apply beyond the marriage to being open to women in general in Christ. This is congruent with our earlier discussion of the passing away of the institution of marriage but not of the "marital virtues" within the feminine and masculine soul. Man's deep ontology to "embrace" woman is expressed eternally in his willingness to be open to woman as woman and all that she is to be, give, and contribute to the good of mankind. In turn, woman's interdependence with man is qualified by her having been created *for* the man (v. 9) and originating *from* him (v. 8). Consequently, *man is as much dependent upon woman for his completion in the new covenant community (the church) as he was of woman in marriage as expressed in the creation account ("It is not good for the man to be alone," Gen. 2:18).*

For this completion and mutual dependence to occur, man must take great efforts in the church and society as well as in marriage to be *with* her in the sense of being open to her as a person, open to her impact upon him, to allow room for her giftedness to impact the community, to embrace her place and role in giving and living *for* the other. This is at the core of the complementary view: men spiritually being open to women in the church for the sake of mutual growth in union with the living Christ. This need not always require close intimate relationships, though there will be meaningful and morally appropriate contact. It primarily requires a certain attitude on the part of man toward supporting woman. What this looks like practically in the church will be left for the final discussion of this chapter. What is clear, however, is that man's "embracing" role of being with woman is not reserved only for marriage but is to take some universal role in the church if mankind is to be whole.

The vice propensity or temptation since the Fall is that man will crush, ignore, or in some way choose to not relate to the woman or treat her as a fellow heir in life or marriage. This often is on account of his own selfish choice or unwillingness to risk being ensnared in what looks to him like her overwhelming needs and unwillingness to look out for his good. This particularly occurs in the church and the workplace whenever the woman looks out for her own welfare and is not consciously seeking to fulfill her complementarity toward the man and the common good. In such cases, man unconsciously (and unfortunately) calculates that being open to such a woman jeopardizes his selfish preoccupation with his own needs. Certainly, a woman's selflessness often provides the needed motivation for man to risk being open to her. Nevertheless, it is the responsibility of man to take the initiative in the relationship to risk involvement and openness toward her person and contribution to life. This, in turn, encourages the woman to seek the man's good and helps lay to rest the temptation to believe that she is being used by a male who thinks her entire existence is merely to serve his goals outside of a relationship of mutual interdependence. This belief is engendered by the domineering male who is threatened by the woman's presence or seeks to use her. However, the "sheepish man" does no better in opening himself, the church, and society to woman and her impact, for he has withdrawn into himself, entertainment, or work and abdicated his responsibility to be involved with the woman's life.

Interestingly, even the "soft male" fails to truly relate to the woman despite the fact that he rejects the strategy of crushing or using women and is sensitive and nurturing to her as a person. The soft male is *for* woman but is not really *with* her, for he is still working out his own masculine identity in the context of unresolved childhood relations and too much interpersonal enmeshment with mother, resulting in unconscious mirroring of Mom in adulthood. Thus, the soft male is incapable of relating to woman with his true masculinity, whether it be in marriage, business, or the church. He merely mirrors her contribution. As a result, the relational dynamics become dominated by the feminine elements alone, resulting in a loss of a complementary relationship in which both genders bring a unique element to the relationship.

On the other hand, there is the male who in excess seeks to find his *identity* in being with the woman, his wife, and his family. Here the individual may be healthy enough to relate to the woman as a person in all her significance. Nevertheless, this man is unwilling to relate to the woman "in Christ," to embrace Christ before all else. The marriage, family, and society may be embraced, but not with the profundity that repentance and brokenness before the living God affords. One's relationship with Christ needs to transform all gender relations.

In contrast, by being faithful to his gender and his capacity for "with-ness" in being open to woman, man learns "in Christ" from the female about his end or teleology, viz., to be in union and relationally submissive to Christ in his eschatological participation in the "bride of Christ" (cf. Eph. 5:31–32; Rev. 19:7–9). Here, the female's distinct gender-specific dimension of "devotion and surrender" (see discussion on pp. 224–26) models to man the feminine horizon and intensity of devotion and spirituality to which he also is called. By being open to her and her impact upon him and others, he receives a lesson in virtue from the feminine, a lesson in "bridal love," submission and devotion, which informs him at the core of human personality about his union with Christ. The man who fails to be faithful to be "with" and open to woman fails to learn from woman how to nurture, love, and sit at the feet of Jesus. This is the Man-as-Philistine who, by denying his masculinity of "with-ness," denies the woman into his life lest he be too affected by her nurturing touch. As a result, the male fails to grasp in experience the meaning of the "union" element in love and abandons himself to a solely objective mode of existence. This is especially relevant to men in the church who so objectify the faith that they and their sons know little of why or how to sit at the feet of Jesus and "[choose] the good part, which shall not be taken away" (Luke 10:42).

Female Typology Overview: Woman as "For-ness"

As we turn to the feminine gender-specific dimension of humanness, the woman's capacity of "for-ness" most centrally captures her nature. She was created *for* the other and, thus, is that individual of the gender pair who was explicitly made for the purpose of complementing the other. The creation account is clear on this point. God created her specifically for the man, so that he would not be alone (Gen. 2:18). Unlike the animals, who were taken out of (Heb. translit. *law-kakh*) the ground, woman was taken out of (Heb. translit. *law-kakh*) the male Adam, and as such is suitable to (lit., "corresponding to") him in order to complete him (Gen. 2:18, 22–23). The fact of her being created second impresses upon her forever the reality that she is *for* the sake of the other (man and God). Like man, all that she does must be conditioned by love in this relational dimension: he with her and she for him, all in Christ.

Paul reiterates these claims in 1 Corinthians 11, where he universalizes insights on male-female relations from the creation account to male-female relations in Christ. Thus, the woman's "for-ness" dimension of her nature is not related merely to the marital relationship but captures a deep element of the feminine soul (married or single) that is for man and the common good of mankind. As we discussed above under "Male Typology," woman is the glory of man insofar as she was created for the man and not the man for the woman. As Paul stated, "For man does not originate from woman, but woman from man; for indeed man was not created for [δια] the woman's sake, but woman for [δια] the man's sake" (1 Cor. 11:8–9).

Paul's use of δια, plus the accusative case of "woman" and "man," clearly points out the idea that woman was created "because of," "for the sake of," and "on account of" the man. This statement is so clear and, yet, often ignored by those writing on gender. Clearly, woman's teleology and purpose, in part, has to do with her being "for" the man, not merely in the family but particularly "in the Lord" (v. 11), for the purpose of helping actualize the union of man and woman with Christ in the church. Woman's "for-ness" does not render her inferior to man. Rather, she is the relational "other" who is sufficiently *more than* or different from man in order to complete him, yet not so different that she is an unsuitable helper to him. For Paul, male and female are so radically interdependent both in creation and in the Lord that neither can realize himself or herself apart from the other (1 Cor. 11:11). No other human relational dynamic can compare to this; only together do the man and woman make up full humanity in the church.

It is important to clarify any misunderstandings concerning what is and what is not necessarily involved in woman living out her "for-ness" with respect to man. First, in no way does the woman need to be married to fulfill her role in being *for* man. Furthermore, woman can live out her "for-ness" apart from a constant face-to-face relationship with a man. Her relatedness to man stands more in giving of herself for others than in making intimacy a goal. Though some contact with the other sex is important for relatedness, spatial proximity need not be a constant in order to live for the good of another. Finally, woman's living for the good of man must always be conditioned by her more primary love of God.

Being *for* man, on the other hand, is most fundamentally an attitude within woman, a perspective about the meaning of her own existence, which ushers forth in giving of herself for others, in being *for* man, being *for* what God has ordained through man, and being for the common good of the "other" in society, the church, and the family. In such a relationship, one is not afraid of the opposite sex, for one knows the intrinsic value of the other. No doubt some relational contact with those of the opposite sex is necessary for growth and has many natural and morally permissible avenues. Thus, face-to-face relatedness is never shunned, only at times abstained from for the sake of purity in the relationship. Intimacy is protected by wisdom and love of God and the common good. This is all true even of marriage, where self-giving love is the font of potential intimacy, though both may kiss in the best of conjugal relationships. Nevertheless, only the eschatological kingdom will fully and freely unite intimacy with moral relatedness, where means and end are blended in one.

The woman's vice propensity and temptation in the Fall, in general, is that she will not give of herself for man and mankind's good but only for herself or, in some cases, for the need to be needed, a subtle way to appear to be *for* the other while living for herself. In recoiling from her hurts and, particularly, the male's selfishness, rejection, and unwillingness to be open to her, she may decide that it is either not possible or not worth the emotional cost to be for man and the other's common good. As a result, a deep relational cleavage occurs in the home, society, and the church, for she models fallen man's attempts to find personal identity in human autonomy and meet one's needs in isolation. The remedy to this situation is not to force herself into service for the other, but in the context of brokenness and the Cross, to turn back to the good of the other in the risk of unrequited love. What a disaster it became when man devalued the woman in his overvaluing of himself and his petty pursuits, tempting woman to follow suit and forget the other in pursuit of feeling herself significant.

However, for the female whose own identity has not been well established by a healthy relationship with her father or God the Father, the result can be such radically permeable boundaries that she does not know herself apart from the other and her finite "for-ness." That is, she feels as if she has no value and is hollow inside unless she is living *for* some other, whether it is her friends or her employer, husband, children, parents, or cause. This creates all types of enmeshing relationships along with an inability to experience the fruits of a real relationship with man and God. She is nurturing, but out of a need to be needed and, thus, without the characterological fiber and adequate boundaries that having a relationally healthy identity in Christ and community afford. A deep dependence on and love for God properly condition her being able to give herself for the other without feeling that her identity and significance is only in this. The finite cannot bear such a psychological load.

Though feminine ontology and teleology have to do with being made *for* man, her full teleology points beyond man alone to being made *for* the union of man and woman to Christ by the Spirit in the church.

As in the case of man, who, by being faithful to his gender, learns eschatologically in Christ from the female's gender-specific dimension of submission and devotion, so woman, by being faithful to being *for* the good of man and others, learns from her relationship with man something of the male texture of what it is to be strong in Christ. Interaction with the male's distinct gender-specific virtues related to strength (see discussion on pp. 222–23) encourages woman toward a new horizon of her personhood in Christ. Here the female shows the capacity to receive within herself a lesson in what it is to love God as warrior from a masculine dimension of spirituality.[9] She already fully shares with man in all the salvific benefits of being in Christ (Gal. 3:28). In the case of the unmarried, she is free to join with man courageously in giving her full relationality and "undistracted devotion to the Lord" and the church

(1 Cor. 7:33–35). In that sense, single men and women are capable of joining together in strength and courage with the whole church to model a radical relationality of helping and encouraging one another in their respective roles and experience, which is a life patterned after the gender traits encouraged in marriage that become translated "in the Lord" as brotherly and sisterly traits and functioning one to another in Christ.

Gender Typology: Some Specific Characteristics

In general, a whole range of specific capacities, traits, and virtues flow from man's and woman's fundamental ontology having to do with their capacities for "with-ness" and "for-ness," respectively. The following list of gender-specific traits and functioning grounded in creation and covenant makes up a minimal biblical typology of gender, which helps to support and explain the complementarity assertion that it is something to be a male or female.

Male Typology: Man as "With-ness"	*Female Typology: Woman as "For-ness"*
The Ruling of Man and Woman	
Man as Representative Ruler	Woman as Relational Ruler
The Work of Man and Woman	
Man as Responsible/ Sacrificial Worker	Woman as Helper/ Submissive Worker
The Relation to Truth of Man and Woman	
Man as Representative Truth-Teller	Woman as Open Receptor
The Posture of Man and Woman	
Man as Exalted/Explicit	Woman as Uplifting/Veiled
The Wholeness of Man and Woman	
Man as Incomplete	Woman as Completing
The Spirit and Strength of Man and Woman	
Man as Strong	Woman as Devout Surrender

As we address each of these, it will be helpful to juxtapose a typology of woman next to man to bring out something of the complementarity within gender. Only in relationship, only as male and female are seen within the context of the other, can we properly understand and develop our genders in their fullness.

The Ruling of Man and Woman

Man as Representative Ruler

Man's fundamental manner of demonstrating his "with-ness" toward the earth is in his capacity to be representative ruler of it. As representative authority, man has a capacity to rule by his actions, make something his own by creating it, and enjoy it by possessing it. These functions are evident in the creation account in which man was created first (Gen. 2:7), exercises authority over the animals by naming them without the woman (Gen. 2:19), and shows authority over woman by naming her (Gen. 2:23). Paul concurs with this analogously in his employing the creation account as evidence for the assertion that man, and not woman, is to exercise authority in the church on the account that man was created first (1 Tim. 2:11–15). Being created first is not the *cause* for his representative position in mankind, but is the *result* of having a nature created to be the representative authority on the earth.

The Scriptures also portray man's representative authority in creation as being the "head" of the woman and the glory of God. Paul asserts that man is the head of woman as Christ is the head of man and God is the head of Christ (1 Cor. 11:3). Similarly, man and not woman is "the image and glory [δοξα] of God; but the woman is the glory [δοξα] of man" (1 Cor. 11:7). The concept of being the glory carries with it the sense of weightiness of character or self-expression. Thus, man is the exemplar of God's self-expression of His weighty character, while woman, in part, is to be an expression of who man is and what he is about, which in both cases can only happen in relationship. *It is important to note that these strong comments are not made in a marital context but are universalized for mankind in the church.* Man's headship in all of societal relationships entails a certain texture in his own self-concept as well as in his relationship and attitude toward women. He is to experience a certain sense of responsibility toward the woman and mankind in general, a certain sense of obligation to seek the welfare of all, ensuring that others are able to fully flourish and have their impact on the earth. It does not mean that any one man is concretely the head of any one woman outside of marriage. Rather, it is a general demeanor or quality which should condition male and female relations.

Paul reiterates elsewhere man's representative ruling with respect to the family, that he is the head of the wife as Christ is head of the church (Eph. 5:23) and that if any man cannot rule his own home, then he is not ready to rule the church (that is, he is not really a man as God created him to be—one who rules as representative head, 1 Tim. 3:5). Paul again affirms the representative nature of the male by giving the man full responsibility for sin and its impact on the human family, even though it was the woman who sinned first (Rom. 5:12–21; cf. 1 Tim. 2:14). Similarly, the anointed seed who would eventually crush the Serpent would be a man and not a woman (Gen. 3:15ff.; cf. the lineage of the male "seed" in Genesis 5).

In a more general sense, both the Old and New Testaments employ the masculine gender as the most representative manner to refer to the human race or the church. In the creation account and following, the Hebrew "Adam" is used for both the individual man as well as the generic word for humanity or mankind (cf. Gen. 1:26–27; 2:7, etc.). Nowhere is the woman's name used as a general and universal demarcation, though all are in a relation of dependence upon Eve, as "mother of all the living" (Gen. 3:20).

The New Testament continues this pattern of using the male and not the female as a generic way to refer to both genders in the church. In most cases, the Epistles address both genders in the church with the masculine "brotherhood," "brethren," or "sons of God." A list of their usage is instructive:

> "Honor all people; love the brotherhood (αδελφοτητα) . . . (1 Pet. 2:17).
> "Greet the brethren (αδελφους) who are in Laodicea and also Nympha and the church that is in *her* house" (Col. 4:15 italics added).
> "Now I urge you, brethren (αδελφους) . . ." (1 Cor. 16:15).
> "For you are all sons (υιοι) of God through faith in Christ Jesus" (Gal. 3:26).
> "All who are being led by the Spirit of God, these are sons (υιοι) of God" (Rom. 8:14; cf. also Rom. 8:23; Gal. 4:7).[10]

The only time the biblical writers used the feminine gender to refer to individuals is when it is specifically referring to females only ("Our sister Phoebe, who is a servant of the church," Romans 16:1; cf. also Phil. 4:3; 1 Tim. 5:1–2). If the biblical writers were only accommodating to contemporary usage, they made no point to indicate any apology for this. There was no thought on their part or that of the Holy Spirit, who is involved in the inspiration of these letters, to make certain that women do not feel excluded or pained in this male gender reference. Certainly, if this was a cultural bias that would be harmful to human relations in the church, the New Testament would be a good place to make the correction or at least comment about it as such, much along the lines of how Paul treats slavery.[11]

The vice propensity of man's representative ruling in the Fall has to do with his drive to find his identity in ruling and dominating the earth apart from being open to the female and her overall impact and nurturing element. His relational passivity produces in him a general inattention to leadership in the family and on behalf of the needy, which will become "feminine affairs." The result: the building of culture and better air conditioners and the maintaining of powerful followings at the expense of spousal love, justice, and benevolence, that is, at the expense of relational complementarity in church and society. By failing to be open to the woman and what she contributes to the whole, the female nurturing element fails to impact him as it could. The city under Lamech in Genesis 4 is just such an illustration of violence, pride, and relational distortion. In general, man's unwillingness to be the "head" of woman and mankind in guaranteeing their welfare puts woman at risk of having to take care of herself in autonomy. On the other hand, man may abdicate this representative ruling altogether and give it to another or the woman. In this case, the male does not wish to take responsibility for being the representative ruler of the earth, for it is too much of a hassle to his life and need for comfort. As a result, this male goes into hiding behind his contempt, criticism, or penchant to recreate away his life.

Woman as Relational Ruler

Woman's "for-ness" is best displayed in her relationality. Whereas man is representative ruler to the earth, woman rules particularly in terms of her nurturing and relational strengths and capacities. As nurturer of the earth, her pre-Fall work was to bear children and help her husband rule in the context of his loving embrace. This idea of completing or helping carries with it some sense of tending to, caring for, nurturing, or bringing about what was missing so that he will be informed relationally by her, enabling him to rule in complete personhood, male with female. Thus, man needs to be in a unique relationship with woman, who completes him in order to learn and experience what is necessary for him to rule and lead properly.

A number of biblical texts point to this nurturing quality of woman, so much so that it is almost a background assumption. In the first place, God likens Himself to a woman with nurturing love. God's love is compared to that of a woman's tender love for her child that she has breast-fed (Isa. 49:15). God cares for His people as a woman comforting her son (Isa. 66:13). Jesus Himself said that He loved Israel and often wanted to gather her to Himself as a mother hen gathers its chicks (Matt. 23:37). In each of these attributions of feminine mother-love to God, the metaphor signifies nurturing, tender care, and love.

Paul the apostle reiterates this nurturing quality of the woman. Older women are to encourage the younger women in this familial and nurturing role, to "love their husbands, to love their children, to be sensible, pure, workers at home, kind, being subject to their own husbands, so that the word of God will not be dishonored" (Titus 2:4–5). It is interesting to note that woman's relational-familial drive correlates to the troubles she encountered in the Curse. Her problems are relational in nature with respect to her husband and bearing children (Gen. 3:16), whereas man confronts troubles particularly with respect to ruling and working the earth (Gen. 3:17–19).

This nurturing quality is not only applicable to the married woman. The concept of "mother" and "wife" are fundamentally metaphors that express the universal feminine nature of gentle, loving care for the good and sake of others. We must always view ontology from the perspective of teleology: That is, woman's experience in the eschatological kingdom at the end of time will not be literally as a mother or wife, though the traits of helping, caring for, and nurturing will continue forever. Thus, all women, married or single, are called to participate in their eternal femininity of which "wife" and "mother" are merely this-world ways to begin to express these. With Paul's advocacy of the single life of perpetual virginity (cf. 1 Cor. 7), there is the clear opportunity for the single woman to live out her spousal and motherly love in society and the church. Edith Stein, the famous Jewish philosopher turned Carmelite nun at the beginning of World War II, discusses this.

> Woman's nature is determined by her original vocation of *spouse* and *mother.* One depends on the other. The body of woman is fashioned "to be one flesh" with another and to nurse new human life in itself. A well-disciplined body is an accommodating instrument for the mind which animates it; at the same time, it is a source of power and a habitat for the mind. Just so, woman's soul is designed to be subordinate to man in obedience and support; it is also fashioned to be a shelter in which other souls may unfold. ***Both spiritual companionship and spiritual motherliness are not limited to the physical spouse and mother relationships, but they extend to all people with whom woman comes into contact.*** The soul of woman must therefore be *expansive* and open to all human beings; it must be *quiet,* so that no small weak flame will be extinguished by stormy winds; *warm,* so as not to benumb fragile buds; *clear,* so that no vermin will settle in dark corners and recesses; *self-contained,* so that no invasions from without can imperil the inner life; *empty of itself,* in order that extraneous life may have room in it; finally, *mistress of itself* and also of its body, so that the entire person is readily at the disposal of every call. That is an ideal image of the gestalt of the feminine soul. (italics her own; bold italics added)[12]

I think Edith Stein as a single woman given to a life of service to God, has beautifully captured the notion that the wifely and motherly metaphors and traits lie at the core of the universal feminine soul. The concrete institution of marriage is a mere finite metaphor for the deeper ontological truth of male and female gender. Of course, a single woman does not submit herself to any concrete man, just as a single man is not the head of any concrete woman. Rather, each embodies the *attitudes and concerns* reflected in the best of married couples as they give of themselves for others in faithfulness to their genders. Thus, in one sense, being a brother or sister in Christ involves the marital virtues deeply understood.

Woman's vice propensity (married or single) is that her relational drive will find expression outside living for the good of mankind in God, particularly in the case where the man is not open to her as a person and to her impact upon him and others. She will still tend to be relational in general, but more in the sense of attempting to get her relational needs met from her husband, lovers, children, friends, work, or whatever cause to which she gives herself. This kind of relationality becomes a vice insofar as it is not tempered and made morally strong by her nurturing quality that manifests in healthily living *for* the benefit of others and God. Of course, she may have many relationships that do, in fact, meet her needs. However, these relationships are conditioned by her attitude and self-concept of caring for the other. She is not afraid of receiving love, but is not solely intent on this. There may also be the woman who has been so hurt or rejected by others that she is tempted to repress her relational and nurturing drive altogether. The result is the slow development of a mono-gendered culture at work, at home, and in the church—a relationally cooler place to live than God intended.

The Work of Man and Woman

Man as Responsible/Sacrificial Worker

Man's relational capacity for "with-ness" is expressed functionally in his being the responsible/sacrificial worker of the earth. This dimension of his nature is grounded in his being created as representative head who is responsible for ruling and subduing the earth while embracing woman (Gen. 1:26–28). Initially, however, he embraces his task of *responsible* rule even prior to the creation of woman in his naming the animals and Eve (2:20, 23; 3:20). He is characterized as responsible *worker* of the earth insofar as the Curse mainly affects him in his toil of the earth (3:17–19), whereas woman is cursed in familial relations (v. 16).

Man's role as responsible/sacrificial worker is further applied to the family, church, and social justice in general. In the family, man is called upon to be responsible for providing for his own family; failure to do so is judged as being worse than an unbeliever, who typically, according to Paul, fulfills this minimal masculine responsibility (1 Tim. 5:8). Furthermore, husbands are to sacrifice and give themselves up for their wives as Christ did for the church, to help in their sanctification process (Eph. 5:21–31), while learning to live with the weaker vessel in an understanding way "since she is a woman" (1 Pet. 3:7). Thus, the man is portrayed as being in some sense responsible for his wife in a way that she is not responsible for the man. Fathers are also responsible for not exasperating their children (Col. 3:21). In general, the sign of masculine spiritual virtue in the eldership is his being responsible for ruling and taking care of his own home, for this is one indicator among others that he can rule and take care of the church (1 Tim. 3:5). He is responsible for shouldering the needs of his extended family and of widows instead of this responsibility falling on the church (1 Tim. 5:8).

In general, then, man (single or married) bears a certain responsibility for the well-being of the earth. He is to be concerned for the welfare of the other, to ensure that the other is well-situated and not merely himself. If things are not well for others, then he is responsible to do something on their behalf. In particular, man is responsible for woman in general (whether in marriage, the workplace, or the church) to develop a context and circumstances that are conducive to providing her opportunity to flourish and properly impact others with her unique, feminine giftedness.

Man's vice propensity and the temptation in the Fall will be to escape his task of ruling the earth sacrificially and responsibly, particularly by submerging himself in lust and intoxicants (cf. the "Kingly Man" text of Prov. 31:1–9). The temptation of man is not so much an attempt to escape from toil in the earth, in which he tends to find so much of his false identity. Rather, he will tend toward *relational* laziness and shirk his responsibility regarding love and justice by immersing himself in pleasure. In particular, he may be intimidated by woman and shirk his responsibility to free her to be and do all she can for the earth. Of course, there may be those who embrace their masculinity and sacrificially take responsibility for the plight of others, but not in relationship with God. This man is unwilling to bear the responsibility of his own sin and, thus, fails to bring his natural responsible/sacrificial virtues to their telos in Christ for the benefit of family, church, and society.

Woman as Helper/Submissive Worker

Another fundamental dimension of woman's "for-ness" is her universal call to be a helper/submissive worker to mankind. The creation account makes clear that her way to complete man is, in part, to be a "helper" (Heb. translit. *ayzer,* lit., an aid or help, Gen. 2:18), a term used often in the Old Testament for God's role toward mankind. Helping man provides the content to her function: She is to work to aid man and mankind in general in a way that another man or an animal could not. Apart from her, mankind is rendered help-less. Of course, this helping role is entirely conditioned by her telos of union with man in Christ. That is, helping man is not by itself the ultimate end of her existence.

Woman as helper/submissive worker to man is particularly brought out in the "Excellent Woman" of Proverbs 31.[13] The emphasis of the text is not upon her relationality or capacity for intimacy; this is assumed. Rather, the emphasis is upon her capability and willingness to use this for the welfare of man, to help man. The thesis statement of the discussion is as follows: "An excellent wife, who can find? For her worth is far above jewels. The heart of her husband trusts in her, and he will have no lack of gain. She does him good and not evil all the days of her life" (Prov. 31:10–12).

The remainder of the discussion from verses 13–31 tells of her many abilities, all of which are, at least to some degree, conditioned by the idea that she has won the trust of her husband, for he is now convinced *by her actions* that her intent is to help him, to do him good and not evil all her days. She fulfills the intent of God in creation. Thus, the excellent woman is not merely an entrepreneur, though certainly she is very capable: She makes clothes (v. 13), is a good trader (v. 14), rises early to prepare her household (v. 15), considers investments (v. 16), is strong (v. 17), tends to the needs of even those beyond her home (v. 20), is interested in beautiful clothes to adorn herself and her family (v. 22), demonstrates inner qualities of strength and dignity (v. 25), shows wisdom and kindness in speech (v. 26), and attends to her relationship with God (v. 30). In no way is she idle, but she "looks well to the ways of her household" (v. 27). As a result, she is praised by her children and husband (v. 28) with the added benefit that the man's overall reputation has been enhanced ("Her husband is known in the gates, when he sits among the elders of the land," v. 23). The text gives the indication that the man's position of being an elder at the gates is, in part, the result of her loving and sacrificial efforts.[14]

The New Testament reiterates this idea of the woman as helper/worker, with respect both to a married woman's actions toward her family and a woman's actions toward others in the church in general. Both older and younger married women were to have lives characterized by being "workers at home" (Titus 2:3–5). In fact, the church was to take care only of those widows who were known for "having a reputation for good works; and if she has brought up children, if she has shown hospitality to strangers, if she has washed the saints' feet, if she has assisted those in distress, and if she has devoted herself to every good work" (1 Tim. 5:10).

What is true of woman in the creation account of woman as helper/worker is transformed "in the Lord" to apply to married and single alike in their relationships in the church. The church's model woman gives her life not only for her family, if married, but also for the sake of others in the church and the world. Thus, her nurturing, relational skills are transformed for the common good by her willingness to help and *work* for others. This is in contrast to the younger widows who, according to Paul, were tempted to be "idle, as they go around from house to house; and not merely idle, but also gossips and busybodies, talking about things not proper to mention" (vv. 11–13). Their relationality had not had sufficient time to be tempered by work for the saints and, thus, they are encouraged to marry, keep house, and take care of children so that this will not be cause for any slander from non-Christians (v. 14).

Thus, the New Testament's virtuous woman is no different from Proverbs' excellent woman who extends her hands beyond the home "to the poor" and the needy (Prov. 31:20) with all her femininity. In particular, the single woman is able to participate in this work for the church in her single-minded devotion to service and work in the Lord (1 Cor. 7:32–35). She and the single man have the relational potential and availability for modeling service to the common good in the gendered community of the church. This work of woman on behalf of others can be instituted wherever she is. As Edith Stein says,

> Certainly, there is an entire range of vocations which can be practiced effectively by women, but these are not specifically feminine activities which require or allow their real nature. In such vocations—in the factory, office, etc.—it would always be good for women that they be ready momentarily to stand by another person's side: through sharing, helping, and promoting, they can preserve their true womanliness. They always have opportunities to do so beyond the professional work itself—in their place of work, home, or community.[15]

The virtuous woman's work will naturally find opportunity to express its particular feminine dimension of nurturing, caring for, and promoting the good of the other. What is individuated in her desire to help and work for her husband is universalized in the feminine soul for the sake of all.

As man is a responsible/*sacrificial* worker, so the woman is a helper/*submissive* worker. That is, her willingness to help and work has a submissive and respectful texture to it. In both the church and the family context, Paul reiterated a number of times that the woman is to submit herself to the man (1 Cor. 14:34; Eph. 5:22; Col. 3:18; 1 Tim. 2:11; Titus 2:4–5).[16] Although there is a general mutual subjecting of the genders one to another (Eph. 5:21), nevertheless, the female's gender-specific dimension toward man manifests in specific ways of seeking to place herself under the other for the sake of helping and working for his common good. *Her work is not merely that of her own initiative in autonomous self-authority; rather, it is the complementary response in submissive love to the other.* Her capability as evident in her work has a quality of submissiveness, which always comes from a position of being under authority and for the sake of the other. This does not manifest itself in abject obedience to her husband or, if single, to any particular man. Rather, it is reflected in her person, as a quality of her being, that she is not her own authority, that her life is not her own but consciously given for the sake of the other.

Thus, the woman may exhibit a powerful personality in her own right with a good deal of forceful character and personal zest. Nevertheless, she is psychologically able and desirous to do this in *light* of her relationship with man and others, not in *spite* of it. In the best of situations, this is in the context of man being relationally open to her as a person in all her giftedness, which, in part, provides her the trust to give of herself for the good of him and others. Ultimately, however, it is within the embrace of Christ that woman finds the heart of submissive love, for only His embrace never fails—unlike man's.

This same "subjecting oneself" dimension in the feminine nature is also seen in the fact that she is to respect man. The woman's "respect" is to condition the manner and attitude in which she helps the man, others, and God. This is true in marriage (Eph. 5:33) and particularly in difficult marriages, in which she is to win the erring husband by her "respectful" behavior, that is, behavior exhibiting a certain attitude of submission and respect for the man, which is to humble him in his work in life (1 Pet. 3:1–2). This submissive attitude is the initial spark, according to Peter, that may open man to honesty and acting according to his nature. When woman takes man's gender-specific tasks upon herself, she is only giving man another excuse to forsake his representative responsibilities in order to pursue his false identity. Whenever possible, it would be better for woman to refuse man's role and, by her submissive and respectful heart, "call" him to be himself in God. Of course, in a fallen world, this is not always possible or beneficial. In general, the relational openness of man to woman and the circumspect submission of woman to the good of man and others go a long way to reciprocally encouraging faithfulness to their gender, though ultimately only the love of Christ is sufficiently constant to encourage this.[17]

The vice propensity regarding woman as helper/submissive worker is that she can be tempted to withdraw herself from man's need for completion and the common good in order to meet her own storehouse of psychological needs due to the Fall. This is often done out of a desire to protect herself from hurt in light of man's unwillingness to accept, value, and be open to her as a significant person in the workplace, the church, or the home. Of course, she is responsible to help despite his failure to respond to her, just as he is responsible to be open to her despite her failure to seek his good. When woman fails to be herself, the earth is bereft of the gender who is to model subjecting of oneself in helping the common good in all spheres of life. Autonomy and isolation are encouraged and modeled, as she again is tempted to take the man's "safety first" approach to life by making her own needs central. Interestingly, Proverbs presents the woman of folly and vice as one who is fixated upon her own psychological needs and need for romance such that she forsakes the good of her husband and seeks private rendezvous with other lovers (cf. Prov. 7:18; 9:17). Though it is difficult to determine all that drives this woman to rebellion and forsaking of marriage fidelity, what is clear is the fact that she cares nothing for the good of the man or for those she seduces. She joins sinful man in being driven by self-concern. According to Paul and Peter, such women give the Enemy cause to slander, to think that something is wrong with how Christians live in gender relations (1 Tim. 5:14; 1 Pet. 2:12; 3:1–5).

Furthermore, the "contentious woman" of Proverbs portrays another way in which woman is unwilling to help man. This woman does not necessarily contend for mastery of the home and society; rather, the text indicates that her ever-badgering words appear to contend for man's energies and time (Prov. 21:9, 19; 25:24; 27:15–16). Her emotional needs dominate the home and work with the result that, when possible, the man and family avoid her. This is exacerbated when there is no man or other sufficiently selfless and loving to embrace her and be responsive to her needs and significance as a person. It is sad that a woman's life can be reduced to this by developmental injury or choice.

Of course, a woman can by fortitude mimic the Excellent Woman of Proverbs 31, giving herself in abject submission to the man and the familial/societal common good, but in such a way that her response is not tempered by devotion and submission to God. A healthy submission in Christ would help spare men, the family, and the culture from thinking that they are the ultimate ends of her life and love. Woman, whether single or married, is to give herself for man and the common good in a way that communicates her ultimate love and devotion to God. How much poetry, music, literature, film and other human endeavors are the fruit of this romantic illusion that the male-female relationship is the ultimate end of human life?

The Relation to Truth of Man and Woman

Man as Representative Truth-Teller

One way man displays his capacity for "with-ness" is his willingness to take responsibility to tell the truth and not withdraw into a lie. It is interesting that man in the Garden was given the responsibility for the commandment and "story" from God regarding how they could eat from all the trees of the garden except from the Tree of the Knowledge of Good and Evil. Throughout the Old and New Testaments, men, and not primarily women, are given the responsibility and authority to *representatively* express the truth. This does not mean that women have less of an affinity for the truth or cannot affirm or teach the truth.[18] The point is that man was given a *representative* responsibility for facing the truth and retelling it.

Following the pattern of Adam having proclamation responsibility, the Scriptures primarily assign to men the mission of public proclamation of the divine message.[19] Women are not prohibited from teaching roles in the church. In general, however, there is little indication in the New Testament, particularly in Paul's writings, that the woman is encouraged in the role of representative or apostolic proclamation of the truth in the church. This appears to fall to the man, who was created with a special function and responsibility to understand, integrate, and represent the truth for the common good.

Though men are made to be truth-tellers and authoritative proclaimers, in the Fall there is a tendency or vice propensity toward psychological dishonesty and verbal passivity regarding crucial intrapsychic, interpersonal, and societal problems. Sometimes man's dishonesty and outright lies are merely an attempt to protect his image of strength, autonomy, and self-sufficiency and not be exposed in his weaknesses. Certainly, man has opened his mouth in places of power (at work, in government, in the pulpit). Nevertheless, in areas that do not affect this strong identity motivation and search for glory, man has often been passive to speak against evil. This was evident in Adam in his failure to address the Serpent and Eve (Gen. 3:1–8) and in his unwillingness to tell the truth about his own failure (v. 12). Paul would have us believe that Adam, unlike Eve, knew what he was doing in spite of the consequences (1 Tim. 2:14). The indictment by God against man is prophetic for the ages: "Because you have listened to the voice of your wife . . ." (Gen. 3:17). Ever since, man has been tempted to not tell the truth in his relationships, particularly in relationship to woman by either crushing or avoiding her in order to escape the inner struggles that result from truly relating to the woman and being open to her.

Woman as Open Receptor

Another fundamental manner in which woman expresses her "forness" is by means of her being an "open receptor," particularly with reference to man and the truth. Whereas the Bible portrays man as a truth-teller gone awry, woman is portrayed as possessing a special gender-specific intensity to "hear" the word of the other, to be moved by wisdom, and to act upon it. This is, in part, due to her natural drive to help, complete, and nurture, which gives her an appetite for practical knowledge and means to growth. Her power is less in telling the truth, though she can and certainly will do this. Rather, her impact upon others is in her receptivity to the truth and *acting* upon it. This receptivity is evident in the creation account where she, and not man, is approached by the Serpent and is open to his apparent wisdom for living ("When the woman saw that the tree was . . . desirable to make one wise," Gen. 3:6).

In general, as man embraces woman, woman is to help inform him for his good by her quiet and submissive attitude. As Peter says regarding a woman's behavior toward her erring husband,

> In the same way, you wives, be submissive to your own husbands so that even if any of them are disobedient to the word, they may be won without a word by the behavior of their wives, as they observe your chaste and respectful behavior . . . but let it be the hidden person of the heart, with the imperishable quality of a gentle and quiet spirit. (1 Pet. 3:1–2, 4)

The woman best teaches her husband less by her words as a truth-teller and more by her life and example. Of course, there will be words of instruction, encouragement, and rebuke from women to men. In applying this marital virtue of respect to the eternal feminine nature, it seems that the Bible asserts *there exists a dynamic in women toward men in which her silent acts of love have an almost irresistible power.* Thus, her openness to God, receptivity of the truth, and respect toward the man is her incarnated manner in exegeting God's Word. When she does speak, the virtuous woman "opens her mouth in wisdom, and the teaching of kindness is on her tongue" (Prov. 31:26). That is, she has words of wisdom for the sake of society, her husband, family, and employees, which are made accessible by her kindness.

This receptive, open demeanor is also evident in the Bible's view of woman and her relation to the authoritative spoken word in the church assembly. In texts having to do with regulating teaching in the church, woman is generally asked to keep silent and not to teach in an authoritative position in the church: Women are told to "quietly receive instruction with entire submissiveness" (1 Tim. 2:11), and "if they desire to learn anything, let them ask their own husbands at home; for it is improper for a woman to speak in church" (1 Cor. 14:35).[20] My point is not that women are forbidden from teaching or from speaking truth to men in the church, but that the emphasis of the Bible is on the woman's ability to learn, to be receptive to others and the male, and to be a model of one who "hears" the truth from another. Her gender specificity models to the man his need to hear and receive the Word of God in all humility.

Due to the distortion of sin, women and men can be tempted since the Fall to be open to the wrong thing, though in woman it may be due to her unique penchant toward pragmatism, the desire for what works, and lack of discrimination. As Paul indicates, the woman was deceived and not the man (1 Tim. 2:14), indicating that woman believed incorrectly that she was getting a good, whereas man knew that he would get something bad as a result of his action. Interestingly, however, Paul lays the blame of original sin to man and not woman (cf. Romans 5). In any case, the Serpent shrewdly goes after the woman and not the man. Man is foolish, to be certain, but perhaps is more often "wide eyed" in his folly. Eve was blinded by the apparent good to be gained. Thus, it may be that woman's passion for wisdom and skill of living, coupled with her openness to this, can at times be reduced to the "end justifying the means" in her behavior. This does not imply that woman is more liable to sin than man, but only that her sin may have a different texture to it, perhaps involving more self-deception than the male's outright rebellion, more justifying of her actions to be good than the male's simplistic repression in going on with sin. Again, these observations are not meant to apply universally to all situations but may indicate certain gender tendencies. Moreover, her capability coupled with her penchant for wisdom can work to verbally dissuade the irresponsible man from what he might know to be the truth, for he is unwilling to do anything about it. In any case, the woman who opens herself to the right things in the right manner is a blessing to the earth and a model to man, family, church, and society.

The Posture of Man and Woman

Man as Exalted/Explicit

Man's capacity or willingness to embrace responsibility is related to his having a certain posture or place in life that he must embrace; namely, in having a sufficiently assertive and open character to be exalted and explicit in contrast to woman who is uplifting and veiled. This male-female ontology of exalted/explicit and uplifting/veiled is analogically related to the very nature of God—the Father as exalted and made explicit by the Son, the Son as exalted and manifested by the Spirit, and the Spirit as One who uplifts and is more veiled. We bless the triune God, but each is blessed within the economy of Their eternal relationships. The Spirit is no less God for magnifying and revealing Christ to the world than are the Father and Son for being exalted and revealed; neither is woman any less person within the male-female relational matrix for her uplifting/veiled nature than is man who is exalted and made explicit.

Adam's being created first as the representative ruler of mankind has certain implications that Paul draws out and applies universally to the church in a crucial text in 1 Corinthians 11. The following are relevant issues raised by Paul that he relates to the creation account and that betoken man's role as exalted and explicit.

> "For a man ought not to have his head covered, since he is the image and glory (δοξα) of God; but the woman is the glory (δοξα) of man." (v. 7)
> "For man does not originate from woman, but woman from man." (v. 8)
> "For indeed man was not created for the woman's sake, but woman for the man's sake." (v. 9)

As man is the image and glory of God, the radiant and weighty self-expression of God, the chief agent to exalt Him, so woman is created out of man and, as such, is his glory, the radiant and weighty expression of man, the chief agent to exalt him as well as God. Man was not created for woman, to uplift her, to make her explicit, to be her glory; rather, woman was created for man. This is not limited to the context of marriage but is applied by Paul to men and women in general. These claims fly in the face of the contemporary view that woman's flourishing is not necessarily tied to the man's or vice versa. Man's and woman's growth in Christ is still, in part, connected to functioning in their roles one to another in church, home, and society.

Man's vice with respect to his capacity to be exalted and explicit can take the direction of either excess or deficiency. In the first place, males have had a tendency to desire to be exalted and revealed more in areas of life in which they find their own personal identity and search for personal glory (work) than in their relational endeavors (the love of God and neighbor, family, social justice, etc.). Thus, a man may be very assertive and explicit in his dealings at work while being an entirely absent and passive member in those areas that he has relegated to women, namely, rearing children, developing the marriage, and taking initiative in matters of social justice and helping the needy. This may even be true in the church, in which men have sought more the explicit places of honor but less those roles that have little prominence.

On the other hand, some males have passively abdicated their role as exalted and explicit on account of an unwillingness to put themselves out for others to see or to confront painful dimensions of life they wish to avoid. The task is often shuffled to the woman who, as helper exemplar, traditionally embraces whatever job needs to be done that no man is willing to do. This, in turn, may tap into her unresolved need to be recognized for who she is.

Woman as Uplifting/Veiled

Whereas man needs to accept being rightly uplifted and explicit in his general posture, the woman's general demeanor seeks to be uplifting and, as a result, is often veiled. This gender-specific dimension is fundamental to her being created *for* the man, as his glory (1 Cor. 11:7–9). It is perfectly expressed in the Excellent Woman of Proverbs 31 who, in God, gives herself for man's good and his reputation as a leader in the community (cf. Prov. 31:10–12, 23, 31). She uplifts; he is exalted. She is veiled, not due to inability, but, because of her extreme capability, she is not afraid of living for the other. As Gertrud von le Fort says,

> In keeping with the veil motif [of 1 Cor. 11:13–15], the unpretentious more than anything else belongs to the domain of woman, and this means all that belongs to love, goodness, compassion, *everything that has to do with nursing and fostering the hidden, the betrayed things of the earth.* Therefore, *the times when woman is crowded out of public life are not in the least detrimental to her metaphysical significance.* On the contrary, probably these very periods, for the most unknowingly, throw the immense weight of womanhood into the scales of the world. (italics added)[21]

As she says later, woman represents the hidden side of God in creation, the "anonymity of God," whereas man represents the "perceptible forces" of God in creation, both cooperating together in the totality of His creative love and handiwork.[22] Thus, the virtuous woman knows who she is and what she stands for in God. The genius of true femininity is the willingness to foster this hiddenness and, thereby, empathize with and tenderly care for the ignored and shunned of the earth.

Not only do her works seek to uplift the man and others within her own veiledness, but woman's heart attitude mirrors this as well. She willingly subjects herself to him (Eph. 5:22; Col. 3:18; 1 Pet. 3:1), and she respects him (Eph. 5:33). As Peter states regarding marriage,

> In the same way, you wives, be submissive to your own husbands so that even if any of them are disobedient to the word, they may be *won without a word* by the behavior of their wives, as they observe your *chaste and respectful behavior.* Your adornment must not be merely external—braiding the hair, and wearing gold jewelry, or putting on dresses; but let it be the *hidden person of the heart,* with the imperishable quality of a *gentle and quiet spirit,* which is precious in the sight of God. For in this way in former times the holy women also, who hoped in God, used to adorn themselves, being submissive to their own husbands; just as Sarah obeyed Abraham, calling him lord, and you have become her children if you do what is right without being frightened by any fear. (1 Pet. 3:1–6, italics added)

Woman at her best does not need to uplift herself or show herself off by her outward beauty or her apparel. Rather, it is the "hidden person of the heart" that is precious to her and God, and is the manner in which she portrays herself to her family and society. Specifically, she wins her erring husband by her silent, chaste, and respectful behavior. This woman calls her husband "lord," as did the godly women of old. She is not diminished by lifting him up; she knows who she is. By so doing, she becomes a protégé of Sarah, a model of a virtuous woman. These traits are not merely for married woman but are eschatologically part of the eternal feminine soul, whose respectful behavior is capable of silently winning the man to honesty and the truth.

We should not think of woman's veiledness as absence; she is not squelched or repressed. The complementary view of the Bible is that she is fully present, so much so that she is capable of living for the other without notice to herself. That others will notice her is likely, just as we will notice the Excellent Woman of Proverbs 31.[23] The point is that she does not psychologically need to seek being noticed. The apostle

Peter believes that even the pagans can recognize the goodness of her quiet and gentle spirit when they see it (cf. 1 Pet. 2:12ff.; 3:4). This respect and uplifting attitude is not due to an unhealthy fear of the man or an impaired self-concept, but on account of her hope in God (3:5) so that she is "without being frightened by any fear" (v. 6). This is a woman who has transcended natural virtue, whose excellence motivated by the Spirit of God takes her beyond pathological fear, a thing to be respected by any erring husband. This is a mighty woman.

Woman in the Fall can be tempted out of personal injury, hurt, or selfishness to move toward a life of calling no man lord. She will be her own master; she will look out for herself, her own career or happiness. This is often exacerbated by the refusal of men to truly be open to women and their potential impact upon society. In response to man's closedness, woman has been tempted to mimic corrupt man's way of getting along in the world by seeking the higher place, by looking out for herself, and by being noticed. As a result, she denies the earth opportunity to see the inner strength of being obscure, of uplifting another, of what the church as bride is to do to Christ. This does not imply that the woman should seek obscurity; she should seek to lift up others and give of herself for the common good without care for notice. If she is noticed or lifted up by others, it is on account of her good works. It is not her intention or desire to be so. If it is, then you know there are deficit needs driving her actions that are at least linked to an erring male, be it a father, husband, or man in general.

On the other hand, a woman may be tempted in another way to uplift the other and remain veiled, not out of strength and hope in the Lord, but out of a need to be needed or a sad, dejected sense of self as a way to find her identity in the other and not in God. In this case, the woman does not know who she is, and the recipients of her care are not confronted by her strength being *in the Lord.*

The Wholeness of Man and Woman

Man as Incomplete

A correlate of man's fundamental "with-ness" is the fact of his deep drive or need to be filled and completed. Man is incapable of fully flourishing in himself or his work. Even prior to the Fall, God said of man that it was not good that he was alone (Gen. 2:18). Unlike the animals, in which male and female were created coextensively, God created the human male-female pair in stages, first creating the individual Adam as the only living creature created with an unmet need—a need to experience "the other" of himself and not merely some "other" outside himself. This is his need to experience that part of humanity who is female.

This male drive for completeness relates existentially to man's search to find meaning or to find himself by looking outside of himself. Man's ontological loneliness cannot be met by himself, and woman was given to him to demonstrate this. By embracing or being psychologically open to woman in marriage and the church, man discovers in a deeper way than is possible in isolation that he is relational to the core, that he fundamentally needs the other, which ultimately is fulfilled in his union with Christ and relationships with others in the church. His being open to woman and her impact upon him, whether in the home, church, or society, calls him to the truth that he cannot flourish or find his identity in himself.

Unfortunately, man in the Fall has tended to search for completion in external or material endeavors or finite relationships outside what is meaningful or moral. The result has been a selfish, autonomous preoccupation with his happiness at the expense of initiating true openness of relationship to woman and her contribution to the world. In response, woman has felt alone and unappreciated in her endeavors at being a woman, tempting her to embrace the safe and autonomous lifestyle of the man. This tension of man's inability to find himself by reference to himself alone and yet the impossibility to find himself outside of himself is resolved in the *nexus* of himself, woman, and Christ—all in union in the mystical body of Christ.

Woman as Completing

Woman's capacity of "for-ness" is grounded in her being created to "correspond" to and help man, that is, to complete him (Gen. 2:18). This is not only true in marriage but eschatologically reflects a deeper, eternal truth of man and woman in general. Whereas man is searching for something due to his incompleteness in being alone, woman desires to be found out by man and others and complete them. Nowhere in the creation account is it said that she is lonely and incomplete, as it is said of

Adam. They certainly need one another, though their needs seem to have a different texture according to gender. Man longs for and finds woman; she is present to complete and preserve. The Bible explicitly says that she is made for him, and not he for her (1 Cor. 11:9). This does not deny that woman longs for a meaningful and true relationship with man and others, whether in or outside of marriage. The fact that she has a strong relational and nurturing capacity indicates that perhaps she, even more than the man, hungers for relationship. But her hunger is to fill another; his is to be filled. Her desire is to complete, his is to be completed. His need comes more from an emptiness, hers from a need to in-fill herself into another, to give of herself for the other.

Even in the Fall and in broken relationships, she recognizes that something profound will take place in the relationship, and, thus, is committed to working on this. Man, on the other hand, longs for woman and, having once attained her, often continues his search "to find himself." Man fails to recognize what woman seems to intuit, namely, that it is in their relational journey together, with man being open to her at home, work, or the church, and her helping him that they discover the meaning of their lives in the midst of conflict, growth, and love. Their willingness to be open to their natures and one another, in turn, opens them both to a new relational horizon that points to a deeper need that can only be met in a more profound embrace by God. In this way, woman completes man and humanity by pointing to the fact that life is primarily a relational journey. Her role to complete another is not merely directed toward a husband but is universalized and finds its fullness "in the Lord" as being for the completion of mankind in general (1 Cor. 11:7–9, 11). Thus, the single woman has as much opportunity to complete mankind as the married.

Because of the strained relationship between man and woman in the Fall, she often seeks to fulfill her capacity or need to complete, help, and perfect whatever will respond to her assistance, namely, her children, her protégés, or her "cause." To help complete another is typically a virtue, except in this case when it is done in reaction to her being shunned or devalued by man. In this case, her benevolence toward others is not conditioned by a general interest, concern, and submissive attitude toward man and his goals in general. Rather, they engender personal autonomy, self-interest, and self-fulfillment as is so typical to sinful man. These relationships are not conditioned and balanced by the virtue gained from the conflict, growth, love, and selflessness that can emerge from the female coming to grips with her nature to complete the male-other and not merely herself, whether it be in the context of marriage or other contexts of life. Thus, this applies to both the married woman and the single woman who may not have much intimate contact with other males. The issue is not necessarily one of spatial proximity and the need to be face-to-face with man but of *attitude*. The reality is that no one is truly completed by the woman who cares little for man, for there is something distorted in her love and attempt to complete others. As a result, serious boundary problems emerge in which others' needs and her need to be needed become enmeshed. This is not only evident in the home with children but also in relationships in general that repress the feminine drive to be concerned for the man's good.

In more extreme cases, woman may altogether deny her drive to complete, turning her back on others and the common good. Out of hurt, she becomes like man, who is ever searching—though her search is perhaps less for identity as in the case of his search for glory, and has more to do with a longing for love and security from pain—a kind of perfect love without being willing to give to the other. Only a relationship with God offers woman the courage to turn back to complete humanity and give of herself at the risk of being hurt.

The Spirit and Strength of Man and Woman

Man as Strong

Strength is often closely associated with the male gender in the Bible, which is one dimension of his nature to embrace his responsibility for the earth. Several of the biblical texts that associate strength with the man may be mere accommodation to a particular culture's understanding of masculinity.[24] Other biblical texts, however, are more clearly universal and normative in their association. For example, the Proverbs account of the Mighty Man expresses the concern that men would give away their "strength" to women and intoxicants, a strength associated with the moral courage to stand up for social justice and those who were unable to speak for themselves (Prov. 31:3–9). Other texts in the Old Testament clearly relate God *as Father* with strength and sovereign power: as a Father who is associated with the strength of delivering Israel from Egypt (Deut. 32:6), as a Father who like a potter exercises sovereign power over the people, who are merely the works of clay and of His hands (Isa. 64:8), as a Father who will discipline David with the rod of men (2 Sam. 7:14), and as a Father with the sovereign power and authority to give to the Son (Jesus) the nations as an inheritance (Ps. 2:7–8).

In the New Testament, Paul associates masculinity with strength in his universal command to "Be on the alert, stand firm in the faith, *act like men, be strong*" (1 Cor. 16:13, italics added). The context clearly indicates that this injunction is given to all the "brethren," both men and women (v. 15). Thus, Paul is encouraging all to embrace and grow in a capacity that is gender-shared but that has overlapping gender-specific dimensions and intensities of which man is the exemplar by nature and in potential.

The vice propensity is that man is tempted to exercise strength as a defense or psychological cover-up of deep feelings of failure, inadequacy, and moral and relational weakness. As a result, this man fixates upon physical or material strength by which to give himself some semblance of being a man, while growing more and more relationally impotent. He refuses to find strength from the Lord in looking at himself truly and at his need for the other, particularly the woman. As a result, man's relational weakness to support and encourage the woman, to be open to being affected by woman, results in discouraging her in reaching out to him and others. His isolation from her forces or at least tempts her into a life of autonomous isolation and selfishness as well. His isolation also may discourage her development of or appreciation of masculine "strength," not only due to his lack of meaningful contact with her, but on account of her response to his nonrelational display of strength. Strength, in his case, may be abusive or at least unduly philistine, which she clearly recognizes. Perhaps a number of "soft males" have emerged from such broken homes, having been raised by mothers responding to man's distorted exercise of strength.

On the other hand, some males are tempted to deny their strength in order to let others toil with life's problems. Here we have the tragicomedy of the sluggard whose laziness is notorious in the Proverbs, who has not even the ambition to bring his hand back to his mouth from the dish, let alone to take up the cause of the widow and orphan (Prov. 19:24). The cure for such failings lies in man's being receptive to both woman and Christ from the heart.

Woman as Devout Surrender

If physical strength is closely associated with the male gender, the Bible frequently associates the woman with being devout and surrendered to the other as very much part of her being. This is one way in which her "for-ness" expresses itself for the good of others. She is often portrayed, particularly in the New Testament, as being an exemplar of devotion and surrender to both family and God. With respect to devotion to God, the accounts in the Gospels continually cast a light upon female devotion unparalleled in the man. It was women who broke ointment upon and kissed Jesus' feet in utter devotion, not the male disciples or the Pharisees, who were onlookers (Matt. 26:6–13: Luke 7:36ff.). It was Mary who had found favor with God and was an example in her response to the angel ("May it be done to me according to your word," Luke 1:28–38), in contrast to Zacharias who, when told of his wife's pregnancy with his son, John, expressed doubt in the words of the angel (Luke 1:18–20). It was Mary, sister of Lazarus, who was a model of one who had chosen the better way of sitting at the feet of Jesus, listening to His word (Luke 10:42). It was the Canaanite woman whose "faith was great," evidenced by her humble response to Jesus' words that it was not good for the dogs to take the children's bread, saying, "Yes, Lord; but even the dogs feed on the crumbs which fall from their masters' table" (Matt. 15:25–28). Women contributed to Jesus' ministry out of their private means (Luke 8:1–3). A number of these same women who were "ministering to [Jesus]" throughout His ministry were present at the cross when most of Jesus' male disciples had fled (Matt. 27:55–56), stayed with Jesus at His burial (Matt. 27:61), came to the tomb first on Easter Sunday (Matt. 28:1), wept at the tomb (John 20:11), were first to see and believe in the resurrected Jesus and "took hold of His feet and worshiped Him" (Matt. 28:8–9), and continued with the apostles to devote themselves to prayer in the Upper Room after His ascension (Acts 1:14).

Though these women discussed in the Gospels are not participating in any spiritual acts peculiar to women alone, nevertheless, the *manner* and *intensity* of their devotion is emphasized (weeping, kissing feet, lingering at the feet of Jesus, choosing the better part, etc.). These women are portrayed as exemplars of love, surrender, and devotion to Christ, which, in contrast, put the men in context to shame. Gertrud von le Fort comments on this dimension of woman.

> *Wherever woman is most profoundly herself she is not as herself but as surrendered;* and wherever she is surrendered, there she is also bride and mother. The nun dedicated to adoration, to works of mercy, to the mission field, carries the title mother . . .[25] (italics added)

Woman portrays the very mystery of gospel living, that we gain everything when we surrender all, that we live when we die, that we are first when we are last. According to von le Fort, "Surrender to God is the only absolute power that the creature possesses."[26] Surrender and devotion are the paths to finding oneself, and woman is an incarnational model to man of this mystery.

The woman's penchant for devotion may have some correlation to women's involvement in false religion, witchcraft, sorcery (magic), and religious prostitution. According to W. F. Adeney,

> The OT contains evidence of the lead taken by women in idolatrous rites. Maacah, the mother of Asa, introduced the worship of Astarte (I Kings 15:13). Jezebel in the Northern kingdom supported the prophets of the Phoenician cults and persecuted the followers of YHWH (I Kings 18:4). Her daughter Athaliah apparently played the same part in the Southern kingdom (cf. II Kings 8:18 and II Chron. 21:6 with II Chron. 22:2 and 24:7). Jeremiah describes the devotion of the women of Jerusalem to the rites of Ishtar, kneading dough and making cakes which would be shaped like the moon . . . to represent the goddess (Jer. 7:18). . . . Ezekiel mentions the devotion of Jerusalem women to the worship of the Babylonian Adonis, saying, "There sat the women weeping for Tammuz." (Ez. 8:14)[27]

How much one can make of these narratives is difficult to tell, for men were also involved in idolatry. Nevertheless, it is interesting to note in the Old Testament that women seemed to take a leadership role in witchcraft and sorcery insofar as there is no mention of a male sorcerer.[28]

On account of sin, the woman's passionate and surrendering heart of devotion for God can be turned pathologically away from the truth in order to meet her more urgent need for the mystical and transcendental. No doubt many modern women have hardened themselves to this dimension altogether and model the philistine man's bent for more hard secular realities. However, others may become deceived by false religion, particularly the magical, astrological, and mysterious, believing that it holds secrets and wisdom for living that mere human reasoning and effort cannot afford (cf. Eve's curiosity in Gen. 3:6 coupled with Paul's comment in 1 Tim. 2:14). In some cases, her drive to find herself in abject surrender may manifest in unhealthy relationships in which she attempts to find the transcendent in romantic love. In either case, delusion and not devotion enter the family, the culture, and even the church.

Gender Implications for Complementarity in the Church

The irony of human self-exploration is that the self only truly finds itself outside of itself in Christ and the new community of the church. All self-descriptors, including gender ones (I am a man; I am a woman; I am a husband; I am a wife; I am one who can think, feel, act, etc.), find their ultimate meaning and telos in God. Life for the theologically autonomous person is a study in *mis*identification. Persons living apart from Christ go wrong in either direction, whether it be in finding their identity in their gender or in a contemporary understanding of personhood and the shared humanity between genders.

Nevertheless, it *is* something to be male or female, which ultimately is to be servant to human growth in Christ and the church. In general, males, whether married or single, are to be open to women and their impact upon them and others; females, whether married or single, are to give of themselves for the common good with an attitude of seeking man's general good. This mutual submission to one another's good by living out one's respective gender is at the heart of the complementarity position, which envisions a corporate and fully gender-conditioned spirituality and life of worship to God. Unfortunately, in more conservative circles, the woman is often repressed or set aside due to insecurities in male leadership in being truly open to her and her impact upon the church and themselves, as well as not wanting to appear to be acquiescing to egalitarian sentiments. In more egalitarian environments, the female is psychologically embraced, though perhaps by a "soft male" leadership at the expense of the masculine dimension in spirituality and the church.

I used to think that much of this gender imbalance could be repaired in the church by husbands truly embracing their wives in their needs, desires, and contributions to others, as well as by wives giving of themselves to the good of their husbands. I still believe that married men and women who are willing to do this are guaranteed to go on the spiritual journey of their lives. The woman's relational long-suffering and willingness to help the man within his embrace will help keep him submerged at levels of insight and wisdom that the external search for glory do not allow. In turn, the feminine would find its way into the church by way of the heart of the embracing man, resulting in a church that resembles IBM less and looks more like a living, relational organism. I still believe a lot can be remedied in this manner.

As a result of this study, however, I believe that the gender-specific "with-ness" and "for-ness" dimensions of personhood are not only for marriage but need to be intentionalized and universalized for all male-female relating "in the Lord" in the church. Gender conservatives have shied away from this, perhaps due to fidelity concerns that arise when crossing over gender lines outside of marriage. The concern is whether a full-blown complementary gender relatedness in the church will result in greater sexual and fidelity temptations. This is a serious concern that must be addressed in every church and every heart. Perhaps greater openness to the significance of persons of the other gender may lead some to see how lonely and dissatisfied they are in their marriages and singleness. In those cases, gender relating should thrust individuals back into a deeper sense of their need for Christ and for working on their relationships in and outside of marriage. There will be need for much wisdom.

Nevertheless, I do not think that true complementarity necessarily entails that healthy boundaries cannot be appropriately upheld. Though there will be increased relationality and personal contact between the genders in this environment, it does not necessitate the pursuit of inordinate or morally inappropriate intimacy between singles or married couples. As I have argued before, spatial proximity is not the only element to relatedness. It has as much to do with an attitude and concern by men and women in the church to be faithful to their gender, to be open to the truth and impact of the other gender upon them and others, and to not repress, deny, or overlook the truth of what gender calls one to be in oneself and the other. This attitude will be reflected to all others they serve, that God has created an order in human nature between man and woman that works beautifully and harmoniously together toward an end that cannot be accomplished by one gender alone. I am not certain what this will look like, for I have yet to see this perspective worked out well in a church. It may, in fact, not always look that much behaviorally different to what we see in some church communities, though the heart attitude toward one's own gender and the other's is the telling issue.

By learning to relate in our "with-ness" and "for-ness," each member of the body is called to be what he or she can be in Christ. Man is called to be open to woman and really hear the woman as woman, to learn from her gender-specific dimension regarding devotion, relational long-suffering, openness, living for someone else, and of surrender as the bride of Christ. For this to work, he must relate to and consider her in the context of all his masculinity, as one who has grieved and repented deeply over his failure to be a man so that he does not merely relate to her as a soft male. Woman, in turn, is to give of herself for the common good of man and mankind, to live for the sake of others, to really consider how she can nurture, exalt, and lift up mankind and the man's work in leading the church and in making it all it can be in Christ, and by learning from the male about what it is to be a fellow warrior in the Lord. She must do this in the fullness of her femininity and devotion to Christ and not merely as a naturally virtuous woman. What a different world this could be were we faithful to our genders. God give us wisdom and grace to open our hearts to such freedom.

CHAPTER TEN

PSYCHOLOGICAL EVIDENCE OF GENDER DIFFERENTIATION

Judith TenElshof

Introduction

On August 22, 1965, Ron and Janet Reimer became the proud parents of identical twin boys whom they named Bruce and Brian. Eight months later, on April 27, 1966, both Bruce and Brian were brought to St. Boniface Hospital in Winnipeg, Canada, to be circumcised. On this fateful morning, Bruce lost his entire penis to a botched circumcision; Brian was never circumcised. The parents took Bruce to a renowned sex research expert at Johns Hopkins Hospital in Baltimore, who convinced them to submit their son to a surgical sex change. The change involved a process, that included clinical castration and other genital surgery when he was a baby, followed by a twelve-year program of social, mental, and hormonal conditioning to make the transformation take hold in his psyche. A process that was not only invasive to the body, but like brainwashing to the mind, created psychological warfare in Bruce. Contrary to reality, medical literature claimed the case to be an unqualified success. Bruce became famous in the annals of modern medicine and was used in the 1970s as proof that the gender gap was purely a result of cultural conditioning, not biology.[1]

Why is this case so important to the discussion of male and female differences? The experiment was a failure, but that was not revealed until 1997 in the medical journal *Archives of Pediatrics and Adolescent Medicine.* Bruce, who was renamed Brenda, struggled against his imposed girlhood from the start, inwardly knowing that something was not right. At age fourteen, he reverted to his created male gender, determined by his genes and chromosomes, and permanently changed his name to David.

This case is a paradigmatic example of the "nature vs. nurture" debate, conclusively demonstrating that nature, as God's creation, is the foundation for the differences between the genders.

In Scripture God said,

> "Let Us make man in Our image, according to Our likeness; and let them rule over the fish of the sea and over the birds of the sky and over the cattle and over all the earth, and over every creeping thing that creeps on the earth." God created man in His own image, in the image of God He created him; male and female He created them. (Gen. 1:26–27)

Here God refers to Himself in the plural, alluding to the distinctive persons of Father, Son, and Holy Spirit, but all in collective union. Mary Stewart Van Leeuwen observes that "God is intrinsically social: Creator, Redeemer and Holy Spirit working in cooperative interdependence throughout the whole of the biblical drama."[2] This view perceives God as more interrelational and interdependent than typically presented. Van Leeuwen continues: "If God is a social tri-unity whose image is in all persons, then it comes as no surprise to read in Gen. 2 that it is 'not good' for the man to be alone. So God creates the woman. Once they are together, God's clear intention for male and female is equality and interdependence in the context of differing sexuality." As God is a relational Being, then so are we as humans. Dan Allender and Tremper Longman assert in their book *Intimate Allies*, "One implication of the Trinitarian nature of God is that the core of the universe is relational. We reflect God as we relate to others in a way that mirrors his character."[3]

The Trinitarian image in its essence has a number of characteristics that bring some enlightenment to the human image as male and female. The image is a relationship in which the three members of the Godhead have distinct roles that are divided up in responsibilities of creation, redemption, and administration. These responsibilities are often overlapping, but Their purposes are one, Their value to Their purposes are equal, and They function in an intimate unity.[4] The key words for complete understanding of the Trinitarian image are *ordered, distinct,* and *unity*. Ordered involves the greater purpose of this book and is discussed in other chapters. Unity will be discussed fully in the last chapter on the relationship of man and woman. The word that concerns this chapter is *distinct*. Specifically, what the distinct differences are in male and female that, when functioning properly, bring complementarity and unity to their relationship. This complementarity then reflects the selfless, other-centered, noncompeting unity of the Trinity.

Donald Joy, in his book *Bonding: Relationships Created in the Image of God*, examines God's created reflection in male and female:

> Suppose that some aspects of God's character are best illustrated by a female, and that some are best illustrated by a male. All this adds up to a magnificently rich portrait of God. And, as always, the metaphor written in the male and female humans is likely only a pale representation of the reality toward which they point.
>
> Now we can imagine that the male side of God's image and the female side of that image are sufficiently different—intrinsically different—that they may be magnetically charged and attracted to each other. The magnetic pull may be fueled as (1) the search for balance and completeness as each "half" yearns for its matching counterpart; or (2) the sense that coming together makes a cosmic statement or nonverbal witness to the character of God, who created them partial facets of a grand image which is larger than either of them.
>
> What this suggests further is that there may be a core of intrinsic differences between male and female, and that these differences are elegant statements about the complex and glorious nature of God.[5]

It is important to recognize here that understanding these distinct differences between male and female is not for the purpose of creating rigid roles for each by boxing them in. Instead, this understanding should free each gender to live fully what it was created to be rather than feeling pressure to be what it is not. Whenever freedom to be one's created self is held in or controlled, intimacy is hindered. This has been experienced by both men and women. Larry Crabb reinforced this when he stated,

> Those who believe that . . . the differences between men and women have no bearing on how each was designed to relate are moving in directions that I think are dangerous and wrong. If our approach to relationships and responsibilities reflects not only our personality and gifts but also our sexual nature, then eliminating the unique element that each sex brings to their community will distort a good design.[6]

It is only through full expression of each one's truly distinct gender that complementarity between man and woman can wholly represent God's image. By selfless other-centeredness, each gender needs to use its distinctiveness to promote the complete fullness of the other. Male and female distinctiveness is enhanced when men and women are growing in other-centeredness.[7] Crabb explains that marriage offers a special kind of intimacy that singleness does not provide, but this does not exclude singles from the fulfilling joys that can be experienced in opposite gender, other-centered relationships.

As woman and man are beings created in the image of God, they reflect His infinite and perfect beauty. They "are able to do so only in the complexity and distinctiveness of both sexes. Both men and women are made in the image of God. Both are necessary to reflect God; one alone is not only incomplete but also inadequate to reflect his glory."[8] The rest of this chapter will pursue a discovery of the differences that help create the complement. These differences are evident empirically, but discounted in the societal trend toward blurring the gender distinctions, thus making the theological evidence provided in Dr. Coe's chapter vitally important.

Fetal Development (Biology)

Biologically, men and women are both very similar and very different. When an embryo starts out, the sex is indistinguishable. But Yves Christen, in the book *Sex Differences,* asserts that it is these indistinguishable differences that start a chain of events that eventually get played out in the biological traits of each sex. So, although the similarities are a reality, it is the inherent differences that begin to develop each embryo into a distinctly male or female baby. The similarities are what link each sex to the human race, but the differences are what differentiate males from females even in the womb.[9]

Genetically, male and female are very similar. Human beings have twenty-three pairs of chromosomes, totaling forty-six. Out of the twenty-three, one pair consists of the sex chromosomes, the only chromosomes that differ between man and woman. A man has an X chromosome and a Y chromosome, whereas a woman has two X chromosomes. A woman can therefore only contribute an X chromosome to her offspring, and thus the father's sperm determines the sex of their offspring.

According to *The Sexual Brain*, by Simon LeVay, one's sex is determined by one gene, called TDF, located on the Y chromosome. "This gene causes an individual to develop as a male. TDF works by causing the undifferentiated gonads to develop as male gonads or testes. The testes in turn influence the remainder of the body to develop in the male direction; this influence is exerted by hormones, chief among which is the sex steroid testosterone."[10]

In their scholarly work entitled *Sexual Differentiation and the Brain*, Robert Goy and Bruce McEwen asserted, "[B]ehavioral traits that exhibit sexual dimorphism are influenced only by the gonadal hormones, regardless of whether these hormones are secreted by the gonads, the adrenals, or both. Restriction of behavioral sexual dimorphisms to gonadal hormone influence reflect the fact that many or all of these traits are directly or indirectly related to reproductive fitness."[11] Hormones are key in the sexual differentiation of persons.

During the first trimester of human fetal development, the fetus starts to develop organs of the female sort, including reproductive cells with fallopian tubes and a vaginal tract. If the fetus possesses a Y chromosome, the androgens, or male hormones, masculinize it between the sixth and ninth weeks. "Thus the male can be regarded as a female transformed by testosterone."[12] Joy explains that "the mother's androgens, responding to XY chromosome command, permit the Y chromosome to produce an alien androgen protein which coats the cells programmed to become ovaries. The coating begins the transformation process which turns them into testicles . . . the testicles then begin to pump out two androgens . . . [one of which is] testosterone, which causes a penis to develop where the clitoris would have developed in [a female baby]."[13]

During the sixteenth week of gestation, the androgen hormones again act as change agents on the male baby's developing brain. The left hemisphere and corpus callosum are saturated by the androgens, both reducing the connections between the right and left hemispheres and providing for increased specialized function in the left hemisphere.

> The findings about this differentiation of the brain are . . . an entirely new set of insights about male and female differences . . . pointing to the absolute interdependence of male and female and of their complementarity.[14]

It is important to remember here that the degree of androgen exposure of the brain is dependent on the mother's stress during the release of the hormones, the possibility of an overproduction of estrogens, or serious hormone depletion. Therefore, dependent on these factors, male-female differentiation may extend across a spectrum.[15]

The sex hormones' interactions with the brain do not stop at this point, however. The interaction continues throughout life. The hypothalamus controls the pituitary gland, which regulates the other glands primarily responsible for hormone production (sex glands, adrenal glands, and thyroid), concluding in the notion that the brain is the regulator of hormonal activity. Goy and McEwen take this interaction a step beyond that conclusion when they assert that

> if the brain intervenes in sexual activity, it is itself influenced by sex hormones. Sex hormones interact with the brain; they possess special receptors on the nerve cell membranes. From here to the thought that, in the course of our development, the most precious of our organs is permeated with the very substances that define gender, is just a short step, which experience invites us to take.[16]

Typically, the cognitive profiles of men and women are different, although there is much overlap, points out Karen Phillips in her article "Why Can't a Man Be More Like a Woman . . . And Vice Versa?" For instance, on spatial tests, both women and men perform well. But Sandra Witelson, professor of psychiatry at McMaster University in Hamilton, Ontario, notes that when large numbers of men and women are averaged, a noticeable difference is apparent. Although some women may do better than some men in spatial tests, the mean male score is better than the mean female score. One also can tell how the brain is going about the task. In lab tests, there is evidence that the differing sexes' brains go about their functioning in different ways.[17]

Structural differences have been identified in at least two parts of the brain by neurobiologists: the corpus callosum and the hypothalamus, both previously mentioned. The corpus callosum connects hundreds of millions of neurons between the two hemispheres, while the hypothalamus controls and coordinates the integration of many basic behavioral patterns, involving brain and endocrine functions.

Marie de Lacoste was one of the first to measure the corpus callosum. This thick, boomerang-shaped band of fibers connects the brain's hemispheres and is the massive midline conduit for processing and relaying information between the two cerebral halves. De Lacoste suspected she would find a significant difference in callosum size between men and women. And she did. Her research was the first study of the human corpus callosum showing a possible anatomical basis for sexual differences in intellect, skills, and behavior.[18]

Roger Sperry, who received a Nobel laureate for his trendsetting work in split-brain theory, set the foundation for understanding further research aimed at understanding the differences in the sexes. De Lacoste's research coincides with this dominant "split-brain" theory, which asserts that male brains have fewer connections across the corpus callosum than female brains. This results in men having an increased capacity for either-side specialization. Men tend to be more left-brain oriented, which affords them with the characteristics of being more analytical and spatially astute than women. Women, on the other hand, tend to function with a more general capacity for both, affording them the ability to more easily verbalize their thoughts and feelings than men.[19]

In light of these biological differences, women and men tend to deal with life in different ways. The research findings about the two hemispheres of the brain provide insight into the daily variances between the sexes. Since women have more connection between the two sides of the brain, they may have a "bi-hemispherical representation of emotion."[20] This would result in a woman's ability to integrate the experience of emotions with the rational process of analytical thought. Men, in contrast, can disassociate themselves from their feelings and operate out of the left side of the brain. Neither one is ideal for every situation in life, but it is evident that each sex may approach similar circumstances in very different ways.

In his article "Two Challenges for Feminist Thought," Richard Epstein highlights an important point:

> The differences between men and women, then, are not simply matters of size, or even matters of size and strength—although these should never be ignored in any overview of the basics. They are also matters of psychology and behavior. The differences are not polar in any category. It would be foolish to say that all men are categorically different from all women. But by the same token, it would be irresponsible to claim that the shape of the distribution with respect to certain traits, its median, and its variance is the same for both males and females when it seems so clear that they are not. The evidence on these matters seems to be accumulating . . . [and] it all seems to run in the same direction. There are important and enduring differences in the behavior and psychology of males and females that must be understood before they are either praised or blamed.[21]

Returning to the story of David Reimer, no surgery, hormones, indoctrination, or therapy could erase his maleness. He had been created male not only outwardly but inwardly in ways that could not be changed. His own words later in life give this message of truth. "If you lose your arm," he says, "and you're dying of thirst, that stump is still going to move toward that glass of water to try to get it. It's instinct. It's in you."[22]

These created biological differences within the male and female show that there is an intrinsic physical difference between men and women. The question now is how these distinct physical differences are given expression externally in terms of masculinity and femininity.

Masculinity and Femininity

Did God create something called masculinity and femininity into our very natures? It seems that He did. This can not only be seen in biology, but also in how we relate. Leon Podles, in his book *The Church Impotent,* distinguishes between maleness and masculinity. He says that the facts of biology and masculine identity are not the same thing. Biology makes one an adult male, but one must choose to be masculine.[23] This is true also about women; they can be born female, but they need to choose to live and act in feminine ways. When made, these choices would create a much better "fit" for the complement God intended.

Although some have sought to deny any significant differences between man and woman beyond the physical, there is considerable evidence to the contrary. Biological differences lead to distinct gender-specific psychology and actions, which is only natural given the holistic nature of the human being.[24] This empirical evidence is borne out by practical experience. Swiss psychiatrist Paul Tournier, after years of counseling both men and women, concludes, "Man and woman are basically different, far more so than they believe. . . . I will go so far as to say that never can a man completely understand a woman, nor a woman a man."[25]

Deep down inside, David Reimer knew he was male, in spite of not being told for the first fourteen years of his life. Even the title of the book that tells his story reflects the truth of his God-created masculinity: *As Nature Made Him: The Boy Who Was Raised as a Girl*. His body developed like a man's, he thought like a man, and he felt like a man. Even in everyday living he questioned whether he wasn't really a man. One day, David found a pair of his mother's black kid gloves, which he tried on. They reminded him of "cool Italian race car gloves that you see in the movies," and he was thinking, "these would give a good grip on the steering wheel."[26] But his mother was standing behind him and encouraged him to put them on because she thought he was trying to be feminine. In less dramatic ways, I wonder how much gender identity is confused for us through television, movies, books, magazines, and in our culture in general.

In Crabb's discussion of masculinity and femininity, he highlighted two concepts that one must not forget: "The design that God created, and the power and joy of His people who are to live by this design."[27] Not only can this created design go wrong in the womb, but sin enters into the development of God's design and corrupts it. Many men and women have lost sight of their created design in God's image and are confused about what it means to be masculine or feminine. In this confusion, men can become "macho" or "wimpy," and women can become "passive doormats" or isolated and independent (rather than interdependent) without the love of their complement. These responses are all self-centered rather than other-centered, keeping the complement from fulfillment. It is important that men and women turn their focus from themselves and begin to understand the other. Crabb's counsel is "to look hard at your spouse, to identify his or her hurts and wounds and frustrations, and then to do whatever is within your power to help. The obstacles you need to remove are those that interfere with your progress toward other-centeredness, not with self-expression."[28] Let's discover what relational differences men and women really have.

Relational Differences

The popularity and widespread cultural reference to Dr. John Gray's book *Men Are from Mars, Women Are from Venus* serves to illustrate the differing relational goals and strategies employed by each gender. Women tend to be oriented more toward their relationships and affect, while men tend to be more objectively and judicially oriented. Carol Gilligan, in her priceless work *In a Different Voice,* tells of how the women in her study described themselves in terms of their relationships.

> In response to the request to describe themselves, all of the women describe a relationship, depicting their identity in the connection of future mother, present wife, adopted child, or past lover. Similarly, the standard of moral judgment that informs their assessment of self is standard of relationship, an ethic of nurturance, responsibility and care. Measuring their strength in the activity of attachment, these highly successful and achieving women do not mention their academic and professional distinction in the context of describing themselves. If anything, they describe their professional activities as jeopardizing their own sense of themselves, and the conflict they encounter between achievement and care leaves them either divided in judgement or feeling betrayed. . . . Thus in all of the women's descriptions, identity is defined in a context of relationship and judged by a standard of responsibility and care. Similarly, morality is seen by these women as arising from the experience of connection and conceived as a problem of inclusion rather than one of balancing claims.[29]

Men, on the other hand, used quite different parameters to describe themselves.

> For the men, the tone of identity is different, clearer, more direct, more distinct and sharp edged. Even when disparaging the concept of self, they radiate the confidence of certain truth. Although the world of the self that men describe at times includes "people" and "deep attachments," no par-

> ticular person or relationship is mentioned, nor is the activity of relationship portrayed in the context of self-description. Replacing the women's verbs of attachment are adjectives of separation—"intelligent," "logical," "imaginative," "honest," sometimes even "arrogant" and "cocky." Thus the male "I" is defined in separation, although the men speak of having "real contacts" and "deep emotions" or otherwise wishing for them. . . . In these men's descriptions of self, involvement with others is tied to a qualification of identity rather than to its realization. Instead of attachment, individual achievement rivets the male imagination, and great ideas or distinctive activity defines the standard of self-assessment and success.[30]

It can be seen, then, that women define themselves in terms of relational attachment, while men in terms of individual achievement. Donald Joy emphasizes that men are able to process information in a single-minded way, analytically and logically considering it, while women are more open to interruptions and "whole-minded" in their responses. Generally, women integrate feelings with logic, beliefs with reality, and worship with theological reflection more easily than men. However, men are "more at the mercy of their feelings, since right-handed, right-eye dominant men tend to speak from their logical analytical left hemispheres. They have to work harder to articulate their 'right mind' where feelings, emotions and experiences with God are processed."[31]

Deborah Tannen, in her groundbreaking work, *You Just Don't Understand*,[32] assessed and analyzed the communication of men and women. Her conclusions include the tendency of men to "one-up" one another when in conversation, in a competitive manner, and women to use what she calls rapport-talk. Women are more interested in and attuned to connection, while men are more interested in and attuned to hierarchy. Women work to preserve intimacy, while men work more to preserve independence.

Allender and Longmen assert, "A woman is no stronger or weaker than a man; she is a helper who is jointly to engage creation and enter into relationship to bring glory to God. But her calling is to do so as a warrior of relationship, a guardian of truth in relationship, one who is made to uniquely reflect God's heart for relationship and his hatred of loneliness."[33]

There is far more evidence for conversational style differences between women and men to support Tannen's work; for instance:

> [C]ompared to men, women have been described as more polite speakers (Holmes, 1995), both in terms of negative politeness, which recognizes the autonomy of others and avoids intrusion, and in terms of positive politeness, which emphasizes connectedness and appreciation (Brown & Levinson, 1978). Women are generally more cooperative (Coates, 1989), more socioemotional in orientation (Gilligan, 1982; Leaper, 1987), and more facilitating of conversational interaction (Cameron, McAlinden, & O'Leary, 1989; Holmes, 1995). They perform the bulk of the interactional work that maintains a conversation (Fishman, 1977, 1978). Women's conversational goals and strategies focus on establishing affiliation with their conversational partner, gaining trust, sharing confidences, and building rapport. Women are more likely to use discourse strategies that reduce inequalities in status and power and that emphasize solidarity. They attenuate criticisms and avoid reproach as well as give compliments and express appreciation (Troemel-Ploetz, 1991). They are responsive listeners and considerate speakers who offer frequent and encouraging minimal responses (e.g., "uh-huh," "mmmm") (Fishman, 1977; Roger, 1989; Zimmerman & West, 1975), and they use more indirect forms of influence (Lakoff, 1990).[34]

On the other hand, men have been characterized as less cooperative contributors to the conversation of others.

> They are eager to hold the floor and control the topic of conversation (Fishman, 1977). They tend to use language to establish status and to gain or convey information (Aries & Johnson, 1983; Tannen, 1990). Their conversations are organized around mutual activities rather than relationships (Aries & Johnson, 1983). Men tend to talk more than women, at least in formal or public situations (Holmes, 1995; Swacker, 1975, 1979), but they have been found to talk less in intimate relationships (DeFrancisco, 1991; Fishman, 1978). They show delayed minimal responses (Zimmerman & West, 1975) and reduced eye contact with the conversational partner when they are listening (Dovidio, Brown, Heltman, Ellyson, & Keating, 1988)—both of which may be experienced by the speaker as signaling a lack of interest in what is being said.[35]

Within this summary of gender conversational styles, the themes of males being more separate or individualistic and women being more interdependent and relational can be seen.

David Reimer, raised as Brenda for fourteen years, experienced these relational differences. When Brenda rescued "her" brother from bullies, "she" acted as his protector, but "she" also sometimes bullied Brian herself. As David moved into puberty, he had feelings for girls while he himself was supposed to be a girl. He became envious of the guys who knew where they belonged, for there was no place for him to be comfortable in relationships. His assigned sex could not override the biologically based sex differences in relating.

Crabb emphasizes that the distinct differences of masculinity and femininity are most fully expressed and recognized within relationship as the two genders understand each other more fully. He said,

> True masculinity and femininity emerge and develop only in the midst of other-centered relating. The more a man understands a woman and is controlled by a Spirit-prompted other-centered commitment to bless her, the more "masculine" he becomes. And he will become more masculine in an unself-conscious fashion.[36]

Masculinity will then be experienced by moving confidently and decisively toward God's purposes while being compassionate and understanding of his family, knowing he can promote good in his wife and children as he gives freedom for them to become all they were created to be. Crabb expressed it this way:

> Masculinity might therefore be thought of as the satisfying awareness of the substance God has placed within a man's being, that can make an enduring contribution to God's purposes in this world, and will be deeply valued by others, especially his wife, as a reliable source of wise, sensitive, compassionate, and decisive involvement.[37]

Femininity, on the other hand, Crabb sees as the satisfying awareness of the substance God has placed within a woman's being expressed primarily through matters that affect the heart. A woman will feel most feminine when she is actively encouraging, affecting, deepening, and nourishing relationships. Allender and Longman agree when they call women "the guardians of truth in relationship."[38] Involvement with others to deepen attachments is what brings rich femininity to a woman.

As men and women learn to focus on bringing out the richness of their opposite, they will experience a truer sense of what it means to be masculine and feminine. But this is particularly difficult in a society that values individualism over community. A primary point of Gilligan as a result of her study assessed psychology as being a discipline developed by men and around men's way of relating. This results in women being considered emotionally inferior or immature, because psychological health is assessed in terms of independence.

> Thus there seems to be a line of development missing from current depictions of adult development, a failure to describe the progression of relationships toward a maturity of interdependence. Though the truth of separation is recognized in most developmental texts, the reality of continuing connection is lost or relegated to the background where the figures of women appear.[39]

Women as a result are viewed as being stuck in relationship, unable to complete their separation. Often they are seen as fused with their mothers and unable to move in their development from independence in adolescence to interdependence in young adulthood. Because our society rewards separation and individualism, women are left at risk when seen as fused. The truth that is omitted in psychological texts is that separation may look different for women because of their being attached in infancy to the same gender. Gilligan supports this when she says,

> In young adulthood, when identity and intimacy converge in dilemmas of conflicting commitment, the relationship between self and other is exposed. That this relationship differs in the experience of men and women is a steady theme in the literature on human development and a finding of my research. From the different dynamics of separation and attachment in their gender identity formation, through the divergence of identity and intimacy that marks their experience in the adolescent years, male and female voices typically speak of the importance of different truths, the former of the role of separation as it defines and empowers the self, the latter of the ongoing process of attachment that creates and sustains the human community.[40]

This is the tension in human development, and women tend to be silent or not heard as to how their process is different. Gilligan's research study was an attempt to enlarge developmental understanding by suggesting that less emphasis needs to be placed on women's lack of separation and more on knowing how to attach and maintain relationship. This change then highlights the difference in men's and women's development, making it possible to recognize not only what is missing in women's development, but also what is there, as well as what might be missing in men's development. It also raises a different standard by which psychological maturity can be assessed.

The question that begs to be asked here is: How does this lack of emphasis on the development of interdependence affect male and female adult relationships, particularly in developing community so vital for relational and spiritual maturity? As a church, are we not far more concerned with individual achievement than intimate relationships with God and others?

Psychologist Paul Vitz, in a paper he wrote titled "Theism and Postmodern Psychology," asserts the following about modern psychology. Note the similarity to Gilligan's critique:

> I will begin with a description of the secular self or individual, as it is normally called in contemporary psychology. This psychology of the self has permeated much of our culture, and today we describe the ideal individual with such terms as "self-actualized," "independent," "autonomous," and "high in self-esteem." The essential idea is that each secular self is an autonomous being whose fulfillment is guided entirely by self-defined values and goals, without serious concerns for others or community. The heavy emphasis on autonomy or freedom implies independence or separation from others, and in many cases results in a kind of social isolation or social "atomism." Furthermore, this self is created by itself—that is, all of us are supposed to be self-made. The best-known psychological theorists who have emphasized this autonomous self include Carl Rogers and Abraham Maslow; their influence has been enormous, especially on education. However, much of the same emphasis is found in many other schools of psychology.[41]

As Gilligan says, this description of developmental psychology fits men better than women. In his work, a man can secure identity through power and separation, but it leaves him unconnected and at a distance from God and others to whom he needs to attach. In order to see the effects of his independent actions on others, he needs intimacy. It is in the experience of relationship that he will no longer be isolated and will show concern rather than indifference to others.

It is interesting to note that the idea expressed earlier of both male and female being created in God's Trinitarian image is an understanding of creation that emphasizes interdependence, while the traditional Western understanding of Eve's sole function was as a helper and procreator to the more autonomous Adam, emphasizing hierarchical relationship. Throughout much of church history, fundamental theologians such as Augustine and Luther (who held to that traditional view of creation hierarchy) have regarded the relational aspects of womanhood in general, and Eve in particular, as quite negative and inferior to the man's more autonomous, justice-emphasizing qualities, rather than valuing the need of each for the other as completion of the complement.

Conclusion

It can be seen from the evidence shown that there are definitely clear differences between the genders. What should be concluded about this differentiation? That God created two people who are able to come together and experience what they could never experience alone.

> Deep body-and-soul intimacy with another person is rare. We all desire it. We yearn for someone to know us and then desire to know even more. We long for someone to know us beyond the perceptible to the depths of what even we do not comprehend. We want a person with whom we can be "naked," a person who will not judge us and who will find in our presence an unreserved delight.
>
> Such a relationship was God's gift to Adam and Eve. God responded to Adam's loneliness by creating Eve. And he created her so they would literally fit together as unity in diversity. He meant them to have a union without loss of uniqueness. He gave them an intimacy that drew their hearts not only to each other but also to delight in and desire God more passionately.[42]

Much of our culture fights against the uniqueness of the genders and their complementarity, instead working toward being undifferentiated. Wendy Shalit, in her book *A Return to Modesty,* writes about the prescription of Prozac for women. She quotes an article from *American*

Woman: "Over six million Americans are now taking the drug, mostly women between the ages of 20 and 50. . . . Some say this little green-and-cream colored pill not only chases away the blues, but PMS, anxiety and overeating too." She asserts, "A girl can do whatever she wants to do, become anything she wants to be—with one crucial exception. Prozac teaches us that there is only one thing nowadays that a girl is not allowed to grow up to be, and that, strange as it may seem, is a woman."[43]

In her work, Shalit comments on the impact culture has had on behavioral expectations regarding each gender:

> The need is not for nonsexist upbringing, but for precisely a good dose of sexist upbringing: how to relate as a man to a woman. Today we want to pretend there are no differences between the sexes, and so when they first emerge, we give our little boys Ritalin to reduce their drive, and our little girls Prozac to reduce their sensitivity. We try to cure them of what is distinctive instead of cherishing these differences and directing them towards each other in a meaningful way. We can never succeed in curing men and women of being men and women, however, and so these differences emerge anyway—only when they do, they emerge in their crudest, most untutored form, such as swearing, stalking, and raping.[44]

So the challenge for each of the genders is to be able to acknowledge, accept, and live out the uniqueness of their genders, and value not only what they have been given, but what they need to find in the other. As the two genders complement each other by appreciating the other, the full image of God is reflected from the oneness that is created. This was confirmed by Karl Barth when he wrote,

> All other conditions of masculine and feminine being may be disputable, but it is inviolable, and can be turned at once into an imperative and taken with the utmost seriousness, that man is directed to woman and woman to man, each being for the other a horizon and focus, and that man proceeds from woman and woman from man, each being for the other a center and source. This mutual orientation constitutes the being of each. It is always in relation to their opposite that man and woman are what they are in themselves.[45]

Beyond David Reimer, whose case was a rare genital accident, a study in Baltimore of twenty-seven male children who were born without penises and raised as girls found that most of them considered themselves boys, suggesting that gender identity is determined in the womb.[46] Not only did the study call into question the practice of surgically changing the sex of infants, but it contradicts those who argue that gender identity develops after birth. Dr. Marianne Legato, a professor of clinical medicine from Columbia University who studies differences between men and women, said,

> When the brain has been masculinized by exposure to testosterone, it is kind of useless to say to this individual "You're a girl." It is this impact of testosterone that gives males the feelings that they are men.[47]

The import of this data to theology is staggering. It not only confirms that men and women are different, but that these differences are by design and were intended by God at creation. When will we learn to hear what our Father said of what He had created, "It is good"? We need to reaffirm gender difference rather than working against God's blueprint. Complementarity does this by seeking to magnify and nurture these God-given differences.

PART FIVE

WOMAN AND MAN IN HUMAN HISTORY

CHAPTER ELEVEN

GENDER ROLES AND AUTHORITY: A COMPARATIVE SOCIO-CULTURAL PERSPECTIVE

Sherwood Lingenfelter

Introduction

Becoming a disciple of Jesus brings dramatic transformation to the personal and communal life of people. As they receive the Holy Spirit and allow the Word of God to take root in their lives, they begin a lifelong journey of being conformed to the image of Christ. As part of that journey, the words of Scripture and the Word of Life challenge men and women to new understandings of their relationships with one another. Each person and each community of believers must wrestle with the meaning and application of the narratives and teachings of the Old and New Testaments to their way of life.

In this process, it is necessary to realize that we all live in a particular historical and social culture that influences our worldview, including our understanding of God's revelation in the Scriptures. Because of our imperfect condition, it is impossible for us to distill a theology or interpretation of scriptural texts totally free from the bias in our languages and worldviews. Nevertheless, the transforming power of the gospel works to set us free from the bondage of sin in our personal and communal life.

A Look at Gender in Human Cultures

In seeking to more fully understand and practice God's pattern of the relationship of men and women and their roles in the practical ministry of the church, it is essential that we understand the particular cultural and historical background within which our church and personal understanding have been shaped and nourished. A comparison with other cultures helps us understand our own biases as well as opening our minds to other possibilities of implementing God's patterns of communal life.

As we approach the question of culture, men and women have many questions about the influence of culture in the defining of gender roles and about the relationship between cultural standards and principles and the standards and principles of Scripture. Some of the typical questions that have been raised on this issue include:

How do cultures vary in their definitions of family and gender roles?
To what extent is marriage the defining relationship in gender roles?
What universals have anthropologists found regarding gender roles?
What is the role of men and women in matriarchal societies?
Is it natural for men to be in authority over women?
How widespread is the abuse of women across cultures?
How do roles of women in leadership vary across cultures?
How do cultural expressions of gender roles oppose principles in Scripture?
Does the Bible set forth gender role absolutes that apply to all cultures?
Which cultures are more biblical in their gender roles and values?
What would the church look like if it valued women more?
What leadership options in the church are culturally and biblically legitimate for gifted Christian women?

The objective of this chapter is to provide some illustrative answers for the cultural issues raised in these questions and then explore the relevance of culture to the questions of appropriate roles for women in the ministry of the church.

A patrilineal society counts as members only those individuals, male and female, who can trace their descent through males to a common male ancestor. Although women belong to the social group of their fathers, their children belong to the social group of their husbands. Likewise, a matrilineal society counts as members only those individuals, male and female, who can trace their descent through females to a common female ancestor. Although men belong to the social group of their mothers, their children belong to the social group of their wives. To help the reader gain a mental picture of some of the diversity that exists in cultures and in Christian life, I will begin with three case studies that highlight some specific variations in culture and how they illuminate the question of gender roles and life in a church community.

Case Study: Betty and Sebastian—A Pacific Island Divorce

Betty was born in 1944 on an island in the Pacific north of the equator in western Micronesia. Her mother came from one of the highest-ranking villages on her island, but her father was a foreigner. As a young woman Betty met Sebastian, and they fell in love and were married. Sebastian came from a second-ranking village located about ten miles north of Betty's home. Because the culture of the island is patrilineal and patrilocal, Betty left her village and became a member of Sebastian's household in the village of his birth. Sebastian built her a house just across the road from his older brother and his family. The older brother gave Betty and Sebastian the land on which to build their house and land to produce their food. The agricultural land included a swamp for growing taro and hill plots for growing yams and fruit. In the traditional division of labor, it was Betty's responsibility to maintain the taro swamps and to develop, with the help of her husband, yam gardens on the hills in the plots that had been given to them. Sebastian in turn was expected to provide the protein for the family by fishing daily in the reef or by getting a job and using his income to purchase meat. When Betty and Sebastian married, she was already pregnant with their first child.

Sebastian had been very successful in high school, and soon he received a scholarship to attend the University of Hawaii. He left Betty and his children in the care of his older brother, and for the next several years spent he most of his time in Hawaii. He returned to his home village for the Christmas and summer vacation periods, but the rest of the year he was busily engaged in his studies. Each year when he returned home, Betty became pregnant with another child. By the time he had earned his master's degree and returned to his home island to work, he had fathered seven children. During his last year at the university, he had an affair with one of the college girls, a daughter of a chief in his home island in Micronesia. After he had returned home to begin his work career, this young woman followed him and continued to pursue her interest with him.

During the years that her husband had been in the university, Betty had been faithful to him and had worked hard to care for their children. Betty had been raised in the Roman Catholic Church, and she was faithful in her commitment to Christ and to the teaching of the church with regard to marriage. She was, therefore, distraught when she discovered that her husband was having an affair with another woman. For a while she confronted him in traditional ways, like refusing to wash his clothing or refusing to cook for him when he did not come home at night. When he complained about how she took care of their home and their gardens, she worked harder to try to please him by being the best wife she knew how. However, one day Sebastian came home and told her that he was divorcing her to marry the girl that he had met in the university. By this time Betty had given birth to her eighth child. She took the three youngest children and moved back to her home village to live with her relatives. The older children stayed with their father and their father's brother. However, some of the older children did not like their father's new wife and left to live with their mother in her home village.

Sebastian had rejected any commitment that he had to Christianity during his university days. The fact that he and Betty had been married in the church was of no consequence to him, since the church no longer had any influence over him. He married his new wife in the traditional cultural way, taking her home with him to his household. Although his marriage to Betty in the church was never annulled, from this time on he lived with his second wife and started a new family of children. After several years of struggling to care for her children alone, Betty remarried in the traditional way to another man in a village near her home. While she continued to attend church, she lived in fear that God would never forgive her for her remarriage.

Case Study: Aswinda—A Polygamist Conversion

Aswinda was born about 1950 in the interior of Surinam in South America. Aswinda was born of the descendants of slaves who escaped into the interior of Surinam and established an independent culture and language called Saramaccan. The Saramaccans are matrilineal people who trace their ancestry to the women who were the founding ancestors of the villages in which they live. Aswinda grew up in the village of his mother, learning the respective roles for men and women by watching his mother, his mother's brother, and his father. The men in his life were itinerant. His father would spend some time with his mother, and other times he would return and live with his sisters in the village of his birth. Likewise, his mother's brother would spend some time with Aswinda and the family, helping them, and other times he would be off living with his wives and his children. The women in Aswinda's life—his mother, his mother's sisters, and his own sisters—were constant for him as he grew up. Working with his mother, he developed skills for gardening and the care of the basic needs around the household. Working with his father and his mother's brother, he learned the roles of men in the wider society.

As a young man, Aswinda ranged far from his village for hunting and other activities. Over a period of years, Aswinda traveled to the different Saramaccan villages on the river, and in the course of his travels married three different wives. During a typical year he would spend a few months with each of his wives and a few months with his mother and sisters. In each of these places, Aswinda participated in the daily economic life of his family and supported the village cults of the ancestors in which they dealt with the fundamental matters of birth and life and death.

One day, in the course of his traveling from one place to another, Aswinda met an evangelist who told him the gospel of Jesus Christ. In all of his roaming, Aswinda had not found anything that provided satisfaction and meaning for him in his life. In time Aswinda accepted the gospel and became a committed follower of the Lord Jesus Christ. He began to witness to his wives and to the other members of his family. His conversion produced great concern among his wives and their brothers, and within a short period of time all three of his wives divorced him. They refused to see him again and refused to allow him to come to their village even to visit his children. Although his mother and sisters did not refuse to see him, they chastised him for running away from the cult of their ancestors. However, Aswinda continued to grow in his walk with the Lord Jesus Christ and dedicated himself to reaching his people with the gospel. He joined a fellowship of Saramaccan believers and committed himself to a life of celibacy and service for the Lord Jesus Christ. Aswinda became a key participant in the translation of the Scriptures into the Saramaccan language. During all of this time, he continued to pray for the salvation of his family and at least one Christian wife.

Case Study: Katherine—A Reluctant Pastor's Wife

Katherine was born in 1924, the fourth in a family of five children. Her mother was an unusual woman for her time, being a college graduate and a schoolteacher who gave up her career and married Katherine's father at the age of thirty. Katherine's father was a farmer and a lay minister in the local community. During the Depression, her father lost his farm, and the family moved to a different town where her father took part-time employment as a pastor in a local church. He was very active in the Bible prophecy movement of the 1930s and became embroiled in a liberal/conservative controversy in his local church. The controversy caused great stress in their family and led to a church split in which her father led the conservatives to start a new church a mile down the road. Her father died suddenly of a heart attack when she was thirteen years of age.

Katherine married when she was sixteen, not finishing her high school education. Seeing the difficulty of her father's life in the church, she resolved not to marry a man who was involved in Christian ministry. Her young husband came from a large family in which all of the men were laborers for the Pennsylvania railroad. After five years of marriage and two sons, Katherine's husband felt called to prepare himself for ministry, and they moved to California, where he attended the Bible Institute of Los Angeles. Upon graduation, he took his first church in a small town in Virginia.

Although Katherine was a gifted seamstress and pianist, she felt inadequate for her role as a pastor's wife. She was extremely sensitive about the fact that she had not finished high school, and so she studied hard on her own to improve her English grammar so that she would not be an embarrassment to her husband in his ministry. Katherine was a shy, introverted person and not skilled at interpersonal relationships. She preferred to be a background supporter for her husband and her family.

Over the years Katherine experienced many frustrations as a pastor's wife. Although all of the churches appreciated her skill as a pianist, most of them had social expectations that Katherine could not fill. Katherine was exceptionally talented with her hands, which was reflected in her piano playing, sewing, upholstering furniture, and even remodeling her home. She also had good management skills, but there was no place for a woman manager in the church. What she lacked were the social skills for public entertaining, counseling, and social networking that many expected of her. For Katherine, life as a pastor's wife was often frustrating and stressful, especially when the expectations of people did not match her gifts of service.

Five Distinctive "Ways of Life"

How do cultures vary in their definitions of family and gender roles? In the three case studies presented above, we see three distinctive variations in the expression of family and gender. How do these variations fit into the bigger picture of society and culture?

Michael Thompson, Richard Ellis, and Aaron Wildavsky suggest that there are five, and only five, distinctive ways of life.[1] These ways of life are formed by particular social preferences and cultural biases. Cuing from the works of Mary Douglas, they see social preferences defined in reference to a society's emphasis on group membership and upon the degree of autonomy that individuals have in reference to their social roles.[2] Some societies give very weak emphasis to membership within groups (weak group, see figure 1), whereas others give highest value to belonging, and make very strong distinctions between insiders and outsiders (strong group). Likewise, some societies allow a great deal of individual freedom in the definition of personal roles (weak grid), whereas others define social roles fairly explicitly and articulate clear standards as to how one must behave within a given role (strong grid). These social preferences lead people to embrace particular sets of social values that Mary Douglas has termed "cultural bias." The social preference in the cultural biases combine together to constitute the five distinctive ways of life.

The *individualist* way of life is one that gives relatively weak value to the group and great autonomy to individuals in the definition of their roles in relationships in society. The story of Isaac and Rebekah is a good illustration of the individualist way of life as expressed in family. Isaac and Rebekah lived at a distance from both of their families, and they were self-sufficient economically. They raised their sons, Jacob and Esau, with a great deal of freedom and little role restriction. Isaac affirmed Esau for his interest in hunting and work in the fields, whereas Rebekah affirmed Jacob for his interest in life among the tents that included cooking, sewing, and taking care of the flocks.

The *authoritarian* way of life, like the individualist, places little value on group membership, but constrains the life of the individual through a much more rigorous definition of role and rules for behavior. In the authoritarian way of life, every social role is clearly defined with a rigorous set of expectations that the individual occupying it must fulfill. The case study of Katherine is an illustration of this way of life. Katherine's frustration came from the fact that the role "pastor's wife" had very clear and rigid expectations for which she was not gifted. The church community evaluated her on her role performance rather than on her personal capabilities. In the authoritarian way of life, role performance is more important than any other specific value.

In the *hierarchist* way of life, the social preferences include both a strong commitment to group and membership and also a high definition of role and clear expectations for role performance. The case study of Betty and Sebastian is a reflection of a hierarchist way of life. Marriage in this Pacific island community requires a woman to leave her own group and to join the group of her husband. The new wife who enters that group becomes an inferior member of the group community. The members of the community place the new woman on trial to see if she performs her role appropriately as a wife and as a new member. The community has very clear standards as to what is expected of a wife. When Sebastian returned from the university, he was critical of his wife's role performance on certain economic and social expectations in the family community. Of course, this criticism was a rationalization for rejecting his wife because of his infidelity. At the same time, Sebastian rationalized his preference for his new wife on the basis of her higher social origins, her superior education, and the higher status the relationship with her would give him in the larger social and economic structure of the islands.

Figure 1. Five "Ways of Life"

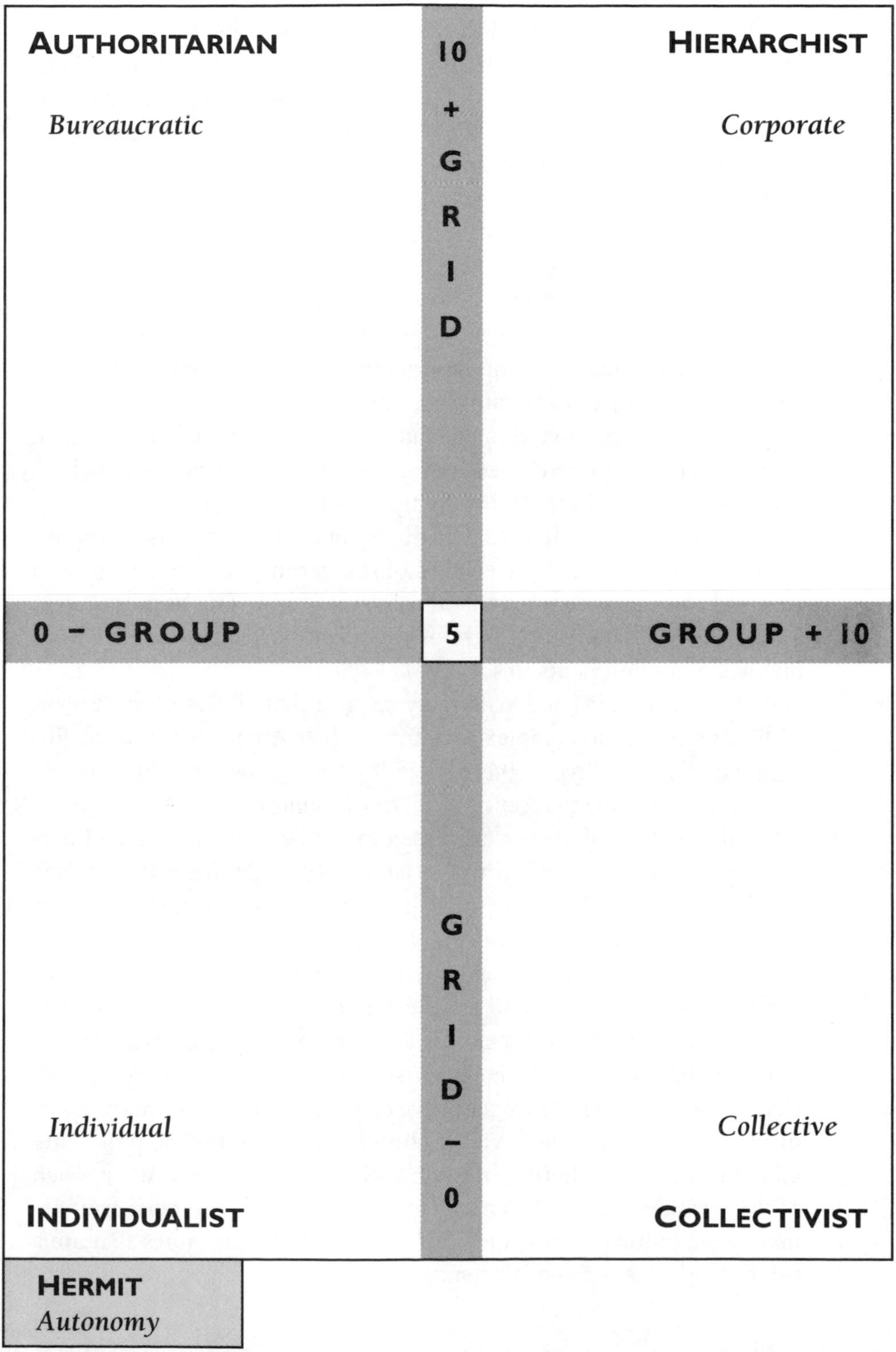

AUTHORITARIAN *Bureaucratic*

HIERARCHIST *Corporate*

10 + GRID

0 – GROUP | 5 | GROUP + 10

GRID – 0

Individual **INDIVIDUALIST**

Collective **COLLECTIVIST**

HERMIT *Autonomy*

The social preferences of the *collectivist* way of life focus on a very strong commitment to membership in a group. This commitment entails conforming to group value, consensus with group decisions, and participation in all group activities. The primary value with regard to individuals is one of equality. Role differences are minimized, and very little role specialization is encouraged. Even men and women may exchange roles when convenient, and individuals have a great deal of freedom and autonomy within the context of the group. The Aswinda case study illustrates the collectivist way of life. Aswinda had a great deal of freedom as an individual to choose his wives, travel up and down the river, and define his own economic activities as he pleased. At the same time, he was not free to violate the commitments of the group to its ancestral cults. When Aswinda made that decision, he immediately became an outsider and was excluded from most of the primary relationships that had been significant in his life up to that time.

The fifth way of life is that of the *hermit*. The hermit is a dropout from society. The social preferences of the hermit are to live alone and to avoid the social distinctions of role and group. The hermit prefers autonomy to relationships and, for the most part, survives apart from any wider commitments to society.

Thompson, Ellis, and Wildavsky suggest that all five of these ways of life are present in complex societies such as America, China, or Europe.[3] People who live in these societies may choose to follow one or more way of life. In my recent book, *Transforming Culture,* I have shown how all five ways of life are expressed in the denominational and personal preferences of American Christians. Each denomination forms its ways of life out of specific social preferences and cultural bias. Some contemporary groups, such as the Vineyard and Calvary Chapels, prefer an individualist way of life. More traditional denominations such as Presbyterian, Methodist, and Southern Baptist reflect a corporate hierarchist way of life. The Plymouth Brethren and Independent Baptist churches have embraced a collectivist way of life, whereas the Roman Catholic and Orthodox churches have emphasized the authoritarian way of life. The hermit is not a viable church option, but some professing Christians choose a hermit lifestyle and claim to worship alone. Each of these expressions of the church grows out of specific social arrangements and cultural constraints. All of them embrace values that are a product of these social arrangements.

Thompson, Ellis, and Wildavsky argue that these five ways of life are functionally necessary for one another and cannot exist without one another.[4] Each of them has relative strengths and weaknesses, and each depends upon some of the corrective contingency of the other ways of life.

Although it is typical of persons who have adopted a particular way of life to view that way of life as the best one, all of them are in fact deficient in significant ways. Their deficiencies arise specifically out of the social preferences that they have rejected. And to adopt any single way of life is to reject the preferences of the other ways of life. Further, when one concludes that one's way of life is the best, one also concludes that the other ways of life are inferior. This can produce a judgmental attitude that can lead to the rejection of others who are different.

The Scriptures speak of these arrangements as "empty way(s) of life" (1 Pet. 1:18 NIV). Although it is clear that God has created us with the capacity for culture and that our cultures are essential for our well-being, at the same time our cultures imprison us.[5] We often see our way of life as something that is more important than our relationship to God and our relationship to our neighbors. I have argued that we may best understand our cultures as "communities of the flesh."[6] The apostle Paul tells us in Galatians and Romans that we have been redeemed from life in the flesh and we are empowered through this work of Christ to live a new life in the Spirit. The church constitutes a community of the Spirit, not a community of the flesh. At the same time, we must continue to live in our bodies, which are flesh, and we must continue to live in our cultures, which are communities of the flesh. Every discussion then of the role of women in the church must take into account the five ways of life and their significance as part of the soil, or communities of the flesh, in which the church is rooted.

Gender Roles in Household and Family

The variation of gender roles in human cultures is a product of the unique histories and ways of life of each society. Households and families learn a particular way of life from their ancestors, and that way of life is then shaped in the struggle for subsistence and reproduction of each generation. The religious and social ideas of the culture also play an important part in the definition of gender roles and in their practical outworking in the daily lives of the people. Although personal and social histories create many particular characteristics in society and culture, it is possible to see gender patterns across cultures that reflect the five distinctive ways of life and that show some fundamental ideas that are part of the great idea traditions of culture.

Family as a Defensive Social Unit

In their study of household and family, Netting, Wilk, and Arnould have concluded that family is fundamentally a defensive social unit, focused on the reproduction of people and their culture.[7] When Aswinda's wives and families rejected him because of his newfound Christian faith, they did so based upon their understanding that his conversion was a threat to their identity and survival as a people and a culture. American Christians who have chosen to homeschool their children see it as a defensive act that will ensure that their children will acquire the values and beliefs that are important to them rather than the values and beliefs that will be taught in the public schools. Human families then see their domestic organization as the proper system to ensure the survival of their children and the reproduction of their way of life.

The definition of gender roles in society has its fundamental roots in the definition of family. Mary Douglas outlines Basil Bernstein's distinction between positional and personal family role systems in society.[8]

The first type of role structure she terms positional authoritarian families and the second, personal egalitarian families.

In positional authoritarian families, gender and other social roles are defined with reference to position, authority, and social expectations. For example, in our opening case study, Betty and Sebastian came from paternal hierarchist families in which authority is focused on the eldest in the senior generation of the family. The hierarchy is based upon relative age and sex. Elder women have authority over younger women, women past menopause have authority over women who are still bearing children, and so on. Men have authority over women; elder men have authority over younger men. The eldest brother acts as head of the family, and his younger brothers succeed him until all of his generation is dead. The case study of Katherine shows another variation of the positional authoritarian family. Katherine's mother gave up her career as a schoolteacher to become a wife. Her father was clearly head of her home, and her mother was subject to her father. In turn, she had a similar subordinate relationship to her husband and her family. However, in contrast to Betty and Sebastian's family, Katherine's mother and father established their own independent household and did not look to their siblings for assistance when they lost their farm in the Depression. Rather, her father and mother chose to endure a time of deprivation until they were able to re-establish themselves as an independent, self-sufficient household. Her father used the lumber from an abandoned building to build a temporary house for his family until he was able to re-establish himself economically and build a new home in a different location.

Personal egalitarian families define their genders and other roles on the basis of a sense of equality, skill, and relationship. In this type of family, roles are open and their content negotiable. We noted earlier that Isaac and Rebekah did not have rigid role expectations with regard to their sons, Jacob and Esau. Rather, each son was encouraged to pursue his personal interests and giftedness. Jacob became a man of the tents and Esau a man of the fields. I have personally observed families among the Deni Indians in Brazil occasionally reversing gender roles for men and women.[9] In these small Indian villages, people will sometimes arise early in the morning and decide that on this day the women will fish and the men will stay in the village and take care of the children and cook. At the end of the day, all bring the product of their labors to the center of the village plaza for a public feast. The men and women laugh and joke with each other about their competence and incompetence in doing one another's work. Although this on the surface seemed just to be joking behavior, when a spouse dies this experience is extremely valuable, as it enables the surviving spouse to continue to support his or her children in the essential functions of subsistence. A widow knows how to fish and to provide food for her children. A widower knows how to cook and process manioc for his children. Having these skills is utterly essential for their survival.

The case study of Aswinda provides another variation of the personal egalitarian family. Aswinda grew up in a household in which he learned the economic responsibilities of both men and women. Boys and girls learned to do all of the activities that are essential for the livelihood of their families. After they marry, women tend to focus on gardening and domestic chores while men focus on hunting, fishing, trading, and the heavier work of clearing the forest for new fields. In all of these personal egalitarian societies, gender roles tend to be flexible, and domestic authority involves negotiation and dialogue among men and women.

As is illustrated in figure 2, there is considerable variation in the structure of human households. Some families emphasize relationship between brothers (fraternal), whereas others emphasize the relationship between sisters (sororal). More commonly, however, families emphasize parent and grandparent generations in the organization of families and households. The independent nuclear families that are characteristic of middle-class American society focus on the married couple and their parental role in the establishing of that family unit. More traditional societies emphasize parental roles rather than those of husband and wife. This is evident in the story of Jacob and his sons in the Old Testament and in the paternal hierarchy of Jewish families as even evidenced in the New Testament account of Zacharias and Elizabeth. The Saramaccans are one of many illustrations of maternally focused families found in the matrilineal societies of the world. In these social groups, the relationship between mother and daughter has greater priority than other relationships within the family unit. And finally, societies such as the Samoans in Polynesia emphasize the grandparent, parent, grandchild linkage with equal emphasis on the descendents of men and women.

Marriage Defines Gender Roles

Anthropologists have spent much time and energy on the definition of marriage cross-culturally. Marriage in one form or another is found in every human society and is central to gender-based division of labor, the reproduction of children, socialization of those children, and the sharing and distribution of family resources. In preindustrial societies, gender roles are inextricably linked to the reproduction and socialization of children. In the vast majority of societies, reproduction of children outside of marriage is not acceptable. Although there are some societies in which this is not the case, they are typically societies that have been subject to dysfunctional economic exploitation. For example, in African-American societies in the Caribbean and in the United States, the reproduction and socialization of children has often been left largely to women, producing what anthropologists call matrifocal families. However, if one studies the African societies from which these people were brought, such families are nonexistent. This particular form of organization is the product of slavery, in which slave masters forcibly

Figure 2. Structural Variation in Households

	INDEPENDENT		CORPORATE
POSITIONAL	**AUTHORITARIAN** *Fraternal – Kansas farmers* *Sororal – Blacks in Chicago* *Paternal – Middle class whites*	10 + GRID	**HIERARCHIST** *Paternal – Yapese, Zacharias* *Maternal – Hopi of Arizona* *Grand Parental – Samoans*
	0 – GROUP	5	GROUP + 10
PERSONAL	*Fraternal – Deni Indians, Brazil* *Sororal – Sranan, Surinam* *Parental – Bonggi, Sabah* **INDIVIDUALIST**	GRID – 0	*Paternal – Jacob and his sons* *Maternal – Saramaccan, Navaho* *Grand Parental – Kapinga atoll* **COLLECTIVIST**
	HERMIT		

removed men from family relationships and promoted the women-centered family that slave owners designed to obtain more slaves through the reproduction of children.

It is important to recognize, however, that a gender-based division of labor varies significantly across cultures. For example, in the islands of Micronesia, the men of Yap fish and the women of Yap farm. But just a few hundred miles away, on the islands of Truk, the men farm and the women fish. The particulars of the gender-based division of labor vary from culture to culture, economy to economy. Similar variations occur in the patterns that are prescribed for the socialization of children and for the sharing and distribution of family resources. In some societies, resources are inherited through matrilineal lines; in other societies, resources are inherited through patrilineal lines. In some societies, resources are shared equally among male and female children; in other societies, the oldest child, male or female, will inherit, and the younger ones will be required to make their way and establish their own households.

Male Public Authority, Female Domestic Authority

The widespread occurrence of male authority has been debated in the current feminist literature in anthropology. Whether or not it is natural, the fact is that men exercise public authority in every known human society in the ethnographic literature.

Although there is much variation, a common theme in culture is that men exercise public authority and women exercise domestic authority for their families. There is much variation in terms of what is defined as public and what is defined as domestic. For example, in Betty and Sebastian's household, Betty has the responsibility to see that her children are taught the standards of the culture and that they learn the basic skills necessary to survive in the household. Betty is responsible for the daily provision of food for the household and for her husband. Sebastian, in contrast, is responsible to provide meat for the daily meals, and he steps in to take responsibility for any public action of his children or his wife that may be of concern to the wider community. If one of Sebastian's sons has stolen from another member of the community, Sebastian must go and plead on behalf of his son. Sebastian will be the one who acts on behalf of his sons and daughters to obtain permission for their marriages.

The Illusion of Matriarchal Societies

When we discuss this subject, some always ask, "What is the role of women in matriarchal societies?" It is important to distinguish between matrilineal and matriarchal societies. A matrilineal society is one in which inheritance patterns and social organization is structured around the relationship between mothers and daughters. In these societies, it is not the mothers and daughters who exercise public and political power. Rather, it is the mother's brother and the sister's son who provide the male leadership for the community. The matriarchal society, in contrast, is one that excludes males from leadership. In its ideal conception, the matriarchal society is one in which women exercise authority, and the structure proceeds from mothers to daughters to granddaughters, parallel to that understood for patriarchy.

Over the past hundred years, anthropologists have researched nearly all of the existing societies that have been accessible to them and have examined the literature available on cultures from the Greek and Roman period to the present. In all of this research, no living example has ever been found of a truly matriarchal society.[10] The idea of a matriarchal society is merely that—an idea. It does not exist to the best of our knowledge in living human cultures.

What then about matrilineal societies? In the study of matrilineal societies around the world, we find first of all that men are always in charge. In the classical matrilineal case studies from North America, Africa, and the Pacific Islands, the men in authority are the brothers of the women who constitute the core members of the kinship group. For example, in Aswinda's case on pp. 253–54, Aswinda was raised by his mother's brother as well as by his father. When his wives chose to divorce him, it was his wives' brothers who forcibly excluded him from returning to the villages to visit with his children. Because men are typically more powerful physically than women and it is men who are the fighters in societies, men exercise public power for their kinship groups.

In the Saramaccan case, if there is an important decision to be made, men and women gather together in the village and discuss the matter. The discussion is public and open and everyone may speak. Even the young are included in the conversation and may voice their views. However, after an extensive time of discussion, the elder men in the community will begin to speak and articulate what they believe is a consensus growing out of the discussion. When the community finally makes a decision, it is the elder men who articulate it and the elder men who implement it.

The Illusion of Biblical or Best Family Structures

Are any of the forms of household and family superior to the others? Each form of family clearly has social costs and benefits for its members. If one is to determine superiority or inferiority, one has to decide which of the benefits are superior and which are inferior to the others. If belonging to a group were superior to not belonging, then either the hierarchist or collectivist forms of family would be superior. On the other hand, if individual freedom or autonomy is valued, then the individualist or authoritarian families provide more of that benefit. Each of these benefits must be selected at the cost of others.

How do cultural expressions of gender roles oppose principles in Scripture? In my view, the ethnographic evidence overwhelmingly supports the complementarian perspective taken in this volume. Men exercise public and domestic authority in all four ways of life available to family and community. Women have a childbearing and nurturing role in all societies excepting modern industrial societies where gender-based roles are still the rule in households, but not necessarily in the workplace. These practices are consistent with prior conclusions in this book that the order of creation in Genesis defines gender roles for men and women along these precise lines.

Yet Scripture seems to say little about preference for one or another of the five ways of life. Rather, it has much to say about domestic relationships in all of them.[11] Although biblical texts do not have much material on families, the places where we do see it show evidence of more than one way of life (See figure 3). Earlier we described Isaac and Rebekah as embracing an individualist way of life. A study of the life of David shows the family relationships in Israel having adopted a hierarchist way of life. We see a similar pattern in the case material provided on Zacharias and Elizabeth in the Gospel of Luke. I have shown elsewhere that the story of the Prodigal Son illustrates the sins of the hierarchist family way of life. The key principle derived from the Prodigal Son is that of the loving father. What Jesus is teaching in this parable is that the roles of the hierarchist way of life, which are best illustrated

Figure 3. Family Social Games in Scripture

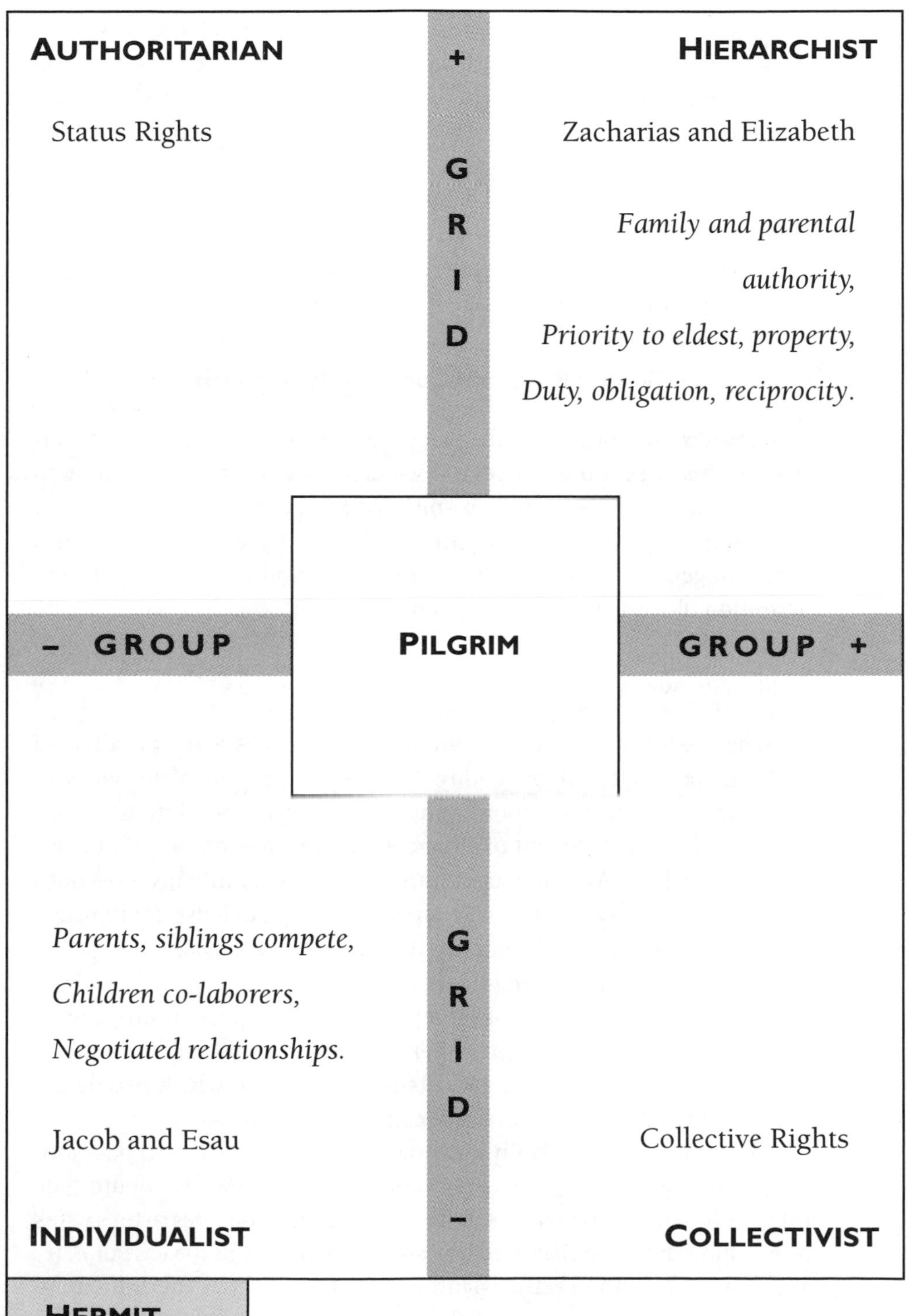

by the elder brother, are not the rules by which God relates to us. God is like the father in the story, the loving father who welcomes back the son who has violated every norm that is proper for a family of their kind. The elder brother, in contrast, acts in accord with the expectations of the hierarchist way of life. He rebukes his father for his generosity, reminds him of his own obedience, and demands proper treatment because of his obedience to the Law. Culture seeks to obtain righteousness through law. The story of the Prodigal Son illustrates that God's righteousness is a gift of a loving Father to sinful sons.

Gender Roles and Community Authority

How do roles of women in leadership vary across cultures? The answer to this question is essential if we are going to understand how to provide biblical guidance for women with regard to the questions of leadership in the church. The patterns that we have already seen with regard to gender roles in the household and family carry over into the definition of women's roles in community.

Public Authority: The Domain of Men

The definition of authority and community has many parallels to authority in household and family. The general purpose of authority in community is to provide coordination for labor, the resolution of conflict, and the establishment of alliances and defenses on behalf of community members. Although community labor frequently involves both men and women, conflict resolution, alliance, and defense are typically the prerogative of males. Regardless of the particular way of life engaged, public authority and leadership are exercised by men.

In spite of this general observation, a more important question is what role women have within the community decision-making context. By looking once again at the two distinctive ways in which people define social roles, we can gain deeper insight into this issue.

When authority in family and community are focused on positional authoritarian type roles, women generally are assigned to subordinate roles within these contexts. As in the case of Katherine, the pastor's wife's role is subordinate to that of pastor and husband. Or in the case of Betty and Sebastian in the Pacific island community, Betty is subordinate to her husband, his older brother, and their older sisters in the community. In those islands, an older sister would not inherit property unless she had no brother at all. A similar situation characterized the Greek city of Corinth to which Paul wrote his first and second epistles to the Corinthians. Greek families and communities were positional authoritarian in their definition of social roles, and women in those contexts were placed in roles that were subordinate and inferior to men. Although the book of Acts makes several references to prominent Greek women, those prominent women were recognized because of their social class. In the context of their families or their community relationships, these prominent women would have been subordinate to prominent men.

In families and communities where social roles are defined on a personal egalitarian basis, we find the definition of gender roles more flexible, providing for greater participation for women in family and community decisions. We have already observed how men and women in Saramaccan society participate together in public discussion before community decisions are made. From conversations with Saramaccan informants, it is clear that the opinions of women are very important and are considered in these community discussions. At the same time, the articulation of consensus is done by the elder men at the conclusion of the public discussion. The story of Isaac and Rebekah shows similar dialogue occurring from time to time between Rebekah and Isaac. Although one might argue that this is a reflection of Rebekah's personality, careful study of the whole extended family shows similar personal negotiating between men and men, as well as between men and women.

The case study of Deborah, the prophetess and judge in Judges 4 and 5, illustrates how communities that define roles on a personal egalitarian basis may allow women significant roles of leadership. A careful analysis of the social context in the book of Judges suggests that the people were engaging in a patrilineal expression of either the individualist or the collectivist way of life.[12] In each of these ways of life, roles are defined in reference to personal egalitarian standards rather than positional authoritarian ones. The details are too extensive for us to analyze here, so I will just invite the interested reader to examine more deeply the social context, evident in the text, that characterized this time period.

The text in Judges 4 makes it clear that Deborah had a leading role in Israel because of her relationship to the Lord—He spoke through her as a prophetess. Her effectiveness as a leader was not on the basis of a particular social role that she occupied. In fact, the text makes it clear that she was a wife, which in a positional authoritarian community would exclude her from any kind of leadership role. It is her personal giftedness that was recognized by the people in Israel. They came to her for the resolution of their disputes, and they responded to her when she called them in the name of the Lord to follow her into battle. The text makes an interesting contrast between the people of Israel and the Canaanites. The Canaanites operated with the positional authoritarian role system that had clear authority placed in kings and generals. Israel, in contrast, had no one with an ambition for generalship or kingship. Barak was unwilling to accept leadership unless Deborah would go with him.

We see then that the social preferences of the community with regard to the definition of role are very important in understanding the potential for women in leadership. When the social preferences prescribe positional authoritarian roles, then the very nature of those definitions may preclude women from leadership responsibilities. On the other hand, when the social preferences allow for personal giftedness and flexible definition of roles, then women may have many more opportunities for participation and for leadership in community activities. Each of the ways of life defines different types of coordination and centralization that are possible, and each defines in distinctive ways how women may or may not participate in leadership. Each of these ways of life then has consequent costs and benefits to the people who participate in them.

Spiritual Authority: Open to Men and Women

A fascinating variation in the study of authority cross-culturally is the fact that spiritual power and knowledge are open to both men and women. The key variable in this question is one of spiritual power. As we have already seen in the case study of Deborah, Deborah had access to spiritual power that other people did not have. This is not a peculiar incident in the history of Israel, as is noted in chapter 3, but something that is more widespread in human cultures. People around the world have recognized that spiritual powers are not the prerogative of men alone. In fact, in some situations (such as that with Deborah), women appear to have greater access to spiritual power than men.

Issues of spiritual power and knowledge are also affected by the social preferences that people choose. In positional authoritarian societies, knowledge tends to be held by men and transferred to men. In these societies if women seem to have unusual spiritual power, they are often considered dangerous and may be accused of witchcraft or other dark powers. If that particular society precludes women from legitimate spiritual power, then it is probably inevitable that those who have power will be condemned for it. This is illustrated by such famous examples as Joan of Arc in France and the many women saints in European history; however, persecution is not always the end result for women with spiritual power.

In societies where gender roles are defined in a personal egalitarian framework, knowledge and power are also seen as personal and thus available to both men and women. Deborah the judge and Huldah the prophetess are examples in the history of Israel. In Saramaccan society in Surinam, there are both men and women who have access to ancestral spirits. Although men typically lead in ritual performances, they are not the ones who have exclusive insight or power.

In some very hierarchical societies, one finds countercultural movements that reflect a correction to the abuses of the major themes in the culture. For example, traditional Korean society is extremely authoritarian and violent. The male rulers and military leaders exercise absolute authority and are at times abusive to their own people as well as to their enemies. As a countercurrent within Korean society, one finds a strong clan structure with a traditional religious belief system that focuses on spirit mediums and curing rituals. In the clan context, Korean women provided spiritual leadership as shaman and spirit mediums. The shamanist expression of Korean life was personal egalitarian in its definition of roles, providing a striking contrast to the positional authoritarian governing structure.

Which Cultures Are Biblical?

Which of these ways of life, or which of the cultures of the world, are more biblical in their gender roles and values? If we were able to do an item analysis of cultural values and biblical values, we might, with some very rigorous and detailed research, show some societies having more overlap with biblical values than others. Yet, in my opinion, this would be an unprofitable exercise. We might be able to do a cluster analysis ranking cultures that are more or less biblical, but it would not lead us to the biblical solution for the question.

I have argued that all cultures constitute prisons of disobedience to the people who live in them.[13] All of them seek to impose on their people standards of righteousness that come by cultural law. Although specific values in a given culture may be biblically centered, the power games of every culture are evidence of the rebellion of its people and their leaders against God.

The danger in seeking to validate one of these five ways of life as "biblical culture" is subsequent drifting toward idolatry. Once we believe we have the right system, then we are tempted to trust the system instead of God to lead us into righteousness. Samuel's retirement sermon in 1 Samuel 12 warns precisely against this error. The people in Israel were convinced that if they could shift from the collectivist way of life that characterized the period of the judges to the hierarchist way of life that was found in the Canaanite communities around them, they would thrive against their enemies. Samuel gave them the king and the way of life that a kingship entailed, but he warned them that only their obedience to God would save them.

I have argued elsewhere that Christians are not called to a biblical culture, but rather they are called to lives of pilgrimage.[14] The book of 1 Peter provides a powerful argument for living in whatever culture you have been planted and living as people of God, a "spiritual house" (2:5), and as aliens and strangers who live such good lives that the people around you glorify your Father in heaven. The goal of Christians is to live within whatever culture God has called them, but to live transformed lives as pilgrims and strangers who are the people of God.

Cultural Universals re: Gender?

What universals have anthropologists found regarding gender roles? The first and most obvious are biological. Women give birth to children and nurse them. Men are physiologically stronger than women (but perhaps not biologically stronger) and therefore take the heavy-labor tasks that are essential to the well-being of their wives and children.

Anthropologists also recognize that every society has a gender-based division of labor. However, they note that this gender-based division is highly variable and that oftentimes tasks assigned in one society to men will be assigned to women in another. The universal is the gender-based division, but the actual tasks of labor are highly variable in terms of whether they are done by men or women.

Many aspects of human society are nearly universal. What “nearly universal” means is that anthropologists have found a few exceptions to these patterns, but they are clearly exceptions and not the rule. I have referred earlier to the male public authority/female domestic authority dichotomy. This is very widespread in human societies, although anthropologists have found some exceptions.[15]

A second nearly universal characteristic is the centrality of marriage to the definition of gender roles. Again, there are some notable exceptions, such as the matrifocal family I have described for the Caribbean among ex-slave populations. However, marriage does not define gender in a singular way, but rather in accord with the ways of life. When gender roles in marriage are flexible and negotiable, then gender roles in the wider community also tend to be flexible and negotiable. When gender roles in marriage are positional and prescribed, then gender roles in the wider society also tend to be positional and prescribed.

Gender Roles in the Church Community

In concluding this chapter, we will reflect on the meaning of a cross-cultural framework for gender roles in the church community. The universal or near-universal pattern of male public authority in every human society suggests that this is a natural pattern for human communities, including the church. This would be consistent with the complementarian understanding of the relationship of man and woman from creation. However, this must be balanced with the evidence we have seen concerning spiritual authority. A very brief observation of the distribution of authority in societies shows a much higher prominence of women with spiritual wisdom, insight, and power than one finds in terms of political authority. In fact, one can point to thousands of women in human history who have had dramatic spiritual impacts on their cultures, whereas only a few have occupied such significant roles as queen or chief ruler in their political context. Since by definition the church is a spiritual context, and by cultural evidence women have much more prominence in spiritual than in political context, women should be expected to have spiritual roles in the context of the church community.

Although there are official leadership roles in the church such as bishops or elders, spiritual leadership does not focus on positional authoritarian status. David Bennett has observed that the words *leader* and *leadership* do not appear in the Gospels, and infrequently in the Epistles.[16] Jesus did not use any of the metaphors from the Greek root *arche,* to rule, for His disciples. Rather, Bennett suggests that the biblical metaphors used by our Lord "describe the followers as members of a spiritual family (brother, child), and . . . picture them as servants (of the Lord and of one another)."[17] If we focus on leadership as service through the power of the Spirit, such spiritual leadership is then exercised in the community of believers by both men and women.

Pilgrim Lifestyle for Gender Transformation

Recognizing that both men and women have spiritual gifts, and that both men and women experience the power of the Holy Spirit to serve the kingdom of God, we may then ask, What are appropriate social and cultural roles for men and women in the practical and spiritual life of the church? To respond to this question, it is important for us to understand that our local churches are rooted in culture and are participants in specific ways of life.

Once we have understood that the church is a participant in a way of life, then we may examine the special problems that arise because of that way of life. Figure 4 illustrates how spouses sin against one another differently in each of the four ways of life. Authoritarian spouses demand that the other play by the rules, and the rules become more important than the person. Collectivist spouses demand equality and conformity, to the exclusion of individuality. Individualists place "me" first, and hierarchists manipulate one another with demands for conformity to rule and group. It is my perception that the sins men and women commit against one another in the home are the same sins that they commit against one another in a public place or the church.

The church then will be subject to the same social sins that affect a family in a given way of life. Once we understand the root of these problems, we may begin to discover the steps required for a church to become a "spiritual house" as opposed to a community of the flesh.

The greater question is, How do we live transformed lives as pilgrims and strangers, serving in the church of the Lord Jesus Christ? To put it bluntly, the application of Scripture varies with the blindness toward sin.

Figure 4. Sins of Husbands in Four Social Games

AUTHORITARIAN	**+**	**HIERARCHIST**
Status Rights		Corporate Rights
Self-sufficiency, isolation, *Authority without love,* *Rules over persons.*	**G R I D**	*Dependency relationships,* *Conditional love,* *Social humiliation of spouse.*
– GROUP	**PILGRIM** *Loving fathers* *Loving husbands*	**GROUP +**
Advance self-interest, *Ends justify the means,* *Deception, intrigue.*	**G R I D**	*Controlling relationships,* *Forced conformity,* *Group threat, manipulation.*
Individual Rights		Collective Rights
INDIVIDUALIST	**–**	**COLLECTIVIST**
HERMIT		

Like a pair of glasses, the prescription must correct the problem of sight. This will lead to different corrections for members of a Plymouth Brethren Church (where the members participate in a collectivist way of life) than for Presbyterians (where members value hierarchy as well as commitment to the group). Likewise, participation in an individualist community such as the Vineyard or Calvary Chapel will require a different correction toward defining appropriate roles for men and women in ministry. All of them will be much more effective if they abandon the preoccupation with leadership and focus once again on the metaphors of ministry that are clearly articulated in the New Testament. When we understand that our roles are servants, brothers and sisters, lowly shepherds, it changes how we see our significance and our service to one another.

PART SIX

WOMAN AND MAN IN CHURCH MINISTRY

CHAPTER TWELVE

THE EPHESIAN BACKGROUND OF PAUL'S TEACHING ON WOMEN'S MINISTRY

Clinton Arnold and Robert Saucy

Introduction

In the belief that the ministry of women and men in the church flows out of their created nature, we have sought insight from Scripture teaching and example as well as pertinent secular studies concerning the real nature of men and women and how they are designed by their Creator to live together in this life. With this background, we must now turn to the teaching of Scripture specifically addressed to the question of women's church ministry and the whole topic of men and women working together in ministry. In this chapter and the next, we will look at the three scriptural texts that directly give instructions concerning women's ministry in the church: 1 Timothy 2:9–15; 1 Corinthians 11:3–16; and 14:34–36.

These teachings are vital to the question of women's ministry and important in the contemporary debate between complementarians and egalitarians. However, the fact that only three passages give specific instructions supports the belief stated above that a full understanding of the relationship of women and men in the ministry of the church must be derived from the entire biblical portrayal of man and woman according to God's design in creation. How all of this works in the ministry of the church will be explored in the final chapter.

The apostle's teaching in 1 Timothy 2:9–15 forbidding women to "teach or exercise authority over a man" is the most explicit directive in Scripture related to the question of women's activity in the church. Located within a passage dealing with the gathered church meeting (2:8–15), the section opens with concerns for men's prayer "in every place" (terminology indicating "meeting-places"[1]) and is followed by the various instructions related to women's adornment and limits in ministry without any indication of a change of context. Although set within the context of the church service, these instructions also have wider meaning for the Christian community. The concern for appropriate dress and the adornment of "good works" for women surely goes beyond the meeting time. So also the issues of "teaching" and "authority" are probably related to the ministry of elders or bishops, which is applicable to the Christian community whether gathered or not.[2] The instructions of our passages therefore cannot be limited to the gathered church meeting as if they have nothing to say relative to Christian situations other than the formal church worship service.

Because of their centrality to the discussion, the instructions concerning women in the church have rightfully evoked much discussion with almost every important word and phrase subject for debate.[3] What exactly is Paul prohibiting? All teaching? Erroneous teaching? Is it legitimate authority or domineering authority that is forbidden? Is this teaching intended to be applied universally to all churches at all times, or only to a specific situation?

We will be looking at the passage itself in search of the answers to these questions in the next chapter. But, before we do, it is important to consider the historical background into which Paul's instructions came. Where this can be ascertained, knowing something of the situation of those addressed is helpful in understanding what is said to them. This is all the more important in the case of this text, because those who reject Paul's prohibition of women teaching as not being normative for today do so on the basis that it relates only to the situation in Ephesus at that time. In this chapter, therefore, we will briefly consider the overall situation of women in the culture at Ephesus and the specific nature of the problem related to women that provided occasion for the apostle's teaching.

The Cultural Context of Social Roles for Women in Ephesus

Our ability to understand the social context of Ephesus—the city where Timothy was ministering when Paul wrote to him—has been greatly assisted in recent years by archaeological discovery. Numerous inscriptions have been discovered in Ephesus and in many other cities from the west coast of Asia Minor. These inscriptions shed some very important, and somewhat surprising, light on the issue of the status and role of women in the civic and cultural life of the city.

Although it is sometimes portrayed that women in the Roman Empire were totally excluded from civic life, political power, business affairs, and the ability to gain an education, the situation for women in Asia Minor was different. There is evidence that women were afforded a much greater freedom than is often thought.

Women in Public and Civic Life

In a very important recent study, Paul Trebilco has accumulated and presented the inscriptional evidence attesting to the role of women in civic positions in western Asia Minor.[4] The chart on the following page summarizes this evidence.

It is frequently assumed in some of the literature that women in Ephesus (and in Asia Minor and the entire Roman world, for that matter) lacked education and the opportunity for an education. This has been drastically overstated. The women who held the various offices listed on the chart clearly had to have a high level of education in order to fulfill the duties of their offices.

But, more important, there is now inscriptional evidence that women served in some of the cities in a position that would be a close functional equivalent of our "superintendent of schools" that is, in the capacity of a gymnasiarch *(gymnasiarchos)*. The "gymnasium" was the center for education in a Greek city. It was also a place for exercise and athletic events. The "gymnasiarch" had oversight of the intellectual training of the citizens and for the general management of the facility. Inscriptions dating from the first to the third centuries attest to forty-eight

Prytanis

- The highest civic office, comparable to our office of mayor. In some cities, however, the administrative power of the city resided more with the town council *(boulē)* while the *prytanis* still remained a position of very high rank.
- There is evidence of twenty-eight women who held this post in eight different cities in Asia Minor. The inscriptions date from the first to the third centuries.

Stephanophoros

- Literally, "the one who wears the crown." This was the title for the principal civic official in certain cities of Asia Minor.
- There is evidence of thirty-seven women who held this post in seventeen different cities in Asia Minor. The inscriptions date from the second to the third centuries.

  (To attain either of these offices, the women would have already had to hold lesser civic or religious offices.)

Dēmiourgos

- A significant civic office in certain Asia Minor cities.
- There is evidence of eighteen women who held this post in fourteen different cities in Asia Minor. The inscriptions date from the first to the third centuries.

Agōnothetis

- The official responsible for athletic contests and competitions in music and drama connected with the games and festivals of the city.
- There is evidence of ten women who held this post in six different cities in Asia Minor. The inscriptions date from the first century B.C. to the third century A.D.
- There is also inscriptional evidence for women holding a variety of other offices in cities in Asia Minor, including:
  - *Panēgyriarach*—the official in charge of the festivals.
  - *Hipparchos*—the highest civic office in the city of Cyzicus, Phrygia.
  - *Gerousia*—an aristocratic society of elders.
  - *Stratēgos*—an official who served on the city council.
  - *Asiarch*—the foremost title of Asia, usually given to wealthy benefactors.
  - *Dekaprōtos*—one of the ten principal tax officers of a city.

women who served as gymnasiarchs in twenty-three cities of Asia Minor and the coastal islands. This suggests that women not only had access to education, but also that in many places they were leading the educational system.

This evidence stands in contrast to what we generally know of the plight of women at the beginning of the Roman Empire. The Roman family was known to be very patriarchal. The man was clearly the head of the household (the *paterfamilias*), and women were expected to fulfill an exclusively domestic role. With few exceptions, women were not given the opportunity of education, had no vote, and were given no role in government. But beginning in the late republic (second century B.C.) and early imperial period, a much greater array of opportunities opened up for women. The famous British classicist Michael Grant observed that "the Roman women of the late Republic possessed a freedom and independence almost unparalleled until the present century. . . . But it was during the tormented years that followed Julius Caesar's death that powerful women really came into their own."[5] He continued, "This period was an unparalleled phenomenon in the ancient world. . . . [W]omen never attained such pinnacles of power again."[6]

Nevertheless, there appears to be more evidence for women participating in all levels of civic life in western Asia Minor than elsewhere in the empire. As we will see later, this may be due not only to broad cultural trends in the empire, but also to the influence of the religious traditions and practices of Asia Minor.

In spite of the fact that women were participating broadly in public leadership, one must still recognize the overwhelming male leadership in the culture. The Roman man is still the *paterfamilias*, and there is a far greater proportion of men in civic leadership than women. What is important for us to recognize, however, is the fact that women were involved in public positions of leadership at all levels.

Women in the Local Cults

Goddess worship predominated among the religions of Asia Minor. In Ephesus alone, Artemis/Diana, Aphrodite, Athena, Cybele (*Magna Mater*), Demeter, Kore/Persephone, Hestia Boulaia, Hekate, Isis, Tyche, Agathe Tyche, and Tyche Soteira were all worshiped.[7] In most of these cults, women held significant positions of leadership.

This is particularly true in the cult of Isis, an Egyptian deity worshiped in Ephesus. Archaeologists have discovered the foundation of her temple in the middle of the State Agora in Ephesus. In an important monograph entitled *The Cult of Isis Among Women in the Graeco-Roman World,* Sharon Kelly Heyob suggested that the Isis cult was an important advocate for freedom and opportunity for women.[8] One of the strongest pieces of evidence is a well-known Isis aretology (an ascription of praise) in which the goddess is praised for giving women power equal to that of men (*P. Oxy.* 1380. 214–16). Women held the places of prominence in the cult of Isis, functioning as priestesses of the cult during the Roman imperial period.[9] For this and other reasons, Isis is extolled as the goddess of women. In the Isis-hymn of Cyme, in Asia Minor (about 95 kilometers north of Ephesus), Isis claims, "I am the one who is called goddess among women."[10]

Of course, the most popular deity of all in Ephesus was the goddess Artemis (also known as Diana, her Roman name). Because she was celebrated as a goddess of fertility and childbirth, Artemis was often allied (and sometimes identified) with Isis as well as the principal fertility goddess of Asia Minor, Cybele (known as "the great mother," *Magna Mater*). Anyone who has seen the cultic image of the Ephesian Artemis has been immediately struck by the conspicuous rows of bulbous objects on her breasts. Interpretations vary as to precisely what they are, but most scholars are in agreement that they illustrate the fertility motif in some way.

Both in the cult of Artemis and in the cult of Cybele, there is a prominent theme of fertility and potency independent from male virility and strength. The top order of priests in both cults were eunuchs—called *megabyzoi* in the Artemis cult and *galloi* in the Cybele cult. Although it is not unusual for a deity to be served by eunuch priests, their physical transformation was carried out voluntarily and in a crude manner by their own hands in an ecstatic worship of their goddess. This drastic measure appears to have arisen from the desire to assimilate themselves to the goddess in a mystical unity and even extended to the donning of female clothing and having their hair dressed and waved like women to complete the process.[11] Markus Barth intimates that male castration may have been understood by the devotees as enhancing the glory of the female deity at the expense of the male.[12]

Although the *megabyzoi* stood at the top of the priestly ranks, many priestesses ministered in the cult of Artemis at Ephesus. In fact, three classes of priestesses have been discerned: the *mellierai,* the *hierai,* and the *parierai.*[13] References to priestesses in the cultic ritual of Cybele also appear quite often in the literature.[14] There is one account, for example, of a Cybele sanctuary at Piraeus in Achaia where there were no priests; the sanctuary was run by a priestess selected annually by a cultic society.[15]

Women were thus accustomed to having prominent positions of leadership in the goddess cults of Ephesus and western Asia Minor. In some ways, the cults served as symbols of freedom from the constraints placed upon women in traditional Greco-Roman society.

Women in Judaism

Given the prominence of women in the civic and religious life of Asia Minor, it is natural to wonder if this had any impact on the role of women in the Judaism of the area. At first glance, one would be inclined to assume not. The literature of Rabbinic Judaism contains many statements clearly limiting the role of women:

- Rabbi Eliezer says, "If any man gives his daughter a knowledge of the Law it is as though he taught her lechery." (Mishnah, *Sotah* 3.4)
- Philo insisted that women should avoid civic affairs. He also taught that "women are best suited to the indoor life which never strays from the house. . . . A woman, then, should not be a busybody, meddling with matters outside her household concerns, but should seek a life of seclusion." (*De specialibus legibus* 3.169–71)
- Rabbi Judah ben Elai taught, "One must utter three doxologies every day: Praise God that he did not create me a heathen! Praise God that he did not create me a woman! Praise God that he did not create me an illiterate person!" (Tosefta, *Berakot* 7.18)[16]
- "The woman does not read out of the Torah for the sake of the honor of the congregation." (*Megillah* 23a [Baraitha])[17]

Archaeological discoveries of Jewish inscriptions in Asia Minor have cast doubt on the extent to which statements like the above typified the beliefs and practices of Jews throughout the empire. Specifically, three inscriptions have been discovered that identify women as rulers of their local synagogues. The most important is a second-century inscription from Smyrna (just north of Ephesus) that says, "Rufina, a Jewess, head of the synagogue *(archisynagogos)*, built this tomb for her freed slaves and the slaves raised in her house."[18]

The notion of a woman as a ruler of the synagogue seemed so inconsistent with Judaism as we know it from the rabbis that older interpreters thought that the title must simply be honorific and not functional. Some scholars therefore thought it was simply a title of honor given to the wife of a synagogue ruler. Others said it was simply a title of honor (perhaps for the donation of a large sum of money), but devoid of any overtones that a woman actually performed the duties of a synagogue ruler.

In an important dissertation for Harvard University, Bernadette Brooten has convincingly argued that the title was functional.[19] Since then, many scholars have agreed that the title was functional and that there were a few instances of women rising to the office of *archisunagogos*.

One of the main lines of argument in support of the functional interpretation of the title is the discovery of inscriptions giving women other leadership titles for the synagogue in Diaspora locations. These include "leader" *(archēgissa, archēgos)*, "elder" *(presbytera, presbyteressa, presbytis)*, "mother of the synagogue," and "priestess" *(hiereia, hierissa)*.[20]

How is it possible for the Jewish communities of Asia Minor to have moved so far away from the rabbinic convictions about the role of women? In his Cambridge monograph on *Jewish Communities in Asia Minor*, Paul Trebilco rightly concluded, "It seems that local factors were a strong formative influence on the Jewish communities."[21] In other words, the Jewish communities in Ephesus, Smyrna, and elsewhere in Asia Minor were not able to resist the prevailing cultural trends of the day. If women ascended to leadership in all levels of the civic life of the city as well as in many of the local religions, why were Jewish women prohibited from exercising leadership in their synagogues?

The Significance of the Cultural Social Role of Women for Interpreting 1 Timothy 2

How does the picture of the role of women in the cultural context of Ephesus affect our understanding of Paul's instructions concerning women in his letter to that church? Surely some of the Gentile and Jewish women in Ephesus who had received Christ and joined the Christian community were accustomed to participating in leadership, either in the civic affairs of the city or in the religious cults from which they came. Would they not have automatically assumed that they could work into positions of leadership in the house churches they had joined? This now seems to be a very likely scenario for understanding why this issue surfaced in Ephesus.

At the very least, the historical evidence we have presented demonstrates that some other reconstructions of the situation at Ephesus are far less likely. It is not probable that Paul was advocating a conformity to the prevailing culture on the issue of women's roles as a means of facilitating the evangelistic outreach of the church to the community. Those who have taken this position typically assume a far greater limitation on women than what appears to have been the case. Nor is it likely that Paul was addressing a situation in which the women were uneducated and, therefore, were disqualified from teaching on that basis alone.[22] Clearly, the women who attained civic offices were educated and, assuredly, a woman serving as "superintendent of schools" was very well educated.

We are left, then, with the recognition of a situation in Ephesus where women were converting to Christianity and desiring to attain leadership roles in the church similar to what they held in society. Aware of this situation, Paul addressed this issue because he did not want these churches to cave in to the cultural pressures of the day and violate a deep-set theological conviction about order between men and women.

False Teaching and Women in Paul's Instruction

Beyond the general roles of women in the Ephesian culture, the apostle's concern for "sound doctrine" that is echoed throughout both letters to Timothy indicates that the health of the Christian community at Ephesus was threatened by false teaching. Attempts to articulate the nature of this false teaching and how it informs Paul's instruction, particularly concerning women in 1 Timothy 2, have led to a variety of conclusions. In a book-length study, Richard and Catherine Kroeger concluded that the teaching combated by Paul was a combination of Gnostic or proto-Gnostic traditions and female-dominated religions centered around the cult of the great goddess Artemis, whose shrine was located at Ephesus. Included in this heretical teaching was the belief that the feminine was the primal source of all life and that special revelation through certain women brought true knowledge for mankind. All of this made Ephesus "a bastion of feminine supremacy in religion." Women were not only influenced by such teaching, but became propagators of the teaching themselves.[23]

How this postulation of the problem behind Paul's teaching became the lens for understanding the text is evident in the following explanation. "If 1 Timothy 2:12 is translated as prohibiting women from claiming the power of origin, it fits with the refutation which follows. Women are forbidden to teach that female activity brought man into existence because, according to the Scriptures, Adam was created first. Eve, for all her desire to bring enlightenment, did not bring gnosis but transgression."[24] The assumption of this particular problem as the background for Paul's teaching thus easily leads to the conclusion that his instruction concerning women is limited to a specific historical problem and says nothing about a normative relation between men and women.

Neither the passage itself nor anything in the Pastoral Epistles provides any evidence that this was in fact the nature of the false teaching at Ephesus at the time of the writing of 1 Timothy. The evidence adduced in support of this hypothesis is actually from much later, leading one reviewer of the Kroegers' work to conclude that it is "really nothing more than a hypothetical reconstruction based on disparate features of pagan religion in Ephesus and Anatolia, and on a few much later [3rd–4th century] Gnostic documents."[25] The same basic theme of the prominence of the feminine in religion, but focused more narrowly on the influence of the cult of the mother goddess Artemis, is proposed by others as the object of the apostle's concern.[26] This also, however, finds no supporting evidence in any of the statements of the Pastoral Letters.

Another suggestion for the false teaching is that it was a form of overrealized eschatology. According to this view, believers were already resurrected spiritually (2 Tim. 2:15–18; cf. 1 Tim. 1:18–20). This led to an otherworldly ascetic practice of abstaining from certain foods and prohibiting marriage (1 Tim. 4:3; Titus 1:14–15). It may also have promoted a tendency toward an eschatological emancipation from all social orders, including those related to women. This would account for the apostle's instructions concerning women in the text before us (cf. also

1 Tim. 5:11–15) and slaves (1 Tim. 6:1–2; Titus 2:9–10).[27] Although this proposal has the advantage of seeking support from statements of the Pastoral Letters themselves and provides an explanation for some of the apostle's teaching, the evidence is not sufficient to make it conclusive.

It is probably best to acknowledge that the specific nature of the heresy of Paul's opponents in the Pastorals is not clear. From statements in the letters themselves, we know that it had "certain Jewish aspects (e.g., its special handling of the law and its interest in specifically Jewish 'myths'), . . . certain esoteric aspects (myths and genealogies, controversial questions, and 'antitheses' identified as knowledge . . .), and in Ephesus at least . . . strongly ascetic rules requiring abstention from marriage and certain foods—and two false teachers there maintained that the resurrection was already past."[28] It thus appears to be "a kind of Judaizing Gnosticism" similar to that found elsewhere in the New Testament era, especially in Colossians.[29] What does seem clear is that the identification of the false teaching in question with a Gnostic teaching of a later time is erroneous. Kelly rightly concludes,

> It is in fact unrealistic to look to the well-known Gnostic, or near-Gnostic, systems of the second century for light on the teaching which provoked the Pastorals. Everything suggests that it was something much more elementary; and it is significant that much of the writer's polemic is directed, not so much against any specific doctrine, as against the general contentiousness and loose living it encouraged. It is perhaps best defined as a Gnosticizing form of Jewish Christianity. . . . There is no need, unless we are driven by compelling evidence to the contrary, to look outside the first century, or indeed the span of Paul's life, for such an amalgam of Jewish and Gnostic traits.[30]

Conclusion

No doubt there was something in the false teaching and the entire cultural environment of Ephesus related to the apostle's instructions concerning women in 1 Timothy 2. Our knowledge of the social roles of women in the cultural context of Ephesus suggests that a problem may have been women in the church desiring leadership roles similar to those they held in society, which would have denied the creation order between man and woman.

In sum, our knowledge of the cultural background and of any false teaching that is particularly related to women from historical study as well as the biblical context is limited and, therefore, makes it impossible to interpret Paul's words as a specific reply to a particular issue. It should be added emphatically that even if we did have a thorough knowledge of the problem that the apostle was addressing, it would not mean that the content of his corrective teaching involved truth that was limited to that specific problem. Paul frequently addressed occasional problems troubling particular churches in his letters. In most instances, his solutions to the problems are not ad hoc statements, but applications of some permanent truth concerning God, His creation, or redemption in Christ. For example, he addresses the problem of disunity in the church at Corinth by reminding them that they were all baptized into Christ who is not divided, i.e., a permanent truth for a situational problem. Thus, even if we knew unquestionably the full nature of the problem that prompted Paul to include these instructions concerning women in 1 Timothy 2, that background information could not tell us whether his teaching is to be considered normative for the church of all time or applicable only to that situation. The answer to that question must be derived from the teaching itself.

CHAPTER THIRTEEN

PAUL'S TEACHING ON THE MINISTRY OF WOMEN

Robert Saucy

Introduction

Having looked in the previous chapter at the Ephesian cultural and church background for the apostle's instruction concerning women in 1 Timothy 2:11–12, we must now turn to the teaching itself. What exactly was the apostle telling the church in his day, and how does it apply to us in the church today? In addition to this primary passage, we will also consider the teaching of 1 Corinthians 11:3–16 and 14:34–36 in relation to women's activity in the church.

Instructions Concerning Women's Learning, Teaching, and Exercising Authority (1 Tim. 2:11–12)

The General Meaning and Application of Paul's Instructions

The primary concern of the apostle in his instructions concerning women's teaching and exercising authority in relation to men in 1 Timothy

2:11–12 is evident in a term that he uses twice in these two verses. He begins by saying, "A woman must *quietly* receive instruction . . ." (v. 11) and concludes in verse 12 with the injunction that she is "to remain *quiet*" (italics added). "Quietly" and "quiet" both translate the Greek phrase *en hesuchia* ("in quietness"). Although *hesuchia* could involve absolute silence, its use in verse 2 of this same chapter and other New Testament passages suggests more the idea of a quietness associated with peace, good order, or tranquility (cf. 1 Thess. 4:11; 2 Thess. 3:12; 1 Pet. 3:4). Paul is thus not forbidding all speaking, but rather "speaking that creates a disturbance."[1] This is supported by the addition that the learning must take place with entire "submissiveness," which, as we noted earlier in chapter 6, has the meaning of being "ordered under." In other words, "quietly receiving instruction" involves submission or subjection, probably, as the context of learning suggests, to the one doing the teaching. Thus, while Paul encourages women to learn, he is concerned that their learning not take place in a way that violates proper order, which in this case concerns the relationship between man and woman.

Having expressed his general concern with the manner of women's learning in a positive way, he goes on in verse 12 to disallow certain activities of women in relation to men: "But I do not allow a woman to teach or exercise authority over a man, but to remain quiet." Before we can look at the specific meaning of this problematic verse, we must answer some more general questions. First, what is the *nature* of the "teaching" and "exercising authority" that are being prohibited? Are they to be viewed as positive or negative activities? Is this a prohibition against the activity of teaching or against the teaching of false doctrine? Similarly, is the apostle referring to the exercise of legitimate authority or to a "domineering authority"?

A second question concerns the *application* of this instruction. Is this injunction against women teaching and exercising authority over men related only to a particular historical situation, or is it intended to apply to the church throughout history?

The Nature of the Activities Prohibited

The apostle's concern throughout the Pastoral Letters for sound teaching leads some to conclude that what is being prohibited is not "teaching" but "false teaching." This is usually supported by the claim that women were either uneducated at the time or influenced by heretical teaching (cf. 1 Tim. 5:6). Aside from the fact that the older women are specifically encouraged to "teach" younger women (Titus 2:3–5), which would suggest that they could teach truth, the obvious question in relation to this view is, why prohibit only women? All of the false teachers specifically named in the Pastorals are men (1 Tim. 1:20; 2 Tim. 2:17–18; cf. 2 Tim. 4:14). There is no indication in these letters of women purveying false teaching. They are rather seen as coming under the influence of the false teaching (cf. 1 Tim. 5:11–15; 2 Tim. 3:5–9). If Paul's reference to teaching meant "false teaching," it is difficult to understand why he did not include men or simply give a general statement applicable to all. The exclusive application to women thus suggests that the prohibition is not speaking of false teaching, but the activity of teaching itself.

The unqualified use of "teach" points in the same direction. Köstenberger notes that the term *teach* is "consistently viewed positively in the New Testament, including the Pastorals, when used absolutely." That is, when the verb *teach* is used without any qualifications showing its nature or its content, it always refers to teaching in a positive light.[2] For example, when false teaching is in view, the apostle clearly indicates its nature either by using a term that means heterodox teaching (e.g., 1 Tim. 1:3, ἑτεροδιδασκαλειν, "teach strange doctrines") or by clearly indicating its nature in the context (e.g., Titus 1:11, "teaching things they should not teach"). Thus we conclude that it is "teaching" that is prohibited, not just "false teaching."

As for the nature of the authority prohibited, the meaning of the Greek word in 1 Timothy 2:12 (αὐθεντέω, *authenteo*), translated "exercise authority over" (NASB) or "have authority over" (NIV, NRSV), has been much debated. Suggestions range all the way from simply "having authority" to "beginning or instigating something," "instigating violence," or "murdering."[3] On the basis of a thorough lexical study, H. Scott Baldwin demonstrates that the concept of "authority" is the root meaning of this word. However, as used in 1 Timothy 2:12, this meaning could be taken either positively (i.e., "having authority" or "exercising authority"), or negatively (i.e., "usurping illegitimate authority," "domineering," or "flaunting authority"). If taken in the positive sense, then Paul's prohibition simply forbids women from having or exercising authority over men. On the other hand, if understood negatively, women are not prohibited from having authority over men. Rather, they are only prohibited from a wrong kind or use of authority.

Although the word itself could carry either sense, its grammatical link with the activity of "teaching" here shows that the author intended it positively in this text. When two terms are joined by the coordinating conjunction *oude,* as in this verse—"to teach *or [oude]* exercise authority"—the activities denoted are either both viewed positively or both negatively.[4] Since, as we have seen previously, "teach" has a positive meaning in this verse, the exercise of authority must also be taken positively. What is prohibited to women, therefore, is not the idea of "domineering" or "flaunting authority," but simply the "exercising of authority" over men. Further evidence for the positive understanding is seen in the fact that the prohibition of exercising authority is specifically said to be "over a man." Only a positive meaning makes sense of this addition, as surely the apostle would have prohibited women from "domineering" or "flaunting authority" over all people, not just men.

The Universal Application of the Instructions

The universal application of this instruction concerning women's teaching and exercising authority over men is denied by many today. Some who reject the inspiration of the apostle's writings explain his words simply as the product of one influenced by the patriarchal culture of his day and therefore erroneous. Others who accept his authority attempt to explain his injunctions as applicable only to the current situation at Ephesus and perhaps other similar situations, but not to all churches everywhere at all times. A common explanation is that women were prohibited from teaching because they were untaught at that time and in danger of being influenced by false teachers. When they become educated, which the apostle encourages in the same section (1 Tim. 2:11), then the prohibition would no longer be applicable.[5] In addition to the concern for educated teaching, the restrictions on women's activities are viewed as expressive of a "concern for the reputation of the church within the larger Greco-Roman society."[6] Paul's instructions in verses 11–12 therefore relate to a particular situation in which women are being influenced by false teaching to violate the generally accepted norms of the society in which they lived. They are "not to be understood as universal principles encoded in a suprasituational 'church order manual' that limit women in all times and places."[7]

Some egalitarians also point to the particular form of the verb used to express the prohibition as indicating a restricted application. Because the Greek word translated "I do not allow" (v. 12, *epitrepo*) is a present active indicative form rather than an imperative, it is suggested that Paul is saying something like, "I am *presently* not allowing a woman to teach or exercise authority over a man." The verb form thus shows that Paul intends his instructions only for a particular situation in the Ephesian church at that time and perhaps, by analogy, similar situations elsewhere, but not as permanently and universally applicable.[8]

Other uses of the present active indicative form for instructions or commands, however, clearly demonstrate that this form does not *necessarily* signify such a restricted application. The exhortations to prayer in the immediately preceding context are present indicative forms: "I urge [or "am urging"] that entreaties and prayers . . . be made" (v. 1); "I want [or "am wanting"] the men . . . to pray" (v. 8). So also is the well-known exhortation of Romans 12:1: "I urge [or "am urging"] you . . . to present your bodies a living . . . sacrifice" (cf. also Rom. 16:17; 1 Cor. 1:10; 4:16; 7:10; Eph. 4:1; 1 Thess. 4:1; 5:14; 2 Thess. 3:6). These uses by the same writer clearly show that this particular form can be used for instructions and exhortations that have universal applicability. It is only from the context of its use that we can determine whether a particular exhortation or command is intended to be restricted in application or have unlimited applicability. Shreiner aptly illustrates this point: "If I say to my daughter, 'You are not permitted to drive the car one hundred miles per hour,' it is obvious (or should be!) that this is a universal prohibition. But if I say, 'You are not permitted to go into the street,' it is also plain that this is a temporary restriction given to a young girl of two years of age who is not yet able to handle herself safely in the street."[9]

Looking at the context of Paul's use of this word for the prohibition regarding women's activities, it is difficult to see anything that points to a limited application. None of the reasons suggested for limiting the prohibition (e.g., uneducated women, testimony to culture) are mentioned in the context. On the other hand, there is evidence supporting an unlimited application. As we have seen in chapter 6, the apostle is concerned in his prohibitions with maintaining a certain order between man and woman expressed by the word *submissiveness* on the part of the woman as she learns from church leaders (1 Tim. 2:11). This concern, as we saw, is not only mentioned here, but in many other references as well, none of which contains any evidence of limitation. We also noted that the apostle grounded his instructions on the creation order of man and woman, which is likewise permanent (vv. 13–14). The context thus gives strong support for the understanding of these prohibitions as intended to be *permanent* and *universal*. The question is: Exactly what do they mean in practical church life?

The Concept of "Teaching"

The meaning of "teach" in Paul's prohibition is complicated by the fact that we tend to think of all speaking ministries as some form of "teaching" or "preaching," (which includes "teaching"). The resultant prohibition against women's "teaching" often excludes women from all forms of both of these activities when men are present. But is this what the apostle meant in 1 Timothy 2:12 when he prohibited women from teaching men? To answer this question, it will be helpful for us to look at the various ways the same word for "teach" used in this passage, *didasko,* is used in other passages of Scripture. We will also consider some other terms used for verbal ministries that express concepts closely related to teaching and that in most of our churches today might be seen as forms of teaching.

The Meaning of Didasko (Διδάσκω)*: "Teach"*

The basic meaning of *didasko* ("teach") in the New Testament is derived from the Old Testament, where it is frequently used to translate the Hebrew למד *(lamad)* in the Septuagint (The Greek version of the Old Testament). Like the secular Greek concept of teaching, Jewish teaching involved the communication of knowledge. The task of the New Testament teacher, therefore, involved the two functions of passing on tradition and interpreting it.[10]

But the biblical concept of teaching differed quite radically from secular Greek teaching in the matter of its goal. Whereas the Greek teacher sought to impart knowledge and skills, teaching for the Jew sought to change the entire life. As Wegenast explains, *didasko* in the Septuagint "does not primarily denote the communication of knowledge and skills (e.g., 2 Sam. 22:35), but means chiefly instruction in how to live (e.g.,

Deut. 11:19; 20:18 and passim), the subject matter being the will of God."[11] This Old Testament sense of teaching was carried over to the early church where "teaching" was concerned "with the whole man and his education in the deepest sense."[12] It included the intellect, but its final goal was the will. As Filson says, "Where information was handed on, or any skill developed, this was done in order to promote the fullest possible achievement of God's will. . . . Such teaching was directed not merely to the mind, but to the whole man, and especially to his will."[13]

How central this idea is to the biblical concept of teaching is clear in Rengstorf's explanation that "to the Jewish ear διδάσκειν ["to teach"] suggests the successful and total molding of the will of another by one's own."[14] Thus one interpreter explains the meaning of "teach" in the Pauline prohibition against women teaching men as "an activity involving personal direction and an exercise of authority."[15] No doubt it had this authority in some uses, but we will see that there are gradations of authority among the various New Testament uses of this term for "teaching." Moreover, even in the most authoritative instances, care must be taken not to make the teacher in the church the equivalent of a Jewish rabbi who drew disciples under his personal authority. For the members of the early church, including the authoritative teachers, Jesus remained the Rabbi or Teacher preeminent and they His disciples (cf. Matt. 23:8). As Dunn notes, "Where a teacher-pupil relationship, such as we find in Judaism between rabbi and pupil, developed in Corinth, Paul was quick to denounce it, and to rally the community as a whole under the one banner of Christ (1 Cor. 1:10–17)."[16]

Various Uses of "Teach" in the Early Church

The words *teach (didasko)* and *teacher (didaskolos)* are used in a variety of ways throughout the New Testament.[17] In the Gospels, their primary application is to Jesus as the Teacher. In fact, while the teaching function is attributed to Jesus' disciples in the Gospels, they are never termed "teachers." Only John the Baptist (Luke 3:12), Nicodemus (John 3:10), and the scribes (Luke 2:46) are "teachers," along with Jesus in the Gospel records. In the remainder of the New Testament dealing with the early church, both the function of "teaching" and the title "teacher" are used to describe ministries in the church.

This teaching ministry in the church took place in a variety of ways by different people. First, there were those who were called "teachers."[18] Mentioned third after apostles and prophets in 1 Corinthians 12, "teachers" were those who were recognized as having this regular ministry in the church. It is perhaps not going beyond the truth to speak of them as holding the "teaching office." Their function "would involve learning and studying, and would thus more or less from the first be a part or full time work or 'profession,' with teachers dependent for their material support on their fellow Christians, particularly those whom they taught (Gal. 6.6)." It would therefore have "more the character of 'office' than any other of the regular ministries."[19] This understanding is supported by the close connection of "teacher" with "pastor" in Ephesians 4:11, possibly signifying the same person here.[20] Whether all those recognized as "teachers" actually held the office of pastor or elder is not certain. Later evidence from church history indicates that some known as "teachers" traveled from church to church and therefore probably did not hold the office of bishop or elder in a church. It is Lindsay's conclusion that "teachers" did not necessarily hold church office in the sense of elder or bishop, but that they could be chosen to do so.[21] Similarly Lincoln, commenting on "pastors" and "teachers" in Ephesians 4:11, says, "It is more likely that they were overlapping functions, but that while almost all pastors were also teachers, not all teachers were also pastors."[22] Paul's reference to some "teaching things they should not teach" (Titus 1:11), and the warning against seeking "teachers" who would simply tickle ears, may also indicate the possibility of teaching outside of an office. The objection against such teachers is not that they are functioning illegitimately, but that they are teaching error.

The function of teaching, however, was not limited to those known as "teachers" or those holding church office. The apostle appears to conceive of many bringing a "teaching" for the edification of the gathered church (1 Cor. 14:26). Even as it was possible for some to prophesy who did not have this as their regular ministry and would therefore not be known as "prophets" (cf. 1 Cor. 14:31),[23] so the apostle thought of teaching "in terms of particular teachings given by those not necessarily regarded as teachers."[24]

Finally, most interpreters see the New Testament ascribing a teaching ministry to all church members when Paul writes to the Colossians, "Let the word of Christ dwell in you richly as you teach and admonish one another with all wisdom" (Col. 3:16 NIV).[25] The exact nature of this teaching is never explained. Banks may be correct when he says that here Paul probably has in mind "the informal teaching and exhorting of one another that went on throughout the Christian meetings rather than some formal exhortatory address."[26] The picture in this text may be similar to that in 1 Corinthians 14:26 discussed previously, where various people were able to share a teaching. At any rate, it indicates, as Knight points out, that "Paul does not restrict teaching to ministers in distinction from other Christians."[27] Nor does it seem that there is any restriction here to men. Similar reference to the general teaching function of all members of the church is found in Hebrews 5:12, where the writer rebukes his readers for their lack of growth by telling them that they should by now all be "teachers." As Hughes explains, it is not that they should all be "in official teaching positions in the church." But they should be sufficiently knowledgeable to be able "to instruct and edify those who are still young in the faith."[28] This survey of the "teaching" *(didasko)* function in the New Testament shows that it was carried on through a variety of means, involving not only stated teachers, but finally all members.

The Range of Authority in Teaching

Although a certain authority is probably present in all of the uses of *didasko,* there appears to be quite a latitude of gradations. Christ amazed His hearers with the authority of His teaching (e.g., Matt. 7:28–29; Mark 1:22). To His disciples, His teaching carried absolute authority because of who He was.[29] The apostles, as the commissioned and inspired representatives of Christ, likewise claimed canonical or normative authority for their teaching (e.g., 1 Cor. 14:37).

When we move to the nonapostolic "teachers" within the church, there is obviously some lesser degree of authority. Probably the highest authority under the apostles was assigned to the regular teaching of a recognized leader, i.e., an elder/bishop/pastor. Teaching by those who were not elders or pastors, and therefore had no authority as official leaders, was no doubt somewhat less authoritative in the church. Similarly, the various "teachings" that individuals may have brought in the gathered church, and the mutual teaching of all, would not have functioned with the same authority as that of leaders.

Consideration of the ministry of teaching in the New Testament church therefore reveals a considerable variety both in terms of its functioning and the authority of the content.

Other Ministries of the Word in the Church

Contrary to the common identification of all the ministries of the Word in today's church as essentially "teaching" or "preaching," a variety of terms are used in relation to the communication of Christian truth. In some instances, these different terms are used as the equivalent of *didasko*. But they also appear to describe ministries that are not identical to this term. One such is *katecheo* (κατηχέω), from which we get our words *catechize* and *catechumen*. In the New Testament it carries the sense of "to tell about something" (see Acts 21:21, 24) or "to give instruction concerning the content of faith."[30] It is used twice in this latter sense in Galatians 6:6, where Paul wrote, "The one who is taught *[katecheo]* the word is to share all good things with the one who teaches *[katecheo]*," and again in 1 Corinthians 14:19, where he asserted that, rather than speak to the church in tongues, he would speak with his mind "that I may instruct *[katecheo]* others also." It is used again by Luke to describe Apollos as one who had "been instructed *[katecheo]* in the way of the Lord" (Acts 18:25; cf. Luke 1:4).

It may well be, as Beyer states, that these uses of *katecheo* are the equivalent of *didasko*.[31] Nevertheless, this term may indicate a certain kind of teaching that was actually carried on by those who were not elders or bishops. The word became the standard term for baptismal instruction given to catechumens in the early postapostolic church. Thus Wegenast states that *katecheo* may be regarded as a "technical term for 'to instruct in the faith.'"[32] The postapostolic writings also show that this instruction was frequently carried on by deacons, although under the authority of the bishops.[33]

Luke uses yet another term, *ektithemi* (ἐκτίθημι), to describe the ministry of Priscilla and Aquila in instructing Apollos (Acts 18:26). The same word is used in connection with Paul's explaining of the truth of Christ to the Jews who came to him in Rome (Acts 28:23). *Ektithemi* simply means "to explain, set forth,"[34] as in Acts 11:4, where Luke records that "Peter began and explained everything" (NIV) to those at Jerusalem concerning his experience of being directed to the house of Cornelius.

The term thus indicates something different from "teaching" in the sense of *didasko*. Priscilla and Aquila simply explained "the way of God more accurately" to Apollos without the aim at the will and change of life that is found in the *didasko* biblical teaching. A further term, *dianoigo* [διανοίγω], which literally means "to open," is also used for the explanation or interpretation of God's truth (Luke 24:32; Acts 17:3),[35] again, probably with less weight of authority than *didasko*.

A frequent ministry that involved the communication of the Word is expressed by the word *parakaleo* [παρακαλέω]. Depending on the context, this word can signify "to beseech," "to comfort," or "to exhort." The mention of this term in the list of spiritual gifts in Romans 12 (v. 8) indicates that the ministry designated by this word was a prominent one in the church. Following immediately after teaching in the Romans 12 list, *parakaleo* is probably best understood here as exhortation. But it may also carry some idea of entreaty.[36] Although the activities of teaching and exhortation in the church surely overlapped, they also had "certain differences of emphasis and method."[37] Exhortation was no doubt a part of the teaching/preaching ministry done by the leaders of the church. But it was also to be exercised by the members of the congregation in relation to one another, although the exact form in which it was carried out is not revealed (cf. 1 Thess. 4:18; 5:11, 14). A closely related term refers to the giving of admonition (*noutheteo*, νουθετέω), which was also the responsibility of all believers (Rom. 15:14; Col. 3:16; 1 Thess. 5:14; 2 Thess. 3:15) toward each other, as well as a function of the pastor.[38]

Beyond these terms, and no doubt others, that were used for the ministry of the Word within the Christian community, we can add the terminology used primarily in the proclamation of the Truth to the world in evangelism. This includes the various word groups connected with *anggello* (ἀγγέλλω, "announce") and *kerusso* (κηρύσσω, "proclaim") and the concepts of "witness" and "confession."[39] This great variety of terminology used for the ministry of the Word toward both believers in the church and the outside world demonstrates a wide variety both in nature and authority in relation to the activity of communicating God's truth in the early church.

The Specific Teaching Prohibited in 1 Timothy 2:12

The variety of teaching functions expressed by the usual Greek word *didasko*, along with the other terms used for what we might often call "teaching," raises the question of the exact meaning of "teach" in Paul's prohibition of that function to women over men. Is the apostle forbidding teaching in general or a specifically limited concept of that function within the church?

The Prominence of Teaching in the Pastoral Epistles

In studying the concept of "teaching" in the Pastoral Epistles, one is immediately struck with the prominence given to that ministry in these writings. If my counting is accurate, there are some thirty uses of words related to the basic word *didasko*. Perhaps most significantly, out of twenty-one occurrences in the entire New Testament of the word *didaskalia* ("teaching," either in the sense of the activity of teaching or that which is taught), fifteen of these are found in the Pastorals. In addition to the frequent use of the vocabulary of "teaching," many expressions relate to the content of teaching. The phrase *pistos ho logos* ("it is a trustworthy statement," πιστὸς ὁ λόγος) is found five times in the Pastorals (1 Tim. 1:15; 3:1; 4:9; 2 Tim. 2:11; Titus 3:8), but nowhere else in the New Testament. The apostle also frequently speaks of "sound words," "the faith," and "that which has been entrusted."[40] Finally, the description of the church as "the pillar and support of the truth" (1 Tim. 3:15) underlies the importance of right teaching and opposition to false teachers in these epistles.[41]

The Purpose of Teaching in the Pastoral Epistles

This prominence of the teaching function in the Pastorals is directly related to the great concern of the apostle that is evident throughout the Epistles, namely, the preservation and transmission of the Christian tradition. The various expressions for the content of that which was rightly believed in the church (e.g., "the faith," "sound words," "trustworthy" or "faithful word") reflect a definite body of teaching present in the church.[42] The frequently used *didaskalia* ("teaching," διδασκαλία) in the singular was "particularly adapted to emphasize the binding character of the historical proclamation."[43] It is this fixed body of teaching that Paul has in view when he speaks of that which had been "entrusted" to those who were to "guard" it. The words that the apostle uses for "guard" (*phulasso*, φυλάσσω) and "that which had been entrusted" (paratheke, παραθήκη) were technical terms for the idea of passing some commodity securely from one party to another "by entrusting it to an authorized agent." This concept was present among the Greeks, Romans, and Jews, but it is used only three times in the New Testament, all in the Pastorals (1 Tim. 6:20; 2 Tim. 1:12, 14).[44] The same thought, however, is probably also to be understood in Paul's exhortation to the Thessalonians to "hold to the traditions" (2 Thess. 2:15).

The fact that the concept of preserving and handing down the faith comes to the fore in the Pastorals is explained by the development that is taking place at this time in relation to divine revelation. At its inception, the church received something new in the revelation of Christ. The apostles and prophets, described by the apostle Paul as "the foundation" of the church (Eph. 2:20), spoke under the direct inspiration of the Spirit. But as this manner of revelation diminished, the need to preserve the truth of Christianity rose in importance. Although Dunn may go too far in the contrast between the earlier and later Paul, he aptly delineates this movement when he writes of the Pastorals,

> [T]he finely tensed balance Paul had achieved between prophecy and teaching, that is between new revelations of the ever present eschatological Spirit and the passing on and interpretation of established tradition, seems to have gone. Wholly dominant is the concern to preserve the doctrinal statements of the past. . . . The Spirit has become the power to guard the heritage of tradition handed on from the past (II Tim. 1.14—φύλαξον διὰ πνεύματος ἁγίου, ["guard through the Holy Spirit . . ."]). And even Paul himself is depicted more as the keeper of tradition than as its author (II Tim. 1.12).[45]

Schweizer sees the same emphasis, noting that it is "characteristic of the Pastoral Letters that all the stress is on 'guarding,' which is to be ensured by the men who represent the connection with the apostle who has been entrusted with the doctrine—men who faithfully take over this teaching and hand it on unchanged."[46]

According to the Pastorals, this task of keeping the tradition and faithfully passing it on is specifically related to the function of teaching. The ideas threatening the church are described as contrary "teaching" (e.g., 1 Tim. 1:3, "strange doctrines"; 4:1, "doctrine of demons"), and those bringing them in are called "teachers" (e.g., 1 Tim. 1:7, "teachers of the Law"; cf. 2 Tim. 4:3; Titus 1:11). Similarly, those exhorted to counter them are termed "teachers" who are to "teach" (cf. 1 Tim. 4:11; 2 Tim. 2:2) and so pass on the "teaching" that they have received from the apostle (2 Tim. 3:10), who himself is pictured as a "teacher" (1 Tim. 2:7; 2 Tim. 1:11). All of this leads us to the conclusion expressed by one scholar that in the Pastorals "invariably 'to teach' involves passing on a tradition which is more or less fixed."[47]

The "Authority" of the Pastoral Teachers

The emphasis on teaching, and the vital importance of its function in maintaining true Christian doctrine, already suggest that considerable authority is attached to this ministry in the Pastoral Letters. This is further borne out by the fact that in these letters this function is particularly associated with the community leaders. Besides the apostle Paul, who, as we have seen, identifies himself as a teacher (1 Tim. 2:7; 2 Tim. 1:11) and refers to his teaching (2 Tim. 3:10), the activity of teaching is to be a central part of the ministry of Timothy and Titus as apostolic delegates (1 Tim. 4:11, 13; 6:2; 2 Tim. 4:2; cf. Titus 2:1, 2:7).[48] It is also clearly linked to the office of elder/bishop or pastor. To be appointed in the church, an elder needs to be one who holds fast to the "faithful word which is in accordance with the teaching, so that he will be able both to exhort in sound doctrine and to refute those who contradict" (Titus 1:5, 9). Apparently referring to the same office, one of the qualifications of an "overseer" or bishop is expressly stated as "able to teach" (1 Tim. 3:2). Interestingly, this qualification does not appear for the deacon. Teaching is also explicitly related to the office of elder in the apostle's instruction that double honor be given to those elders who work hard at "preaching and teaching" (1 Tim. 5:17).

It is probably impossible to conclude that the function of teaching in the Pastorals is limited to the official leader of the community, since false teachers are also given this title (cf. 1 Tim. 1:7; 4:3). Moreover, the prohibition of only women may imply that there were some men other than the elders/bishops who had the right to teach. Also, there is no clear indication that the "faithful men" to whom Timothy was to entrust the teaching, so that they could teach others, were all elders/bishops (2 Tim. 2:2).

Nevertheless, the strong association of teaching with the official leaders suggests that the primary responsibility of passing on the tradition according to the Pastorals rests with the authoritative teaching of the stated leaders. As Fitzmyer says,

> Here the function of the teacher is clearly predicated of the delegates of the apostle and of those whom they appoint as *episkopoi* ["overseers" or "bishops"]. It echoes, in effect, the gifts given to the Church in Eph. 4:11, which may reflect something of the same tendency. This does not mean, of course, that such officials are the only teachers in the (local) Christian community, but the Deutero-Pauline letters suggest that concern and wariness for sound doctrine rest with such appointees.[49]

This strong relationship of the function of teaching to the leaders in the Pastorals clearly suggests that there is an authoritative element attached to it.

Certain terminology related to the ministry of teaching also bears this out. The menacing presence of heresy causes the teaching of the Pastorals to take on a certain apologetic and polemical character, which demands authority for the protection of the faithful.[50] Thus Timothy is exhorted to "command and teach these things" (1 Tim. 4:11 NIV). The Greek term translated "command" *(paranggello, παραγγέλλω)* is used "of all kinds of persons in authority" and means generally to *"give orders, command, instruct, direct."*[51] The authority implied in this terminology that is to characterize Timothy's teaching is explained by Knight:

> The apostle of Christ (1:1) commands the servant of Christ (4:6) to continually command (παράγγελλε, present imperative) that which the apostle has communicated (cf. 4:6). δίδασκε ["teach"] refers to the communication of the truth to which παράγγελλε seeks obedience. ταῦτα ["these things"] indicates the content to be taught.[52]

This same term expressing "command" is found in two other instances in connection with Timothy's instruction (1 Tim. 5:7; 6:17).

Teaching is also associated with "exhortation" (παρακαλέω, *parakaleo*), as when Paul told Timothy, "These are the things you are to teach and urge *[parakaleo]* on them" (1 Tim. 6:2 NIV; 4:13). The elder is to hold the "faithful word which is in accordance with the teaching, so that he will be able both to exhort *[parakaleo]* in sound doctrine and to refute those who contradict" (Titus 1:9; cf. 2:6). As this verse indicates, in addition to exhortation the leader must "refute" or "reprove" (ἐλέγχω, *elencho;* cf. also 1 Tim. 5:20; 2 Tim. 4:2; Titus 2:15) as well as "rebuke" (ἐπιτιμάω, *epitimao*, 2 Tim. 4:2) as part of his ministry. These various terms are not the equivalent of "teaching" *(didasko)*. Nevertheless, their explicit association with teaching in some instances, and the realization that it would be hard to exhort, refute, or reprove without some teaching of truth, suggests that the teaching ministry in the Pastorals that was primarily associated with the community leaders was one of authority. When it is recognized that the tradition to be passed on by the teacher was at that time still primarily oral rather than written, the significance of the authority attached to the teacher and his function may be even more readily understood.

The Specific Teaching Forbidden in 1 Timothy 2:12

In attempting to determine exactly what Paul means in prohibiting women from "teaching" men, it is imperative that we place it in the context of this picture of the teaching function in the Pastorals. When we do so, it seems impossible to say, as one interpreter does, that the verb *teach* "is simply a general one for teaching and does not suggest in itself a limitation to a particular kind of teaching, such as 'authoritative' preaching or teaching."[53] The teaching of the Pastorals clearly suggests an authority that cannot be attributed in the same way to every use of teaching in the New Testament.

The authority involved in the specifically prohibited teaching is further emphasized when it is viewed in connection with the additional prohibition of "exercising authority over a man." Whether "teach" (*didasko,* διδάσκω) and "exercise authority over" (*authenteo,* αὐθεντέω) are to be taken as two distinct activities,[54] or as two elements that "convey a single coherent idea,"[55] it is generally agreed that being joined together by the Greek term *oude* ("or"), they are closely related ideas, where in many instances the latter activity appears to further elaborate or extend the first, e.g., "to accept or to observe" (Acts 16:21); "speak or teach" (Acts 4:18); "not to teach strange doctrines . . . nor to pay attention to myths" (1 Tim. 1:3–4).[56] Since the thrust of the entire discussion related to the prohibition concerns women's learning and teaching, the exercising of authority mentioned would also seem to be primarily related to that issue. This suggests that the teaching proscribed is one that carries a certain authority over the ones taught.

On the basis of the entire pastoral concept of teaching and the mention of exercising authority in the immediate context, most interpreters understand Paul as prohibiting women from that "teaching" that is done in the capacity of a leader of the church. Dunn, for example, says, "The teaching in 1 Tim. 2:12 is probably envisaged as an official function."[57] Similarly, Blomberg concludes that "the only office or role forbidden to women in the NT is that of the highest 'authoritative teaching' position in the church."[58] Others, while acknowledging that the prohibition excludes the official teaching as elder/bishop, nevertheless see it as more than a restriction from holding this office. Pointing out that functional rather than office language is used, Knight argues that the apostle is prohibiting "women from publicly teaching men, and thus teaching the church."[59]

Although the activity of teaching in the Pastorals is closely related to the official leaders of the community, it is probably impossible to be dogmatic in limiting Paul's prohibition to a certain office holder. As we have noted, there may have been those who carried on a regular ministry of teaching without holding office. But it is also probable that these carried considerable authority in the community. Whether limited to office or not, what is clearly at issue in the prohibition is the relationship of man and woman. In our opinion, whatever the specific application of "teaching," it is the kind of teaching that gives woman a position of authority over man. Perhaps Clark expresses it best when he says, "[T]he passage concerns relationships of authority and subordination, and forbids a woman to hold a position of authority over men in the Christian community." Or again, as he summarizes Chrysostom's understanding of the passage: "Paul in 1 Tm 2:12, does not forbid a woman all teaching. Paul is only prohibiting the headship of women in the Christian community."[60]

Instructions Concerning Order and Conduct in the Church (1 Cor. 11:3–16 and 14:34–36)

The two passages that touch on the relationship of men and women in the church addressed to the Corinthian believers add little to our understanding of women's ministry in the church over what we have seen in 1 Timothy 2. The apostle's concern in 1 Corinthians 11:3–16 is the proper relationship of man and woman in the church with nothing specifically said about ministry. No matter how the difficult issues of the nature of woman's "head covering" and its relation to "authority on her head" are understood, two principles are clear in the passage.[61] First, a distinction between man and woman is to be maintained; women are not to look like men and vice versa. In addition there is a "headship" of man over woman that, as we saw in chapter 6, involves a loving leadership. Since this responsibility of leadership in the New Testament church rested with those known as elders or bishops, this passage supports the rest of the New Testament evidence that indicates that this office was held only by men. The reference to women praying and prophesying in this same passage (v. 5), along with the picture of women's ministries seen in chapter 8, indicates that they exercised significant ministries, both public and private, under the "headship" of the elders.

The apostle's instruction in 1 Corinthians 14:34–35 is similarly fraught with questions: "The women are to keep silent in the churches; for they are not permitted to speak, but are to subject themselves, just as the Law also says. If they desire to learn anything, let them ask their own husbands at home; for it is improper for a woman to speak in church." Is Paul demanding total silence of all women? Is he speaking of submission just to husbands or to all church leaders? Did Paul want women to learn only from their husbands at home? And so forth.

Some of these questions are easily answered by the apostle's own words in the same letter. The command to silence cannot mean that no woman can speak in church, for he previously, as just seen, had instructed women concerning the proper decorum (i.e., head coverings) when they prayed or prophesied (1 Corinthians 11).[62] The idea that women were only to learn from their husbands at home also would appear to be ruled out by the apostle's concern for "all" to learn through the prophetic ministry in the church service (1 Cor. 14:31; cf. also v. 6).

Most commentators therefore agree that the call for women to "keep silent," which is further explained as "not permitted to speak" (v. 34) and "improper ["disgraceful," NIV] for a woman to speak in church" (v. 35), refers to the prohibition of a particular kind of speaking by women in church, not all speech. Some suggest that this instruction relates to the situation where women and men were separated in the church service. Asking questions of their husbands in the service would then create noisy confusion and was therefore prohibited. There is no evidence, however, of such a segregated arrangement in the early church of this time. Others have suggested that the silence commanded relates to the abuses of spiritual gifts, especially speaking in tongues. The usual response of the apostle to abuses, however, is regulation and not total prohibition. Moreover, why only women? Were there no disorderly men?

Another proposal is that the "speaking" forbidden is asking questions as a form of teaching (cf. v. 35). Dialogue of questions and answers was a common form of teaching in the first century among Jewish rabbis as well as Greeks. In the synagogue, the rabbi or official teacher asks the questions, not students. If the church followed this rabbinical style, then women asking questions would be considered a form of authoritative teaching, which was forbidden.[63]

A more likely suggestion is found in the immediately prior context dealing with "weighing" (NIV) or "evaluating" prophecies that were given in the service (v. 29). As different individuals gave prophecies, they needed to be evaluated as to whether they were truly from God. In addition, the meaning and application of the prophecy to the community had to be determined, tasks that would ultimately fall to the authoritative leadership that rested with men.

We cannot be sure of the exact scenario behind this particular injunction. However, the underlying concern of the apostle's negative prohibition is evident in the positive counterpart. After calling for women's silence and declaring that they "are not permitted to speak," he adds that they are to "subject themselves [order themselves under], just as the Law also says" (v. 34). Paul's language here is similar to that found in his instructions concerning women in 1 Timothy 2:11. Here in 1 Corinthians 14:34 he calls for *silence* and asks that women *subject themselves, [hupotasso]*. In the Timothy passage he instructs that women "*quietly* receive instruction with entire *submissiveness* [*hupotage,* the noun form related to *hupotasso*]" (italics added). As in the 1 Timothy 2 instruction, Paul's underlying concern in this Corinthian passage is with the relationship of man and woman. Whatever the particular speaking that he forbids, it was of such a nature that its practice violated God's created design for woman and man.

Thus, although our present knowledge precludes a sure understanding of the specific speaking that is prohibited and other details concerning this passage, the underlying principle is clear and remains so for the church today. Care must be exercised so that men and women, as they live and minister together in the church, do so in a way that fulfills the complementarian order in which they were created and in which they can best fulfill God's purpose for them together.

Conclusion

We have seen that the overriding concern of all three passages dealing with women's ministry in the church is the upholding of the relationship between men and women, which has repeatedly and consistently been taught and exemplified throughout Scripture. This complementarian relationship in which man has the responsibility of leadership is to be practiced in the church as well as in the family. As the message of God's truth is the ground and sustenance of spiritual life, the maintenance of truth against all erosion and pollution is vital to the life of the church. This task belongs to the whole church as "the pillar and foundation of the truth" (1 Tim. 3:15 NIV). In the words of one interpreter, "Each local Church has it in its power to support and strengthen the truth by its witness to the faith and by the lives of its members."[64] As in all matters, however, the ultimate responsibility for the protection and proclamation of truth rests with the leadership, which, in accord with the complementarian order and exemplified in all human communities, rests with some men.

The specific instructions prohibiting women from teaching or exercising authority over men (1 Tim. 2:12) and from a certain kind of speaking (1 Cor. 14:34) are to be understood in light of this background. It is a prohibition of the kind of authoritative "teaching" that belonged to the leadership of the community, not a prohibition against all ministries of the Word. The New Testament, as we have seen, contains a wide variety of teaching activities and other avenues of instruction and proclamation that were exercised by women to the benefit and nurture in the truth for all. Similarly, it is not all exercise of authority over men that is prohibited. In the family, there are certain areas over which the wife and mother exercises considerable authority and is respected for such by her husband, all without destroying his headship. So in the church not all authority in relation to men is forbidden, only that which denies the divine order of the complementarian relationship in the community. How this complementarian relationship, in which men and women work together in the practical functioning of the church community, actually functions remains to be worked out in the following chapter.

CHAPTER FOURTEEN

THE COMPLEMENTARY MODEL OF CHURCH MINISTRY

Judith TenElshof and Robert Saucy

Introduction

Created as equal persons before God and each other, man and woman were designed by their Creator to live together in harmonious unity. This created relationship, as we have seen throughout this study, is one of complementarity in which man and woman in their created differences give themselves for the good of the other and their union together. The choice of both woman and man to "be like God" (Gen. 3:5) in disobedience to God brought a self-centeredness that ruptured the original unity. Where there was loving delight in the other resulting in union, there was now blame, distrust, and prideful competition leading to alienation and strife.

But God has begun a new creation in which these effects of sin are overcome through the saving power of Christ. As believers in Christ, we are this new creation called to live in the world as new people in which the power of Christ by the Spirit overcomes the effects of sin. In relation to our topic, this entails living as men and women together in a new way, a way that is different from the world about us, which is still dominated by gender conflict.

To do this requires both an understanding of God's plan and His power to live it. As in our personal lives, the task of becoming new will never be perfectly completed in our earthly walk. So in the church the work of understanding and living in the perfection of God's design for the relationship of man and woman will never be completed short of glory. But both the impetus of the new heart within and God's command calls us to growth toward the goal.

It is our purpose in this final chapter to suggest something of the pattern of this complementary relationship of man and woman in the life of the church. This involves an understanding of what complementarity means in relation to man and woman, especially as it relates to Christian ministry. It also entails the application of this to the practical activities in the church. Finally, and perhaps most importantly, living in light of the biblical pattern of complementarity transforms the personal attitudes of both men and women who recognize their complementary nature. Without recognition and acceptance of these values, there can be no true complementary functioning. Our thoughts, especially with regard to the actual implementation of complementarity, are not proposed as a final word. Our concern is more with principles, the actual implementation of which may take somewhat different forms according to the situation. But the suggestions are attempts to show, at least in a beginning way, how the principle of complementarity relates to the actual functions of church ministry.

The Complementary Relationship of Man and Woman

The Need for Both to Accomplish the Mission of the Church

Scripture tells us that by our very nature as man and woman, we were created to need each other. God made it evident to Adam that it was "not good" for him to exist alone, and it is only after the first woman was created as his helping partner that God pronounced humanity and all that He had made as "very good" (Gen. 1:31; cf. 2:18). Although the Hebrew word for "good" in this context carries our thought of "beautiful" or "nice," its primary thought is utilitarian. It is "goodness for something." When God "saw" His creation as "good," He saw that they were "in good order," good for the purpose for which they were fashioned."[1]

If we apply this to God's evaluation that it is "not good" for man to be alone, it suggests that man cannot accomplish the purpose for which he was created without another, which is not another man, but a woman. This, of course, is obvious in procreation, which was part of God's original command for mankind (cf. Gen. 1:28). But there is no basis for restricting the application of man's need for woman to anything less than her complementary help in accomplishing all of God's purpose for mankind. To phrase it another way, man needs woman and vice versa in the fulfillment of God's purpose for human existence. This purpose includes not only their task in relation to the rest of creation placed under their care, but their overall purpose to glorify God through personal and spiritual maturation and the proclamation of His glory to others. As the church is the expression of the new creation through which this purpose of mankind is being carried out today (Eph. 3:21; cf. 1 Pet. 2:9), it is especially in the community of believers that the truth of the complementary participation of man and woman must be operative.

Models of Complementarity

The question that is difficult to answer is exactly how this complementarity is intended to operate. It could be argued that a clear gender-based division of labor in which men and women function separately in their distinctive tasks is a form of complementarity in ministry. As we saw in the example of the early church in chapter 8, a form of this was operative among Paul's co-laborers in the planting of churches with women ministering to women and men to men. It is also seen in the apostle's exhortation for older women to teach the younger women in matters pertaining to their lives and responsibilities as women.[2] Something of this may also be seen, for example, when the functions of leadership and teaching mixed groups in the church are carried on without any involvement of women, and other activities such as children's work and social fellowship are allotted to women.

On the other hand, complementarity may be conceived as involving the distinctive gender strengths of both men and women together in ministries. In this form of complementarity, contributing to the whole is not done primarily by performing certain distinct gender tasks, but by supplying complementary differences to the various tasks.

In actuality, these two forms of complementarity probably never function in their pure form in isolation from the other. In relation to church ministry, both forms are always present. Churches that tend to have a sharp gender division of labor in certain areas also have areas where both genders are free to minister. Those who seek the second form, in which both men and women contribute to various tasks, no doubt have some areas where women are prevalent and some in which men predominate. The two forms of complementarity, however, do represent somewhat different perspectives on the functional relationship of women and men in church ministry.

The Family as a Model for the Church

We would suggest that something of the biblical perspective on the complementarity of man and woman in the church can be learned by consideration of their relationship in the family. The many family terms used in relation to the church suggest that the church bears some resemblance to social family structures and practices (e.g., "the household of the faith," Gal. 6:10; "God's household," Eph. 2:19; 1 Tim. 3:15; 1 Pet. 4:17).[3] Although his discussion is limited to the question of leadership, Poythress rightly says, "The Bible invites us to use this family teaching to draw some particular inferences about the respective roles of men and women within the church."[4] The concept of the family as the model for church structures is particularly evident in the Pastoral Letters. According to Verner, "The author of the Pastorals conceptualizes the church as the household of God. He thus conceptualizes the social structure of the church on the model of the household."[5] Describing the church as the "household of God" (1 Tim. 3:15), the apostle depicts the order of the church like that of a human household in which the members "treat one another as they would the members of their own family (1 Tim. 5:1–2)."[6] Timothy is told not to "sharply rebuke an older man, but rather appeal to him as a father, to the younger men as brothers, the older women as mothers, and the younger women as sisters, in all purity" (1 Tim. 5:1–2). Clark sums up the import of the biblical teaching of the church as a family in terms of actual practice, stating that "the correspondence between the family and community goes to the heart of how the early Christians understood their life together. If the life of the Christian people is lived as a family rather than as a social institution, the same roles are needed in both family and community."[7]

Chrysostom's suggestion that "a household is a little church" and "a church is a large household" raises the question of how men and women would function together in church if their relationship was analogous to that in the home. In particular, what would ministry of women and men together look like if it resembled the relational functioning of men as husbands and fathers, and women as wives and mothers, in the social family? Speaking of a Christian husband and wife, the early Latin church father Tertullian wrote, "Together they pray, they work, they fast, teaching, exhorting, supporting one another. . . . Together in the church . . . willingly the sick is visited, the poor is helped; alms without afterthought, sacrifices without hesitancy, daily zeal without obstacle."[8]

Within a nonegalitarian framework, Tertullian's description of the relationship of man and woman in the marriage relationship suggests a complementarity that is less one of strict gender division of labor than one in which both genders are involved in various activities together, each contributing his or her own uniqueness to their mutual benefit and, as the statement suggests, to the service of others. It is not that each gender participates equally in each task, but that both work together with significant participation in various tasks according to their genders and giftedness.

The family metaphor thus challenges the church as God's household to a complementarity of ministry of men and women similar to that of husband and wife in the family. Like husband and wife, father and mother, each member in the family serves together according to his or her abilities for the good of the whole. The church is a household in which, as we have seen in the New Testament, the ministry of the church is not primarily conceived of as a male function, but women are recognized as "co-laborers" serving in vital ministries in the church alongside men.[9]

Complementarity in Practice

What would a complementarity of men and women in church ministry be like, in which both functioned as a team using all of their spiritual gifts fully in accord with their created order? In some areas of ministry, this is already a reality in most churches, at least to some degree. The ministry of caring for the physical needs of people, and even to some extent emotional and spiritual counseling, requires the service of both women and men. In certain aspects of physical care, propriety calls for the ministry of women with women and men with men. The apostle's instruction for older women to "train" (Titus 2:4 NIV, the Greek term means to "encourage, advise, urge"[10]) the younger women also suggests the usefulness of some separate-gender counseling. This no doubt occurs informally in all churches, but complementarity as well as the biblical teaching above would suggest less emphasis on the centrality of counseling by the pastor (male) in favor of a counseling ministry by both men and women. In the case of marriage, counseling could be done by couples.

These ministries, many of which are associated in Scripture with the service of the deacons, provide a rich opportunity for both women and men to exercise the gifts of service, show mercy, and even give exhortation or encouragement. As we saw in chapter 8, these kinds of ministry were not only prominent in the New Testament and postapostolic church, but were central to the life and witness of the church right along with the ministry of the Word. Unfortunately, in many contemporary churches, a diaconate ministry of practical care has lost its significance, being reduced, as someone has said, to "sporadic acts of charity." This has not only diminished the effectiveness of the church in its mission, but has robbed many women as well as men from opportunities for significant ministry and the personal fulfillment that comes with it.

The diaconate ministry of practical service provides one example of a complementarity of ministry in which women and men serve together, each according to their particular gender characteristics and spiritual gifts. One can imagine them working together in a holistic way in serving a family in need. Both genders would be functioning with similar gifts (i.e., helps, showing mercy) complementing each other according to their gender strengths and characteristics, making the whole body rich beyond what either could do without the other.

Does such a complementarity of men and women working together, using the same spiritual gifts, apply to all areas of church ministry? In particular, does it apply to the ministries of teaching and leadership? Is it possible to have a complementarity of ministry in which men and women exercise similar spiritual gifts of teaching and leadership in their own ways within the overall biblical teaching of an order between man and woman?

Complementarity in the Ministry of the Word

An assessment of the overall ministry of the Word in most evangelical churches today shows very limited participation by women beyond that with children. This is due in part to seeing Paul's instruction that women are not to teach men (1 Tim. 2:12) as prohibiting women from any teaching when men are present. But the structure of most ministry situations in churches also contributes to this phenomenon. Little of the reality of the ministry of member to member or of various individuals participating in the ministry of the Word when the community is gathered (cf. 1 Cor. 14:26) is seen in today's churches. In relation to this, someone has described the church today as a body with one big mouth and two big ears. With the "mouth" being restricted to men, this model not only precludes women, but also severely limits the participation of men as well. Although this is an exaggeration, it is difficult to deny that in many of our churches the participation in the various ministries of the Word is limited in comparison to that seen in the New Testament church.

Several factors lead to the conclusion that Scripture supports a complementarity of the ministry of the Word in which women have more participation than in many churches today.

Women's Ministry of the Word to Women

As we have already noted in chapter 8, one significant ministry of women involves the teaching of other women. Although this is universally recognized, it is not frequently implemented in the contemporary church. Clark argues that in the early church "wherever a position for a man existed there also existed some complementary position for a woman." This is illustrated in the following statement from Clement:

> The apostles, giving themselves without respite to the work of evangelism, as befitted their ministry, took with them women, not as wives but as sisters, to share in their ministry to women living at home: by their agency the teaching of the Lord reached the women's quarters without arousing suspicion.[11]

This ministry of women teaching women in evangelism continued among the believers in the church. The older women taught the younger women "what is good" and trained them how to be mature Christian women (Titus 2:3–5). In general, "the care of the younger women is entrusted to the older women."[12] This practice provided the opportunity as well as the responsibility for women to be involved in the activity of teaching along with men.

Women's Ministry of the Word to Both Men and Women

In addition to the women's ministry of teaching other women, the New Testament also shows the participation of women in ministries related to the speaking of the Word in which both genders participated. As we saw in more detail in chapter 8, women participated in prophecy. In addition to the prophetic ministry, which does not have the same presence in the church today as it did in New Testament times, the gathered church practiced ministries involving the Word in which any could contribute. When they came together, the apostle writes, "each one has a psalm, has a teaching, has a revelation, has a tongue, has an interpretation" (1 Cor. 14:26). This description of the church meeting does not describe all that went on in every meeting of the church. Nothing is said, for example, of corporate prayer or the reading of Scripture. There was probably also a time for the authoritative teaching by one of the elders of the church. But this text does tell us that there were contexts in the life of the church in which there was opportunity for many to exercise spiritual gifts including "teaching," described by Barrett as "the elucidation or application of Christian truth."[13] The mention of "revelation" suggests prophecy, and we know from the context that women participated in this important ministry (cf. 1 Cor. 11:5). Nothing suggests here that they were excluded from the exercise of any of these gifts, including teaching. Unfortunately, such a context is no longer normative in most of our churches, thereby limiting the participation of many in this ministry, including women.[14]

Something similar to this Corinthian passage is seen in Paul's instructions to the Colossian church that the believers should be "teaching and admonishing one another" (Col. 3:16). Although there is some question as to whether the teaching here is done through speech or song, there seems little question that women as well as men participated in this ministry of teaching in the Christian community.[15] Finally, the complaint of the writer of Hebrews that his readers "ought to be teachers" by this time (Heb. 5:12) suggests a perspective that maturity in the faith brought the responsibility to teach those less mature. How this teaching was to be practiced, whether in the gathered community, privately, or among the same gender, is not indicated. The generality of the statement, however, suggests that it would apply to all, women and men alike.

In the example of Priscilla, we clearly saw a woman instructing a man (Acts 18:24–26). As Clark notes, this instruction "must have proceeded at a fairly high spiritual and intellectual level, because Apollos was a learned man and he went on to continue teaching afterward. Therefore, Priscilla must have been well-educated as a Christian and capable of a high level of instruction."[16] As noted in the previous chapter, this "instruction" was more of the nature of "explaining" than authoritative "teaching." But it probably did not differ much from that which we call teaching in many situations in the church today.

Some would see the fact that this was done in a home as an important factor, drawing a distinction between public teaching said to be limited to men and private teaching in the home, in which women shared.[17] One wonders, however, how far such a distinction may be pressed given the fact that the primary meeting places for churches of the New Testament and on until the third century were private homes. In fact, the "home" of Priscilla and Aquila where they instructed Apollos was the place of meeting for the church at Ephesus (cf. 1 Cor. 16:19). If there had been another person along with Apollos, would Priscilla's instruction no longer have been private, or would another person have prohibited her from participating with her husband in that ministry? What takes place in some situations in our contemporary churches, such as Sunday school classes or Bible studies, does not seem unlike what may have taken place in homes in the early church. In reality, the place where the teaching occurs is less significant than the kind of teaching or instruction taking place.

Another distinction in relation to women's teaching is similarly questionable. In this view, women are prohibited from publicly teaching with men present, but are encouraged to teach through writing, including scholarly scriptural studies. It is interesting to note that the writings of some women have significantly influenced the thought even of some men who reject their public teaching of men. It is difficult to understand why, if men can learn from women through writing, they cannot learn from them through oral teaching. Again, the biblical issue seems more concerned with the manner or the attitude in which this ministry is carried out rather than the mode.

If we add to "teaching" other forms of the ministry of the Word with which believers served one another, such as exhortation and admonition,[18] we find a New Testament church in which women had a significant role in the ministry related to God's truth. Obedience to the Pauline prohibition of women exercising authoritative teaching over men did not mean an exclusion of women from any ministry related to the speaking of the Word. The issue was the context and manner of their ministry.

The Complementary Relationship in Teaching

The complementary nature of man and woman also suggests the value of the participation of women in the teaching ministry of the church. As has been reiterated throughout this work, God did not make woman simply as another person, but as one who is different from man—and not only different but complementary. Do the differences between men and women that make them indispensable to each other and therefore to the wholeness of the community also have a bearing on the ministry of the Word in the church?

Without attempting to review all of the distinctions between masculinity and femininity discussed in chapters 9 and 10, it is generally recognized that men are more likely to view "the world in terms of objects, ideas, and theories," whereas women see it "in personal, moral, and aesthetic terms."[19] Man is more task-oriented and woman is more relational-oriented. Created as helper and mother, woman is more supportive and nurturing, whereas man is more adventurous and initiatory.[20] Emotional differences between man and woman are also generally recognized.

It must be acknowledged that the ministry of the Word is channeled through human personality. The message of God's judgment on the one hand and His loving mercy on the other come through more or less powerfully, depending on the individuals communicating the message. We must all admit that our nature tends to lead us toward emphasizing certain aspects of God's truth. This is not to suggest that the lack of women's participation in the ministry of the Word has resulted in the total absence of certain themes of Scripture in the church. But we would suggest that, given their gender differences, women are intended by God to contribute certain emphases and dimensions of God's truth that would enrich, in a complementary way, the church's hearing of the Word. The learning of authentic tenderness, compassion, and sensitivity to others could be enhanced through a woman's influence as she models spiritual nurturing. Maybe with more female wisdom in the functioning and healing of relationships, the church today would be less an organization and more an organism that combined the subjective and practical side of knowledge with objective truth.

The Family Model

The family model for the church is also suggestive of a ministry of teaching for women. Although biblically the father bore the ultimate responsibility for teaching in the household, the wife and mother also played a major role. Proverbs speaks of the necessity of heeding the father's instruction and the mother's teaching (cf. 1:8; 6:20). The "excellent wife" of 31:26 is described as one who "opens her mouth in wisdom" and has "the teaching of kindness . . . on her tongue." The picture of this woman managing the household and family business affairs while her husband was concerned with the public business of community affairs presents the strong possibility that there would be servants, both men and women, in her household. Clark is probably correct in saying, "She instructs the household, possibly men and women alike, in how to live according to God's teaching."[21] Is it not possible to see women in the church involved in an analogous ministry under the leaders of the church? If a wife can at times lead family devotions, even with her husband present, with blessing and edification for all, is it not possible for women to have something of a corresponding ministry in the church family?

No doubt every thoughtful husband and wife would also acknowledge the value of the mutuality described by Tertullian when he speaks of husband and wife "teaching, exhorting, supporting one another." Is there also a place for such a mutuality of teaching and instruction between women and men in the church as the family of God? Although this takes place in the home, the fact that not all believers live with other believers in the home leads to the conclusion that such a mutual teaching is needed in the church.

Summary

The complementary nature of man and woman from creation includes both an ordered relationship and the mutual need of the other for our personal fulfillment and the accomplishment of our God-given tasks as His people. We find in Scripture the Pauline prohibition of women's teaching or exercising authority over men. But along with this we also find much evidence for a significant participation of women in various ministries of the Word. The truth of the prohibition representing the order in the complementarity between men and women must not be allowed to stifle the latter truth of the mutual need of man and woman for the ministry of each other, including the ministries of the Word. Participating as part of a team ministry in which the headship of man is recognized, women would minister as women, "supporting and supplementing" the teaching ministries of the male leaders.[22]

Complementarity in Leadership

How does the complementary relationship of woman and man apply to the ministry of leadership in the church? Does the Pauline prohibition against women exercising authority over men exclude women's participation in the functions of providing vision and direction for the believing community? Or does God's evaluation that "it is not good for man to be alone" also relate to this ministry?

According to biblical complementarianism, the ultimate responsibility for community leadership rests with men. This male leadership, however, as Lingenfelter's evidence from anthropology shows, can take a variety of forms—all the way from a hierarchical, dictatorial approach to leadership of community consensus. The leadership of men in the church has likewise been practiced with a wide diversity. We would suggest that the nature and function of biblical leadership is most effective when it functions on the basis of the belief that women's gifts and abilities are a valuable complement to those of men in accomplishing this ministry.

In this discussion, it will be helpful to remind ourselves of the nature and function of true leadership in the church. Jesus made it plain that leadership among God's people is quite different from the secular leadership around them. We might not want to describe all secular leadership today with the same language that He used—they "lord it over them, and . . . exercise authority other them" (Matt. 20:25). Nevertheless, the same patterns of organizational relations of authoritarian positions are the norm, even though in some instances they are practiced with more sensitivity. In contrast, leadership in the church is not a matter of authoritative status, but of humble service.

This countercultural leadership pattern for the church rests on the reality that human leaders (in contrast to secular leaders in their organizations) are not the ultimate authority. Jesus profoundly established the situation of Christian leadership when He said, "But do not be called Rabbi [lit, "my great one"]; for One is your Teacher, and you are all brothers. . . . Do not be called leaders; for One is your Leader, that is, Christ. But the greatest among you shall be your servant" (Matt. 23:8, 10–11). Leadership in the church is servant leadership *among* the people ("you are all brothers") and not hierarchical authority *over* them. Christ alone is Lord and head of the church, not human leadership. There is leadership in the church, but it is radically different from the natural leadership of the world.

As part of the body, such leadership serves the members of the church for their growth in relationship to the Head and to each other. Several characteristics inherent to such a leadership function may be noted. As has been suggested, the crucial element in the growth of the church is relational. The church grows as members are "fitted and held together by what every joint supplies, according to the proper working of each individual part" (Eph. 4:16). Leadership in the church involves the promotion of relationships. Church leadership also aims at an inner response from the people and not simply an outward behavioral change. Its style, therefore, cannot be one of command-type authority, but must be that of a servant whose influence reaches the heart through the less outwardly impressive mode of love, gently instructing and modeling the truth.

Several truths concerning the need for effective leadership in the church are obvious from this very limited consideration of its nature and function. To effectively serve the needs of the members of the body and encourage the members' growth and ministry to others, leadership must know the members personally. With that knowledge, they must have wisdom on how best to meet the particular needs of individuals and use their gifts in the body. In addition, they need wisdom on how best to serve the body with the Lord's vision and direction for the maturity of the church as a whole.

Such leadership of the church cannot be effectively accomplished without the participation of women. In the words of the creation account, man needs the woman as "helper" in the ministry of leadership. The apostle Peter tells husbands to live with their wives "in an understanding way" (1 Pet. 3:7), so church leadership requires understanding of all members. Such understanding in both the home and the church cannot be attained without the voice of woman. Women not only provide the vital knowledge of their own situation—their needs, their desires, their vision—but also their perception of the whole, which is necessary for full understanding.

In addition, the leadership of the church needs the complementary strengths of both genders. Being different, each gender brings its unique contribution to the leadership functions. After a careful study of men in the Bible, Gordon MacDonald brings together some characteristics for biblical masculinity.

> Biblical masculinity paints a picture of man that begins with an ear turned to Heaven. It further describes a man whose energies are directed at protecting, inspiring, motivating, and freeing others. This man is a giver, not a taker; he lives by design, not by default. He knows how to run toward the action, how to stand in the heat, and how to kneel in a moment of quietness.[23]

Each of these characteristics is necessary for effective leadership, but even more so for the office of elder. The crucial aspect of the office of elder is not so much the ministry roles the elders fulfill, but the responsibility and authority for overseeing the ministry in the church. They have the responsibility to see that the congregation is being cared for. That is why the characteristics of protecting, inspiring, motivating, and empowering others is so important. Even more necessary is that they are listening to God as to when and how to take action and stand firm. Although elders perform many of the ministry roles associated with the care and instruction of the people, those roles are not unique to them. Elders are to equip the congregation, but all members of the body are to use their gifts to build up the body (Eph. 4:12–16). Elders are to care for the church, but everyone is to care for one another (1 Cor. 12:25). Elders must be able to teach, but many others taught the Word of God in the New Testament church. What is limited to elders is the official responsibility and authority to ensure that the teaching that is done is in accord with the teaching of the Bible. Elders also have the responsibility to see that all persons are using their gifts for the good of the body.

Women also bring a uniqueness to leadership in their femininity. They are uniquely focused on relationship with strengths in communication, emotional connectedness, helping, submission, and vulnerability, with a strong desire for deep relationships. As one thinks of the relational nature of the church, it is clear that these strengths are central to the health of the church. But their presence is also necessary in the matter of effective leadership. As leadership envisions programs, structures, and general directions for the healthy growth of the church, these feminine strengths and ways of looking at things are a needed complement to the masculine strengths of the elders for a holistic perspective.

In sum, as no wise husband would seek to provide directions for his family without seeking the wisdom and perspective of his wife, so the elders in the church cannot fulfill their responsibility of leadership without the contribution of women in the church. The husband seeks and values his wife's input, not only to better understand the situation, but also to hear her complementary perspective on what best can be done for the good of the family. For the same reasons, the elders need to value and seek the wisdom and perspective of women in the church.

To successfully accomplish this, a purposeful structure would need to be developed in which women would become part of a church leadership team. Perhaps this could take the form of a regular meeting where men and women who served in various leadership capacities in the church (e.g., deacons, deaconesses, various men's, women's, youth, and children's ministry leaders, and worship leaders), would regularly come together to discuss the affairs of the community of believers. Elders could share their vision and projected plans for discussion, but others would have opportunity to tell their visions as well. Matters of church concern could be discussed and the complementary input of both men and women heard. Certain issues would still be the province of elders alone, such as some matters of discipline and perhaps other areas. But like decisions in the home that most often are made by husband and wife together, the direction of the church body, in most instances, would be provided by the consensus of this body. Even as the wife respects her husband, so this body should respect the elders among them. But as the husband likewise values his wife and respects her contribution in reaching decisions, so the elders would respect the input of the other leaders. The process would be somewhat reminiscent of the collectivist model noted by Lingenfelter in which both men and women of the community participated in the discussion, after which elder men articulated the consensus (chapter 11, p. 258). Some such model would not only have the value of the complementarian strengths of both genders in reaching decisions, but it would be a strong impetus to the other pole of complementarity, namely, unity.

Personal Relationships of Men and Women in Complementarian Ministry

A complementary church ministry demands biblical principles of practical relationships between all people, and, in particular, special attention to the relationships between men and women. Loving, trusting relationships between men and women that are geared to supporting, encouraging, and building self-worth and personal identity in Christ are vital to the biblical functioning of ministry. Sadly, in many churches today, the opposite is true, and the interpersonal functioning of pastors and leaders in the church is a matter of much concern. This concern is related to reports that relational immaturity can be tied to many of the problems that are prevalent among pastors and Christian leaders.[24] Marital and family life in the church today is in crisis and in desperate need of a model of true communion between men and women. The restoration of a true relationship between men and women in church leadership would model, help motivate, and enhance individual families to make the necessary changes for restoration in their gender relationships. This section will address a model of relationship between men and women in the church that more fully reflects God's created image of male and female.

After God created Eve, humanity no longer consisted of just one gender. Rather, it was made up of men and women working together toward a common goal. This goal was to reflect fully the glory of the created image by working and relating together in harmony and unity. Our world today needs practical evidence of Christ's redemptive power in the area of gender relations. Although Ruth Barton holds to egalitarianism, she rightly says,

> Men and women all over the world struggle with the issue of gender relations. Some are trying to confront the inequities of the past while others cling to "the way it's always been." As Christians, we should model healthy relationships between men and women characterized by true teamwork. We were created for this. (Gen. 1:26–28)[25]

The biblical models for the development of a theology of gender relations are found in the relationships between the three persons of the Godhead and between Christ and His church. Christ brings committed love, grace, and empowerment to the church while the Trinity as a whole exemplifies unity, order, and intimacy. A closer and deeper understanding of each of these six characteristics needs to be explored.

Committed Love

The unconditional love of God is demonstrated in the New Testament in 1 John 4:19: "We love, because He first loved us." It is also beautifully articulated in Romans 5:8, which reminds us that God's love is lived out for us in the fact that while we were still sinners, Christ died for us. Practically, how do men and women in the church exercise this kind of committed love? First, we need to recognize that we are on the same team, God's team, and our love comes from Him. We will not be able to come close to the mutual respect and committed love for each other that is needed if we are not abiding in God's love for us. It is not easy to love and respect someone so different from ourselves, so we will need God's help. His help will develop in us a mutual respect for one another.

Second, committed love will mean mutual respect that avoids stereotyping and recognizes our need for the distinctiveness the other brings. Why? Our purpose will not be accomplished alone but rather with the help of a complement. God said that Adam *needed* a helper. Male and female together reflect the fullness of who God is as we complement each other in love. This respect is grounded in the fact that we are equal in value before God, both responsible for filling, ruling, and subduing the earth, and dependent on one another in the body of Christ as reflected by Barton:

> Our attitudes and relationships will be transformed as we consciously remind ourselves, This man (or woman) reflects the image of God to me. She (or he) is a royal priest just as I am, and I need her (or him) to work alongside me to carry out my priestly responsibilities.[26]

First Peter 2:5, 9 teaches that all Christians (male and female) are priests responsible to build a spiritual house by offering spiritual sacrifices acceptable to God. Paul argues, "To each one is given the manifestation [gift] of the Spirit for the common good. . . . The eye cannot say to the hand, 'I have no need of you'" (1 Cor. 12:7, 21).

Third, committed love that brings mutual respect will drive us toward effective communication. Effective communication involves active listening by being direct, clarifying, and reflecting to develop mutual empathy. Rather than women pursuing and men withdrawing in conversation; or women being seen as having a problem and men having the answer; or women looking for connection and men looking to get the task done, mutual respect should encourage mutual empathy. Empathy in relationships helps men and women build bridges of understanding that model Christ's incarnation. He loved us enough to leave His heavenly home and come to walk in our shoes, thinking, feeling, suffering, and experiencing with us. Are we willing to leave our thoughts and feelings long enough to experience those of the opposite gender? If we do, people of the other gender will feel safe, accepted, listened to, and loved, and will not be intimidated. Mutual empathy through effective communication will give rise to acknowledging conflict between the way we think, feel, and act, which will require a large component of grace.

Grace

In all relationships, conflict is to be expected, but the depth of not understanding the conflict and how to work through it may be exacerbated between opposite genders. This is given evidence in the amount of marital conflict that results in divorce in half of all marriages. Not only should conflict be seen as inevitable, but also as beneficial and growth enhancing. Healthy conflict takes place best in the atmosphere of grace that offers acceptance and forgiveness.[27]

Unconditional love necessitates the grace to accept and forgive in light of one's flaws, shortcomings, and differences. God the Father models this by graciously accepting us through His Son's incarnation, death, and resurrection. Christ's coming in human form makes our own forgiveness possible, which in turn gives us the ability to forgive others.

Just as God does not expect us to trust Him without first showing His immeasurable love, men cannot expect their wives or ministry partners to respond to their lead without first providing a loving context in which to understand what is intended for the good of the other or the body. As men are trustworthy in giving love and acceptance, women can trust them to love and provide direction. Direction, just as the Law, guides the way to God, and should not be present just to restrict or punish. A practical example of love and grace could be demonstrated by looking at the emotional expression of men and women. It is important that women, who are generally more emotionally expressive than men, don't lose respect and credibility when their emotions are expressed. Rather, their emotions are seen as giving important information about themselves, others, or the topic at hand; and others need to demonstrate grace and acceptance and learn from the emotion expressed.

A wonderful story is told about Abraham Lincoln that demonstrates the love and grace that is necessary for women to submit to their husbands and the men who are elders with whom they minister.

> Abraham Lincoln went one day to a slave market to see for himself the injustice of the practice. A young woman was brought out on the slave block, her face registered her anger, her bruised body gave evidence of her having been mistreated, and as men made their examinations her eyes flashed with hostility. When men began to bid for ownership, Abraham Lincoln also bid until he bought her. Walking up to the slave block he reached up and took the rope that bound her wrists and led her to the edge of the crowd. Stopping, he untied the rope to give her freedom. As she rubbed her wrists for the circulation he said simply, "You are free to go."
>
> The young woman looked at him with surprise, "What did you say, Master?"
>
> Again he said, "You are free to go."
>
> "Do you mean that I can go where I want to?"
>
> "Yes," he said, "you are free to go."
>
> "I can think like I want to?"
>
> "Yes, you are free."
>
> "I can say what I want to?"
>
> "Yes," he said, "you are free now."
>
> Her eyes filled with tears. "Then, Sir, I want to go with you!"[28]

Abraham Lincoln truly demonstrated acceptance and grace, allowing this woman to grow and become all that God created her to be, which is an act of empowerment.

Empowerment

Another biblical theme that is needed for men and women to reflect their complement is empowerment. The resources of each gender are to be used to empower rather than control one another. To empower means to be active and intentional in the process of enabling another person to acquire power. Jesus rejected the use of power to control others; rather, He demonstrated and affirmed the use of power to serve others, lift the fallen, forgive the guilty, and encourage growth and responsibility in the weak. God's work in people's lives is empowering. Jesus said, "I came that they may have life, and have it abundantly" (John 10:10). John 1:12–13 says that those who believe in Him, He gave power or authority to become children of God. There is no law keeping us from reflecting the fruits of the Spirit, which will result in perfect unity (Gal. 5:22–23). Men and women in a complementarian ministry need to apply this truth by reflecting their strengths of love, joy, peace, longsuffering, gentleness, goodness, and faith. Successful empowerment allows the other gender to gain in personal power while retaining one's own power, resulting in unity of spirit.

This transfer of power is demonstrated by Elaine Stedman as she relates to submission.

> Peace, freedom, wisdom, beauty, fidelity, love—all are symbolized in the female gender. Are they then exclusively female characteristics? Of course not! But may it be that the godly woman, whose gentle, quiet spirit is her love-response to God's loving authority, in a unique way releases others to understand and experience these qualities of life. Is it not possible that the woman who responds with wise and loving submission to the authority of her husband might set him free to headship in the home? And this headship would, if universally practiced, set in motion a cycle of redemptive social responses which would restore order and love to humanity.[29]

Overseers or elders in the church need to make sure that everyone in the body, but particularly the male and female leaders, have an awareness of their gifts and resources as male and female. The strength and power of these gifts and resources need to be other-focused rather than self-enhancing. For example,

> In staff meetings, women may not feel the same freedom most men do to express opinions or to jump into the middle of a discussion. Because of their focus on relationships, women may not want to risk offending or contradicting others. But they must not assume that men are being insensitive and take offense. Because of the way men approach tasks, they may assume that women experience the same kind of freedom they do in arguing a point. Both must continue to learn how the other thinks and empower each other in order to work together.[30]

Focusing on individual performance, whether in preaching or helping, with no thought of the other, is no longer operating as a body. This means that elders need to be aware of what is happening at the levels of the heart as well as the head and encourage both to grow and be active in the body so it is operating as a whole in unity.

Unity

Relating in perfect unity is best seen by looking at the relating patterns of the Father, Son, and Holy Spirit. Jesus expressed it best in John 17:20–23 (*The Message,* italics added):

> I'm praying not only for them
> But also for those who will believe in me
> Because of them and their witness about me.
> The goal is for *all* of them to become *one heart and mind*—
> Just as you, Father, are in me and I in you,
> So they might be *one heart and mind* with us.
> Then the world might believe that you, in fact, sent me.
> The same glory you gave me, I gave them,
> So they'll be *as unified and together as we are*—
> I in them and you in me.
> They they'll be mature in this oneness,
> And give the godless world evidence
> That you've sent me and loved them
> In the same way you've loved me.

Men and women who relate in unity will be putting God's needs and desires first, rather than their own. When men and women are trusting

God first, their needs will be unified by Him, and they will reflect one heart and one mind, that of God. Oswald Chambers put it this way:

> Our Lord trusted no man; yet He was never suspicious, never bitter, never in despair about any man [or woman], because he put God first in trust; He trusted absolutely in what God's grace could do for any man [or woman]. If I put my trust in human beings first, I will end in despairing of everyone; I will become bitter, because I have insisted on man [or woman] being what no man [or woman] can ever be—absolutely right. Never trust anything but the grace of God in yourself or in anyone else.[31]

Having the ability to trust God's grace in another person's life, particularly in another gender who is not easily understood, is not often experienced today. It is here that we see relational immaturity in so many. The ability to trust is developed through our experiences of attachment and separation in relationships throughout life, beginning with our parents. Many have not experienced secure attachment that empowers autonomy and the ability to trust others and God. This lack will cause one to trust in self more than others or God and bring disunity to the body.

This disunity in the body, resulting from the inability to trust, is one of the greatest challenges to the church of this century. Most people in the brokenness of family life have not experienced what Crabb defines as a good relationship: "one in which each member willingly and actively devotes whatever he or she has to give to the well-being of the other."[32]

This kind of other-centeredness is what is needed today for primarily two reasons. The first is to bring unity to the body of Christ like that of the persons of the Trinity. The individual roles of the Godhead flow out of the relationship They have with each other.

> The Father loves the Son (John 3:35). He shows him all that he does (John 5:20). The Son in response always does what pleases the Father (John 8:29), and his obedience springs from his love for his Father (John 14:31). The Spirit is self-effacing. He does not speak of himself, but he takes the things of the Son and shows them to believers. He glorifies Christ (John 16:13–14).[33]

The role of each gender needs to be empowered and given direction by one's relationship with God, which requires the ability to trust.

Role confusion and distortion results when one's role is self-empowered and self-directed, rather than God-directed, because of an inability to trust. For example, women may rise up and take over because of an inability to trust male leadership; and men may respond in anger and apathy when they no longer feel necessary because they are unable to trust that women's strength can complement their own and strengthen them rather than weaken them. The church needs to provide contexts of one-on-one relationships, i.e., mentoring, counseling, or friendship, where people can learn to trust if they have not had experiences that have empowered them to trust others. Without this, how will men and women ever trust that their complementary gender has God's and their best interest in mind? The focus of each instead will be on their own needs and fears of being rejected, intimidated, and angered again.

This struggle in gender relationships in the church is reflected as men abdicate leadership when women become more involved. This causes women to become better trained to take over ministries and do a better job than men or to build auxiliary structures such as mission organizations when denied ministry of their giftedness in the church. When competent women are threatening to men and the working atmosphere becomes competitive, common results are power struggles or male passivity. What is lost is the value of interdependence when women give up their femininity and become like men to have power and authority. This struggle will be one of the greatest challenges to the church in the new millennium. Will we rise to the challenge with commitment, grace, empowerment, and intimacy to create the model, fulfill our true purpose, and reach the goal of reflecting His glory to a lost world?

Second, other-centeredness will enhance the distinctiveness of each gender, because each will want to do service for the other that brings forth the other's strength and enhances its glory. As each gender trusts God first, its need for the other will be more clearly understood through the work of the Holy Spirit within. Trust in God and His power brings humility of how little one can do alone and heightens the awareness of our need for others who have strengths different from our own. For example, when a woman honors a man's wisdom and comes alongside and adds the relational component to his wisdom, in unity they reflect a more complete image than either could alone. Then in being faithful to the ultimate goal of reflecting the fullness of God's glory, each will serve the other to enhance its gifts and strengths of gender. This will reflect to the world not only unity and distinctiveness, but also order.

Order

Although order is clearly seen in the biblical passages discussed in this book, and is also seen in the persons of the Godhead, it is most difficult for men and women to live out.

> It is legitimate to question how the three Persons of the Godhead manage to get along so well. Certainly they never quarrel. We never read of the Spirit getting jealous of the Son's top billing. When they met in committee to discuss creation, no decision had to be tabled due to bickering over what should be created first or who would do what. If it's true that two's company and three is a crowd, one might expect that in all the years they've been together some trouble would have developed. But most couples can't make it through their first night without fussing about something.[34]

We believe primarily the human tendency to fight is true because of our sin of pride and self-centeredness. Not only do we struggle in giving value to the gender we are not, but we also often have many other gods we value for the enhancement they bring to ourselves. These other gods range from money, status, or education, to identifying with someone we hold up as greater than God, and they are more valuable to us than serving the enhancement of someone else.

> Headship and submission, when defined as opportunities to uniquely give to our spouses what they long to receive, become the route to enjoying the difference between men and women.
>
> The differences are real and deep. Men are designed to enter their worlds of people and responsibilities with the confident and unthreatened strength of an advocate. Women are designed to invite other people into a non-manipulative attachment that encourages the enjoyment of intimate relationship.[35]

We honor and give glory to God when men and women live out their created design as male and female.

> Women honor their God-created femininity when they learn to operate in their strengths. It does not honor God when women try to act like men, or to convince men to become more like them. Both men and women should focus on becoming more like Christ—maturing in character but keeping the male or female characteristics distinguishable in the process.[36]

Let's take one more look at the order and focus for both Adam and Eve in Genesis 2. Adam first had a relationship with God, and second was told what his responsibilities were, and third was told of his need for a human relationship to help him. Eve too first had a relationship with God, and second was taken by God to Adam, and third was given her task in the context of her relationship with Adam. We can see from this passage that both Adam and Eve received their identity and security from their relationship with God, but their approach to their tasks was different. Adam was to focus on completing his responsibilities, and Eve was to help in these responsibilities through her relationship with Adam, making relationship her key focus. In completing God's overall purpose, both were necessary and needed.

Women as helpers share this role with Christ, who was given this role by His Father, and with the Holy Spirit, who is our Helper. Just as Jesus knew His purpose and was secure in His relationship with the Father, so women should find their security with God. They then bring to ministry their relational skills and their care for others, which are so necessary for the building of the community in the body. Women's time spent on relationships may seem unproductive to some, but women know it is the key to the task they were given.

> Jesus also acknowledged the difference between men and women. When He spoke to the woman at the well (John 4), he was specific about her sin. But He called her to a lasting relationship with Him that would satisfy her deepest longings. When He called the disciples to follow Him, He challenged them to assume the task He had for them. He did not speak of relationships until much later.[37]

Communication skills is also one of the primary ways women influence. Research shows women to be far more verbal than men, and in Scripture we see women's communication skills being a tool God uses for His purposes. Two positive examples are Priscilla with Apollos (Acts

18) and Abigail with David (1 Samuel 25). These women were submitting to God's leadership, whereas Rebekah influenced Jacob and Delilah manipulated Samson for their own purposes. Men can be especially susceptible to women's influence, so women too need to be on their knees listening to God. When women are called to submit, it will not always be easy, but it is a position of great strength. "It is a voluntary release of one's rights and privileges for a higher purpose."[38] We see this in the life of Christ as He submitted to the Father's will both throughout His life on earth, as well as in the garden when He prayed, "Not my will, but Yours be done" (Luke 22:42).

As we have looked at the order of men and women in leadership and their unique contributions of influence, we can see that both men and women must continue to learn how the other thinks and feels in order to work together in an intimate way.

Intimacy

Most often when we think of intimacy, we think in terms of the sexual intimacy between husband and wife. Therefore, questions overtly or covertly arise: Are you sure intimacy between men and women in ministry is necessary? Isn't intimacy what should be really feared and therefore avoided? In answer to these questions, we avoid commitment to the opposite gender instead of developing the discipline of self-control and the integrity that is held accountable in our same-gender relationships. Paul's teaching to Timothy concerning relationships in the body reflected the intimacy of relationships in the home, appealing to older men as fathers, younger men as brothers, older women as mothers, and younger women as sisters with the emphasis that it be done in all purity (1 Tim. 5:1–2). It is not a matter of whether these relationships should exist, but rather that they exist with the integrity of purity.

Intimacy as defined by the Balswicks, "to know and be known," brings caring, understanding, and communication with others.[39] "A concerted effort will be made to listen, understand, and want what is best for the other. Not only will differences be accepted, but valuing and respecting uniqueness will be a way of confirming the other person."[40]

Rather than discounting differences, men and women's differences bring fullness and completeness to our expression of godly, intimate wholeness. We must be respectful of God's investment in every man and woman and be willing to learn to know each other in order to nurture the life God has placed in them. Elaine Stedman emphasized the hard work that this is.

> In order to nurture life in others we must be willing to learn to know them. This cannot be rushed. It requires a willingness to be imposed upon and a commitment to listening. And a willingness to be candid about our own lives. I wonder if the well-known "woman's intuition" may not be at least partially due to a more highly developed faculty for listening than is commonly found in men. We must learn to know one another according to God's wisdom, evaluating our needs and desires by His standards, so that we may nurture His life and character in one another. This is "body life" relatedness, growing together through mutual response to God's will and purpose for our lives.[41]

Galatians 3:28 points toward such a spiritual partnership in mutual love. Clark noted,

> Galatians 3:28 and related passages teach that men and women are one in Christ, joint-heirs to the grace of eternal life, both fully part of the body of Christ, both sons and daughters of God, both with full access to the Father and fully responsible before him. Both are therefore called to build up one another and the body of Christ in love and to worship the Father in Spirit and in truth.[42]

Intimacy has to be expressed directly and indirectly and experienced objectively and subjectively, bringing comfort, adventure, negotiation, and stability to the relationship.[43] Anderson explains that comfort comes through nourishing the bond of attachment. Adventure is experienced through creative communication and interaction. Negotiation in conflict resolution reinforces the relationship. And, finally, stability is established with loyalty to a commitment to the relationship. Men and women ministering in a complementarian relationship will nourish the relationship as they bring Christ's love, grace, and empowerment to one another as they work side by side. Adventure with the unknown will require courage and boldness. As they venture forth into where God has called each of them, they will need to creatively negotiate the rough places and rocky cliffs but will begin to experience the stability of relationship that comes with commitment over time.

> To better love God and other people is the goal of the Christian life. But before we can love them, we must see them. And we must see them not as we would like to see them or as they would like to be seen. We must see them as they are. Otherwise we don't love the person. We love the image we perceive the person to be. If we are to love people as they are, we must see them as they are. Which means seeing all that lies hidden within them.[44]

The relationships between men and women in the church have a long way to go to reach this level of knowing and understanding. But that should not stop us from moving forward with boldness and courage, leaning on God for His guidance.

CONCLUSION

Modern feminism has stimulated the church to consider anew the question of the nature and relationship of man and woman. Evangelicalism has often tended to ignore these matters of everyday experience in favor of focusing on what are deemed more important and more "theological" issues. But created as relational beings in the likeness of God, our relationship with one another, and especially man with woman as the first human relationship, is vital to our experience of true human life. As the church proclaims the good news of the restoration of human life in Christ, a godly relationship between men and women in the church is indispensable to its witness to the world.

As we have seen, Scripture teaches that the design for the relationship of man and woman was established at creation and grounded in their very nature. Created as equals in God's image, man and woman are nevertheless different—male and female. We are not simply human beings; we are either male or female. Our gender difference was designed for more than procreation. It was to bring wholeness to human existence as man and woman complement each other in all of life. Only with the creation of woman, in addition to man, was creation "very good" (Gen. 1:31), i.e., able to be and do that for which it was created.

Two central truths emerge from the creation account and are consistently seen thereafter in the teaching of the entire biblical record. Man and woman are designed by God to live together in unity as equals, whether in marriage or other social units. From the creation account where they are equally human beings ("man") to the example of Jesus in His dealings with women and the apostle's teaching that there is "neither male nor female . . . in Christ" (Gal. 3:28), man and woman are viewed as equal human persons. They stand before God with equal personal spiritual responsibility and opportunity for relationship with God through His gracious redemption. Woman and man are thus equally valuable, important, and necessary in God's purpose for human life.

A second truth evident from the creation account is that the equality of man and woman includes complementary gender differences. Man needs woman and woman needs man, both for personal fulfillment as human beings and the accomplishment of the divinely given tasks for humanity. Their differences thus draw them together in the promotion of unity. According to Scripture, the gender difference includes some functional distinction in which the man is commissioned to serve in the responsibility of ultimate oversight of the human community and woman to serve as his complementary helper. This relational order, according to apostolic teaching, is grounded in creation where man is first formed and commissioned to his task and then woman. It is apparent in the first events of their existence together that after both man and woman fell into sin, God first addressed the man, although the woman sinned first. Relational order is thereafter consistently expressed throughout all of biblical history in divinely given teaching and structuring of the life of His people. As we have seen, anthropological studies showing the leadership of men in all human societies throughout history also suggest that this order is structured into our very nature.

Sin disrupted all human relationships, bringing self-centered competition instead of self-giving complementarity. But God's purpose for humanity remained the same, and His redemptive grace worked to fulfill His original goal for man and woman. Redemption reaches its zenith in the work of Christ and the gift of the Spirit to indwell all of His people and join them into one body, the church. As partakers of God's eschatological salvation in Christ, men and women are called to live together in the "goodness" of God's creation design for their relationship. We are to "work out" our "salvation" in this realm and live it before the world as lights even as in our individual holiness.

The present gender confusion and conflict owes much to modern feminism's demand for a general gender sameness, contrary to historical human practice. However, the magnitude of the struggle even in evangelical circles suggests that it is not simply a problem of unbiblical demands, but as the history of the church demonstrates, it is also a failure to live according to God's design. Desiring to be faithful to the text of Scripture, the male-led church has often tended to adhere to the prescribed order, but failed to actualize the fullness of the created complementarity of man and woman. Although appreciated for what they do, women have, to a great extent, been limited in their participation in what are publicly portrayed as the most important and valued church ministries. Few evangelical churches today model the prominence of women in the biblical picture of the New Testament church. The result is not only the loss of the gifts of many women to the church, but the sense on the part of many (especially women, but also men) that women are of less value and inferior in the church.

As believers in the church, we need to use the present controversy as an opportunity to look carefully at God's design of man and woman and their relationship revealed in Scripture. Created as complementary in nature, they were intended to function as complements. Without denying some gender-specific tasks (e.g., in relation to childbearing), the created complementarity of man and woman calls for the mutual need of the partnership of both genders for fullness of life. As in the Christian family where husband and wife work together under the headship of the husband, helping each other in most areas, so the church needs to consider the ministry of men and women together in all areas of church life, including teaching and leadership within God's design of order.

Finally, men and women must recognize the need of each other so that their different contributions in church ministry are equally valued in the accomplishment of the mission of the church and its growth toward maturity in Christlikeness. Christian love that wills to understand the other and minister for his or her true good is the only power that can bring true complementarity of women and men in ministry.

The present gender struggle highlights the problem. But only the

Word of God gives our Creator's design for man and woman and thus the solution. The church must renew its faith in the goodness of God's plan as taught in His Word, despite its overwhelming rejection by contemporary culture. And in doing so, we must study and pray together so that we may more fully demonstrate the "goodness" of life together as men and women by living in obedience to our Lord.

NOTES

Abbreviations Used:

ABRL	Anchor Bible Reference Library
BAR	Biblical Archaeologist Reader
JBL	Journal of Biblical Literature
NAC	New American Commentary
NICNT	New International Commentary on the New Testament
NICOT	New International Commentary on the Old Testament
SNTSMS	Society for New Testament Studies Monograph Series
WBC	Word Biblical Commentary
ZNW	Zeitschrift für die neutestamentliche Wissenschaft
EPRO	Études preliminaries aux religions orientales dans l'empire Romain
JSOT	Journal for the Study of the Old Testament

Chapter 1: A Problem in the Church

1. John Piper and Wayne Grudem, eds., *Recovering Biblical Manhood and Womanhood : A Response to Evangelical Feminism* (Wheaton, Ill.: Crossway, 1991), xiii.
2. The words of Adam in the rhythmic pattern of poetry represent speech in the form of a cry, in this instance, one of joy, cf. Claus Westermann, *Genesis 1–11: A Commentary* (Minneapolis: Augsburg, 1984), 231.
3. U. Cassuto, *A Commentary on the Book of Genesis,* part I (Jerusalem: Magnes Press, 1961), 135.
4. Victor P. Hamilton, *The Book of Genesis: Chapters 1–17* (Grand Rapids: Eerdmans, 1990), 179, with reference to W. Brueggeman, "Of the Same Flesh and Bone (GN 2, 23a)," *Catholic Biblical Quarterly* 32 (1970): 532–42; cf. also N. P. Bratsiotis, "בָּשָׂר, *basar,*" *Theological Dictionary of the Old Testament,* vol. 2, ed. G. Johannes Botterweck and Helmer Ringgren (Grand Rapids: Eerdmans, 1975), 328.
5. Walter L. Liefeld, "A Plural Ministry View: Your Sons and Your Daughters Shall Prophesy," in *Women in Ministry: Four Views,* ed. Bonnidell Clouse and Robert G. Clouse (Downers Grove, Ill.: InterVarsity, 1989), 127.
6. Alvera Mickelsen, ed., *Women, Authority and the Bible* (Downers Grove, Ill.: InterVarsity, 1986), 20.
7. Ibid., 24.
8. A few evangelicals would agree that Paul was in error in some of his teaching relative to the relationship of men and women; cf. Paul K. Jewett, *Man as Male and Female* (Grand Rapids: Eerdmans, 1975), 119; cf. also some who identified themselves as evangelicals at the time of writing: Virginia Ramey Mollenkott, *Women, Men, and the Bible,* revised ed. (New York: Crossroad, 1988), 77; Letha Scanzoni and Nancy Hardesty, *All We're Meant to Be* (Waco, Tex.: Word, 1974), 28.

9. For a discussion of the various interpretations of 1 Timothy 2:12, see chapter 12.
10. It should also be noted that there is some variation among evangelical egalitarians on the question of practice today. Some seek immediate implementation of the egalitarian position both in the home and church. Others would see egalitarianism as the ideal toward which to strive, but would attempt to work within the cultural norms so as not to hurt the cause of Christ. Their stance would be somewhat similar to the issue of slavery in the New Testament world, which most believers would agree is not biblical and yet for the sake of testimony, the apostles did not strive for emancipation of all slaves.
11. For indications of the variety in application among those who hold to a permanent order, see Robert D. Culver, "A Traditional View," in *Women in Ministry* ed. Bonnidell Clouse and Robert G. Clouse (Downers Grove, Ill.: InterVarsity, 1989), 25–52; Susan Foh, "A Male Leadership View," in *Women in Ministry* ed. Bonnidell Clouse and Robert G. Clouse, 69–105; Douglas Moo, "What Does It Mean Not to Teach or Have Authority Over Men?" in *Recovering Biblical Manhood and Womanhood,* ed. John Piper and Wayne Grudem, 186.
12. Robert D. Culver, "A Traditional View," in *Women in Ministry,* 29.
13. Susan Foh, "A Male Leadership View," in *Women in Ministry,* 102.

Chapter 2: The Background of the Contemporary Situation

1. Vern L. Bullough with Bonnie Bullough, *The Subordinate Sex* (Urbana, Ill.: Univ. of Illinois, 1973), 58. Bullough's work presents a good general history of the place of women throughout the world.
2. Plato, *Republic,* ed. and trans. Paul Shoren, 2 vols. (London: Heinemann, 1935), 454D–456C; cited by Bullough, *The Subordinate Sex,* 60.
3. Bullough, *The Subordinate Sex,* 60.
4. Aristotle, *Generation of Animals,* trans. A. L. Peck (London: Heinemann, 1953), 729A, 25–34; cited by Bullough, *The Subordinate Sex,* 62.
5. Bullough, *The Subordinate Sex,* 62.
6. Bullough, *The Subordinate Sex,* 64; referring to Aristotle, *Generation of Animals,* I, xx (728A), 18–20; and Nichomachean, *Ethics* VIII, vii, 2–3.
7. Bullough, *The Subordinate Sex,* 95–96.
8. Ibid., 114; referring to Clement of Alexandria, *Paedagogus,* bk. 1, iv in vol. 2, *The Ante Nicene Fathers,* ed. and trans. Alexander Roberts and James Donaldson, American ed. A. Cleveland Coxe (reprinted, Grand Rapids: Eerdmans, 1961).
9. Mary Daly, *The Church and the Second Sex* (New York: Harper & Row, 1975), 85.
10. St. Thomas Aquinas, *Summa Theologica,* ed. and trans. the Fathers of the English Dominican Province, 3 vols. (New York: Benzinger, 1947), vol. 1, pt. 1, ques. 92, "The Production of Women"; cited by Bullough, *The Subordinate Sex,* 174–75. See Augustine, PL 34, 395–6., *De Genesi ad litteram* IX, cap. 5; referenced in Mary Daly, *The Church and the Second Sex,* 85.
11. Ignatius, "Rules for the Discernment of Spirits," First Week, Rule 12, in *Spiritual Exercises;* cited by Mary Daly, *The Church and the Second Sex,* 101.
12. Bullough, *The Subordinate Sex,* 114; citing Tertullian, *On the Apparel of Women,* bk. 1 in vol. 4, *The Ante Nicene Fathers.*
13. Williston Walker, *John Calvin* (New York: Schocken, 1969, rpt), 236.
14. John Knox, "The First Blast of the Trumpet Against the Monstrous Regiment of Women," in *The Works of John Knox,* coll. and ed. David Laing, vol. 4 (Edinburgh: Bannatyne Club, 1855), 373.
15. Bullough, *The Subordinate Sex,* 298; referring to Julia Cherry Spruill, *Women's Life and Work in the Southern Colonies* (Chapel Hill: Univ. North Carolina, 1938), 202.
16. Bullough, *The Subordinate Sex,* 308.
17. Ibid., 155.
18. St. Teresa of Avila, *Way of Perfection,* chap. III in *The Complete Works of St. Teresa of Jesus,* trans. and ed. E. Allison Peers (London: Sheed & Ward, 1949), II:298.
19. Mary Daly, *The Church and the Second Sex,* 95–97.

20. Mary A. Kassian, *The Feminist Gospel: The Movement to Unite Feminism with the Church* (Wheaton, Ill.: Crossway, 1992), 15–201, see especially the helpful charts on pp. 255–57.
21. Elizabeth Gould Davis, *The First Sex* (Baltimore: Penguin, 1972), 335–37; cited by Kassian, *The Feminist Gospel*, 87.
22. The following survey is based primarily on Kassian's *The Feminist Gospel*.
23. William Douglas, "Women in the Church: Historical Perspectives and Contemporary Dilemmas," *Pastoral Psychology* (June 1961): 14.
24. Ibid., 13.
25. Rosemary Lauer, "Women and the Church," *Commonweal* 79, no. 13 (1963): 366.
26. Kassian, *The Feminist Gospel*, 40.
27. Ibid., 41, referring to Daly's thought.
28. Letty Russell, *The Feminist Interpretation of the Bible*, ed. Letty Russell (Philadelphia: Westminster, 1985), 16. Her citation is from Elisabeth Schüssler Fiorenza, "A Feminist Biblical Hermeneutics: Biblical Interpretation and Liberation Theology," in *The Challenge of Liberation Theology: A First-World Response*, l. Dale Richesin and Brian Mahan, eds. (Maryknoll, N.Y.: Orbis, 1981), 107.
29. Kassian, *The Feminist Gospel*, 98.
30. Ibid., 135–47.
31. Rosemary Radford Ruether, "Feminist Theology and Spirituality," in *Christian Feminism: Visions of a New Humanity*, ed. Judith Weidman (San Francisco: Harper & Row, 1984), 13.
32. Letty Russell, *The Feminist Interpretation of the Bible*, 144, 139.
33. In her collection of texts and essays entitled *Womanguides: Readings Toward a Feminist Theology*, Ruether included writings both from biblical and nonbiblical texts, including such diverse sources as ancient mythology, Christian Science, and goddess worship (Rosemary Radford Ruether, *Womanguides: Readings Toward a Feminist Theology* [Boston: Beacon, 1985], xi.). Out of all of this a new canon emerges to which even contemporary stories of women's redemptive experience may be added (ibid., 247).
34. Kassian, *The Feminist Gospel*, 179–82.
35. For evangelical involvement in the earlier women's movement, see Nancy A. Hardesty, *Women Called to Witness: Evangelical Feminism in the Nineteenth Century* (Nashville: Abingdon, 1982); Janette Hassey, *No Time for Silence: Evangelical Women in Public Ministry Around the Turn of the Century* (Grand Rapids: Zondervan, 1986); Ruth Tucker and Walter Liefeld, *Daughters of the Church: Women and Ministry from New Testament Times to the Present* (Grand Rapids: Zondervan, 1987).
36. Mark Chaves, *Ordaining Women: Culture and Conflict in Religious Organizations* (Cambridge, Mass.: Harvard Univ., 1997), 66.
37. Catherine Brekus, "Female Evangelism in the Early Methodist Movement, 1784–1845," unpublished manuscript (Chicago: Univ. of Chicago Divinity School, 1996), 39; cited by Mark Chaves, *Ordaining Women: Culture and Conflict in Religious Organizations*, 66.
38. Virginia Mollenkott, in a letter to *His* magazine, June 1973.
39. Ruth Haley Barton, *Equal to the Task* (Downers Grove, Ill.: InterVarsity, 1998); Gilbert Bilezikian, *Beyond Sex Roles: A Guide for the Study of Female Roles in the Bible* (Grand Rapids: Baker, 1985); Mary J. Evans, *Woman in the Bible* (Downers Grove, Ill.: InterVarsity, 1983); Stanley J. Grenz and Denise Muir Kjesbo, *Women in the Church: A Biblical Theology of Women in Ministry* (Downers Grove, Ill.: InterVarsity, 1995); Rebecca Merrill Groothuis, *Women Caught in the Conflict: The Culture War Between Traditionalism and Feminism* (Grand Rapids: Baker, 1994), and *Good News for Women: A Biblical Picture of Gender Equality* (Baker, 1997); Patricia Gundry, *Woman Be Free* (Grand Rapids: Zondervan, 1977); *Heirs Together* (Grand Rapids: Zondervan, 1977); *Neither Slave nor Free: Helping Women Answer the Call to Church Leadership* (San Francisco: Harper & Row, 1987); Roberta Hestenes, ed., *Women and Men in Ministry* (Philadelphia: Westminster, 1984); E. Margaret Howe, *Women and Church Leadership* (Grand Rapids: Zondervan, 1982); Gretchen Gaebelein Hull, *Equal to Serve: Women and Men in the Church and Home* (Old Tappan, N.J.: Revell, 1987); Paul Jewett, *Man as Male and Female* (Grand Rapids: Eerdmans, 1975); Craig S. Keener, *Paul, Women and Wives: Marriage and Women's Ministry in the Letters of*

Paul (Peabody, Mass.: Hendrickson, 1992); Richard Clark Kroeger and Catherine Clark Kroeger, *I Suffer Not a Woman: Rethinking 1 Timothy in Light of Ancient Evidence* (Grand Rapids: Baker, 1992); Alvera Mickelsen, ed., *Women, Authority and the Bible* (Downers Grove, Ill.: InterVarsity, 1986); Virginia Mollenkott, *Women, Men, and the Bible* (Nashville: Abingdon, 1977); Dorothy R. Pape, *In Search of God's Ideal Woman* (Downers Grove, Ill.: InterVarsity, 1976); Letha Scanzoni and Nancy Hardesty, *All We're Meant to Be* (Waco, Tex.: Word, 1974); rev. ed. (Nashville: Abingdon, 1986); 3rd rev. ed. (Grand Rapids: Eerdmans, 1992); Aida Spencer, *Beyond the Curse: Women Called to Ministry* (Nashville: Nelson, 1985); Elaine Storkey, *What's Right with Feminism* (Grand Rapids: Eerdmans, 1986); Ruth A. Tucker and Walter L. Liefeld, *Daughters of the Church: Women and Ministry from New Testament Times to the Present* (Grand Rapids: Zondervan, 1987); Ruth A. Tucker, *Women in the Maze: Questions and Answers on Biblical Equality* (Downers Grove, Ill.: InterVarsity, 1992); Mary Stewart Van Leeuwen, *Gender and Grace: Love, Work and Parenting in a Changing World* (Downers Grove, Ill.: InterVarsity, 1990); Don Williams, *The Apostle Paul and Women in the Church* (Ventura, Calif.: Regal, 1977).

40. Gretchen Gaebelein Hull suggests that some of the passages be bracketed off as impossible to understand and therefore outside of the present discussion (*Equal to Serve* [Old Tappan, N.J.: Revell, 1987], 189).

41. A comparison of the latest edition of *All We're Meant to Be* (1992) by Scanzoni and Hardesty with their original edition (1974) clearly reveals some erosion from traditional evangelical positions. In a discussion of biblical interpretation, they speak approvingly of "women speaking out of the authority of their own experience" (Letha Dawson Scanzoni and Nancy A. Hardesty, *All We're Meant to Be,* 3d rev. ed. [Grand Rapids: Eerdmans, 1992], 15). Instead of men defining them, women are to define themselves by listening to "the inner voice" (ibid., 318). In relation to the composition of the biblical canon, the latest edition of their work also tells us that "we must remember that the book was primarily written by men in patriarchal cultures; that the canon was defined by men, *who left out many books now known to us to be more favorable to women*" (ibid., 9, italics added). Although they still claim to be "evangelical" and "biblical feminists" holding to "a commitment to the authority of Scripture" (ibid., 2, 14), it is obvious that they have departed considerably from the historical meaning of that commitment.

The philosophy of secular feminism, and to a great extent liberal feminist theology, that all distinctions within humanity lead to oppressive domination, has influenced some within the evangelical tradition to begin to acknowledge the validity of homosexuality. Although their first edition uniformly saw homosexual behavior as sinful, Scanzoni and Hardesty in their latest revision sound very much like their nonevangelical feminist counterparts. Noting that the liberal feminist theologian Rosemary Ruether referred to "all duality, all polarity" as evil, Scanzoni and Hardesty go on to declare, "All distinctions between people—male and female, rich and poor, black and white, *gay and straight,* Western world and Third World, Christian and non-Christian—are attempts to deny our common humanity" (italics added). Such divisions, we are told, are the essence of sin involving "the desire to lord it over one another that we see so graphically displayed in sexism, racism, homophobia, classism, nationalism, and militarism" (ibid., 14, 16). Similarly, Virginia Mollenkott, a leader of the evangelical feminist cause in the mid-1970s, has subsequently condoned both homosexuality and sexual relations outside of marriage (Virginia R. Mollenkott, *Godding: Human Responsibility and the Bible* [New York: Crossroad, 1987], 87–88, 106; *Sensuous Spirituality: Out from Fundamentalism* [New York: Crossroad, 1992]. See also her work written with Letha Scanzoni, *Is the Homosexual My Neighbor?* [San Francisco: Harper & Row, 1978]).

Erosion in broader theological concepts is also apparent in the thinking of Mollenkott. Beginning with the call for the equality of men and women in church ministry in her first book published in 1977, she moved to the promotion of inclusive God language in her second work in 1983. God, she said, "may be referred to as *He, She,* or *It.*" That this has developed along the lines of liberal feminist theology in a changing concept of God is evident in her statement that "He/She/It [is to] be recognized in everyone and everything" (Virginia R. Mollenkott, *The Divine Feminine: The Biblical Imagery of God as Female* [New

York: Crossroad, 1983], cited by Kassian, *The Feminist Gospel,* 238). Mollenkott explains, "To be one with God means to recognize our oneness with all those who also have derived their being from the same Source: Muslims; Jews; post-Christians or post-Jewish feminists; gay people or heterosexual people; liberal or fundamentalist people; communist or capitalist people; black, white, red, or yellow people" (*Godding: Human Responsibility and the Bible,* 10). "God is *both* 'other' *and* ourselves, more fully ourselves than our superficial body-identified personalities could ever be. . . . God is becoming God's Self through the process of my living" (ibid., 4).

Mollenkott is no doubt an extreme example of one whose feminism has clearly led her away from her conservative evangelical roots. But others claiming the evangelical position also acknowledge that feminism impacts theology far beyond the issue of equality of men and women or the question of women's ordination.

42. Letha Dawson Scanzoni and Nancy A. Hardesty, *All We're Meant to Be,* 337–38.
43. For a description of the movement of some feminists toward liberal theology and in some instances completely away from the church, see Kassian, *The Feminist Gospel,* 225–40.
44. Donald G. Bloesch, *A Theology of Word and Spirit: Authority and Method in Theology, Christian Foundations,* vol. 1 (Downers Grove, Ill.: InterVarsity, 1992), 89. For a more complete discussion of the impact of inclusive God language, see Donald G. Bloesch, *The Battle for the Trinity: The Debate over Inclusive God-Language* (Ann Arbor, Mich.: Servant, 1985).
45. Feminist theologian Letty Russell provides an interesting example of the power of feminist interpretation to extend over more and more of the Bible. In 1976, she wrote in the introduction of a book on nonsexist interpretation that "the message of the Bible can become a liberating word for those who hear and act in faith but that this same message also needs to be liberated from sexist interpretations which continue to dominate our thought." In a later book, she explains that this earlier work was a "'premature' guide to feminist interpretation of the Bible. As the contributions to feminist interpretation have continued to grow in volume and maturity, it has become abundantly clear that the scriptures need liberation, not only from existing interpretations but also from the patriarchal bias of the texts themselves" (Letty M. Russell, "Introduction: Liberating the Word," in *Feminist Interpretation of the Bible,* ed. by Letty M. Russell [Philadelphia: Westminster, 1985], 11).
46. Samuele Bacchiocchi, *Women in the Church* (Berrien Springs, Mich.: Biblical Perspectives, 1987); Stephen B. Clark, *Man and Woman in Christ: An Examination of the Roles of Men and Women in Light of Scripture and the Social Sciences* (Ann Arbor, Mich.: Servant, 1980); Susan T. Foh, *Women and the Word of God: A Response to Biblical Feminism* (Phillipsburg, N.J.: Presbyterian & Reformed, 1980); James Hurley, *Man and Woman in Biblical Perspective* (Grand Rapids: Zondervan, 1981); George W. Knight III, *The Role Relationship of Men and Women: New Testament Teaching* (Chicago: Moody, 1977, rev. 1985); Werner Neuer, *Man and Woman in Christian Perspective* (Wheaton, Ill.: Crossway, 1991); John Piper and Wayne Grudem, eds., *Recovering Biblical Manhood and Womanhood: A Response to Evangelical Feminism* (Wheaton, Ill.: Crossway, 1991).
47. The Council on Biblical Manhood and Womanhood has set forth its rationale, goals, and affirmations in the *Danvers Statement.* Information on CBMW may be obtained by writing CBMW, P.O. Box 317, Wheaton, IL 60189. Christians for Biblical Equality has also published a position paper entitled "Men, Women and Biblical Equality." Information on the CBE may be obtained by writing Christians for Biblical Equality, 380 Lafayette Road South, Suite 122, St. Paul, MN 55107-1216.

Chapter 3: The Relationship of Woman and Man in the Old Testament

1. The reader should also consult Susan T. Foh's excellent discussion, *Women and the Word of God: A Response to Biblical Feminism* (Phillipsburg, N.J.: Presbyterian & Reformed, 1980), especially chapter 3, "What the Old Testament Says About Women," 50–88.

2. John Sailhamer, "Genesis," in *The Expositor's Bible Commentary* (Grand Rapids: Zondervan, 1990), 2:38.
3. Foh, *Women and the Word of God,* 55. She has a lengthy discussion (52–59) that refutes Paul Jewett's view that "Man's creation in the divine image is so related to his creation as male and female that the latter may be looked upon as an exposition of the former" (*Man as Male and Female* [Grand Rapids: Eerdmans, 1975], 13).
4. Stanley J. Grenz, "Theological Foundations for Male-Female Relationships," *Journal of the Evangelical Theological Society* 41:4 (1998): 618.
5. Genesis 2 does not teach this view, either. "The *adam*" (or simply *adam*) occurs consistently throughout Genesis 2–4 to refer to the man both before and after the creation of the woman. God took the *material* that He used to form the woman from the man's side, even as He used the "dust of the ground" to form the man. The woman had a separate creation from the man; she did not spring whole from his side.
6. Sometimes it is translated "people," as in Isaiah 6:11 (NASB and NRSV). See also Genesis 6:3, 5–7; 7:21, 23; 8:21; 9:5–6; Exodus 4:11; 9:9; etc.
7. The Septuagint (an ancient Greek translation of the Old Testament) uses the same Greek words for "male" and "female" that Paul uses, and this makes it clear that Paul alludes to Genesis 1.
8. Lillie Devereux Blake in *The Woman's Bible* (New York: Arno, 1972 [repr. of 1895 ed.]), 1:19.
9. David J. A. Clines, *What Does Eve Do to Help? and Other Readerly Questions to the Old Testament,* JSOT Supplement Series 94 (Sheffield, England: Sheffield Academic Press, 1990), 36–37.
10. Clines, *What Does Eve Do,* 35.
11. Gordon Wenham, *Genesis 1–15,* Word Biblical Commentary 1 (Waco, Tex.: Word, 1987), 68.
12. John Piper and Wayne Grudem, eds., *Recovering Biblical Manhood and Womanhood: A Response to Evangelical Feminism* (Wheaton, Ill.: Crossway, 1991) 102–3.
13. Cf. Wenham, *Genesis 1–15,* 70–71. In ancient Hebrew culture, the woman would also leave her family and become a part of her husband's family (cf. Gen. 24), but the account is told from the man's point of view.
14. Wenham, *Genesis 1–15,* 68.
15. Susan Foh, *Women and the Word of God,* 62.
16. Stephen B. Clark, *Man and Woman in Christ: An Examination of the Roles of Men and Women in Light of Scripture and the Social Sciences* (Ann Arbor, Mich.: Servant, 1980), 28.
17. For a popular explication, see Larry Crabb, *The Silence of Adam: Becoming Men of Courage in a World of Chaos* (Grand Rapids: Zondervan, 1995), 11–12.
18. See Wenham, *Genesis 1–15,* 80.
19. Foh, *Women and the Word of God,* 69.
20. Claus Westermann, *Genesis 1–11: A Commentary* (Minneapolis: Augsburg, 1984), 263. I would not agree, however, that Genesis 3 does not narrate the "fall" of mankind.
21. Foh, *Women and the Word of God,* 69. Note, however, that under Foh's view the issues she mentions become significant for *both* the man and the woman. Since verse 16 is still part of the woman's punishment rather than the man's, this could be an argument against Foh's position (cf. Irvin A. Busenitz, "Woman's Desire for Man: Genesis 3:16 Reconsidered," *Grace Theological Journal* 7:2 [1986], 207).
22. Gerhard von Rad, *Genesis: A Commentary,* rev. ed.; Old Testament Library (Philadelphia: Westminster, 1972), 93–94.
23. Also, property was inherited through the sons, but it could be passed on to daughters if there were no sons (Num. 27:1–11).
24. See Wenham, *Genesis 1–15,* 101–2. Possibly Paul alludes to this connection as well in 1 Corinthians 11:12.
25. The name "Eve" *(chavva)* most likely means "life" (*Zoe* in the Greek Septuagint). The explanation is the narrator's comment rather than Adam's, since she had not yet had any

children. However, Adam must have had something like this in mind, perhaps reflecting on the promised offspring of 3:15.

26. Martin Noth, *Leviticus: A Commentary,* Old Testament Library (Philadelphia: Westminster, 1965), 97.
27. Baruch Levine mentions an ancient belief that newborns were subject to demonic influence. Thus there would be a desire to protect the daughter for a longer period because of "the expectation that she herself would someday become a new mother" (*The JPS Torah Commentary: Leviticus* [Philadelphia: Jewish Publication Society, 1989], 250). One problem with this view is that it implies a superstitious belief that is not endorsed in Scripture. Also, the passage focuses on the unclean state of the mother with no hint in the context of how the practice would somehow protect the newborn.
28. J. R. Porter, *Leviticus,* Cambridge Bible Commentary: *New English Bible* (New York: Cambridge Univ., 1976), 95. Some have also referred to "a belief in antiquity that the postnatal discharge lasted longer in the case of a girl [baby]" (G. J. Wenham, *The Book of Leviticus,* NICOT [Grand Rapids: Eerdmans, 1979], 188).
29. Clines, *What Does Eve Do,* 45.
30. A special category of leaders in the OT was called "elders" (Num. 11:16–17, 25), and the people were required to respect their elders (Lev. 19:32; Prov. 20:29). For the blessedness of children, see Psalm 127:3–5; 128:3; Proverbs 17:6.
31. The end of 1 Samuel 1:28 is difficult: "And he [Eli?] worshiped the Lord there." The Hebrew could be taken instead, "they worshiped," meaning that both Eli and Hannah worshiped. A variant from the Dead Sea Scrolls reads, "she worshiped," which makes the most sense in the context.
32. John E. Hartley, *Leviticus,* Word Biblical Commentary 4 (Dallas: Word, 1992), 481.
33. Cf. Gordon Wenham, *Numbers: An Introduction and Commentary,* Tyndale Old Testament Commentaries (Downers Grove, Ill.: InterVarsity, 1981), 206.
34. Targum "Pseudo-Jonathan" and the Mishnah, *Niddah* 5:6.
35. Later Jewish tradition restricted the husband's veto power "to those vows which involve either self-denial or matters of mutual concern to the husband and wife" (Mayer I. Gruber, "Women in the Cult According to the Priestly Code," in Jacob Neusner, et al., eds., *Judaic Perspectives on Ancient Israel* [Philadelphia: Fortress, 1987], 38).
36. God can work through situations that do not reflect His revealed plan. The polygamy in Jacob's family, even his marriage to two sisters, declared illegal under the Mosaic code, would be in the same category with Abraham's lies about Sarah or the brothers' sending Joseph into slavery. It seems as if God could have chosen to build Jacob's family through one wife or to have preserved Abraham's life apart from deception or to have preserved Jacob's family alive through some means other than sibling rivalry. He actually worked through and in spite of the failings of mankind.

Chapter 4: The Ministry of Women in the Old Testament

1. See Micah 3, which describes a time when all of Israel's leaders, including the prophets, were corrupt.
2. See chapter 8 for a discussion of the "deaconess" in the New Testament.
3. I. Howard Marshall, *The Gospel of Luke: A Commentary on the Greek Text,* New International Greek Testament Commentary (Grand Rapids: Eerdmans, 1978), 124.
4. Susan Foh, *Women and the Word of God: A Response to Biblical Feminism* (Phillipsburg, N.J.: Presbyterian & Reformed, 1980), 84.
5. She was called the "queen," but she must have been the queen mother rather than Belshazzar's wife, because his "wives and his concubines" were already present at the banquet (Dan. 5:2–3). History shows that Nebuchadnezzar was not Belshazzar's literal father, but the queen mother may have been Nitocris, Nebuchadnezzar's daughter. Alternatively, Nebuchadnezzar may have been Belshazzar's "father" in the sense of his predecessor (D. J. A. Clines, "Belshazzar," *ISBE*, rev. ed. [Grand Rapids: Eerdmans, 1979], 1:455).
6. See Robert L. Thomas, *Revelation,* vol. 2 (Chicago: Moody, 1995), 234–36.

7. Robert L. Hubbard Jr., *The Book of Ruth,* NICOT (Grand Rapids: Eerdmans, 1988), 24.
8. I have translated the Hebrew literally to bring out an emphasis that the versions miss.
9. Some have identified Lappidoth with Barak, since both have a name that means "lightning" (Robert G. Boling, *Judges, Anchor Bible* 6A [Garden City, N.Y.: Doubleday, 1969], 95). Arthur Cundall rightly calls the evidence for this "flimsy" (*Judges: An Introduction and Commentary,* Tyndale Old Testament Commentaries [Downers Grove, Ill.: InterVarsity, 1968], 83).
10. The NIV renders verse 4, "Deborah . . . was leading Israel at that time." This reads too much into the verb "judging." She simply settled disputes for the people. Acting as a judge or arbiter was something that other women besides Deborah did (see 2 Sam. 20:16–22).
11. In the rest of the passage, the order is "Aaron and Miriam" (Num. 12:4–5).
12. E. J. Young, *My Servants the Prophets* (Grand Rapids: Eerdmans, 1952), 54.
13. She is known traditionally as the "witch of Endor," but the text simply calls her a "medium" (Hebrew *baalat ob*, "possessor/controller of a ghost").
14. Derek Kidner, *Proverbs: An Introduction and Commentary,* Tyndale Old Testament Commentaries (Downers Grove, Ill.: InterVarsity, 1964), 183.
15. David Atkinson, *The Message of Proverbs,* The Bible Speaks Today (Downers Grove, Ill.: InterVarsity, 1996), 168.
16. Cheryl Dunn, "A Study of Proverbs 31:10–31," MA thesis (Talbot School of Theology, 1993), 19.
17. Carol Meyers, in her study based on "archaeological, biblical, and ethnographic data," states: "Considerable expertise—planning, skill, experience, and technological knowledge—was necessary for the performance of a woman's tasks, many of which involved precise chemical and physical processes" ("The Family in Early Israel," in *Families in Ancient Israel,* ed. Leo G. Perdue, et al.; The Family, Religion, and Culture [Louisville: Westminster John Knox, 1997], 27).
18. Dunn, "Proverbs 31:10–31," 146.
19. "The use of 'land' within Prov. 31:23 may therefore indicate that a broader territorial area than a single city was intended by the author" (Dunn, "Proverbs 31:10–31," 115).
20. William McKane, *Proverbs: A New Approach,* Old Testament Library (Philadelphia: Westminster, 1970), 669.

Chapter 5: Women in the Teaching and Example of Jesus

1. For example, note the plurals in the title of the following volume, which are intended to point to the diversity of viewpoints within first-century Judaism: Jacob Neusner, William S. Green, and Ernest Frerichs, eds., *Judaisms and Their Messiahs at the Turn of the Christian Era* (Cambridge: Cambridge Univ., 1987).
2. For a brief overview, see Monique Alexandre, "Early Christian Women," in *From Ancient Goddesses to Christian Saints,* ed., Pauline Schmitt Pantel, volume 1 of *A History of Women in the West,* 5 vols., gen. eds., Georges Duby and Michelle Perrot, (Cambridge, Mass.: Harvard Univ., 1992), 409–44.
3. See the comments in James A. Borland, "Women in the Life and Teachings of Jesus," in *Recovering Biblical Manhood and Womanhood: A Response to Evangelical Feminism,* eds., John Piper and Wayne Grudem (Wheaton: Crossway, 1991), 113–14.
4. Cited in Leonard Swidler, *Women in Judaism: The Status of Women in Formative Judaism* (Metuchen, N.J.: Scarecrow Press, 1976), 80, 199–200 n. 96.
5. For a fairly balanced discussion, see Ben Witherington III, *Women in the Ministry of Jesus: A Study of Jesus' Attitudes to Women and Their Roles as Reflected in His Earthly Life,* SNTSMS 51 (Cambridge: Cambridge Univ., 1984), 1–10.
6. See *b. Berakot* 48a; cf. F. F. Bruce, *New Testament History* (Garden City, N.Y.: Doubleday, 1971), 76. Josephus, with his penchant for negative attitudes toward women, speaks of the peace of her reign, but he is not as generous in describing her overall rule (cf. Josephus, *Antiquities* 13.430–32).

7. Anthony Saldarini, "Babatha's Story: Personal Archive Offers a Glimpse of Ancient Jewish Life," *BAR* 24 (1998): 37.
8. The documents they carried were their marriage contracts, their deed of gift of property from their father, and a renunciation of claims others had against their property.
9. For a brief overview, see Tal Ilan, "How Women Differed," BAR 24 (1998): 38–39, and in the same issue, the article cited above by Anthony Saldarini, "Babatha's Story: Personal Archive Offers a Glimpse of Ancient Jewish Life," 29–37, 72–74. For a scholarly look at rabbinic attitudes, see Tal Ilan, *Mine and Yours Are Hers: Retrieving Women's History from Rabbinic Literature* (Melbourne, Fla.: E.J. Brill, 1997).
10. Cf. Grant R. Osborne, "Women in Jesus' Ministry," *Westminster Theological Journal* 51 (1989): 259–91, who suggests that the negative status of women had begun in the time of Jesus, but the gloomy picture painted by the rabbis is a later development (263).
11. Cf. John Nolland, *Luke 9:21–18:34,* WBC 35B (Dallas: Word, 1993), 724; Borland, "Women in the Life and Teachings of Jesus," 114–15.
12. For a more extensive discussion, see Michael J. Wilkins, *Following the Master: A Biblical Theology of Discipleship* (Grand Rapids: Zondervan, 1992), chaps. 4–5.
13. Cf. John 1:35ff.; Matthew 11:2ff.; 14:12; 22:15–16.
14. Donald A. Hagner, *Matthew 1–13,* WBC 33A (Dallas: Word, 1993), 360.
15. See Wilkins, *Following the Master,* chap. 13.
16. Several authors struggle to distinguish between the women as disciples (believers) and as those who minister (function); e.g., Ruth A. Tucker and Walter Liefeld, *Daughters of the Church: Women and Ministry from New Testament Times to the Present* (Grand Rapids: Zondervan, 1987), esp. 19–48.
17. For a good overview of the subject, see Witherington, *Women in the Ministry of Jesus,* 1–10.
18. A father who was under a vow, which restricted his activities in other ways, "may teach Scripture to his sons and his daughters" (*m. Nedarim* 4:3). This indicates that fathers were to teach all of their children, including both boys and girls.
19. R. Eliezer says: "If any man gives his daughter a knowledge of the Law it is as though he taught her lechery" (*m. Sota* 3:4).
20. In the same passage above, where R. Eliezer excluded daughters from education, R. Ben Azzai says: "A man ought to give his daughter a knowledge of the Law so that if she must drink [the bitter water] she may know that the merit [that she had acquired] will hold her punishment in suspense" (*m. Sota* 3:4).
21. See James L. Crenshaw, *Education in Ancient Israel: Across the Deadening Silence,* ABRL (New York: Doubleday, 1998), 179.
22. Cf. Osborne, "Women in Jesus' Ministry," 281.
23. Robert H. Stein, *Luke,* NAC 24 (Nashville: Broadman, 1992), 240.
24. Joel B. Green, *The Gospel of Luke,* NICNT (Grand Rapids: Eerdmans, 1997), 317. See also Martin Hengel, "Maria Magdalena und die Frauen als Zeugen," *Abraham unser Vater,* Festschrift for O. Michel, ed. O. Betz et. al., Arbeiten zur Geschichte des Spätjudentums und Urchristentums 5 (1963): 243–56; Ben Witherington, "On the Road with Mary Magdalene, Joanna, Susanna and Other Disciples: Luke 8:1–3," *ZNW* 70 (1979): 243–48; Eugene Maly, "Women and the Gospel of Luke," *BibTheolBull* 10 (1980): 99–104; Rosalie Ryan, "The Women from Galilee and Discipleship in Luke," *BibTheolBull* 15 (1985): 56–59.
25. The preposition *sun* occurs in Acts 1:21 as a prefix in the verbal phrase *sunelthontōn hēmin,* "came with us."
26. See pages 106–109 under "The Role of the Women in the Ministry Team."
27. Witherington, *Women in the Ministry of Jesus,* 118.
28. Some suggest that the most that can be stated with certainty is that the women's roles were redefined, but within rather than outside the structure of Jewish society; e.g., Osborne, "Women in Jesus' Ministry," 280; Evelyn and Frank Stagg, *Women in the Ministry of Jesus* (Philadelphia: Westminster, 1978), 121–23, 225, 228. For one who wrestles with the exact role of the women, see Pheme Perkins, *Jesus as Teacher* (Cambridge: Cambridge Univ., 1990), 33–37.

29. Ryan, "The Women from Galilee," 57; Ben Witherington III, "On the Road with Mary Magdalene, Joanna, Susanna and Other Disciples: Luke 8:1–3," 2NW 70 (1979): 243–48.
30. Cf. Kathleen E. Corley, *Private Women, Public Meals: Social Conflict in the Synoptic Tradition* (Peabody, Mass.: Hendrickson, 1993), 24–79; Bernadette J. Brooten, *Women Leaders in the Ancient Synagogue,* Brown Judaic Studies 36 (Atlanta: Scholars Press, 1982).
31. E.g., Susanne Heine, *Women and Early Christianity: A Reappraisal* (English trans., Minneapolis: Augsburg, 1988), 60–62.
32. Green (*Luke,* 317 n.4) argues convincingly against the suggestion that Jesus, the Twelve, and the women are three subjects of the singular verb "traveling through," and hence the accompanying participles "proclaiming and preaching" (cf. Quentin Quesnell, "The Women at Luke's Supper," *Political Issues in Luke–Acts,* ed. Richard J. Cassidy and Philip Scharper (Maryknoll, N.Y.: Orbis, 1983), 68. The more likely grammatical probability is that the emphatic position of the pronoun *autos* ("He") points to Jesus as the singular subject of the verb "traveling through" and accompanying participles, and that Luke has simply omitted the verb "to be" to describe the Twelve and the women as having been with Jesus.
33. E.g., Witherington, *Women in the Ministry of Jesus,* 118; Hengel, "Maria Magdalena," 247–48. A critique against the assumption that the women only provided domestic help for the traveling ministry team is given by David C. Sim, "The Women Followers of Jesus: The Implications of Luke 8:1–3," *Heythrop Journal* 30 (1989): 51–62. Sim does not speculate what their exact role is, beyond providing some economic support.
34. John Nolland, *Luke 1–9:20,* WBC 35A (Dallas: Word, 1989), 367.
35. E.g., Green, *Luke,* 317.
36. Peter, James, John, and sometimes Andrew; e.g., Mark 13:3.
37. Leon Morris, *The Gospel According to Matthew* (Grand Rapids: Eerdmans, 1992), 668.
38. I have developed this "community" aspect of mutual discipleship of women and men more fully elsewhere; see Michael J. Wilkins, *In His Image: Reflecting Christ in Everyday Life* (Colorado Springs: NavPress, 1997), ch. 9.
39. Matthew 27:55–56, 61; Mark 15:40–41; Luke 23:49, 55–56; John 19:25–27.
40. Matthew 28:1; Mark 16:1; Luke 24:1, 10–11; John 20:1–18.
41. Susanna is named in the NT only in Luke 8:3. Although she is not mentioned at the crucifixion or resurrection scenes, this does not necessarily mean that she was not present.
42. Among those who argue that these characteristics imply that women are disciples are Jane Kopas, "Jesus and Women in Matthew," *Theology Today* 47/1 (1990), 20; Osborne, "Women in Jesus' Ministry," 275; Witherington, *Women in the Ministry of Jesus,* 122–23. Among those who argue that these characteristics do not imply that women are disciples is Janice Capel Andersen, "Matthew: Gender and Reading," *Semeia* 28 (1983), 18–24.
43. Matthew and Mark have *akoloutheō* (Matt. 27:55; Mark 15:41), while Luke has *sunakolouthousai* (23:49), a compound for the technical discipleship word, *akoloutheō.*
44. Jack Kingsbury suggests that the presence or absence of two factors—cost and commitment—is the key to understanding whether "following Jesus" should be taken literally or metaphorically in Matthew's gospel (Jack Dean Kingsbury, "The Verb AKOLOUTHEIN ('To Follow') as an Index of Matthew's View of His Community," *JBL* 97 [1978], 58). I would extend those two criteria to the usage in the other Gospels and Acts as well.
45. E.g., Osborne, "Women in Jesus' Ministry," 270.
46. Josephus, *Antiquities* 4:219. See also *m. Shebuoth* 4:1; Rabbi Akiba in *m. Yebamoth* 16:7.
47. E.g., *m. Sotah* 6:4; 9:8; *m. Shebuoth* 3:10–11. In *m. Sanhedrin* 3:3, women do not appear in a list of those who are said to be not qualified to be witnesses. See Witherington, *Women in the Ministry of Jesus,* 9–10, for a discussion of the mixed rabbinic attitudes toward women's ability to give witness. He goes to some length to rightly correct Jeremias, who has influenced many by his statement that women were never considered valid witnesses because the rabbis considered them to be liars by nature: see Joachim Jeremias, *Jerusalem in the Time of Jesus* (1962; 3d ed.; Philadelphia: Fortress, 1969), 374–75.
48. For discussion of the broader issues, see William L. Craig, "Did Jesus Rise from the Dead?" in *Jesus Under Fire: Modern Scholarship Reinvents the Historical Jesus,* ed. Michael J. Wilkins and J. P. Moreland (Grand Rapids: Zondervan, 1995), 151, 155.

49. My thanks to Betty Talbert-Wetler, my research assistant during the 1997–98 academic year, who did an excellent job of tracking down sources, screening the primary materials, and interacting with me on the direction of the research.

Chapter 6: Woman and Man in Apostolic Teaching

1. For a discussion of the nature of the prohibition and the activities involved, see chapter 13.
2. For a discussion of Peter's use of the language of Genesis 18:12 dealing with Sarah and Abraham, see J. Ramsey Michaels, *1 Peter,* Word Biblical Commentary, vol. 49 (Waco, Tex.: Word, 1988), 165.
3. Gerhard Delling, "τάσσω, κτλ.," *Theological Dictionary of the New Testament,* vol. VIII (Grand Rapids: Eerdmans, 1972), 41; see also Markus Barth, *Ephesians 4–6,* The Anchor Bible (Garden City, N.Y.: Doubleday, 1974), 709.
4. The concept of "order" is a favorite with the apostle Paul. Barth notes that "in the Pauline Epistles, the verb 'subordinate' occurs twenty-three times, and nouns *tagma* ('rank,' 'order,' status,' etc.) and *diatage* ('ordinance') once each, *taxis* ('order') two times, *hypotage* ('subjection') four times" (Markus Barth, *Ephesians 4–6,* 709).
5. One additional use of the concept of subjection is found in the apostle's statement that "the spirits of the prophets are subject to the prophets" (1 Cor. 14:32 KJV).
6. The exhortation to "mutual subordination" in Ephesians 5:21 is the last of five actions that are related to the command to "be filled with the Spirit" (vv. 18–21): "Be filled with the Spirit, speaking . . . singing . . . making melody . . . giving thanks . . . [being] subject to one another. . . ."
7. Without using exactly the same words, Peter presented an interesting parallel when he exhorted the younger men to "be subject to your elders" and immediately followed with the statement, "and all of you, clothe yourselves with humility toward one another" (1 Pet. 5:5). An alternative understanding views the exhortation to be "subject to one another" in Ephesians 5:21 not as calling for the submission of all people to each other, but as a general statement covering the specific ways that Christians are to submit to one another in the following verses (5:22–6:9) (cf. James B. Hurley, *Man and Woman in Biblical Perspective* [Grand Rapids: Zondervan, 1981], 140ff.). Even if this interpretation is followed, it does not negate the general principles of humility and love, which call for placing the interests of the other over one's own.
8. Barth, *Ephesians 4–6,* 608.
9. Ibid., 609; cf. also Andrew T. Lincoln, *Ephesians,* Word Biblical Commentary, vol. 42 (Dallas: Word, 1990), 365–66.
10. Lincoln, *Ephesians,* 366.
11. Barth, *Ephesians 4–6,* 609.
12. Walter Grundmann, "ταπεινός, κτλ.," *Theological Dictionary of the New Testament,* vol. VIII (Grand Rapids: Eerdmans, 1972), 21–22. The close relation of the word *hypotasso* ("to order under, subordinate") used in Eph. 5:21 for mutual subjection and *tapeinophrosyne* ("humility of mind") used in Phil. 3:2 is in Delling's assertion that *hypotasso* "bears a material relation to Christian *tapeinophrosyne*" (Gerhard Delling, "τάσσω, κτλ.," *Theological Dictionary of the New Testament,* vol. VIII: 45.
13. Letha Dawson Scanzoni and Nancy A. Hardesty, *All We're Meant to Be,* 3d ed. (Grand Rapids: Eerdmans, 1992), 90–91.
14. For the discussion of the Old Testament evidence, see chapters 3 and 4. For the teaching and example of Christ, see chapter 5.
15. The fact that the apostle uses *plasso* ("formed"), which is used in Genesis 2, rather than the Greek word *poieo* ("make"), which is used for God's creative activity throughout Genesis 1, indicates his clear reference to the creation account of Genesis 2, where the sequence of the creation of man and woman is stated.
16. W. Bauer, *A Greek-English Lexicon of the New Testament and Other Early Christian Literature,* trans. W. F. Arndt and F. W. Gingrich. 2d rev. and augmented by F. W. Gingrich and F. W. Danker from Bauer's 5th ed. (1958) (Chicago: Univ. of Chicago, 1979), 151–52.

17. Philip B. Payne, "Libertarian Women in Ephesus: A Response to Douglas J. Moo's Article, '1 Timothy 2:11–15; Meaning and Significance,'" *Trinity Journal* 2 NS (1981): 175–77; cf. also, Gilbert Bilezikian, *Beyond Sex Roles* (Grand Rapids: Baker, 1985), 179–81; Aida Besancon Spencer, *Beyond the Curse* (Nashville: Nelson, 1985), 88–92.
18. Bauer, *A Greek-English Lexicon,* 151–52.
19. Douglas J. Moo, "The Interpretation of 1 Timothy 2:11–15: A Rejoinder," *Trinity Journal* 2 (1981): 202–4.
20. Hurley, *Man and Woman in Biblical Perspective,* 208.
21. Stephen Bedale writes, "While the word κεφαλή . . . unquestionably carries with it the idea of 'authority' such authority in social relationship derives from a relative priority (*causal* rather than merely temporal) in the order of being" (Stephen Bedale, "The Meaning of *kephalē* in the Pauline Epistles," *Journal of Theological Studies* 5 [1954], 215).
22. Gordon D. Fee, *The First Epistle to the Corinthians* (Grand Rapid: Eerdmans, 1987), 517–18, 522–24.
23. Paul Jewett, *Man as Male and Female* (Grand Rapids: Eerdmans, 1975), 113–14.
24. Cited by Claus Westermann, *Genesis 1–11* (Minneapolis: Augsburg, 1984), 227.
25. Ibid.
26. Ibid.
27. Ibid., 232.
28. C. K. Barrett, *A Commentary on the First Epistle to the Corinthians* (New York: Harper & Row, 1968), 255.
29. Karl Barth, *The Doctrine of Creation,* Church Dogmatics, vol. III, no. 4 (Edinburgh: T. & T. Clark, 1961), 163.
30. For a discussion of different types of subordination, see Stephen B. Clark, *Man and Woman in Christ* (Ann Arbor, Mich.: Servant, 1980), 41.
31. This includes both the active form of the verb and the passive where the latter is used as a substitute for God's name ("the so-called *Passivum divinum*"). See Barth, *Ephesians 4–6,* 709, and Delling, "τάσσω, κτλ.," *TDNT,* VIII, 41.
32. Barth, *Ephesians 4–6,* 709.
33. Ibid., 710. The verb form used in the case of believers is the Greek middle or passive. See Barth, *Ephesians 4–6,* 709–10, and Delling, "τάσσω, κτλ.," *TDNT,* VIII, 41–42.
34. Barth, *Ephesians 4–6,* 710.
35. Fritz Zerbst, *The Office of Woman in the Church* (St. Louis: Concordia, 1955), 71–72.
36. The use of *exousia* ("authority") in relation to the woman's head covering in 1 Cor. 11:10 has been taken by some as an exception to the above (e.g., Charles Hodge, *An Exposition of the First Epistle to the Corinthians* [Grand Rapids: Eerdmans, 1953], 211). But see the preferable interpretation in F. W. Grosheide, *A Commentary on the First Epistle to the Corinthians* (Grand Rapids; Eerdmans, 1953), 257; Archibald Robertson and Alfred Plummer, *A Critical and Exegetical Commentary on the First Epistle of St. Paul to the Corinthians* (Edinburgh: T. & T. Clark, 1911), 232–33; C. K. Barrett, *A Commentary on the First Epistle to the Corinthians,* 254–55.
37. Werner Foerster, "ἐξουσία," *Theological Dictionary of the New Testament,* vol. 2 (Grand Rapids: Eerdmans, 1964), 566.
38. Fritz Zerbst, *The Office of Woman in the Church,* 77.
39. See, for example, C. C. Kroeger, "Head," in *Dictionary of Paul and His Letters* (Downers Grove, Ill.: InterVarsity, 1993), 374–77; A. Mickelsen and B. Mickelsen, "What Does *Kephalē* Mean in the New Testament?" in *Women, Authority and the Bible,* ed. A. Mickelsen (Downers Grove, Ill.: InterVarsity, 1986), 97–110. An article written in the early 1950s by S. Bedale was a major impetus to this new view ("The Meaning of *Kephalē* in the Pauline Epistles," *Journal of Theological Studies* 5 [1954], 211–15).
40. In 1 Corinthians 11:3—"the head of the woman is man" NIV—some have suggested that this passage is limited to the marriage relationship because it uses the Greek terms *anēr* and *gunē* to refer to male and female and should thus be translated, "the head of the wife is the husband" (See, for example, C. L. Blomberg, *1 Corinthians,* NIV Application Commentary [Grand Rapids: Zondervan, 1994], 209–10). Although it is true that Paul frequently uses the two terms to refer to husbands and wives, this more specific

determination must be made by the context alone. The terms themselves are typically used by Greek writers to stress the sexual differentiation between male and female. There is nothing in the context of 1 Corinthians 11 to restrict the usage of the terms to husband/wife relationships. The context clearly has to do with the role relationships between men and women in the community of believers. Thus, the passage goes on to speak of the decorum of women when they pray and prophesy, especially the issue of head coverings, and how propriety is different in this regard for the men.

41. Wayne Grudem, "Does *Kephalē* ('Head') Mean 'Source' or 'Authority Over' in Greek Literature? A Survey of 2,336 Examples," *Trinity Journal* 6 (1985): 38–59. The article is reprinted in the appendix of George W. Knight III, *The Role Relationship of Men and Women,* rev. ed. (Chicago: Moody, 1985), 49–80.
42. Joseph Fitzmyer, "Another Look at *Kephalē* in 1 Corinthians 11:3," *New Testament Studies* 35 (1989): 503–11; idem, "*Kephalē* in 1 Corinthians 11:3," *Interpretation* 47 (1993): 52–59.
43. Wayne Grudem, "The Meaning *Source* 'Does Not Exist.' Liddell-Scott Editor Rejects Egalitarian Interpretation of Head *(Kephalē),*" *CBMW News* 2.5 (December 1997), 1, 7–8.
44. *Griechisch-deutsches Wörterbuch zu den Schriften des Neuen Testaments und der frühchristlichen Literatur,* 6. völlig neu bearbeitete Auflage; Hrsg. K. Aland & B. Aland (Berlin/New York: Walter de Gruyter, 1988), s.v. Now also the new English third edition of Bauer's lexicon: *A Greek-English Lexicon of the New Testament and Other Early Christian Lierature,* 3d. Ed. Rev. and Ed. by F. W. Danker Chicago: Univ. of Chicago, 2000) s.v.
45. The similarity between the relationships of man/woman and husband/wife is strengthened in Genesis 2 when it is said, "A man shall leave his father and his mother and be joined to his wife" (v. 24 NKJV).Thus the relationship of marriage is considered to be the normal state for men and women.
46. See Clinton E. Arnold, "Jesus Christ: 'Head' of the Church," in *Jesus of Nazareth: Lord and Christ: Essays on the Historical Jesus and New Testament Christology,* eds. J. B. Green and M. Turner (Grand Rapids: Eerdmans, 1994), 346–66.

Chapter 7: The "Order" and "Equality" of Galatians 3:28

1. For a discussion of the variety of interpretational approaches to Galatians 3:28, see Klyne R. Snodgrass, "Galatians 3:28: Conundrum or Solution?" in *Women, Authority and the Bible,* ed. Alvera Mickelson (Downers Grove, Ill.: InterVarsity, 1986), 162–66. For a survey of the interpretation of the verse by the major teachers of church history, see S. Lewis Johnson, "Role Distinctions in the Church: Galatians 3:28," in *Recovering Biblical Manhood and Womanhood: A Response to Evangelical Feminism,* ed. John Piper and Wayne Grudem (Wheaton, Ill.: Crossway, 1991), 155–56. For some insightful discussions of the issues involved in the interpretation of Galatians 3:28 and other apostolic teaching related to men and women, see Robert W. Yarbrough, "The Hermeneutics of 1 Timothy 2:9–15,"and Harold O. J. Brown, "The New Testament Against Itself: 1 Timothy 2:9–15 and the 'Breakthrough' of Galatians 3:28," in *Women in the Church: A Fresh Analysis of 1 Timothy 2:9–15,* ed. Andreas J. Köstenberger, Thomas Schreiner, and H. Scott Baldwin (Grand Rapids: Baker, 1995), 155–208; Stephen B. Clark, *Man and Woman in Christ* (Ann Arbor, Mich.: Servant, 1980), 137–63.
2. F. F. Bruce, *The Epistle to the Galatians,* The New International Greek Testament Commentary (Grand Rapids: Eerdmans, 1982), 190.
3. See, for example, Paul K. Jewett, *Man as Male and Female* (Grand Rapids: Eerdmans, 1975), 142–49; Virginia Ramey Mollenkott, *Women, Men, and the Bible,* rev. ed. (New York: Crossroad, 1988), 84–86.
4. Mary Hayter, *The New Eve in Christ* (Grand Rapids: Eerdmans, 1987), 134.
5. Jewett, *Man as Male and Female,* 142. The commanding position of this text in the discussion of the roles of men and women in the church for many egalitarians is illustrated in the thought of Gilbert Bilezikian. Referring to both Galatians 3:28 and Acts 2:15–21

(the spiritual giftedness of both men and women with the coming of the Spirit) he wrote, "The commanding prominence of those two statements as constitutional declarations of the church and their crystalline clarity endow them with normative power." To deny this conclusion, he went on to imply, is nothing less than to destroy the church and incur the judgment of God: "Discrimination of any kind is a monstrous denial of the oneness of the church of Christ. The Scripture promises destruction for anyone who thus destroys the church, the temple of God (1 Cor. 3:16–17) and judgment without mercy to anyone who is found guilty of practicing discrimination within the body of Christ (James 2:1–13)" (*Beyond Sex Roles* [Grand Rapids: Baker, 1985], 128).

6. Jewett, *Man as Male and Female,* 112, 119; cf. also Mary Daly, *The Church and the Second Sex* (New York: Harper & Row, 1968), 41–42. Jewett presents a clear statement of the incompatibility of Paul's teaching in Galatians 3:28 with his other teachings: "Because these two perspectives—the Jewish and the Christian—are incompatible, there is no satisfying way to harmonize the Pauline argument for female subordination with the larger Christian vision of which the great apostle to the Gentiles was himself the primary architect. It appears from the evidence that Paul himself sensed that his view of the man/woman relationship, inherited from Judaism, was not altogether congruous with the gospel he preached" (op. cit, 112–13).
7. J. B. Lightfoot, *The Epistle of St. Paul to the Galatians* (London, 1865), 63; cf. also, F. F. Bruce, *The Epistle to the Galatians,* 22.
8. Richard N. Longenecker, *Galatians,* Word Biblical Commentary, vol. 41 (Dallas: Word, 1990), 136.
9. Longenecker, *Galatians,* 135.
10. Herman Ridderbos, *Paul: An Outline of His Theology* (Grand Rapids: Eerdmans, 1975), 59.
11. While noting that this list is particularly relevant to the Colossian believers, commentators see in this teaching the equivalent of Galatians 3:28. In connection with Colossians 3:11 Peter O'Brien says, "Here the teaching of Galatians [3:28] is expanded, no doubt in accordance with the needs of the Colossian readers . . ." (*Colossians and Philemon,* Word Biblical Commentary [Waco, Tex.: Word, 1982], 192).
12. The closeness of the teaching of equality in Christ in 1 Corinthians 12:13 and the exhortation to the subordination of women in both 1 Corinthians 11:3ff. and 14:34 also lead to the similar conclusion that Paul does not see these teachings as contradictory.
13. E. K. Simpson and F. F. Bruce, *Commentary on the Epistles to the Ephesians and the Colossians* (Grand Rapids: Eerdmans, 1957), 290, n. 139.
14. F. F. Bruce, *The Epistle to the Galatians,* 187.
15. Clark, *Man and Woman in Christ,* 146.
16. H. L. Strack and P. Billerbeck, *Kommentar zum Neuen Testament aus Talmud und Midrasch* (Munich, 1922–26), III, 558; cited by Clark, *Man and Woman in Christ,* 145.
17. The patriarchal nature of the contemporary Jewish culture is noted by Stendahl: "Jewish tradition is rich in sayings which show how the structure of the synagogue and Jewish society is strongly masculine. All the way from circumcision to burial rites it is only the male who is an Israelite in the true sense of the word. Only he is committed to the Law and to the obligation to prayer. When the study of the Torah becomes the center of Jewish existence, this too is a male obligation and honor" (Krister Stendahl, *The Biblical View of Male and Female* [Philadelphia: Fortress, 1966], 27).
18. Clark explains, "The main principle used by the rabbis was that the woman was not obligated to keep those commandments that had to be performed at a specific time. In effect, this ruling meant that she was not obligated to keep the commandments concerning public ritual" (Clark, *Man and Woman in Christ,* 148).
19. K. H. Rengstorf, "δοῦλος," *Theological Dictionary of the New Testament,* vol. 2 (Grand Rapids: Eerdmans, 1964), 271.
20. Klyne R. Snodgrass, "Galatians 3:28: Conundrum or Solution?" in *Women, Authority and the Bible,* ed. A. Mickelsen (Downers Grove, Ill.: InterVarsity, 1986), 168; this Greek prayer is variously attributed to Socrates, Plato, and Thales.
21. J. Jeremias, *Jerusalem in the Time of Jesus* (Philadelphia: Fortress, 1962), 375.

22. A. Oepke, "γυνή," *Theological Dictionary of the New Testament*, vol. 1 (Grand Rapids: Eerdmans, 1964), 781–84.
23. K. H. Rengstorf, "δοῦλος," *Theological Dictionary of the New Testament*, 271; cf. also Klyne R. Snodgrass, "Galatians 3:28: Conundrum or Solution?" in *Women, Authority and the Bible*, 169.
24. Klyne R. Snodgrass, "Galatians 3:28: Conundrum or Solution?" in *Women, Authority and the Bible*, 171.
25. See Finley's discussion of the creation accounts of Genesis in chapter 3.
26. A. Oepke, "ἀνήρ," *Theological Dictionary of the New Testament*, vol. 1 (Grand Rapids: Eerdmans, 1964), 362.
27. N. P. Bratsiotis, "אִישׁ," *Theological Dictionary of the Old Testament*, vol. 1 (Grand Rapids: Eerdmans, 1974), 226.
28. For a good discussion of the question of a parallel between the abolition of slavery and the distinction between male and female, see Clark, *Man and Woman in Christ*, 155–60. Among the dissimilarities between the slave/freeman and male/female categories, Clark aptly notes that "slavery cannot serve as a model for men's and women's roles if simple abolition is the point, since the parallel to the abolition of slavery would be abolition of males and females as *different types of people*, and such abolition is impossible currently" (p. 159, italics added).
29. Something similar is true of one dimension of the male-female distinction that was abolished "in Christ." In the Old Testament, the priesthood was limited to men from the line of Aaron of the Levites. "In Christ," however, this distinction is gone as all believers, both male and female, are part of the "holy priesthood" (1 Pet. 2:5). Again, this distinction was part of God's historical plan of salvation that came into being because of sin and was never intended to be permanent. This change in the priesthood, which was instituted because of sin, does alter the original man-woman order founded in creation.
30. Madeleine Boucher, "Some Unexplored Parallels to 1 Corinthians 11:11–12 and Galatians 3:28: The NT on the Role of Women," *The Catholic Biblical Quarterly* 31 (January 1969): 57. According to Boucher, Jewish rabbis similarly made statements about women's equality with men before God, or assumed its truth, without any implications that all social distinctions or role differences were obliterated (cf. 50–58). Based on these, Boucher states, "It may be that the contrast between the Jews' subordination of women and the Christians' new interest in their equality has been too sharply drawn, indeed, that such a contrast never existed. It is possible that the two religions were alike in teaching at once the religious equality and the social subordination of women, and that no break occurred between the rabbis and Paul in this matter" (p. 55).
31. Klyne R. Snodgrass, "Galatians 3:28: Conundrum or Solution?" in *Women, Authority and the Bible*, 175.
32. F. F. Bruce, "Women in the Church: A Biblical Survey," in *A Mind for What Matters* (Grand Rapids: Eerdmans, 1990), 263.
33. This is in reality the point of the other instructions of the apostle to believing slaves and masters. They both have obligations to each other because both are "in Christ" and equal before Him (cf. Eph. 6:6–9; 1 Tim. 6:1–2).
34. C. F. D. Moule, *The Epistles of Paul the Apostle to the Colossians and to Philemon* (Cambridge: Cambridge Univ., 1962), 121.
35. John Eadie, *Commentary on the Epistle to the Colossians* (Grand Rapids: Zondervan, 1957, rept. of 1856 ed.), 238.
36. The following discussion on distinction and equality of persons relates primarily the arguments of Rebecca Merrill Groothuis in her work *Good News for Women: A Biblical Picture of Gender Equality* (Downers Grove, Ill.: InterVarsity, 1997), 41–63.
37. Groothuis, *Good News for Women*, 44–45.
38. Ibid., 48.
39. M. Scott Peck, *The Different Drum* (New York: Simon and Schuster, 1987), 175.
40. Groothuis, *Good News for Women*, 53.
42. Gordon D. Fee, *The First Epistle to the Corinthians* (Grand Rapids: Eerdmans, 1987), 614. The following comment by Fee is also important: "Crucial to this argument is the fact that they

only 'seem' to be weaker. There is a sense, of course, in which that is true; they are weak and thus protected internally [i.e., internal body organs]. Paul's point seems to be that such apparent weakness has no relationship to their real value and necessity to the body" (p. 613).

43. Groothuis, *Good News for Women*, 54.
44. Ibid., 59–60.

Chapter 8: The Ministry of Women in the Early Church

1. Women were also full members of the covenant community of Israel (cf. Exod. 19; Deut. 29; 31:9–13; 2 Kings 23:1–3; Neh. 8). But the institutional nature of much of the ministry under the Mosaic economy gave them less prominence in the ministry of the community than in the New Testament church.
2. Patricia Ranft, *Women and Spiritual Equality in Christian Tradition* (New York: St. Martin's, 1998), 26–28.
3. C. S. Keener, "Woman and Man," *Dictionary of the Later New Testament and Its Developments*, ed. Ralph P. Martin and Peter H. Davids (Downers Grove, Ill.; InterVarsity, 1997), 1206.
4. See pp. 176–78 for a brief dicussion of the gender of this person.
5. Roger Gryson, *The Ministry of Women in the Early Church* (Collegeville, Minn.: Liturgical Press, 1976), 30; citing Clement of Alexandria, *Strom.* 3.6.
6. The other men specifically named as "co-workers" are Aquila (Rom. 16:3); Urbanus (Rom. 16:9); Clement (Phil. 4:3); Aristarchus, Mark, Jesus or Justus (Col. 4:10–11); Philemon (Philem. 1); Demas, and Luke (Philem. 24).
7. Cf. E. Earl Ellis, "Coworkers, Paul and His," in *Dictionary of Paul and His Letters* (Downers Grove, Ill.: InterVarsity, 1993), 183; cf. also Georg Bertram, "συνεργός κτλ.," *Theological Dictionary of the New Testament*, vol. 7, ed. Gerhard Friedrich (Grand Rapids: Eerdmans, 1971), 874–75.
8. For the assertion of the equality of women with Paul, see Elisabeth Schüssler Fiorenza, *In Memory of Her* (New York: Crossroad, 1983), 169–70. On the other hand, Bertram is surely correct when he affirms that "one is not to see in all this unconditional equality with the apostle" ("συνεργός κτλ.," *Theological Dictionary of the New Testament*, vol. 7, 874).
9. W. H. Ollrog, *Paulus und seine Mitarbeiter,* Wissenshaftlich Untersuchunger zum Neuen Testament 50 (Neukirchen: Neukirchener, 1979), 67, cited by James D. G. Dunn, *Romans 9–16,* Word Biblical Commentary, vol. 38b, (Dallas: Word, 1988), 892.
10. Peter T. O'Brien, *The Epistle to the Philippians: A Commentary on the Greek Text* (Grand Rapids: Eerdmans, 1991), 481.
11. Ibid., 482.
12. Moises Silva, *Philippians* (Grand Rapids: Baker, 1992), 221.
13. For more refutation of this view, see F. W. Grosheide, *Commentary on the First Epistle to the Corinthians* (Grand Rapids: Eerdmans, 1953), 252–53. Grosheide's own view that prophecy was done in public outside of the congregational meeting (cf. Agabus, Acts 21:11ff.) rather than a meeting of the congregation also founders on the purpose of prophecy for the edification of the church.
14. John Calvin, *The First Epistle of Paul the Apostle to the Corinthians* (Grand Rapids: Eerdmans, 1960), 231; Thomas Charles Edwards, *A Commentary on the First Epistle to the Corinthians* (London: Hodder & Stoughton, 1885), 382; Robert L. Thomas, *Understanding Spiritual Gifts* (Chicago: Moody, 1978), 158. See chapter 13, 292–96 for more on the relation of this instruction for women praying and prophesying in public meetings of the church and the command for them to be "silent in the churches" (1 Cor. 14:34).
15. For more on the nature of this teaching, especially in relation to the prohibition against women teaching men (1 Tim. 2:12), see chapter 13.
16. Gryson cites evidence of this ministry of the widows in the post-apostolic writings (*The Ministry of Women in the Early Church,* see esp. 27, 67). See also Gustav Stählin, "Χήρα," *Theological Dictionary of the New Testament,* vol. 9, ed. Gerhard Kittel and Gerhard Friedrich (Grand Rapids: Eerdmans, 1974), 457.

17. E.g., J. N. D. Kelly, *The Pastoral Epistles* (London: Adam & Charles Black, 1963), 240; A. T. Hanson, *The Pastoral Epistles,* New Century Bible Commentary (Grand Rapids: Eerdmans, 1982), 180.
18. William Barclay, *The Letters to Timothy, Titus and Philemon* (Philadelphia: Westminster, 1960), 284.
19. The relation to this kind of general teaching and the apostle's prohibition against women teaching men in 1 Tim. 2:12 will be discussed in chapter 13.
20. P. E. Hughes, *A Commentary on the Epistle to the Hebrews* (Grand Rapids: Eerdmans, 1977), 190.
21. For a defense of the second translation, see Peter O'Brien, *Colossians, Philemon,* Word Biblical Commentary, vol. 44, (Waco, Tex.: Word, 1982), 208–9.
22. O'Brien, *Colossians, Philemon,* 209.
23. Heinrich Schlier, "ᾀδωή, ᾠδή," *Theological Dictionary of the New Testament,* vol. 1, ed. Gerhard Kittel (Grand Rapids: Eerdmans, 1964), 165.
24. Henry Chadwick, *The Early Church* (Harmondsworth, N.Y.: Penguin, 1968), 56.
25. "Widows indeed" indicated those who were "left alone" with no family to support them (v. 5) and in addition were sixty years old and above.
26. E.g., George W. Knight III, *The Pastoral Epistles: A Commentary on the Greek Text* (Grand Rapids: Eerdmans, 1992), 225; cf. also Kelly, *The Pastoral Epistles,* 116–17. Stählin, "Χήρα," *Theological Dictionary of the New Testament,* 457.
27. Stählin, "Χήρα," *Theological Dictionary of the New Testament,* 465; see also Gryson, *The Ministry of Women in the Early Church;* Ranft, *Women and Spiritual Equality in Christian Tradition,* 25.
28. Richard Clark Kroeger and Catherine Clark Kroeger, *I Suffer Not a Woman: Rethinking 1 Timothy 2:11–15 in Light of Ancient Evidence* (Grand Rapids: Baker, 1992), 91. According to the Kroegers, "Phoebe's office as *prostatis* appears to imply authoritative responsibility similar to that of an elder."
29. Bo Reicke, "προΐστημι," *Theological Dictionary of the New Testament,* vol. 6, ed. Gerhard Kittel (Grand Rapids: Eerdmans, 1968), 700–703.
30. For reasons for preferring this view here see, James D. G. Dunn, *Romans 9–16,* Word Biblical Commentary, vol. 38b, 731; C. E. B. Cranfield, *A Critical and Exegetical Commentary on the Epistle to the Romans,* vol. II (Edinburgh: T. & T. Clark, 1979), 626–27.
31. Douglas J. Moo, *The Epistle to the Romans* (Grand Rapids: Eerdmans, 1996), 916; cf. Bo Reicke, "προΐστημι," *Theological Dictionary of the New Testament,* 703.
32. The terms *overseer* and *elder* referred to the same person or function in the New Testament church; see J. B. Lightfoot, *Saint Paul's Epistle to the Philippians* (Grand Rapids: Zondervan, 1953, rept. of 1913 ed.), 95–99.
33. Kroeger and Kroeger, *I Suffer Not a Woman,* 91.
34. For the meaning and uses of these related words, see Walter Bauer, *A Greek-English Lexicon of the New Testament and Other Early Christian Literature,* trans. W. F. Arndt and F. W. Gingrich. 2d rev. and augmented by F. W. Gingrich and F. W. Danker from Bauer's 5th ed. (1958) (Chicago: Univ. of Chicago, 1979), 699–700.
35. Cranfield suggests that the reason the two groups (overseers and deacons) are mentioned in Philippians is that both had to do with the collection of the gifts for which Paul is thanking the church. The deacons acted as agents in the matter under the supervision of the overseers (C. E. B. Cranfield, "Diakonia in the New Testament," in *Service in Christ,* ed. James I. McCord and T. H. L. Parker [Grand Rapids: Eerdmans, 1966], 39. Cf. also Herman W. Beyer, "ἐπίσκοπος," *Theological Dictionary of the New Testament,* vol. 2, ed. Gerhard Kittel (Grand Rapids: Eerdmans, 1964), 616; "διάκονος," ibid., 89; Klaus Hess, "Serve," *The New International Dictionary of New Testament Theology,* vol. 3, ed. Colin Brown (Grand Rapids: Zondervan, 1978), 546.
36. Gryson, *The Ministry of Women in the Early Church,* 3–4; Dunn, *Romans 9–16,* 886–87; Cranfield, *A Critical and Exegetical Commentary on the Epistle to the Romans,* 781.
37. Albrecht Oepke, "γυνη," *Theological Dictionary of the New Testament,* vol. 1, ed.Gerhard Kittel (Grand Rapids: Eerdmans, 1964), 787.

38. For support of these women as the wives of deacons, see Knight, *The Pastoral Epistles,* 171–72.
39. For support of these women as deaconesses, see Gryson, *The Ministry of Women in the Early Church,* 8; J. N. D. Kelly, *The Pastoral Epistles* (London: Adam & Charles Black, 1963), 83–84; Thomas R. Schreiner, "The Valuable Ministries of Women in the Context of Male Leadership," in *Recovering Biblical Manhood and Womanhood: A Response to Evangelical Feminism.*, edited by John Piper and Wayne Grudem (Wheaton, Ill.: Crossway, 1991), 213–14; Walter Lock, *A Critical and Exegetical Commentary on the Pastoral Epistles* (Edinburgh: T. & T. Clark, 1936), 40–41.
40. Beyer, "ἐπίσκοπος," *Theological Dictionary of the New Testament,* 93.
41. Beyer, "διάκονος," *Theological Dictionary of the New Testament,* 91.
42. Although he may be slightly overstating the case, Oepke, pointing to the general usage of *diakonos* (servant) in the New Testament, concludes with regard to Phoebe as a *diakonos* that "we are not to think exclusively or even predominantly of works of charity . . . , but of all kinds of service rendered to the community" (Oepke, "γυνή," *Theological Dictionary of the New Testament,* 787). For a good discussion of the wide and varied ministry of deacons in the early church, see G. W. H. Lampe, "Diakonia in the Early Church," in *Service in Christ,* ed. McCord and Parker, 37–64.
43. Gryson, *The Ministry of Women in the Early Church,* 41–42, citing *Didascalia Apostolorum,* 3, 12, 1–13, 1 (Funk, 208, 8–214, 3; Connolly, 146, 1–148, 22), trans. Connolly.
44. W. Bauer, *A Greek-English Lexicon of the New Testament and Other Early Christian Literature,* trans. W. F. Arndt and F. W. Gingrich. 2d rev. and augmented by F. W. Gingrich and F. W. Danker from Bauer's 5th ed. (1958) (Chicago: Univ. of Chicago, 1979).
45. Ray R. Schulz, "Romans 16:7: Junia or Junias?" *Expository Times* 98, no. 4 (January 1987); Bernadette Brooten, "Junia . . . Outstanding Among the Apostles," in *Women Priests: A Catholic Commentary on the Vatican Declaration,* ed. L. and A. Swidler (New York: Paulist, 1977), 141–44.
46. Cited by William Sanday and Arthur C. Headlam, *A Critical and Exegetical Commentary on the Epistle to the Romans* (Edinburgh: T. & T. Clark, 1902), 423; John Chrysostom, *Homily on the Epistle of St. Paul the Apostle to the Romans* 31 in *A Selected Library of Nicene and Post-Nicene Fathers,* trans. J. P. Morris and W. H. Simcox (Grand Rapids: Eerdmans, 1980), 11:555, cited by Stanley J. Grenz, with Denise Muir Kjesbo, *Women in the Church: A Biblical Theology of Women in Ministry* (Downers Grove, Ill.: InterVarsity, 1995), 95.
47. Cranfield, *A Critical And Exegetical Commentary on the Epistle to the Romans,* vol. II, 789.
48. Ben Witherington, *Women in the Earliest Churches* (Cambridge: Cambridge Univ., 1988), 115, following C. K. Barrett, *The Signs of an Apostle* (Philadelphia: Fortress, 1972), 23ff. and R. Schnackenburg, "Apostles Before and During Paul's Time," in *Apostolic History and the Gospels,* ed. W. Gasque and R. P. Martin (Grand Rapids: Eerdmans, 1970), 293–94. In light of the various uses of the term *apostle* in the New Testament, to simply ascribe apostleship to Junia, leaving the impression that her ministry is parallel to Paul's as a "fellow-apostle," can be misleading (cf. C. S. Keener, "Man and Woman," *Dictionary of Paul and His Letters,* ed. Gerald F. Hawthorne, Ralph P. Martin, and Daniel Reid [Downers Grove, Ill.: InterVarsity, 1993], 589; cf. also, Kroeger and Kroeger, *I Suffer Not a Woman,* 91.
49. John Stott, *Romans: God's Good News for the World* (Downers Grove, Ill.: InterVarsity, 1994), 396; Cranfield, *A Critical and Exegetical Commentary on the Epistle to the Romans,* vol. II, 789; Witherington, *Women in the Earliest Churches,* 115; contra, Dunn who sees Junia as a foundational apostle commissioned directly by Christ, Dunn, *Romans 9–16,* 894–95. Further doubt that Andronicus and Junia are to be understood as foundational "apostles of Jesus Christ" is cast by the fact that clearly Jesus did not appoint any women among the first apostles before the Resurrection. If He did so after the Resurrection and they are equal in every respect to the first apostles, then it is difficult to see why none were included originally.
50. Grenz, *Women in the Church,* 90.
51. Alvera Mickelsen, "An Egalitarian View," in *Women in Ministry: Four Views,* ed. Bonnidell Clouse and Robert G. Clouse (Downers Grove, Ill.: InterVarsity, 1989), 190.

52. Witherington, *Women in the Earliest Churches,* 200. Even earlier in the third century, Clement and Origen, while acknowledging the presence of deaconesses in the time of the apostles, give no indication that they are still present in their churches in Alexandria (Gryson, *The Ministry of Women in the Early Church,* 32).
53. Oepke, "γυνή," *Theological Dictionary of the New Testament,* I:789.
54. The following discussion of the reasons for the decline of women's ministry in the post–New Testament church is drawn largely from Witherington, *Women in the Earliest Churches,* 183–210.
55. Witherington, *Women in the Earliest Churches,* 189–90. On the minimization of the office of deacons associated with the rise of the parochial priesthood, see also Lampe, "Diakonia in the Early Church," in *Service in Christ,* ed. James I. McCord and T. H. L. Parker, 57ff.
56. Gryson, *The Ministry of Women in the Early Church,* 57, 113, citing the *Ecclesiatical Canons of the Apostles.*
57. James Tunstead Burtchaell, *From Synagogue to Church: Public Services and Offices in the Earliest Christian Communities* (Cambridge: Cambridge Univ., 1992), 329.
58. Cited by Witherington, *Women in the Earliest Churches,* 189.
59. Gryson, *The Ministry of Women in the Early Church,* 112.
60. Witherington, *Women in the Earliest Churches,* 192.
61. Keener, "Woman and Man," *Dictionary of the Later New Testament and Its Developments,* 1214.
62. Mary J. Evans, *Woman in the Bible* (Downers Grove, Ill.: InterVarsity, 1983), 37; cf. Oepke, "γυνή," *Theological Dictionary of the New Testament,* I: 781–84.

Chapter 9: Being Faithful to Christ in One's Gender: Theological Reflections on Masculinity and Femininity

1. Charlotte von Kirschbaum, *The Question of Woman: The Collected Writings of Charlotte von Kirschbaum,* ed. Eleanor Jackson (Grand Rapids, Eerdmans, 1944 [1998]), 56.
2. However, God has identified Himself and the angels in revelation primarily, though not exclusively, with the masculine gender. Some argue this is mere accommodation to the cultural views of the day. However, I would argue that this accommodation has to do with His wanting to teach us something by way of analogy of how we are to understand and relate to Him.
3. It also points to the fact that there is an element of relationality in the human person that is more fundamental to personhood than even human gender relations, namely, the capacity to receive the divine, though in such a way that it is always informed by our gender.
4. According to Paul, the indwelling presence of God in human experience is part of the "mystery" or reality in the new covenant not realized in the old, namely, Christ in us, the hope of glory (Col. 1:27). Thus, Pentecost opens a whole horizon of possible relationality in union with God by the Spirit for all mankind. As Paul wrote, "But we all, with unveiled face, beholding as in a mirror the glory of the Lord, are being transformed into the same image from glory to glory, just as from the Lord, the Spirit" (2 Cor. 3:18).
5. This is congruent with Jesus' statements to the Sadducees and the disciples that there was not going to be any marriage or giving in marriage in the kingdom (Luke 20:27–40) and that one could make oneself "single" for the kingdom of God (Matt. 19:10–12). Perhaps this was news to a people who assumed that marriage was necessary for community and relational fulfillment.
6. Charlotte von Kirschbaum, *The Question of Woman,* 55.
7. Along the same lines, I will be assuming that any prescription, judgment, or command related to specific gender roles typically is not merely asking a man or woman to be a good cultural creature. However, there is an example in 1 Corinthians 11 that might indicate a prescription based upon a general gender principle and how this should be worked out in the particular culture (relevant to women wearing a head covering, etc., 1 Cor. 11:4ff.).

8. "Let her breasts satisfy you at all times; be exhilarated always with her love" (Prov. 5:19); "Enjoy life with the woman whom you love" (Eccles. 9:9). It was a man's virtue to be ravished by his wife's body, to know her intimately and to crave her: "I am my beloved's, and his desire [*teshookaw,* literally, craving desire] is for me" (Song of Sol. 7:10; cf. 4:1ff.).
9. Interestingly, Paul encourages both men and women to emulate certain dimensions of spiritual strength of which man is the model ("Be on the alert, stand firm in the faith, act like men [ανδριζεσθε], be strong," 1 Cor. 16:13). Various biblical texts point to this more masculine or warrior dimension of spirituality that are universal for all saints ("Be strong in the Lord and in the strength of His might," Eph. 6:10; "Put on the full armor of God" to do battle against dark powers, Eph. 6:11, etc.).
10. It may be that the use of "sons" is in light of the context of ancient inheritance practices in which the male receives the family's goods, which is employed by the Bible to demonstrate full salvific inheritance to both man and woman. In any case, the use of the "brethren" or "brotherhood" still stands.
11. Paul affirms that freedom is the best state when possible, though he recognizes that practically it may not always be possible and, in those cases, he encourages believers to bear in mind that they are the Lord's freedmen (cf. 1 Cor. 7:21ff. and Philemon). However, he never expresses these type of remarks regarding the woman's role to the man in the church or marriage, a great moral oversight if his comments were only an accommodation to culture.
12. Edith Stein, *Essays on Woman,* in *The Collected Works of Edith Stein,* vol. II, ed. L. Gelber and R. Leuven (Washington, D.C.: Institute of Carmelite Studies Publications, 1996), 132–33.
13. Interestingly, as Kidner notes, the same word (Heb. *hayil*) used for the "excellent" woman in Prov. 31:10 is used for the "mighty men of *valour*" in 2 Kings 24:14 (italics added) and elsewhere, indicating that in some contexts it denotes strength, wealth, and ability (D. Kidner, *Proverbs,* in Tyndale Old Testament Commentaries, ed. D. J. Wisemen [Downers Grove, Ill.: InterVarsity, 1964], 184).
14. It is interesting to note that the Old Testament Wisdom Literature, in general, personifies woman and not man as wisdom (cf. Prov. 1:20–33; 4:6–9; 8:1–9:6). It is possible that the Old Testament sage is merely carrying on the custom of other ancient Near Eastern cultures. However, it also may be that the sage is making some correlation between wisdom and woman-as-helper-worker, both being for the sake of mankind to help make their lives better in every way. In general, the concept of wisdom (Heb. *hokma,* lit. skill or dexterity, hence, the skill for living) carries with it the practical skills and information necessary for excellent living, which may correspond to woman's general interest in helping. It is difficult, however, to ascertain whether this personification indicates that women are characteristically wise or merely that wisdom is good for man as a good woman is a good thing for man and, therefore, to be embraced ("Prize her, and she will exalt you; she will honor you if you embrace her," Prov. 4:8). It is also interesting that folly and lust, man's great nemeses, are also personified as a woman who seeks to lure him into a path of personal and societal destruction (Prov. 9:13–18). This does, at least generally, correspond to the creation account that ascribes to woman the office of one who was to be a great help to man, but who, in fact, was an accomplice to his first sin. For more on this, cf. H. P. Müller, *Theological Dictionary of the Old Testament* (Grand Rapids: Eerdmans, 1980), 4:380.
15. Stein, *Essays on Woman,* 115.
16. See chapter 6 for more detailed analysis of υποτασσω *(hypotasso)* and the relevant texts.
17. I think it is a mistake to relegate this subjection of the woman to man as the result of sin and not creation, or to see it as something done away in the new covenant. As Kirschbaum notes, "Admittedly, the more elevated position of husbands and men and the subjection of wives and women are alleged to be a consequence and sign of sin; however, on the basis of this passage [Eph. 5:22–33] one must contest this allegation. How could a pattern of social order brought about through sin function as an analogy for the pattern of interrelationship between Jesus and His church? Eph. 5:22–33 refers explicitly to Gen. 2:19–24. *Here what is meant is an order established in and with the cre-*

ation of man and woman, and constitutive of their very being" (von Kirschbaum, *The Question of Woman,* 66–67, italics added). The order evident in submission is both a reflection of the order of man and woman in nature and, further, of the transcendental relationship between Christ and His church. Its ontology runs deep in the fabric of reality. In fact, according to Kirschbaum, "Women's subordinate position in relation to men is not abolished—rather, women can see that it is precisely through their obedience to the Lord . . . that their natural existence as women is privileged to function as an analogy for their existence as Christians in the church of Jesus Christ" (ibid., 86).

18. However, I would not be surprised if there were certain interesting and subtle gender differences between the manner in which men and women entertain, evaluate, and interact with issues of truth.
19. Rather than duplicate work, I refer the reader to earlier chapters for detailed discussions regarding the role of man as representative proclaimer of divine truth in the Old Testament, New Testament Gospels, and, particularly, the Epistles.
20. Cf. chapters 7, 12, 13 for more detailed discussions of the role of women in relation to teaching and public proclamation of the Word. Without solving all the controversies surrounding these texts, it is interesting to note that though both men and women were having problems with respect to behaving inappropriately in the church gatherings, particularly at Corinth, there is no instance of men being told to be quiet in the assembly, to not teach or exercise authority over women, or to be quiet and learn from their wives at home.
21. Gertrud von le Fort, *Eternal Woman,* trans. Placid Jordan (Milwaukee: The Bruce Pub. Co., 1962), 7.
22. Ibid., 44.
23. Perhaps the Roman Catholic Church has made some interesting applications of this with its concept of the convent and sisterhood as servant to the church and the male hierarchy. Though this relationship has its problems not entirely consistent with the complementarity view, nevertheless, it does provide an interesting picture in which often very strong and assertive women in these orders are capable of appropriately working and interacting with the male clergy. I am not certain that contemporary Protestants have satisfactorily worked out the place for the single Excellent Woman, let alone the place for the woman in general to serve and uplift the community.
24. For example, the Philistines' use of this in their admonition to their own armies, to "take courage and be men" (1 Sam. 4:9) demonstrates merely how one pagan culture viewed strength and bravery as male virtues. Even the narrative texts in which the Hebrews associate strength with maleness may be only an expression of their cultural view (cf. David telling Solomon as a child, "I am going the way of all the earth. Be strong, therefore, and show yourself a *man,*" 1 Kings 2:2, italics added).
25. Von le Fort, *Eternal Woman,* 6.
26. Ibid., 13.
27. W. F. Adeney, "Woman," *A Dictionary of the Bible* (T. & T. Clark, Edinburgh, 1898), 4:93.
28. See also examples of the witch of Endor of whom Saul inquired in 1 Samuel 28:7 and the young woman with the spirit of divination whom the men of Ephesus were making profit from in Acts 16:16. Cassuto agrees that the Bible does show women as more involved in "magic practices" and sorcery than men, but he believes this is merely a description of women's activity without making any normative point about gender and woman's involvement being more common than that of man (U. Cassuto, *A Commentary on the Book of Exodus* [Jerusalem: The Magnes Press, 1967], 290). See also chapter 11, pp. 270–71 in this work.

Chapter 10: Psychological Evidence of Gender Differentiation

1. John Colapinto, *As Nature Made Him: The Boy Who Was Raised as a Girl* (New York: HarperCollins, 2000), xi–xv. This book covers Bruce's complete story.
2. Mary Stewart Van Leeuwen, *Gender and Grace* (Downers Grove, Ill.: InterVarsity, 1990),

40. This is a well-written work assessing the psychological and biblical implications of gender and gender differences in relating between the sexes.

3. Dan B. Allender and Tremper Longman, *Intimate Allies* (Wheaton, Ill.: Tyndale, 1995), 146. I consider this book to be an excellent resource regarding the roles and interaction of men and women as male and female in Christianity, and more specifically within marriage. Contains beneficial and heretofore unemphasized insight about gender differences and complementarity providing the image of God.
4. Larry Crabb, *Men and Women: Enjoying the Difference* (Grand Rapids: Zondervan, 1991), 139. This book is an excellent resource on the marriage relationship.
5. Donald Joy, *Bonding: Relationships Created in the Image of God* (Waco, Tex.: Word, 1985), 18. This book talks about God's intention for our being bonded to each other, in all relationships in our lives.
6. Crabb, *Men and Women,* 133.
7. Ibid., 143.
8. Allender and Longman, *Intimate Allies,* 19.
9. Yves Christen, *Sex Differences: Modern Biology and the Unisex Fallacy,* trans. Nicholas Davidson (New Brunswick & London: Transaction Publishers, 1991). A book originally published in France, the author talks about sex differences in application to the sociopolitical context. Biological and sociobiological differences are delineated.
10. Simon LeVay, *The Sexual Brain* (Cambridge, Mass.: MIT, 1993), 28. This reference is nonacademic and a liberal perspective with some good content.
11. Robert W. Goy and Bruce S. McEwen, *Sexual Differentiation of the Brain* (Cambridge, Mass.: MIT, 1980), 6. Behavioral, genetic, cellular, and molecular sexual differentiation discussed in detail by the director of a primate center and a professor of neurobiology.
12. Christen, *Sex Differences,* 29.
13. Joy, *Bonding: Relationships Created in the Image of God,* 90–92.
14. Donald Joy, *Men Under Construction* (Wheaton, Ill.: Victor, 1993), 92. A quite valuable book on men, masculinity, and men's styles and potential baggage in relating to others.
15. Joy, *Men Under Construction.*
16. Goy and McEwen, *Sexual Differentiation,* 67.
17. Karen Phillips, "Why Can't a Man Be More Like a Woman . . . and Vice Versa?" in *Omni* 13 (October 1990). She explores research into physiological areas of the brain that appear to indicate biological gender differences in intellect skills and behavior, i.e., structural differences in corpus callosum.
18. Phillips, "Why Can't a Man Be More Like a Woman?"
19. Ibid.
20. Christen, *Sex Differences,* 68–69.
21. Richard Epstein, "Two Challenges for Feminist Thought" in *Harvard Journal of Law and Public Policy* 18 (Spring 1995): 331–49. Raises some common challenges to all versions of feminist theory, e.g., biology of sex similarities and differences; nature of men and women; substantive beliefs about correct choice of political philosophy and political institutions.
22. Colapinto, *As Nature Made Him: The Boy Who Was Raised as a Girl,* 148.
23. Leon J. Podles, *The Church Impotent* (Dallas: Spence Publishing, 1999), 37. A good resource on men in the church, using evidence from anthropology and developmental psychology to clarify the peculiarities of the masculine personality.
24. Gregg Johnson, "The Biological Basis for Gender-Specific Behavior," in *Recovering Biblical Manhood and Womanhood: A Response to Evangelical Feminism* eds. John Piper and Wayne Grudem (Wheaton, Ill.: Crossway, 1991), 280–93. This reference gives a good discussion of gender-specific behavior based upon various biological distinctions in the human male and female.
25. Paul Tournier, *To Understand Each Other* (Atlanta: John Knox, 1967), 38.
26. Colapinto, *As Nature Made Him: The Boy Who Was Raised as a Girl,* 177.
27. Crabb, *Men and Women: Enjoying the Difference,* 151.
28. Ibid., 156.

29. Carol Gilligan, *In a Different Voice: Psychological Theory and Woman's Development* (Cambridge, Mass.: Harvard Univ., 1982), 159–60. Excellent, groundbreaking text discussing a study conducted on men's and women's differing relational styles. Results of study provided a critique of modern psychology, stating that its standards stem from a male psychology and male styles of relating.
30. Ibid., 160–63.
31. Joy, *Men Under Construction* 22–23.
32. Deborah Tannen, *You Just Don't Understand: Women and Men in Conversation* (New York: Ballantine, 1990). Groundbreaking study assessing the verbal cues and signals sent by the different sexes.
33. Allender and Longman, *Intimate Allies,* 148.
34. Annette Hannah and Tamar Murachver, "Gender and Conversational Style as Predictors of Conversational Behavior," in *Journal of Language and Social Psychology* 18 (June 1999): 153.
35. Ibid., 153.
36. Crabb, *Men and Women: Enjoying the Difference,* 155.
37. Ibid., 160.
38. Allender and Longman, *Intimate Allies,* 148.
39. Gilligan, *In a Different Voice,* 156.
40. Ibid.
41. Paul Vitz, "Theism and Postmodern Psychology," a paper submitted to the Life After Materialism, The Implications of the New Science for the New Century Conference; sponsored by Biola University and Discovery Institute, Dec. 2–5, 1999.
42. Allender and Longman, *Intimate Allies,* 213.
43. Wendy Shalit, *A Return To Modesty: Discovering the Lost Virtue* (New York: Free Press, 1999), 164–67. A recent college graduate assessed and articulated the message our culture sends to young women and the impact that it is having on society as a whole.
44. Ibid., 153.
45. Karl Barth, "The Doctrine of Creation," *Church Dogmatics,* vol. III, no. 4 (Edinburgh: T. & T. Clark, 1961), Eng. translation, 163.
46. Seth Hettena, "Study: Boys Born Without a Penis Consider Selves Male" in Health and Science, *The Orange County Register,* 13 May 2000, 22.
47. Ibid.

Chapter 11: Gender Roles and Authority: A Comparative Sociocultural Perspective

1. Michael Thompson, Richard Ellis, and Aaron Wildavsky, *Cultural Theory* (Boulder, Col.: Westview Press, 1990).
2. Mary Douglas, *Natural Symbols: Explorations in Cosmology,* 2d ed. (New York: Pantheon, 1982).
3. Thompson, Ellis, and Wildavsky, *Cultural Theory,* 48–51.
4. Ibid., 83–84.
5. Sherwood G. Lingenfelter, *Agents of Transformation: A Guide for Effective Cross-Cultural Ministry* (Grand Rapids: Baker, 1996), 216–33.
6. Sherwood G. Lingenfelter, *Transforming Culture: A Challenge for Christian Mission* (Grand Rapids: Baker, 1998).
7. Robert Netting, Richard Wilk, and Eric J. Arnould, *Households: Comparative and Historical Studies of the Domestic Group* (Berkeley: Univ. of California, 1984).
8. Mary Douglas, *Natural Symbols,* 24–27.
9. Gordon Koop and Sherwood Lingenfelter, *The Deni of Western Brazil* (Dallas: SIL Museum of Anthropology, 1980).
10. David M. Schneider and Kathleen Gogh, eds., *Matrilineal Kinship* (Berkeley: Univ. of California, 1961).
11. See Lingenfelter, *Transforming Culture,* 107–36.

12. Aaron Wildavsky, *The Nursing Father: Moses as Political Leader* (Univ. of Alabama Press, 1984), 223–24.
13. Lingenfelter, *Transforming Culture* (1992).
14. See Lingenfelter, *Agents of Transformation* (1996) and the second edition of *Transforming Culture* (1998).
15. The exceptions I am referring to here are incidences in a matrilineal society when there is no legitimate heir to a position of "high chief." In such a situation a woman may serve as "high chief" until a male successor, such as her son, is ready to assume responsibility.
16. David W. Bennett, *Metaphors of Ministry: Biblical Images for Leaders and Followers* (Grand Rapids: Baker, 1993), 11, 193.
17. Ibid., 193.

Chapter 12: The Ephesian Background of Paul's Teaching on Women's Ministry

1. C. K. Barrett, *The First Epistle to the Corinthians* (New York: Harper & Row, 1968), 33–34.
2. Cf. George W. Knight III, *The Pastoral Epistles: A Commentary on the Greek Text* (Grand Rapids: Eerdmans, 1992), 130–31.
3. Much discussion of this text is found in works supporting both the egalitarian and complementarian perspectives. Recently, an excellent book from the complementarian viewpoint has been devoted to the discussion of this one text. See Andreas J. Köstenberger, Thomas R. Schreiner, and H. Scott Baldwin, eds., *Women in the Church: A Fresh Analysis of 1 Timothy 2:9–15* (Grand Rapids: Baker, 1995).
4. See chapter 2, "The Prominence of Women in Asia Minor" in Paul Trebilco's monograph, *Jewish Communities in Asia Minor,* SNTSMS 69 (Cambridge: Cambridge Univ., 1991), 104–26.
5. Michael Grant, *A Social History of Greece and Rome* (New York: Scribner, 1992), 30–31.
6. Ibid., 36.
7. For further information, see Richard E. Oster, "Ephesus as a Religious Center Under the Principate, I. Paganism Before Constantine," *Aufstieg und Niedergang der römischen Welt* II.18.2 (1990), 1661–1728.
8. Sharon Kelly Heyob, *The Cult of Isis Among Women in the Graeco-Roman World,* EPRO 51 (Leiden: Brill, 1975), 52.
9. Ibid., 129–30.
10. *I. Kyme* 41 (= *Inschriften griechischer Städte aus Kleinasien V. Die Inschriften von Kyme, Bonn,* 1976). Reproduced and trans. in G. H. R. Horsley, *New Documents Illustrating Early Christianity,* vol. 1 (North Ryde, NSW: Macquarie Univ., 1981), 18–21.
11. Lewis R. Farnell, *The Cults of the Greek States* (Oxford: Clarendon, 1907), 3.300–301; 2.481. See also Friedrich Schwenn, "Kybele," in Pauly-Wissowa, *Real-Encyclopädie der classischen Altertumswissenschaft* 11 (1921), 2260. The Attis legend recounts his self-castration; see Maarten Vermaseren, *Cybele and Attis: The Myth and the Cult* (London: Thames & Hudson, 1977), 11, 96–101. The poet Catullus actually describes such a case of emasculation in one of his poems (no. 13).
12. See Markus Barth, "Traditions in Ephesians," *New Testament Studies* 30 (1984): 16.
13. K. Wernicke, "Artemis," in Pauly-Wissowa, *Real-Encyclopädie der classischen Altertumswissenschaft* 2 (1896), 1372.
14. Schwenn, "Kybele," 2262.
15. Maarten Vermaseren, *Corpus Cultus Cybelae Attidisque* EPRO 50 (Leiden: Brill, 1977–1986), 2.68.
16. Cited in C. Brown, "Woman," in *Dictionary of New Testament Theology* (Grand Rapids: Zondervan, 1978), 3.1058.
17. Ibid., 3.1058.
18. *Corpus Inscriptionum Judaicarum,* 741.
19. Bernadette J. Brooten, *Women Leaders in the Ancient Synagogue,* Brown Judaic Studies 36 (Atlanta: Scholars, 1982).

20. For the references and a discussion of the inscriptions, see Brooten, *Women Leaders,* chaps. 1–5 (5–99).
21. Trebilco, *Jewish Communities,* 126.
22. Forms of this view have been advocated by Gilbert Bilezikian, *Beyond Sex Roles: A Guide for the Study of the Female Roles in the Bible* (Grand Rapids: Baker, 1985), 173–84, and Craig S. Keener, *Paul, Women and Wives: Marriage and Women's Ministry in the Letters of Paul* (Peabody, Mass.: Hendrickson, 1992), 101–21.
23. Richard Clark Kroeger and Catherine Clark Kroeger, *I Suffer Not a Woman: Rethinking 1 Timothy in Light of Ancient Evidence* (Grand Rapids: Baker Book House, 1992), 54, 60, 62, 105–13; cf. also Ruth Haley Barton, *Equal to the Task* (Downers Grove, Ill.; InterVarsity, 1998), 40–41; Alvera Mickelsen, "An Egalitarian View: There Is Neither Male nor Female," in *Women in Ministry: Four Views,* ed. Bonnidell Clouse and Robert G. Clouse (Downers Grove, Ill.: InterVarsity, 1989), 202–3.
24. Kroeger and Kroeger, *I Suffer Not a Woman,* 113.
25. Albert Wolters, "Review: *I Suffer Not a Woman,*" in *Calvin Theological Journal* 29 (1993):208–13. Wolters, along with other reviewers, fault this work in many areas; cf. also Robert W. Yarbrough, "I Suffer Not a Woman: A Review Essay," *Presbyterion* 18 (1992): 25–33; S. M. Baugh, "The Apostle Among the Amazons," *Westminster Theological Journal* 56 (1994): 153–71.
26. Sharon Hodgin Gritz, *Paul, Women Teachers, and the Mother Goddess at Ephesus* (Lanham: Univ. Press of America, 1991), 11–49; 105–16; cf. also Philip B. Payne, "Libertarian Women in Ephesus: A Response to Douglas J. Moo's Article, '1 Timothy 2:11–15: Meaning and Significance,'" *Trinity Journal* 2 (1981): 182.
27. Philip H. Towner, *The Goal of Our Instruction* (Sheffield: JSOT Press, 1989), 30–36.
28. Knight, *The Pastoral Epistles,* 27. Knight details the characteristics of the false teachers found in the Pastoral Letters: "The false teachers are characterized by an interest in myths (1 Tim. 1:4; 4:7; Titus 1:14; 2 Tim. 4:4) and genealogies (1 Tim. 1:4; Titus 3:9), a concern with the law or a Jewish orientation (1 Tim. 1:7; Titus 1:10, 14; 3:9), an interest in 'antitheses' that they identify as 'knowledge' (1 Tim. 6:20), a tendency toward controversy, argumentation, and speculation (1 Tim. 1:4, 6; 6:4, 20; Titus 1:10; 3:9; 2 Tim. 2:14, 16, 23), deceptiveness (1 Tim. 4:1–3; Titus 1:10–13; 2 Tim. 3:6ff., especially v. 13), immorality (1 Tim. 1:19, 20; Titus 1:15, 16; 2 Tim. 2:16, 19; ch. 3), and a desire to get material gain by means of their teaching (1 Tim. 6:5; Titus 1:11; 2 Tim. 3:2, 4). In addition to these aspects mentioned in all three PE . . . , there is the harsh asceticism described in 1 Tim. 4:1–5, according to which some, in Ephesus at least, were apparently forbidding marriage and eating of meat, and a teaching that the resurrection had already taken place (2 Tim. 2:18; cf. 1 Tim. 1:19, 20)," (11–12).
29. Martin Dibelius and Hans Conzelmann, *The Pastoral Epistles* (Philadelphia: Fortress, 1972), 3. Acknowledging the lack of evidence for some of the feminist proposals for a specific teaching related to women as the background to Paul's teaching, egalitarian scholar David M. Scholer concluded that "the heresy is some type of ascetic-Gnosticizing movement within the church (1 Tim. 1:3–7; 6:20–21) but cannot be more specifically defined" ("1 Timothy 2:9–15 and the Place of Women in the Church's Ministry," in *Women, Authority and The Bible,* ed. by Alvera Mickelsen [Downers Grove, Ill.: InterVarsity, 1986], 199, n. 19; cf. also Ben Witherington, *Women in the Earliest Churches* (Cambridge: Cambridge Univ., 1988), 118.
30. J. N. D. Kelly, *A Commentary on the Pastoral Epistles* (London: Adam & Charles Black, 1963), 12.

Chapter 13: Paul's Teaching on the Ministry of Women

1. C. H. Peisker, "ἡσυχία, κτλ." *Exegetical Dictionary of the New Testament,* vol. 2, ed. Horst Balz and Gerhard Schneider (Grand Rapids: Eerdmans, 1991), 125. Peisker says, "The primary meanings in Greek literature, 'rest, peace, tranquility,' are those present in the NT." Noting that the word is more regularly translated "peaceable" or "respectful,"

Blomberg suggests that it here reflects "the characteristic Jewish demeanor required of any learner of either gender." (Craig L. Blomberg, "Not Beyond What is Written: A Review of Aida Spencer's *Women Called to Ministry*," *Criswell Theological Review* 2 [Spring 1988]: 411).

2. Andreas J. Köstenberger, "A Complex Sentence Structure in 1 Timothy 2:12," in *Women in the Church: A Fresh Analysis of 1 Timothy 2:9–15*, ed. Andreas J. Köstenberger, Thomas R. Schreiner, and H. Scott Baldwin (Grand Rapids: Baker, 1995), 90; P. B. Payne, "οὐδέ in 1 Timothy 2:12," paper read at the 1986 annual meeting of the Evangelical Theological Society, 6–8.
3. See H. Scott Baldwin, "A Difficult Word: αὐθεντέω in 1 Timothy 2:12," in *Women in the Church*, ed. Köstenberger, Schreiner, and Baldwin, 67–69. Baldwin (p. 76) argues that the Kroegers' understanding of Paul's prohibition ("I do not allow a woman . . . to proclaim herself author of man") is based on wrongly taking the meaning "to begin or instigate something" to include the sense "to be the organic origin of something" (cf. Kroeger and Kroeger, *I Suffer Not a Woman*, 103).
4. Köstenberger, "A Complex Sentence Structure in 1 Timothy 2:12," in Köstenberger, et al., eds., *Women in the Church*, 81–103.
5. See for example, Gilbert Bilezikian, *Beyond Sex Roles: A Guide for the Study of Female Roles in the Bible* (Grand Rapids: Baker, 1985), 180; Aida Besancon Spencer, *Beyond the Curse: Women Called to Ministry* (Nashville: Nelson, 1985), 84–85, 91, 95 for statements to this effect; Mary J. Evans, *Woman in the Bible* (Downers Grove, Ill.: InterVarsity, 1983), 105.
6. David Scholer, "1 Timothy 2:9–15 & the Place of Women in the Church's Ministry," in *Women, Authority and the Bible*, ed. Alvera Mickelsen (Downers Grove, Ill.: InterVarsity, 1986), 198.
7. Ibid., 203.
8. E.g., Spencer, *Beyond the Curse*, 84–85.
9. Thomas R. Schreiner, "An Interpretation of 1 Timothy 2:9–15: A Dialogue with Scholarship," in Köstenberger, et al., ed., *Women in the Church*, 126.
10. James D. G. Dunn, *Jesus and the Spirit* (Philadelphia: Westminster, 1975), 282.
11. K. Wegenast, "Teach," *The New International Dictionary of New Testament Theology*, vol. 3, ed. Colin Brown (Grand Rapids: Zondervan, 1978), 760. For the difference between the secular Greek and Hebrew meanings of "teach," see also Karl Heinrich Rengstorf, "διδάσκω κτλ," *Theological Dictionary of the New Testament*, vol. 2, ed. Gerhard Kittel, trans. and ed. Geoffrey W. Bromiley (Grand Rapids: Eerdmans, 1964), 135–38.
12. Rengstorf, "διδάσκω," *Theological Dictionary of the New Testament*, 137.
13. Floyd V. Filson, "The Christian Teacher in the First Century," *Journal of Biblical Literature* 60 (1941): 318.
14. Rengstorf, "διδάσκω κτλ," *Theological Dictionary of the New Testament*, 143.
15. Stephen B. Clark, *Man and Woman in Christ* (Ann Arbor, Mich.: Servant, 1980), 196.
16. Dunn, *Jesus and the Spirit*, 283.
17. Wegenast, "Teach," 761–65; 767–71; Rengstorf, "διδάσκω," *Theological Dictionary of the New Testament*, 138–48; 152–59.
18. This terminology is found in only four places (Acts 13:1; 1 Cor. 12:28f.; Eph. 4:11; James 3:1).
19. Dunn, *Jesus and the Spirit*, 283; cf. Wegenast, "Teach," 768; Peter H. Davids, *The Epistle of James* (Grand Rapids: Eerdmans, 1982), 136; James Adamson speaks of an "order of 'teachers'" within the congregations of the Jewish Diaspora (*The Epistle of James* [Grand Rapids: Eerdmans, 1976], 140).
20. Markus Barth, *Ephesians 4–6, The Anchor Bible*, 34A (Garden City, N.Y.: Doubleday, 1974), 438. Barth translates the words in question as "teaching shepherds" adding, "While sometimes in the NT 'teachers' and 'shepherds' (or the equivalent of shepherds) are mentioned separately, and at other occasions the titles 'bishop' and 'elder' occur, all these functions probably belong together." See also Rengstorf, "διδάσκω," 158. Lincoln is more doubtful that "pastor" and "teacher" refer to the same person in this passage.

21. Thomas Lindsay, *The Church and the Ministry in the Early Centuries* (Minneapolis: James Family Publishing, rept. 1977), 103–6.
22. Andrew T. Lincoln, *Ephesians,* Word Biblical Commentary, vol. 42 (Dallas: Word, 1990), 250.
23. C. K. Barrett, *A Commentary on the First Epistle to the Corinthians* (New York: Harper & Row, 1968), 329.
24. James D. G. Dunn, *Romans 9–16,* Word Biblical Commentary, 38b, (Dallas: Word, 1988), 729.
25. For a discussion of whether the teaching in Col. 3:16 is linked to the activity of singing or whether singing is a second thought in the verse, see Peter T. O'Brien, *Colossians, Philemon,* Word Biblical Commentary, vol. 44, (Waco, Tex.: Word, 1982), 208–9. Whichever way one interprets the verse, the thought of all of the believers teaching one another is present. For the significance of song in teaching, see our discussion of this verse in chapter 8.
26. Robert Banks, *Paul's Idea of Community* (Grand Rapids: Eerdmans, 1980), 127.
27. George W. Knight III, *The Pastoral Epistles: A Commentary on the Greek Text* (Grand Rapids: Eerdmans, 1992), 141; cf. Wegenast, "Teach," 765.
28. Philip Edgcombe Hughes, *A Commentary on the Epistle to the Hebrews* (Grand Rapids: Eerdmans, 1977), 190. Bruce similarly explains that "the word διδάσκαλος is used here in quite an informal sense, and not of trained catechists or anything like that. It was an axiom of Stoicism that anyone who had mastered true learning was in a position to impart it to others; and it is equally a Christian axiom" (F. F. Bruce, *The Epistle to the Hebrews* [Grand Rapids: Eerdmans, 1964], 107, n. 80).
29. Rengstorf says that for early Christianity the teaching of Jesus was "in the absolute because with every word He brought His hearers into direct confrontation with the will of God as it is revealed in His Word and as it is constantly revealed in history" (Rengstorf, "διδάσκω κτλ," 140–41). The teaching of the Spirit was similarly seen as carrying a final authority (cf. John 14:26; 1 John 2:27).
30. Herman Wolfgang Beyer, "κατηχέω," *Theological Dictionary of the New Testament,* vol. III (Grand Rapids: Eerdmans, 1965), 638.
31. Beyer, "κατηχέω," 639.
32. Wegenast, "Teach," 771.
33. With reference to the duties of deacons in the early church, C. E. B. Cranfield writes, "The duty of assisting the bishop extended in some measure to the episcopal function of teaching. . . . The *Didache* urges the congregation to appoint *episkopoi* and *diakonoi* . . . as substitutes for the ministry of prophets and teachers. . . . Hermas certainly links deacons with teachers; and deacons are not infrequently mentioned in connexion with catechetical teaching" ("Diakonia in the New Testament," in *Service in Christ,* ed. James I. McCord and T. H. L. Parker (Grand Rapids: Eerdmans, 1966), 58.
34. *A Greek-English Lexicon of the New Testament and Other Early Christian Literature,* 2d ed., rev. and augmented by F. Wilbur Gingrich and Frederick W. Danker (Chicago: Univ. of Chicago, 1979), 245.
35. Ibid., 187.
36. Dunn, *Romans 9–16,* 730.
37. C. E. B. Cranfield, *The Epistle to the Romans,* vol. 2, The International Critical Commentary (Edinburgh: T. & T. Clark, 1979), 623.
38. J. Behm, "νουθετέω, νουθεσία," *Theological Dictionary of the New Testament,* vol. 4 (Grand Rapids: Eerdmans, 1967), 1021–22.
39. On the basic meaning and use of ἀγγέλλω, κηρύσσω, and their derivatives, see Ulrich Becker, Dietrich Müller, and Lothar Coenen, "Proclamation, Preach, Kerygma," *The New International Dictionary of Theology* (Grand Rapids: Zondervan, 1971), 3:44–57.
40. "Sound words" (1 Tim. 6:3; 2 Tim. 1:13; cf. 2 Tim. 2:15); "the faith" (1 Tim. 3:9; 4:1, 6; 5:8; 6:10, 12, 21; 2 Tim. 3:8; 4:7; Titus 1:13; 2:2; "that which has been entrusted" (1 Tim. 6:20; 2 Tim. 1:12, 14); the word "sound" is often used with "teaching/doctrine" as well (cf. 1 Tim. 1:10; 2 Tim. 4:3; Titus 1:9; 2:1; cf. also "good teaching," 1 Tim. 4:6 (NIV), 16; 6:1, 3; 2 Tim. 2:2; Titus 2:10).

41. Eduard Schweizer, *Church Order in the New Testament* (London: SCM Press, 1961), 79.
42. A. Sabatier, *The Apostle Paul* (London: Hodder & Stoughton, 1903), 389.
43. Rengstorf, "διδάσκω κτλ," 162
44. Philip H. Towner, *The Goal of Our Instruction* (Sheffield: JSOT Press, 1989), 125.
45. Dunn, *Jesus and the Spirit,* 348–49; Sabatier expresses this same movement toward preservation when he speaks of the Pastorals as marking a new "phrase of Paulinism, i.e., an era of 'conservative tradition'" (Sabatier, *The Apostle Paul,* 263).
46. Schweizer, *Church Order in the New Testament,* 79–80.
47. Wegenast, "Teach," p. 765; cf. also Joseph A. Fitzmyer, "The Office of Teaching in the Christian Church According to the New Testament," in *Teaching Authority and Infallibility in the Church,* ed. Paul C. Empie, T. Austin Murphy, and Joseph A. Burgess (Minneapolis: Augsburg, 1976), 204–7.
48. David C. Verner, *The Household of God: The Social World of the Pastoral Epistles,* Society of Biblical Literature Dissertation series; no. 71 (Chico, Calif.: Scholar's Press, 1983), 158.
49. Joseph A. Fitzmyer, "The Office of Teaching in the Christian Church According to the New Testament," 206. Verner similarly says of the officers of the church in the Pastorals, "Their most important functions involved the preservation, transmission and defense of the teaching. . . . This strong emphasis on the official leadership as the first line of defense against opposition to the teaching leads one to suspect that the teaching was in fact encountering significant opposition in the church" (Verner, *The Household of God: The Social World of the Pastoral Epistles,* 160).
50. Jacques Schlosser, "La didascalie et ses agents dans les epitres pastorales," *Revue des Sciences Religieuses* 59 (April 1985): 93–94.
51. *A Greek-English Lexicon of the New Testament and Other Early Christian Literature,* 613.
52. Knight, *The Pastoral Epistles,* 204–5.
53. Witherington, *Women in the Earliest Churches,* 121.
54. Douglas Moo, "What Does It Mean Not to Teach or Have Authority Over Men?" in *Recovering Biblical Manhood and Womanhood: A Response to Evangelical Feminism,* ed. John Piper and Wayne Grudem (Wheaton, Ill.: Crossway, 1991), 187; Schreiner, "An Interpretation of 1 Timothy 2:9–15," in *Women in the Church,* 133.
55. Philip Payne explains, "Οὐδέ in 1 Tim 2:12 ought to be translated in harmony with Paul's use elsewhere. Its translation should indicate that it joins together two elements in order to convey a single coherent idea, or if it conveys two ideas these should be very closely interrelated" (*What Does the Scripture Teach About the Ordination of Women?* part II "The Interpretation of I Timothy 2:11–15: A Surrejoinder," a study commissioned by the Committee on Ministerial Standing [Minneapolis: Evangelical Free Church of America, 1986], 104–8; Blomberg, "Not Beyond What Is Written, 412; J. N. D. Kelly, *The Pastoral Epistles* (London: Adam & Charles Black, 1963), 68; cf. also Barnett who argues for the same conclusion based upon the chiastic structure of vv. 11–12 (Paul W. Barnett, "Wives and Women's Ministry [1 Timothy 2:11–15]")," *The Evangelical Quarterly* 61 (January 1989): 232.
56. For more examples of this construction, see Köstenberger, "A Complex Sentence Structure in 1 Timothy 2:12," in *Women in the Church,* 85–89.
57. Dunn, *Jesus and the Spirit,* 412–13, n. 12.
58. Blomberg, "Not Beyond What Is Written: A Review of Aida Spencer's *Beyond the Curse: Women Called to Ministry,*" 418.
59. Knight, *The Pastoral Epistles,* 141.
60. Clark, *Man and Woman in Christ,* 199, 305.
61. For a discussion of the permanence of the relationship of man and woman based in their creation, see chapter 6. For a good discussion of the various problems involved in this passage, with the conclusion that the principles of this passage are permanent although the particular manner in which they are expressed (e.g., head covering for women's submission to her "head") may vary from culture to culture, see Thomas R. Schreiner, "Head Coverings, Prophecies and the Trinity," in *Women in the Church,* 124–39.
62. Some who understand the call for women's silence in church as absolute attempt to explain the discrepancy by seeing the praying or prophesying in chapter 11 as done outside of the church service (F. W. Grosheide, *Commentary on the First Epistle to the*

Corinthians [Grand Rapids: Eerdmans, 1953], 251–52). Most interpreters, however, see the context of these women's activities as the worshiping community. First, it is difficult to envisage where women would commonly be ministering in this way publicly, especially praying. Nor is any reason suggested as to why such ministry would be acceptable in public before the world and not in the church in the presence of believers. Finally, the concern for women's propriety "because of the angels" (1 Cor. 11:10) is normally understood in relation to their observation of the church service, indicating that the instructions likewise related to the gathered community.

Others have suggested that the regulations concerning head coverings were only a concession to what women were doing, but which the apostle really disapproved and now expresses his real desire, namely, that women do not speak in any fashion (Robert L. Thomas, *Understanding Spiritual Gifts* [Chicago: Moody, 1978], 158; cf. also Archibald Robertson and Alfred Plummer, *A Critical and Exegetical Commentary on the First Epistle of St. Paul to the Corinthians* [Edinburgh: T. & T. Clark, 1911], 324–25). This seems very unlikely as the apostle does not seem hesitant to express his disapproval in other situations, and there is absolutely no hint of such disapproval in his instructions in chapter 11.

63. Susan Foh, "A Male Leadership View: The Head of the Woman Is the Man," in *Women in Ministry: Four Views,* ed. Bonnidell Clouse and Robert G. Clouse, 84, 104, n. 20; cf. also the suggestion that in some situations asking questions of respected authoritative teachers such as a rabbi was a sign of disrespect (Samuele Bacchiocchi, *Women in the Church* [Berrien Springs, Mich.: Biblical Perspectives, 1987], 168).
64. Walter Lock, *A Critical and Expository Commentary on the Pastoral Epistles* (Edinburgh: T. & T. Clark, 1936), 44.

Chapter 14: The Complementary Model of Church Ministry

1. I. Höver-Johag, "טוֹב, *tob;* טוּב, *tub;* יטב, *ytb,*" *Theological Dictionary of the Old Testament,* vol. 5, ed. G. J. Botterweck and Helmer Ringgren (Grand Rapids: Eerdmans, 1986), 304.
2. See chapter 8, 163–68.
3. Other family terminology includes "brothers" (e.g., Eph. 6:21; Col. 4:7), and "sisters" (Philem. 2), "mother" (Rom. 16:13), and more. For the various expressions used in Scripture pointing to the church as God's family, cf. V. S. Poythress, "The Church as Family: Why Male Leadership in the Family Requires Male Leadership in the Church," in *Recovering Biblical Manhood and Womanhood: A Response to Evangelical Feminism,* ed. John Piper and Wayne Grudem (Wheaton, Ill.: Crossway, 1991), 233–36; Robert Banks, *Paul's Idea of Community,* rev. ed. (Peabody, Mass.: Hendrickson, 1994), 49–57.
4. Poythress, "The Church as Family," in *Recovering Biblical Manhood and Womanhood,* 233.
5. David C. Verner, *The Household of God: The Social World of the Pastoral Epistles,* Society of Biblical Literature Dissertation Series no. 71 (Chico, Calif.: Scholar's, 1983), 147.
6. P. T. O'Brien, "Church," in *Dictionary of Paul and His Letters,* edited by Gerald F. Hawthorne and Ralph Martin (Downers Grove, Ill.: InterVarsity, 1993), 128. Towner sees the apostle's instructions concerning men and women in 1 Timothy 2:8–15 as analogous to appropriate behavior in the household (P. H. Towner, "Households and Household Codes," in *Dictionary of Paul and His Letters,* 418).
7. Stephen B. Clark, *Man and Woman in Christ* (Ann Arbor, Mich.: Servant, 1980), 69.
8. Tertullian, *Ad Uxorem* II, 9, cited by Clark, *Man and Woman in Christ,* 290.
9. Cf. chapter 8, 163ff.
10. W. Bauer, *A Greek-English Lexicon of the New Testament and Other Early Christian Literature,* trans. W. F. Arndt and F. W. Gingrich, 2d ed. rev. and augmented by F. W. Gingrich and F. W. Danker from Bauer's 5th ed. (1958) (Chicago: Univ. of Chicago, 1979), 802.
11. Clark, *Man and Woman in Christ,* 132, 116 (source of Clement's words not given).
12. Ibid., 108.

13. C. K. Barrett, *The First Epistle to the Corinthians* (New York: Harper & Row, 1968), 317.
14. For a good overview of ministry in the New Testament church involving the exercise of gifts by various members, see Robert Banks, *Paul's Idea of Community.*
15. See chapter 8 for fuller treatment of the meaning of Colossians 3:16, including the teaching value of song.
16. Clark, *Man and Woman in Christ,* 107.
17. Ibid., 107–9.
18. See chapter 8 for a discussion of these additional ministries of the Word.
19. J. I. Packer, "Postscript: I Believe in Women's Ministry," *Why Not? Priesthood and the Ministry of Women* (Sutton Courtenay: Marcham Manor, 1976), 132. See chapters 9 and 10 in this work for more on gender differences.
20. Clark, *Man and Woman in Christ,* 389–90.
21. Ibid., 62.
22. J. I. Packer, "Postscript: I Believe in Women's Ministry," 169, 172–73. This concept of a team ministry is also supported by John Stott, *Decisive Issues Facing Christians Today* (Old Tappan, N.J.: Revell, 1990), 278.
23. Gordon MacDonald, "Biblical Masculinity: What Is a Real Man?" *Discipleship Journal* 77 (1993): 49.
24. Todd W. Hall, "The Personal Functioning of Pastors: A Review of Empirical Research with Implications for the Care of Pastors," *Journal of Psychology and Theology* 25 (Summer 1997): 240–53.
25. R. Ruth Barton, "Working Together," *Discipleship Journal* 77 (1993): 59–62.
26. Ibid.
27. Jack and Judy Balswick. *The Family* (Grand Rapids: Baker, 1991), 26–27.
28. Myron S. Augsburger, *The Christ-Shaped Conscience* (Wheaton, Ill.: Victor, 1990), 39–40.
29. Elaine Stedman, *A Woman's Worth* (Waco, Tex.: Word, 1975), 68.
30. Vollie Sanders, "Biblical Femininity," *Discipleship Journal* 77 (1993): 52–55.
31. Oswald Chambers, "God First" (May 31), *My Utmost for His Highest* (Grand Rapids: Discovery House, 1935, renewed in 1963), 152.
32. Larry Crabb, *Men and Women: Enjoying the Difference* (Grand Rapids: Zondervan, 1991), 109.
33. Ibid.
34. Crabb, *Men and Women,* 108.
35. Ibid., 212.
36. Sanders, "Biblical Femininity," 54.
37. Ibid.
38. Ibid.
39. Jack and Judy Balswick, *The Family,* 30.
40. Ibid., 31.
41. Stedman, *A Woman's Worth,* 156.
42. Clark, *Man and Woman in Christ,* 155.
43. R. S. Anderson, "Spiritual Formation as Family Therapy: A Social Ecology of the Family Revisited" (lecture, Seattle Pacific University, 1997).
44. Ken Gire, *The Reflective Life* (Colorado Springs: Victor, 1998), 134.

SUBJECT INDEX

Information found in the endnotes is designated by an *n* and a note number following the page number.

SCRIPTURE INDEX

Scriptures found in the endnotes are designated by an *n* and a note number, following the page number.

Moody Press, a ministry of Moody Bible Institute,
is designed for education, evangelization, and edification.
If we may assist you in knowing more about Christ
and the Christian life, please write us without obligation:
Moody Press, c/o MLM, Chicago, Illinois 60610.

More From Robert L. Saucy

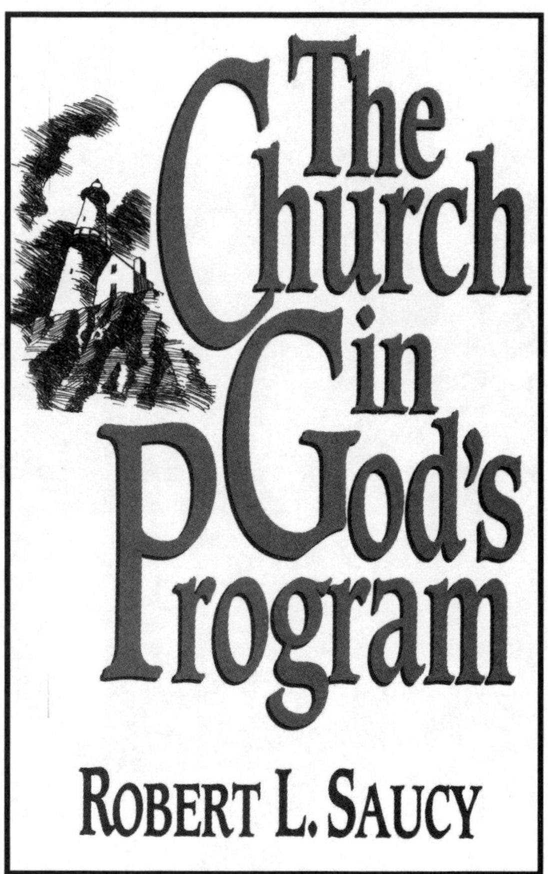

The term "church" can carry with it a number of different meanings from the building where Christians meet to the corporate body of Christ. ***The Church in God's Program*** is a biblical study covering the entire scope of the church, including its beginnings, nature, and purposes. An essential for those deeply commited to Church ministry.

ISBN 0-8024-1544-X